The Indian Civil Sphere

The Indian Civil Sphere

Edited by

Jeffrey C. Alexander and Suryakant Waghmore

polity

Copyright © Polity Press 2025

First published in 2025 by Polity Press

Polity Press
65 Bridge Street
Cambridge CB2 1UR, UK

Polity Press
111 River Street
Hoboken, NJ 07030, USA

All rights reserved. Except for the quotation of short passages for the purpose of criticism and review, no part of this publication may be reproduced, stored in a retrieval system or transmitted, in any form or by any means, electronic, mechanical, photocopying, recording or otherwise, without the prior permission of the publisher.

ISBN-13: 978-1-5095-6381-4
ISBN-13: 978-1-5095-6382-1(pb)

A catalogue record for this book is available from the British Library.

Library of Congress Control Number: 2024946093

Typeset in 10 on 12pt Sabon Lt Pro
by Cheshire Typesetting Ltd, Cuddington, Cheshire
Printed and bound in Great Britain by CPI Group (UK) Ltd, Croydon

The publisher has used its best endeavors to ensure that the URLs for external websites referred to in this book are correct and active at the time of going to press. However, the publisher has no responsibility for the websites and can make no guarantee that a site will remain live or that the content is or will remain appropriate.

Every effort has been made to trace all copyright holders, but if any have been overlooked the publisher will be pleased to include any necessary credits in any subsequent reprint or edition.

For further information on Polity, visit our website:
politybooks.com

Contents

Notes on the Contributors	vii
Preface and Acknowledgments	xi
Introduction: The Indian Civil Sphere between Vitality and Suppression Jeffrey C. Alexander	1

Civil Repair and Anti-Caste Movements

1. *Caste, Incivility, and the Prospects of Civil Repair*   39
   Hugo Gorringe and Karthikeyan Damodaran

2. *The Indian Civil Sphere and the Question of Caste: The Case of the Hathras Movement*   54
   Raju Chalwadi

3. *Can the Brahmin be Civil? The Ambiguous Repair of Caste Privilege*   70
   Ramesh Bairy T. S.

4. *Civil Sphere versus Civil Religion: Hindutva and its Multiple Opponents in Karnataka*   88
   Suryakant Waghmore

5. *The Authoritarian Civil Sphere, Populism, and Secular Sectarianism*   107
   Ajay Gudavarthy

CONTENTS

The Macro Framework

6. *Building Solidarity, Attempting Civil Repair: Pious Altruism and Muslim Politics in Post-Babri Mumbai*   127
Qudsiya Contractor

7. *Financial Inclusion: Private Interventions in the Civil Sphere*   144
Kartikeya Saboo

8. *The British Raj and its Legacy for Democracy and Civil Society in India*   162
Krishan Kumar

   Commentary: India and the Civil Horizons of Political Community   178
   Trevor Stack

   Commentary: Leveraging the Heuristic Potential of the Indian Civil Sphere   190
   Carlo Tognato

   Conclusion: Two Antagonistic Visions of India's National Identity   196
   Peter Kivisto and Giuseppe Sciortino

Notes   207
References   223
Index   247

Notes on the Contributors

Jeffrey C. Alexander is the Lillian Chavenson Saden Professor Emeritus of Sociology at Yale University, Director Emeritus of Yale's Center for Cultural Sociology, and Co-Editor of the *American Journal of Cultural Sociology*. Among his recent publications are *What Makes a Social Crisis: The Societalization of Social Problems* (2019), *Civil Repair* (2024), and *Frontlash/Backlash* (2025).

Ramesh Bairy T. S. teaches sociology at the Indian Institute of Technology. He is the author of *Being Brahmin, Being Modern: Exploring the Lives of Caste Today* (2010).

Raju Chalwadi recently submitted his PhD in the Humanities and Social Sciences Department at the Indian Institute of Technology Bombay, India. For the academic year 2022–23, he was a Fulbright-Nehru Doctoral Research Fellow affiliated with the University of California, Santa Cruz. His research has previously been published in *South Asia Research* and *EPW*, including the chapter "(Re)Constructing Spatial and Social Relations: Valmikis of Mumbai and Their Everyday Challenge to Caste," in *Caste in Everyday Life* (Palgrave Macmillan 2023).

Qudsiya Contractor is a Visiting Fellow at the Centre for Liberal Education, Indian Institute of Technology, Bombay. Her work focuses on the changing salience of religious identity in urban India. Among her recent writings is "Religious Imagination in the Making of Public Muslims in a Mumbai Slum," published in *Culture and Religion* (2022).

Karthikeyan Damodaran is an Assistant Professor, Social Sciences, and Co-Director of the Centre for the Study of Marginalized Communities

NOTES ON THE CONTRIBUTORS

at the National Law School of India University in Bangalore. Prior to entering academia, he worked as a senior journalist with *The Hindu* newspaper for seven years before completing his PhD at the University of Edinburgh. He worked as a Research Fellow in the Centre for Modern Indian Studies, University of Göttingen, and as Assistant Professor at the Department of Asian Studies, School of Creative Liberal Education, JAIN (Deemed-to-be University), before joining NLSIU. His research focuses on caste processions and commemorations in Tamil Nadu and performances of traditional masculinity in contemporary times. He is the author of numerous sole- and joint-authored articles on Dalits, Dalit politics, Dravidian politics, and Tamil cinema.

Hugo Gorringe is a Professor of Sociology and former Co-Director of the Centre for South Asian Studies at the University of Edinburgh, Scotland. His research in India focuses on the sociopolitical mobilization of Dalits and their struggle to achieve equality and deepen Indian democracy. He is an editorial board member of *Contemporary Voice of Dalit* (Sage). He is the sole author of *Panthers in Parliament: Dalits, Caste and Political Power in South India* (Oxford University Press 2017) and *Untouchable Citizens: Dalit Movements and Democratization in Tamil Nadu* (Sage 2005), and he is co-editor of several books, including *Caste in Everyday Life: Experience and Affect in India* (Palgrave 2023, with D. Bhoi) and *Civility in Crisis, Democracy, Equality, and the Majoritarian Challenge in India* (Routledge 2021, with S. Waghmore). He has also published numerous articles and chapters on identity, violence, space, caste, and politics.

Ajay Gudavarthy is currently Associate Professor, Centre for Political Studies, Jawaharlal Nehru University. He is currently Associate Member, Institute for Humanities, Simon Fraser University, Canada. He was earlier Visiting Professor, Centre for Modern Indian Studies, Gottingen University, Germany (2014); Visiting Fellow, Centre for Citizenship, Civil Society and Rule of Law, University of Aberdeen (2012); Visiting Faculty, Goldsmith College, UCL, London (2010); and Charles Wallace Visiting Fellow, SOAS, London (2008). His published work includes *Politics of Post-Civil Society* (Sage 2013), *Maoism, Democracy and Globalization* (Sage 2014), *India after Modi: Populism and the Right* (Bloomsbury 2018), and *Politics, Ethics and Emotions in "New India"* (Routledge 2023); and edited books include *Re-Framing Democracy and Agency* (Anthem, London 2012), *Revolutionary Violence versus Democracy* (Sage 2017), and *Secular Sectarianism: Limits of Subaltern Politics* (Sage 2019).

viii

NOTES ON THE CONTRIBUTORS

Peter Kivisto is the Richard A. Swanson Professor of Social Thought Emeritus at Augustana College. Recent books include *The Cambridge Handbook of Social Theory* (Cambridge University Press 2021), *Populism in the Civil Sphere* (Polity Press 2020, with Jeffrey C. Alexander and Giuseppe Sciortino), and *The Trump Phenomenon: How the Politics of Populism Won in 2016* (Emerald 2017).

Krishan Kumar is University Professor and William R. Kenan, Jr., Professor of Sociology at the University of Virginia, USA. He was previously Professor of Social and Political Thought at the University of Kent at Canterbury, UK. He has also been a Visiting Scholar at Harvard University, a Member of the Institute for Advanced Study, Princeton, and a Visiting Professor at the Universities of Bergen, Bristol, Bocconi, the Central European University, and Hong Kong. Among his publications are *Utopia and Anti-Utopia in Modern Times* (1987), *1989: Revolutionary Ideas and Ideals* (2001), *The Making of English National Identity* (2003), *Visions of Empire: How Five Imperial Regimes Shaped the World* (2017), and *Empires: A Historical and Political Sociology* (2021). He is currently writing a book about the Chinese Empire.

Kartikeya Saboo teaches social anthropology at Wichita State University in Kansas, where he is doing research on political persuasion, sexuality, and culture. He runs a field school of ethnography and applied anthropology in a semi-rural community. He has previously studied racial capitalism and criminal labor in the Northeastern United States.

Giuseppe Sciortino teaches sociology at the Università di Trento, Italy. He is a member of the coordinating committee of the Civil Sphere Theory Network, and the editor, with Martina Cvajner and Peter Kivisto, of the *Research Handbook in the Sociology of Migration* (Edward Elgar 2024).

Trevor Stack is Professor in Spanish and Latin American Studies at the University of Aberdeen. He holds a BA in History and a Masters in Social Anthropology from Oxford University, a PhD in Anthropology from the University of Pennsylvania. Stack founded and directs the interdisciplinary Centre for Citizenship, Civil Society and Rule of Law (CISRUL), which focuses on the study of political concepts in the world. He has been doing research mainly in Mexico since 1992, primarily on aspects of citizenship and civil society. Stack has published *Knowing History in Mexico: An Ethnography of Citizenship* (University of New Mexico Press 2012) and edited the volumes *Religion as a Category of Governance and Sovereignty* (Brill 2015), *Breaching the Civil Order:*

NOTES ON THE CONTRIBUTORS

Radicalism and the Civil Sphere (Cambridge University Press 2020), *Engaging Authority: Citizenship and Political Community* (Rowman & Littlefield International 2021), and *Citizens Against Crime and Violence: Societal Responses in Mexico* (Rutgers University Press 2022).

Carlo Tognato is currently Faculty Fellow at the Center for Cultural Sociology, Yale University. He has been for two years Research Fellow at the Center for Holocaust and Genocide Studies at the University of Minnesota and before that Senior Policy Fellow for another two years at the Schar School of Policy and Government at George Mason University. Before moving back to the United States at the end of 2019, he was, for over a decade, Associate Professor at the Department of Sociology of the National University of Colombia, Bogotá, as well as, for four years, Director at the Center for Social Studies at the same university. Since 2014, his research has focused almost exclusively on civil reconstruction and civil degradation.

Suryakant Waghmore is Professor of Sociology at the Indian Institute of Technology, Bombay. He is author of *Civility against Caste* (Sage 2013).

Preface and Acknowledgments

This volume has a long backstory.

As a doctoral student at the University of Edinburgh in 2008, Waghmore won Best Paper Prize at the university's annual New Directions in Sociological Research conference. He was urged by an anonymous reviewer of the paper to make use of Alexander's *The Civil Sphere* (2006) to further develop his thoughts about caste, civility, and civil society.

Five years later, Waghmore wrote to Alexander about the publication of his own book, *Civility against Caste*. Alexander replied, "I'm asking the Yale Library to order your book so I can read it!" And, after doing so, wrote back enthusiastically.

In 2017, Waghmore invited Alexander to come to IITB in Mumbai to participate in a conference on caste, religion, and civility. Unable to attend, Alexander suggested to Waghmore that they plan a conference on the civil sphere in India.

At the beginning of 2018, Alexander came to Mumbai for a week's lectures on cultural sociology and to plan such a conference with Waghmore. On January 3, 2018, in Jalvihar Seminar Hall, Waghmore chaired Alexander's lecture, "The Civil Sphere." On the IITB website, the topic of that lecture was described thus:

> The Civil Sphere is a new general macro-sociological theory of con-temporary democratic societies. It combines cultural and institutional levels. Comparison with the instrumentalization of political science and political sociology, on the one hand, and the idealism of Habermas on the other. The role of "the binary discourse of civil society." The centrality of solidarity, but one that is exclusive as well as inclusive. Regulatory and Communicative institutions. The contradictions and dynamics of real existing civil spheres.

PREFACE AND ACKNOWLEDGMENTS

The conference was to take place in 2020 but the pandemic caused it to be postponed. It took place in New Haven in spring 2022.

We thank Shivani Choudhary for her assistance throughout the days of the conference as well as for the suggestions she made for the Introduction to this volume. Nadine Amalfi, the Administrator for Yale's Center for Culture Sociology, organized the entirety of the conference with her usual blend of efficiency and good cheer. We gratefully acknowledge funding from the Templeton Foundation and the Edward J. and Dorothy Clarke Kempf Memorial Fund established by Yale University's Macmillan Center for International and Area Studies. Dr. Patti Phillips provided excellent copy-editing before the manuscript went into press with Polity, where John Thompson had already made its publication possible.

We thank the contributors to this volume for their patience, their dedicated attention, and, above all, for their insight.

Jeffrey C. Alexander and Suryakant Waghmore

When a people has lived for centuries under a system of castes and classes, it can only reach a democratic state of society through a long series of more or less painful transformations.

Alexis de Tocqueville, *Democracy in America*

Introduction

The Indian Civil Sphere between Vitality and Suppression
Jeffrey C. Alexander

Indian democracy is in trouble. A highly popular, democratically elected leader stands athwart it, dangerously authoritarian and disrespectful of civil liberties, the independence of the courts and the press, and disputatious vis-à-vis organized counter-powers. Leading intellectuals, Indian and Western, are writing books about the death of Indian democracy and the passage to despotism (e.g., Chowdhury and Keane 2021). These dangers are very real, but I will suggest in this introductory chapter that the death of Indian democracy is greatly exaggerated. To understand why, we must move beyond democracy narrowly understood as a governmental form to a broader theory of the cultural, associational, and institutional life necessary to sustain it. In the seventy-five years since India's independence, there has been an extraordinary development of its civil sphere. As my co-editor Suryakant Waghmore has written, in India, even today, "one easily gets a feel of the vibrancy of democracy and the politicization of public spaces" (Waghmore 2013: xxix).

Model of the Civil Sphere

An independent civil sphere is essential to sustaining democracy as a way of life, a structure of discourse, a mode of experience, and a feeling for others that sustain a wide range of civilly oriented, non-governmental institutions (Alexander 2006). The civil sphere can be conceived as a differentiated social arena with relative autonomy vis-à-vis other, "non-civil" realms, such as economy, religion, family, and state. Defined by feelings of solidarity rather than monetary profit, salvation, loyalty, or power, civil ties transcend narrower, more primordial commitments to kinship, race, religion, ideology, and region. The utopian ideals of the civil sphere intertwine respect for individual autonomy with collective obligations toward people whom we will never actually meet in person but whom we symbolize via discourses that endow them with such sacred democratic qualities as cooperativeness, altruism, independence, rationality, and honesty. Yet, even as we bind ourselves to such brothers and sisters, we inversely symbolize those who are outside the civil sphere – as being so aggressive and selfish, dependent, irrational, and deceitful that to include them in our collectivity would be to undermine our capacity for self-government.

This binary discourse of sacred–civil and profane–anti-civil is a language spoken without thinking, not only by those inside civil spheres but those outside wanting in – by those on the left, right, and center; by rich and poor; religious and secular; male and female; dark skinned and light. Not whether one speaks this language but how and to whom its potent binaries are applied is what decides inclusion and exclusion and triumph and defeat; which social movement is legitimated and which repressed; which social policy applauded and effected and which booed and rejected; which political party lionized and reelected, which humiliated and sent down to defeat.

It is the institutions of the civil sphere that specify this generalized civil discourse, connecting it to policies, parties, movements, and people. Communicative institutions – factual and fictional media, associations, public opinion and polling – create moment-to-moment interpretations of ongoing events in real time, sacralizing them as civil or polluting them as dangerously not. Regulative institutions – law, office, elections, and parties – also create purifying and polluting interpretations, but via judgments that are longer in the making and can be enforced through the coercive arm of the state.

Civil Sphere in Independent India

The cultural and institutional ingredients for creating a civil sphere in India were well in place by the time of its independence from the British empire in the mid-twentieth century. In some part, they were the residue of the more public-facing, "beneficent" face of British colonialism that emerged after, and in opposition to, the grossly abusive domination of the East India Company (Wilson 2023); in another and more substantial part, they were the product of a strenuous struggle, within this newly emerging institutional and discursive framework, of the elite that led the "National" movement and played such an outsized role, from the mid-nineteenth century onward, in bringing a civilizationally relevant version

INTRODUCTION

of "modernity" to India. Regulatory institutions were created that could sustain independent India's democracy. In 1885, this emerging Indian elite, forging ties with British reformers, created the Indian National Congress (INC), and in the early decades of the twentieth century this political party, now called simply Congress, contested and triumphed in British-sponsored elections at local and national levels (Brown 2003: 43), which had increasingly expansive franchises (Jaffrelot 2003a: 11, 47–77). Along with the regulatory institutions of elections and parties, a powerful framework of independent Indian legal adjudication had also formed within the colonial state. "By the 1940's," writes Rohit De in *A People's Constitution*, "India's legal profession constituted a fairly well-defined professional public with common journals, association meetings, and lobbying groups" (De 2018: 27; cf. Austin 1999a [1966]: 206). At the time of independence, India had 72,425 licensed legal practitioners, the second highest in the world outside the United States (De 2018: 27).

The background for these democratically oriented regulative institutions was the energetic effort of the modernizing elite to develop a broadened, national solidarity. Communicative institutions played the central role. By the mid-nineteenth century, there emerged a plethora of voluntary organizations dedicated to "public service," whether motivated by the reformed Hindu notion of *seva* (Gorringe 2005: 91; Watt 2005), Christian charity, or Fabian socialism. "Social service, charitable and philanthropic initiatives," writes Watt in *Serving the Nation*, "were animated by notions of active citizenship and mediated by a growing network of associations [that] aimed at improving and strengthening the 'community', 'race' and 'country'" (Watt 2005: 1, 3).

> Service and self-help groups ... encouraged the efficient use of dana or "charity" for the public good; they promoted the cooperative credit movement and the principles of mutual aid; and they were involved in a wide variety of more mundane activities such as distributing water to third-class rail passengers [and] helping the elderly. [T]here was particular concern about the "uplift" of the lower castes, classes and untouchables. [Such] citizen activism and the culture of association contributed to the shaping of India's sociological landscape, namely its "public sphere" and "civil society." (Watt 2005: 3, 5)

As the sense of a national "public opinion" began to crystallize, so did uncounted numbers of magazines and newspapers, regionally and nationally (Barns 1940; Natarajan 2021 [1955]). Their "news" avidly communicated interpretations of social and political life in colonial India, applying the binaries of civil discourse to the independence movements and their enemies (Sen and Roy 2014; Sen 2017).

3

THE INDIAN CIVIL SPHERE

> Journalism travelled from England to various colonies [and was] constructively adapted by the local elites. [It] prepared the groundwork for the use of the press as a powerful weapon during India's freedom struggle . . . as a site where the first impulses of Indian nationalism were being expressed. Journalism also became an effective tool for social and religious reform. (Sonwalker 2019: 36)

Four decades after independence, there were already 32,000 newspapers in India; two decades later, 94,000 (Rodrigues and Ranganathan 2015: 10); and five years after, with the advent of cable, 825 television channels and 300 24/7 news channels broadcasting in sixteen languages (Rao 2019: 1). Critical investigative journalism flourished, creating explosive revelations that often "shook the nation" (Rodrigues and Ranganathan 2015: 68). In 1987, after *The Hindu* documented kickbacks that Prime Minister Rajiv Gandhi's government had received from a Swedish armaments company in exchange for government contracts (Rodrigues and Ranganathan 2015: 70), the Congress party was defeated in the 1989 national election. In 2011, in the midst of "stories about corruption and a lack of transparency and accountability among politicians and bureaucrats," journalists sympathetically interpreted the anti-corruption sit-ins and hunger strikes of the septuagenarian Anna Hazare, who declared that "a second freedom struggle" had begun (Rodrigues and Ranganathan 2015: 164, 154). "The mainstream media, particularly the 24-hour news channels, could not find a better story – full of drama, conflict, visuals, and popular support," write Rodrigues and Ranganathan (2015: 155). This "media event" (Dayan and Katz 1992) rekindled idealism about office inside the Indian civil sphere, in the face of "forgotten ideas and lexicon [about] 'corruption', 'conflict of interest', 'misuse of office', 'the political-corporate nexus', 'cross-party collusion'" (Rodrigues and Ranganathan 2015: 169). While the liminal drama fizzled out in 2012, due to the fading health of its protagonist and media allegations of financial abuse by some members of Team Anna and Anna himself, the opposition BJP party and its leader Narendra Modi swept to power in 2014, promising "Good Days Are Coming" and launching the "Clean India Campaign" after his victory (Jaffrelot 2014).

If it was the later stages of coloniality that, counterintuitively, had "opened up public spaces" and "spheres of freedom for competitive political mobilization" (Waghmore 2013: xx), it was the Constitution of newly independent India – ratified in 1950 after three years of extraordinary conversation, consultation, compromise, and innovation – that crystallized the legal foundations for the new nation's impressively developed communicative and regulative institutions (Austin 1999a [1966], 1999b). The Constitution laid out a detailed series of negative

INTRODUCTION

liberties (Berlin 2002) guaranteeing individuals and groups freedom *from* constraint – rights to free speech, religion, association, and free press. Yet, equally importantly, the Constitution also inscribed a novel set of positive liberties, promising Indian citizens freedom *for* developing their economic, biological, and cognitive well-being, from women's rights to universal public schooling, to abolishing untouchability and "scheduling" lower castes for affirmative access to wide-ranging opportunities. In the words of the legendary chronicler of the constitutional assembly, Granville Austin, the founders had created not only the lineaments of a political democracy, but the framework for a social revolution (Austin 1999a [1966]). In one fell swoop, the Constitution guaranteed the full panoply of legal, political, and *social* rights that, according to the influential theorizing of T. H. Marshall, had taken three centuries to evolve in Britain (Marshall 1965).

> India's founding fathers and mothers established in the Constitution both the nation's ideals and the institutions and processes for them. [A] democratic and equitable society . . . was to be achieved through a social-economic revolution pursued with a democratic spirit using constitutional, democratic institutions. . . . Representative government with adult suffrage, a bill of rights providing equality under the law and personal liberty, and an independent judiciary were to become the spiritual and institutional bases for a new society – one replacing the traditional hierarchy and its repressions. Other constitutional provisions were designed to spread democracy by protecting and increasing the rights of minorities, by assisting under-privileged groups in society to better their condition, and ending the blatant oppression of the Scheduled Castes and Tribes. . . . The Constitution, by its very existence, was a social revolutionary statement. (Austin 1999a [1966]: xi–xiii)

Contradictions: Independent India's "Actually Existing" Civil Sphere

These foundational articulations of the Indian civil sphere were manifestly utopian, and they exerted extraordinary cultural-*cum*-institutional power.[1] In "actually existing" civil spheres, however, there is a clash between the real and ideal, which creates the contradictions that dynamize social change. Such contradictions create wrenching strains that motivate efforts at civil repair, as well as the backlash that ineluctably reacts against them. The Constitution laid out ideals for practicing democracy and expanding solidarity, and the secular, mostly British-educated leaders of the successful national movement dedicated themselves to

THE INDIAN CIVIL SPHERE

carrying these ideals out. But India's *social* resources were hardly a match for these high *political* aspirations.[2] For one thing, rather than a bourgeois "middle class" that could define its ideal and material interest in democratic terms, most regions of independent India were controlled by landed property owners with an interest in maintaining caste-*cum*-class; they had no objective interest, in other words, in generating the kind of generalized, free-floating resources that the Indian masses would require if their newly promised liberties were to be substantiated (Corbridge and Harriss 2000: 31–9; cf. Moore 1966). The Constitution did gesture toward the public ownership of national wealth, but its insistence on submitting property seizure to legal adjudication effectively blocked the distribution of land in more egalitarian ways.

Resistance to expanding material solidarity was complemented, indeed motivated, by powerful cultural and affective commitments to caste hierarchy. There was a reason that Western social theorists had so often defined their own liberal ambitions by contrasting them with Hindu India's *Homo hierarchicus* (Dumont 1970). Among the great Axial religions (Bellah 2011) that laid the basis for multiple modernities (Eisenstadt 1982; Alexander 2020), Hinduism was least able to generate the distance from primordial attachment that is required to nurture critical universalism and, eventually, equality (Bellah 2011).[3] With its four varnas and the thousands of infinitely differentiated jatis, or subcastes, spreading out amongst them, Indian Hinduism sacralized powerfully primordial over civil attachments – commitments to family, place, occupation, and gods (Alexander 2024). Rather than imagining salvation as equality and liberation, caste imbedded individuals in their local community and demanded loyalty to authority, requiring deference to those above and legitimating domination over subordinates below. What underlays a civil solidarity is the sense of the fundamental sameness of every human being; in caste society, by contrast, "difference is absolute" (Hall 1998 in Waghmore 2013: xxi). B. R. Ambedkar was the only Indian founding father from the *avarna* – one "without varna," the residual outcaste category so polluted that they could be identified only as untouchables, in Hindi *Dalits*. In his impassioned *Annihilation of Caste*, Ambedkar memorably argued that the caste system was actually not "a division of labour," but rather "a division of labourers" (Ambedkar 2016 [1936]: 223). Ambedkar polemized that caste was inimical to democracy: "The effect of caste on the ethics of the Hindus is simply deplorable. Caste has killed public spirit. Caste has destroyed the sense of public charity. Caste has made public opinion impossible. A Hindu's public is his caste. His responsibility is only to this caste" (Ambedkar 2016 [1936]: 259).

INTRODUCTION

Anti-Caste Movements and Civil Repair

It is remarkable that, despite these powerful ideal and material contradictions, for many decades after independence the Indian civil sphere allowed, indeed encouraged, less privileged Indians to make good on the promises of their Constitution and the utopian promises of their civil sphere. In region after region, the lower castes created powerful social movements that leveraged the civil sphere's communicative and regulative institutions to effect (Alexander 2024) that, materially and symbolically, significantly extended national solidarity.

"The constitution has undermined the legitimacy of caste," Hugo Gorringe argues in *Untouchable Citizens*, his ethnography of Dalit movements and democracy in the southern region of Tamil Nadu, demonstrating in copious detail how India's civil sphere "provided the oppressed with the institutional means to challenge their subordinate status" (Gorringe 2005: 21). As a newly "horizontal mobilization" (ibid.) emerged among the once highly fragmented untouchables, they engaged in protest petitions, mass rallies, marches, and organized public disruptions, appealing across caste boundaries to the civil obligations that putatively bound the privileged social groups above them. In the 1970s, the Dalit Panthers exploded onto the social scene, the product of a younger generation who expressed a "fanatical passion for equality" (Gough 1960: 44 in Gorringe 2005: 117). "Time and time again," Gorringe writes, young Dalits "assert[ed] their common humanity: 'If we are cut do we not bleed? Is our blood not as red as yours?'" (Gorringe 2005: 119). In the midst of a steeply hierarchical society, this "rejection of dharma and assertion of equality" certainly "constituted a *cultural* revolution" (Gorringe 2005: 348, italics added). Yet, the Panther leader Thol. Thirumavalavan insisted that, when his people leveraged the broader solidarity that underlaid the promises of a civil sphere, this movement of "the people at the bottom rung of society" aimed not at political revolution but incorporation: "The organization of the Liberation Panthers," he remonstrated, "is a movement aimed at the well-being of the *general* population"; as a *democratic* movement, "it seeks to promote better *understanding* between castes. It is a democratic movement" (Gorringe 2005: 53, italics added). "If we do not exercise our right to vote in the state or general elections," a Dalit activist explained, "our immediate enemies are the ones to gain" (Gorringe 2005: 286). Gorringe observes that "the subaltern seem to think democracy is working for them" (Gorringe 2005: 291), that, despite their exploitation, "the majority of Dalits still place their faith in the democratic process," insisting that what

7

they "wish to see [is] their leaders in power [in order to] render political institutions accountable" (Gorringe 2005: 343).[4] Because their movements were effective, Dalits were "entering the mainstream" (Gorringe 2005: 324; cf. Gorringe et al. 2016).

In his more macrosociological study of northern India, the French political scientist Christophe Jaffrelot traces an equally powerful incorporative process generated by lower-caste social movements, concluding that "North India is going the way South India [has] already gone" (Jaffrelot 2003a: v). He traces the same process of subcaste fusion among Dalit jatis – Dalit caste fragments – into extended groupings reflecting more "horizontal solidarity" (Jaffrelot 2003a: 147, 150). Describing this wider grouping as an "alternative social *imaginaire*," Jaffrelot observes a new "collective identity" that is now much more "conducive to the emancipation of the lower castes" (Jaffrelot 2003a: 151) because its ties more closely align with those that define India's relatively independent civil sphere.

Another new development among the civil sphere's communicative institutions was the emergence of civil associations like BAMCEF, a coalition among the so-called "Backward Classes" dedicated to solidarity and uplift, whose 200,000 members eventually formed a successful political party (Jaffrelot 2003a: 39).[5] And peasant leaders like Charan Singh – the "champion of farmers" who eventually became India's fifth prime minister – organized broad movements of lower castes into powerful political organizations that could successfully compete in state and eventually national elections.

The aim of these social movements was not only to gain subjective recognition, via communicative institutions, but to force regulative institutions to make good on, and deepen, long-promised quotas guaranteeing lower-caste groups entry into education and employment in government. By 1977, the proportion of upper-class MPs in the national parliament had already fallen below 50 percent; ten years later, it was below 40 percent. Singh declared, "a silent transfer of power is taking place in social terms" (Jaffrelot 2003a: 350). By the early 1990s, "scheduled" quotas for Dalits and OBCs ("Other Backward Classes") were expanded to ensure them fully one-half of all new positions in government and higher education. James Manor was certainly right to conclude, in a recent overview, that "the strong influence which higher castes once exercised over local affairs has been substantially eroded over time" (Manor 2021: 134). There has been "a marked increase in inter-caste accommodation which pre-empts violence," Manor insists, and which has "foster[ed] the growth of a certain minimal civility towards Dalits" (Manor 2021: 129). The Indian civil sphere had been wedged open (Stack 2019) by powerful lower-caste movements for social change.[6]

INTRODUCTION

Frontlash/Backlash

As the first two chapters in this volume make vividly clear, the struggle for the civil repair of caste hierarchy was anything but a smooth unfolding process, the kind of "adaptive upgrading and value generalization," for example, that Talcott Parsons theorized in his teleological approach to social evolution (Alexander 2005). Just as the African-American freedom struggle faced fierce resistance, so has the Indian anti-caste movement – not least bigoted judges and police, terrifying violence and brutality. Waghmore points to the "anxieties of the privileged and dominant castes over their eroding control of ex-untouchables" (Waghmore 2013: 161). Manor warns that anti-caste "struggles for inclusion and decency ... only partly succeed," and that even "when they make some headway," their success "often lead[s] to ... fresh dilemmas and disappointments" (Manor 2016: xiv). Even as the relative autonomy of a democratic civil sphere allows "groups [to] coalesce, assert themselves and ... acquire some influence," he explains, the "reactions of adversaries – and even some of their own successes – create new impediments and sometimes trigger disintegration and disempowerment" (Manor 2016: xiii). Mendelsohn and Vicziany (1998: 53 in Gorringe 2005: 133) analyze the many "incidences of high caste retaliation," the "extravagant revenge" triggered by Dalits' "resistance to subordination and claims to social respect." Gorringe recounts "the 'story' of Melavalavu," "known to all Tamil Dalit activists" (Gorringe 2005: 135), that recounts the "premeditated massacre of [Dalit] panchayat president Murugesan, and five of his followers" (ibid.).

> When Murugesan contested and won the seat reserved for SC's [Scheduled Castes] in the Melavalavu panchayat (local elections) in 1977 [he] had to stand against the ... threats of the locally-dominant Thevar caste. [But] the legal recognition accorded to the post of panchayat president was insufficient to protect Murugesan and his followers from being massacred in broad daylight by those who could not countenance the elevation of an Untouchable to a position of responsibility. (Gorringe 2005: 21)

At best, it was two steps forward, one step back; at worst, one step forward, two steps back. Like the Black freedom struggles in America, Dalit and OBC movements to "annihilate caste" (Ambedkar 2016 [1936]) in India triggered right-wing reactions, which not only blocked further advances of civil rights, but sometimes overturned what had already been achieved. To the degree they are successful, movements for empowerment undermine extant ideal and material interests, interests deeply entrenched inside the compromised civil order, not only among elites but among privileged fragments of the masses as well. Civil repair brings greater freedom and equality for the many, but it reduces freedom of action for previously hegemonic others. For Nelson Mandela and the African National Congress, victory over Apartheid felt like "the long walk to freedom" (Mandela 1995), but for those who profited from Apartheid, ideally and materially, the ANC's victory felt more like a car crash. What they experienced was whiplash, an injury that festers unless therapeutic interventions are made. Civil repair is a frontlash movement whose victories create aggrieved parties, with backlash movements the likely result (Alexander 2019b).

Frontlash/backlash polarizes civil spheres. This dynamic can have the effect of pushing left-wing movements to the far left and right-wing movements to the far right, animating hostile, even paranoid antagonisms that can undermine the solidarity whose civil character provides the very underpinning of democracy. The dynamics of polarization are inherent to an open society, a normal feature of democratic social change. In relatively "healthy" civil spheres, there is a pendulum movement, frontlash pushing society to the left, backlash pushing it to the right. The danger is that the pendulum will get stuck on either side, that extreme right or left populism, after legitimately winning state power, will wish to keep it to themselves. If they can suppress the autonomy of the civil sphere, they will be able to prevent the social pendulum from swinging back to the other side. Martin Luther King famously declared, "the arc of the moral universe is long but it bends towards justice" (King 2022 [1963]). But his was a normative profession of faith, not a clear-eyed statement about the dark possibilities of empirical social life. Just as backlash movements have allowed anti-democratic leaders to gain power in the Americas and Europe, so have far right populists in India, like current Prime Minister Narendra Modi, ridden waves of backlash sentiment to gain state power. Skillfully marshalling the binary discourse of India's civil sphere, Modi and his Bharatiya Janata Party (BJP) have gained state power, and they have begun to throttle the nation's independent communicative and regulative institutions.

Layered Backlash in India

There are distinctive dimensions, or layers, that have created the backlash against civil repair in India and the discourse and institutions of the civil sphere that have facilitated it. They reach back centuries into colonial prehistory, yet they are as recent as the nationwide election that

INTRODUCTION

played out as this book was going to press. Each dimension is powerful, but none on its own is dispositive. They are layers of the same cake, whose combinatorial power creates the capacity to block the pendulum of Indian political life from swinging back from the right side to the center and left. Whether such a fateful freezing happens cannot yet be determined. The Indian civil sphere will have its say.

In the space of this introduction, there is not the opportunity to fully explore the many layers of India's democratic achievement and the backlash against it. I am laying out a blueprint, not the building that might be made from it. In what remains of this chapter, I employ civil sphere theory to suggest a new approach to the challenges facing Indian democracy.

Hindutva

The discourse of civil society that so powerfully shaped, and still shapes, the contours of democratic India is a metalanguage. A syncretic structure in Saussurean terms, civil discourse can also be understood in an historical, or diachronic sense, as a developing cultural tradition that amalgamated binaries from classical republicanism, Christianity, and modern liberalism. Emerging from the political discourse of ancient Greece, in the shadow of the declining Roman empire, republicanism became intertwined with Christianity, the three distinct elements creating an ideological compound that informed the democratic breakthrough of the early Renaissance city states, like Florence and Venice (Skinner 1978a). In a more radicalized form, this potent brew later fueled the Protestant Reformation (Skinner 1978b), which in turn triggered the first modern democratic revolution in seventeenth-century Britain – an upheaval that Michael Walzer once described as "the revolution of the saints" (Walzer 1965). One century later, this radical democratic ideology, which Robert Bellah called the American "civil religion" (Bellah 1970), marked the language of the American Revolution (Bailyn 1967; Hatch 1977; Bloch 1985).

Why bother with this strand of Western cultural history in an essay introducing the civil sphere in India? Because it provides the basis for a critical comparison. In the West, democracy emerged from *within* the religious tradition.[7] While the discourse of civil society is not in itself religious, it had metaphysical anchoring.[8] Whereas in the democratic formation of Britain and America, there was hardly any air between civic radicalism and religious salvation, in India exactly the opposite was the case.[9] The discourse of the Indian civil sphere was rooted in an imported, religious-*cum*-secular ideology of the colonizer. It should not

11

THE INDIAN CIVIL SPHERE

be surprising that so many Indians, not only religious elites but religious masses, experienced civil discourse and institutions as threatening, not only to their religion but to their traditional way of life.

"Hindutva" is the ground base for India's backlash against democracy (Nussbaum 2007: 152–85). A Hindi term roughly translated as "Hinduness," Hindutva is more, and less, than the Hindu religion. It is a manifestly nationalistic and backward-looking variation – one that, in the words of Jyotirmaya Sharma, one of its most astute scholarly contemporary critics, constitutes an "emotive call to 'culture' and 'traditional values,'" a cultural movement that aims at eviscerating "India's democratic, republican, rational and secular foundations" and resurrecting, in their place, an "imagined glorious past" in which the metaphysics and social structure of Hinduism reign supreme (Sharma 2015: 4). In its most recent incarnation, Hindutva is the ideology of the BJP, the massively popular political party that recently triumphed in its third successive national election. It is hardly an accident that the BJP was born, three-and-a-half decades ago, as a protest against "Mandalization," the last, and deepest, expansion of the quotas for lower-caste Indians put into place by socialist Prime Minister V. P. Singh in 1990 (Jaffrelot 2003a: 320–49).

Yet Hindutva as cultural movement goes back much further, to the mid-nineteenth century. When Christian missionaries condemned Hinduism for its idolatry and superstition (Jaffrelot 1996 [1993]: 14), Hindutva's foundational thinkers responded by polluting European civilization as materialist, sacralizing Hinduism's putatively higher spirituality. In a work that was foundational to the Hindu revival, *Satyartha Prakash, the Light of Truth*, Swami Dayananda Saraswati declared that the authors of the Western Bible were savages and the Christian God nothing more than a "flesh-eating trickster" (Saraswati 1972 [1875]: 612 in Sharma 2015: 47; cf. Jaffrelot 1996 [1993]: 16–17). India's humiliating subjection at the hands of the British, however, was deemed less the result of colonial power than the degeneration of Hinduism itself. It was "indolence, negligence, and mutual discord" that had allowed India to be "crushed under the heel of the foreigner" and its people "to bear untold misery and suffering" (Saraswati 2002 [1875]: 267 in Sharma 2015: 34). To purify Hinduism, there would have to be a return to the religion's most ancient texts, the Vedas, for "it behooves all good people to hold in due respect the teachings of . . . ancient history" (ibid.). Composed millennia earlier, the Vedas were written in Sanskrit, which the Hindu revivalists claimed as the mother of all languages, and they were composed by Aryans, an early Indian civilization whom Saraswati exalted as having been "sovereign rulers of the whole earth" (Saraswati 1972 [1875]: 266 in Sharma 2015: 32). While revivalists rued later Hinduism's diffusion of the caste

12

INTRODUCTION

system into fragmented jatis, they adamantly insisted that caste hierarchy had been essential to the Vedic Golden Age and would be foundational to the Hindu revival. The Brahmins occupied the first varna, Saraswati suggests, because, quite simply, they deserved to, for it was they who best understood and taught Vedic wisdom. As for the Shudras, the fourth and lowest varna, they had been relegated to that position because of their dismerit, for they were simply unable to learn.

> Wherever it is declared that the Shudras are debarred from the study of the Veda, the prohibition simply amounts to this: that, he that does not learn anything even after a good deal of teaching, being ignorant and destitute of understanding, is called a Shudra. (Saraswati 1972 [1875]: 79 in Sharma 2015: 52)

Alongside the loss of spiritual wisdom and the threat to vertical caste organization, an animating concern of the Hindutva revival was what they viewed as a concomitant withering away of masculinity. In post-Vedic times, they claimed, Hinduism had allowed itself to become dangerously effeminate, which had rendered it vulnerable to outside subjugation. For this reason, Hindu revival would have to depend, not only on Brahminic wisdom, but also on the dharma of the militant Kshatriya varna, a caste category just one rank below it. Sri Aurobindo, another highly influential Hindu revivalist, declared, "the first virtue of the Kshatriya is not to bow his neck to an unjust yoke but to protect his weak and suffering countrymen against the oppressor and welcome death in a just and righteous battle" (Aurobindo 1998 [1906–8] in Sharma 2015: 60–1). Just as Arjuna, the hero of the Hindu epic the *Mahabharata* and the "very symbol of Kshatriya" (Sharma 2015: 61), had chosen to fight to save ancient India rather than surrender to oppressive tyranny, so would today's "weak and unmanly Indians" (Sharma 2015: 65) have to transform themselves in order to shake off their contemporary oppressors. Moral uplift must be accompanied by he-man physical rehabilitation, famously alliterated by another major Hindutva thinker, Swami Vivekananda, as "beef, biceps, and the Bhagavadgita" (Sharma 2015: 56). With rhetorical flourish, the Swami even suggested that young Indians might actually be "nearer to Heaven through football than through the study of the Gita" (Vivekananda 1999 [1951], vol. III: 242 in Sharma 2015: 117).

> You will understand Gita better with your biceps, your muscles, a little stronger. You will understand the mighty genius and the mighty strength of Krishna better with a little strong Blood in you. You will understand the Upanishads better and the glory of the Atman, when your body stands firm upon your feet, and you feel yourself as men. (ibid.)

A less concrete and more generalized effect of these foundational Hindutva ideas was to undermine the origin myth of Indian democracy. Their revised Hinduism displaced India's democratic founding fathers, like Gandhi and Nehru, who had led the fight for national independence, along with the other civilly minded founding fathers who had created the new nation's constitution and whose Congress party ruled India in its early formative decades. The real origins of "Mother India," Hindutva claims, were millennia earlier, in Vedic times, when mythically religious Aryans had created a Golden Age. The national narrative of democratic India was progressive and hopeful: since the nation's founding in 1947, the story went, there had been massive civil repair that worked to resolve contradictions in the Indian civil sphere. Hindutva, by contrast, sketched a backward-looking narrative; according to this story, it had all been downhill since the Vedic Golden Age, a decline that had actually been exacerbated by the birth of democratic India at midnight on August 15, 1947, when India had become putatively, but only superficially, free.[10]

It was the thinking of a fourth foundational Hindutva thinker, Vinayak Damodar Savarkar, that transformed this theological renewal of ancient wisdom and manly militancy into organizational forms that could "consolidate and strengthen Hindu nationality" (Savarkar 1969 [1923]: 140 in Jaffrelot 1996 [1993]: 25) and unleash the final struggle for the "Hindu Rashtra [nation]." In the 1870s, Dayananda Saraswati had created the proselytizing *Arya Samaj*, or Noble Society (Jaffrelot 1996 [1993]: 13–20; Sharma 2015: 54–5); three decades later, in order to "Hinduize all politics and militarize all Hindudom," Savarkar created the revolutionary and violence-prone secret organization *Abhinav Bharat Mandir*, the Young India Society (Savarkar 1967 [1942]: 2). In 1925, Keshav Baliram Hedgewar, a Hindutva militant deeply influenced by Savarkar (Sharma 2019: xxvii–xxix), founded the infamous *Rashtriya Swayamsevak Sangh*, or RSS (Association of National Volunteers). His disciple, M. S. Golwalkar, succeeded him as RSS leader and transformed its ascetic, militant, and largely Brahmin cadre into the most effective extremist organization in Indian history (Jaffrelot 1996 [1993]: 33–79) – "a rigid, codified, monochromatic and aggressively masculine entity" (Sharma 2019: xix; cf. Nussbaum 2007). In every locally organized RSS group, or shakha, the morning would begin with strenuous calisthenics, which were followed by intensive ideological-*cum*-religious training highlighting extraordinary deeds recorded in the Vedas, along with discussion of equally heroic deeds to come. By the end of the Second World War, 600,000 RSS shakhas had spread across India, and they now included lower-caste members who were willing to undergo renunciation for the Hindutva cause. In January 1948, Nathuram Godse, a militant

INTRODUCTION

Hindutva ideologue, assassinated Mahatma Gandhi. Nehru's newly formed government temporarily outlawed RSS and arrested 20,000 of its activists; Godse walked to the gallows singing the RSS hymn "I bow to you always, O loving motherland" (Sharma 2019: xxxiv).

Islam

Rather than hating Gandhi for being secular, an obvious impossibility, Godse believed the Mahatma's original sin to be his lifelong protest against Hindutva-inspired struggles to cleanse India of its Muslim minority. Indeed, while Hindutva stridently resented the British Raj for its Christian and democratic discourse, its efforts at religious reconstruction were also powerfully, if less conspicuously, motivated by antagonism to the six-century long Muslim colonialization of India. Not just the Raj, but this immensely powerful *non*-Western occupier had also made Hindus weak. "Wave after wave of barbarian conquest has rolled over this devoted land of ours," Vivekananda decried: "'Allah Ho Akbar!' has rent the skies for hundreds of years, and no Hindu knew what moment would be his last" (Vivekananda 1999 [1951], vol. III: 269–70 in Sharma 2015: 99). During Mughal rule, Golwalkar declared, "there was no one to protect the Hindus," yet, "despite force and inducements," there remained people "who kept the commitment to Hindu culture intact by singing songs in praise of Lord Ramachandra and Lord Krishan [and] kept faith, tradition and piety alive" (Sharma 2019: 12). The RSS aimed to continue this heroic, Hindutva-inspired resistance in the present day.

Despite the massive intrusion of the East Indian Company, Mughals had managed to sustain their rule over India until the Government of India Act established the Raj in 1858. The British allowed Muslims to maintain their distinct, mosque-centered religious practices. Vis-à-vis the Hindu majority, the Raj treated the minority Muslim population virtually as a "separate but equal" collectivity entitled to incipient social and political rights, including the possibility of voting for their own religiously affiliated representatives in local and national bodies (Brown 2003: 129; cf. Bhagat 2001). Even as Muslim elites actively participated in the independence movement, they developed their own national aspirations and organizations, fearful of becoming a despised minority in a Hindu-dominated post-independence India. This developing Islamic nationalism was fiercely countered by secular and religious leaders of the Indian National Movement, most spectacularly by Gandhi's furious declamations, backed up by dramatic fasts and *yatras* (marches/ pilgrimages) that remonstrated for a more religiously inclusive, all-India form of civil-religious solidarity. These efforts could do little, however,

THE INDIAN CIVIL SPHERE

to stem the tide. By the early twentieth century, an Indian-Muslim elite was demanding independence, not only from the Raj, but from "Hindu India." A Muslim League formed, led by the fiery nationalist M. A. Jinnah (Brown 2003: 131ff), and began pushing for the creation of a physically separated Pakistani state.

Anti-Muslim resentment among the Hindu masses intensified accordingly, and horrific episodes of what came to be termed "communal" violence marked the early and middle years of the twentieth century (Guha 2007: 624–50; Jaffrelot 2011: 343–408; Cooke 2019). In 1946, for example, the Muslim League ordered a "direct Action Day" that triggered murderous religious rioting in Calcutta, leaving more than 4,000 persons dead and 100,000 homeless. When India became independent one year later, the British-mandated "Partition" of India and Pakistan led to an immensely debilitating tragedy. Within hours, the Punjab, a border state with a small Islamic majority, "erupted into flames and violence," as "thousands of Muslims and Hindus found themselves on the assumed wrong side of the new international border" (Brown 2003: 175). As primordial fears fanned panic along the border and beyond, mass carnage ended the lives of more than 1 million Hindus and Muslims, with 15 million more displaced. After Partition, Muslims throughout India were "deeply traumatized [and] fearful of their Hindu neighbors" (Brown 2003: 224); and, during moments of internal and external crisis, Hindu Indians would often condemn Muslim citizens as "anti-national" secret sympathizers with India's enemy Pakistan (ibid.).

Amidst their proud celebrations of national independence, the despair, shame, indeed the humiliation of the Partition trauma was publicly glossed over by leaders on both sides (Alexander 2009). Privately, however, Nehru gave voice to profound worry about how the explosive experience would affect the possibility for civil solidarity. "I could not conceive of the gross brutality and sadistic cruelty that people have indulged in," he wrote to India's future president, Rajendra Prasad (Nehru 1947a in Brown 2003: 176). Framing Hindu revivalism as "the narrowest communalism" (Nehru 1947b in Brown 2003: 175), Nehru described it as "the exact replica of the narrow *Muslim* communalism which we have tried to combat for so long" (ibid., italics added); he feared "that this narrow sectarian outlook will do grave injury [to] the high ideals" of independence (ibid.). Decades later, when public debates and personal testimonies from the Partition trauma finally surfaced, along with public debates about its causes and consequences, Nehru's dark premonitions had seemed to come true. Alok Bhalla, editor of *Stories about the Partition of India*, worried that Partition had forced Indians on both sides "to leave behind a human world . . . in return [for] an empty allegory of religious commu-

16

INTRODUCTION

nity" (Bhalla 1994: xxii); Dipesh Chakrabarty linked Partition violence to "the persistence of religion and caste in post-independence India" (2002: 6); Gyanendra Pandey traced Partition's effects to a "narrow and diminishing view of nationalism" (1997: 3); and Rajeev Bhargava believed Partition had promoted a trope of "communal fanaticism" that "left no space for relatively impersonal principles that could prevent reasonable disagreements from degenerating into hostility" (2000: 199). For decades, Partition had lain like a festering wound in the Indian collective consciousness. Eventually, the sentiments it provoked would provide fertile ground that Hindutva movements cultivated as they moved forcefully from religion into politics, challenging the civil solidarity of India's democratic state.

Cultural Backlash and Political (de)Formation

The primordial inversions of the cultural foundations for civil solidarity traced in the preceding pages have shaped the meanings of social life for many millions of Indians, but they did not, in themselves, shut out the more cosmopolitan and universalistic understandings of millions of others, e.g., the "argumentative Indians" whom Amartya Sen (2005) portrays in his defense of deliberative democracy in India. A culture of critical discourse (Gouldner 1979) continues to proliferate alongside such independent cultural institutions as opinion polls, self-regulating secular universities, professional journalism, and fictional media, both literary and filmic, telling stories about open, embracing, and supra-religious social relationships inside contemporary Indian cinema (Dickey 1993; Sen 2017; Damodaran 2018b; Darshan 2019; Damodaran and Gorringe 2020).

It was far from inevitable, in other words, that the nativistic backlash culture of Hindutva would ascend the heights of national political power, much less assume the overweening status that, despite the encouraging results of the just completed 2024 elections, it continues to occupy today. While its long march to state power had cultural roots, roots alone do not a tall tree make. Democratic and anti-democratic cultural meanings are highly generalized; they have to be funneled and specified through regulatory institutions before they provide access to state power; only then can they even begin the effort to regulate social life in one or another ideological way. In the transition from cultural power in the civil sphere to political position in the state, the regulatory institution of elections is central. Only if election machinery is independent of ideological control can civil power register legitimately. Despite the perambulations of

THE INDIAN CIVIL SPHERE

India's civil sphere and politics, the independence of its electoral machinery, the faith of the masses of Indians in the efficacy of their votes and the integrity of those counting them, has remained remarkably intact. This, in itself, is a paradoxical demonstration of the continuing vitality of civil power in India.

While regulative institutions of the civil sphere, like office and law, remain at some remove from the communicative mobilization that dynamizes public opinion, political parties are, by contrast, intimately responsive to it. Because they aim to win state power for their particular ideological candidate, political parties are much less concerned to maintain a generalizing solidarity: their intent, indeed their obligation, is to *sharpen* the binaries that differentiate and polarize the public's opinion about the sacred and profane opportunities and threats to democratic social life (Alexander 2025b). Parties mobilize voters by staging dramatic political campaigns, writing scripts, and finding candidates to felicitously perform them – all to persuade a majority, or at least a plurality, of the electorate that the current political contest is a matter of social life and death, a struggle in which the very future of democracy is at stake. If elections are transparent, then political victory will go to the political party that has been most effective in crystallizing political opinion, which depends on finding a candidate who has the performative ability to fashion themselves into a collective representation (Alexander 2010; Alexander and Jaworsky 2014). More than the right candidate, parties need an effective staff, which has a powerful esprit de corps and enough discipline to get out the vote.

In the Indian nation's formative decades, it was the Congress party that possessed these political, organizational, and performative capacities. Indeed, it virtually monopolized them. Despite the gathering cultural storm of Hindutva, India remained virtually a one-party state (Kothari 1964). While backlash was well organized and directed in cultural terms – viz. the hundreds of thousands of RSS shakhas – it did not possess an effective vehicle for carrying this cultural mobilization into the political field and, via elections, to transform its primordial visions into state power. Alienation from "modern" institutions and democratic discourse had made Hindutva reticent vis-à-vis the national struggle for independence; yet, it was within that crucible that India's future democratic institutions were formed. When the Partition loomed and Hindutva fears about political Islam exploded, Gandhi's assassination had the effect of pushing its most powerful organizational manifestation – the RSS – completely outside the political scene. RSS was outlawed and thousands of its most effective cadre incarcerated. In the wake of this enormous, if ultimately temporary setback, the backlash religious movement rededi-

INTRODUCTION

cated itself to the cultural task of polarizing India's civil sphere instead of investing energy in what seemed the truly daunting effort of entering the state. It was only many decades later, as civil repair expanded solidarity, challenged caste hierarchy, and widened linguistic and religious plurality, that Hindutva's determined reticence dissolved.[11]

In the first six decades of Indian democracy, it was Congress, the party of civil repair, that held political sway. Because Congress had been leading the independence movement since the late nineteenth century, its leaders built upon their charismatic authority to win elections and control over key offices of the new state. It was not long, however, before the deficiencies of Congress as an organizing and shaping tool became apparent. For one thing, despite its relative unity during the national struggle, its post-independence ideological currency fragmented among socialists, liberals, statists, farmers, large landholders, and big capital. For another, rather than employing a well-trained, organizationally sophisticated, and disciplined cadre to energize and get out the vote, Congress employed "vote banks," relegating the task of turning out voters to local grandees who had long held regional power as a matter of right. Drawing upon traditional obligations of caste and class, these local bigwigs called in electoral chits from blocs of voters. Finally, rather than political ability determining power in the organization, after Nehru's death, Congress descended into a familial dynasty where leadership was ascriptive rather than achieved. Indira Gandhi's principal qualification for succeeding Nehru was having been his daughter; she had never even stood for election, let alone demonstrated a performative ability to win ideological authority or particular organizational prowess. In office, Mrs. Gandhi proved a tone deaf and polarizing leader. Faced with hardening resistance to her policy edicts, she defaulted to non-consensual governance, evoking the "Emergency" clause in the Indian Constitution to establish a dictatorship that, thanks to the continuing vitality of India's civil sphere, lasted only eighteen months (Jaffrelot and Anil 2021). Eight years later, she was assassinated by a Sikh bodyguard after peremptorily, and violently, suppressing a movement for Sikh independence. Congress immediately elevated her eldest son, Rajiv, to succeed his mother. One of his mother's most ruthless, influential, and conspiratorial advisers during the Emergency, Rajiv had trained as an airline pilot not as a politician, never cultivating a political mandate of his own. Gaining party leadership simply on the basis of what Weber called "family charisma," he led a five-year long national government mired in chaos and scandal. After his own assassination, the dynasty was continued by his Italian born and bred widow, Sonia Gandhi, who "presided" over Congress and two victorious national campaigns. The party had become an empty shell, and the rise of political Hindutva guaranteed its defeat, after which the young man Sonia Gandhi had been grooming to succeed her, none other than her own son Rahul, became Congress president, presiding over years in the political wilderness before the extraordinary, and unexpected, revival of his party's political fortunes in 2024.

The BJP was the vehicle for translating Hindutva into political power, and in organizational terms it was a completely different story. Rather than a vote bank run by traditional notables, BJP was staffed by a shakha-trained, disciplined, ascetic, and ideologically fervent cadre, who met and organized voters at the grassroots, even if, in good Leninist style, their orders came from on high. Emerging as a party in 1980, the BJP became a stridently powerful national force only under the leadership of Narendra Modi. A "pure product of the RSS" (Jaffrelot 2021: 34), Modi was a preternaturally gifted political strategist and a master organizer. He was also a brilliant performer in the symbolic sense, deftly dissembling his Machiavellian machinations and often anti-civil ruthlessness behind a seamless veneer of "saintly politics" (Rai 2023). Modi's freshly pressed white kurta, specially tailored to emphasize his thrusting "56 inch chest," is always subtly ornamented with saffron, traditional Hindu color coding (Puri 2019). A proud renunciator, Modi quotes Vedic scriptures in Sanskrit, conducts mass yoga exercises in public, addresses the small and large concerns of tens of millions of his followers in an intimate monthly radio program (Choudhary 2022),[12] and sequesters himself for frequent fasting. He first became an avenging angel of Hindutva backlash in 2002, when, as the Chief Minister of Gujarat – a western state bordering Pakistan – he presided over days of blood-curdling communal violence, in which marauding Hindu mobs, enraged by an alleged attack on their religious confreres, murdered as many as 2,000 Muslims, often burning them alive (Nussbaum 2007). Since then, Modi has been elegized as "The Emperor of Hindu Hearts," deriding Rahul Gandhi as "the crown prince of the Muslim Dynasty" (Jaffrelot 2021: 55). In 2017, the person Modi appointed to be the governor of Utta, India's largest state with a Muslim minority of 45 million, was a Hindu monk named Yogi Adityanath, who speaks about "feeding bullets, not biryani" to Muslim troublemakers, wears his saffron religious robe while conducting state business, and "frequently commission[s] helicopters to shower rose petals on Hindu religious processions" (Travelli and Kumar 2023). In the closing days of Modi's third successful national election campaign, the Prime Minister called out Indian Muslims as "infiltrators" who would steal the gold of Hindu mothers and daughters if Rahul Gandhi were elected (Mashal 2024; Travelli and Raj 2023).

INTRODUCTION

Between Vitality and Suppression

In the ten years of "Modi's India" (Jaffrelot 2021), the fateful contrast in effectivity between the BJP and Congress only deepened, with BJP victories in the national elections of 2014 and 2019 massively depressing Congress morale and further hollowing out its organizational capacities. There was also a highly significant broadening of the cultural mobilization of BJP's mass base. If the party had begun as an upper-caste backlash movement against civil repair and expanded solidarity, in the face of electoral losses during the 1990s and 2000s the BJP broadened Hindutva's appeal to the lower castes comprising fully half of India's citizen audience (cf. Gorringe and Waghmore 2019). Instead of endorsing the critical democratic fervor of rights-bearing anti-caste movements – culturally inconceivable in the Hindutva context – Modi initiated a massive nationwide welfare policy that directly deposits cash into the bank accounts of tens of millions of Indians (Biswas 2024), a policy innovation that Aiyar (2023; Aiyar and Venkat 2024) characterizes as "techno-patrimonial."[13] The move demonstrates that solidarity can be emphasized, and broadened, inside a conservatively anti-civil frame, one that in India continues to be marked by hierarchical deference to higher castes and primordial exclusion (of Muslims).[14] In chapter 5 of this book, Ajay Gudavarthy characterizes this strategy as creating an oxymoronic "Hindu Civil Sphere." Modi's horizontal expansion of the BJP's primordial populism won him extraordinary poll ratings in the "Hindu Belt," the wide swathe of northern Indian states that is much more populated and much less wealthy than those in India's southern region, where the nation's high-tech, financial, and entertainment industries are located, where the primary languages are not Hindi, and into which the Mughal empire only very tentatively was spread.

Ominously, the process of "anti-civil incorporation" that allowed Modi to so broadly secure political power has played out against the background of state interventions vis-à-vis civil sphere institutions: intrusions whose intent is to undermine institutional autonomy via the soft power of cooptation, if possible, or the hard power of financial manipulation and physical coercion, if necessary. While the national English-language newspapers have remained relatively independent in institutional terms, the cutting edge of their critical coverage of government activity has frequently been softened by a process that might be described as "ideological capture," the intoxicating aura generated by Modi's grandiose grasping of great power nationalism.[15] But the effort to control media of communication has also sometimes been hardwired,

21

with billionaire Indians inside Modi's circle purchasing, and neutering, independent television companies, triggering the self-exile of long trusted anchors and reporters (Palepu and Kay 2024). Similar efforts were made to control, or at least neutralize, the critical discourse and democratic functioning of such core regulative institutions as office and law. BJP-controlled government agencies, like tax auditing agencies (Yasir 2024) and police investigation units, have repeatedly conducted state business on behalf of narrow party-political interests rather than on behalf of the civil sphere. Justices in high regional and national position have been influenced in their rulings by implicit offers to bestow or remove government patronage (Mashal et al. 2023); and the infamously slow as molasses decision-making of backed up India courts – the current backlog is estimated at 50 million (Yasir 2024) – has allowed prosecutors to issue warrants for the detention of BJP opponents despite knowing that, when the case eventually comes up for judicial review – months if not years down the road – the arrests will likely be dismissed for want of evidence or judicial justification (ibid.).[16]

In the run-up to the 2024 election, Modi and other BJP authorities made no secret of their ambition to gain a mandate so large that, in their words, India would, once and for all, become "Congress free." This was not a vain hope. Congress was so demoralized and Rahul Gandhi's brand so tarnished that India's grand old party was compelled to enter into electoral coalition with twenty-eight regional and national parties. The ideology of the I.N.D.I.A. coalition suffered from ideological fuzziness, despite the deceptive precision of its acronym.

Yet, in the autumn of 2022, eighteen months before voting began, an extraordinary event unfolded that demonstrated the continuing vitality of India's civil sphere. Securely protected by the constitutional right to peaceful assembly, and motivated by the cultural memories of generations of pilgrimages dramatizing the civil sacred, Rahul Gandhi began a 145-day *Bharat Jodo Yatra*, "Unite India March," on September 7, 2022, walking 2,200 miles from Kanyakurmari Beach in Tamil Nadu, the most southern point of India, to Srinigar in Kashmir, the very tip in the north (Yasir 2024).[17] No longer the clean-shaven pampered scion, Rahul walked stoically, with growing beard in t-shirt and jeans, accompanied by handfuls of mostly young and highly energized Congress staff. As the Yatra progressed, it attracted hundreds and sometimes many thousands of ordinary Indians to what increasingly took on the sacrificial trappings of a spiritual pilgrimage into the India heartland – one that allowed the born-again Congress leader to experience the pure sacrality of the democratic folk. Wending their way slowly up the spine of the Indian nation, the political pilgrims chanted slogans, sang songs,

INTRODUCTION

and recited epic poetry. They organized gatherings for Rahul to give speeches and engage in public dialogues in the hamlets dotted along the way; hosted formal meetings with an unending flow of representatives of "civil society"; and welcomed farmers, factory workers, crafts people, and enthusiasts drawn to what came to seem, for many Indians, an electrifying and esthetically compelling moral drama of physical sacrifice and utopian idealism. So effectively did the Yatra's aura project spiritual ideals that members of local RSS shakhas were known to visit the overnight encampments, immersing themselves in the atmosphere and conversation. While national media did not provide anything like continuous coverage, the October 15 public gathering in Ballari under heavy rainfall was a conspicuous exception.[18] Meanwhile, professional and citizen journalists at the local levels devoted to the Yatra scrupulous reportage, and between 2 and 5 million YouTube subscribers tuned in regularly. Congress staffers believed that the Yatra's organized liminality was recruiting a new and idealistic cadre that would charge the party for years to come. The experience certainly made a profound impact on the party's standard bearer himself.[19]

Whatever the long-term effects, the Yatra compelled Modi and the BJP to cease their derogatory caricaturing of the Gandhi persona. If, for some slice of the Indian citizen audience, Rahul had now entered into a sacred, civil-*cum*-religious space, the BJP would have to be careful not to offend it. The worry was that the Congress leader's newly purified status might allow him to become a magnetic civil symbol, to display an iconic power that might rival Modi's own.

At this point, the velvet glove came off the iron fist.

A few weeks after the Yatra's conclusion, a judge in Modi's home state of Gujarat found Rahul Gandhi guilty of criminal defamation, sentencing him to two years in prison; one day later, government officials ordered Gandhi removed from the Indian parliament – two years being the statutory minimum prison time rendering a sitting member ineligible for office. The intended effect of the ruling was obvious: to prevent Gandhi from leading Congress in the upcoming national elections. The cause of the suppression was also clear: it was the fear of Gandhi's markedly increased post-Yatra popularity. When the *New York Times* reported on the ruling, it provided this background for non-Indian readers: "Mr. Gandhi, 52, had been building up his own profile lately. He had rallied the public with a grassroots march across India – 2,500 miles over five months – in which he rallied against Mr. Modi's power" (Travelli and Raj 2023). While Gandhi was granted bail to appeal his conviction, Cassandras evoked familiar doomsday prophesies about the end of Indian democracy. In a story headlined "With a Pliant Judiciary,

Modi Tightens His Grip on India" (Mashal et al. 2023), an experienced Indian observer of right-wing Hindu politics explained that the government was "subverting the legal process, running the judiciary like the executive, and doing it with impunity and [being] absolutely brazen about it" (ibid.).

It soon became manifestly evident, however, that regulatory institutions of the civil sphere could not be so easily cowed. Within weeks, the Indian Supreme Court, acting with unprecedented alacrity, unanimously overturned Gandhi's conviction, allowing him to return to Parliament, where he would be able to continue his anti-Modi struggle. The Court's ruling evoked the discourse of civil society, criticizing the Gujarat court for demonstrating a "complete lack of reasons" in its allocation of punishment (Rajagopal 2023); "had the duration of the sentence been a day less," a suspicious Court pointed out, "the [removal] provisions would not have [applied]" (ibid.). Such irrationality and sneakiness, the Court explained, not only deprived Gandhi the individual of his liberty, but also undermined the power of the civil sphere as a collective entity, preventing it from translating its will, via elections, into control over the state. It is because "disqualification not only affects the rights of the individual but also that of the electorate he represents in the Parliament," the Court explained, that "the ramifications are wide," for "an entire constituency which elects a person will go unrepresented" (ibid.). Congress party officials rang the same discursive chords. In the wake of his exoneration, Rahul Gandhi maintained that "truth always prevails"; a parliamentary leader, asserting "this is the victory of truth," predicted "it will cost Modi heavily" (Ellis-Peterson 2023); and the Congress president, ascribing the misdirected case against Gandhi to the "BJP's conspiratorial hounding," framed the Supreme Court decision as vindicating the civil sphere *tout court*, as "a win for the people of India, the Constitution and democracy" (ibid.).

Six months later, in the fervid weeks before national voting was to begin, this key regulatory institution of the civil sphere asserted its independent power once again. In what *The Hindu* hailed as "a landmark unanimous judgment," the Supreme Court struck down a widely abused electoral bonds scheme (Rajagopal 2024). It had been put in place seven years earlier by the Modi government, so that corporate donors making large political contributions could maintain anonymity. The rationale for the decision was to prevent market logic from intervening directly into the state, without civil sphere mediation. "Contributions made by companies," the Court argued, "are purely business transactions made with the intent of securing benefits in return" (Kaushik et al. 2024) – without regard for the civil community. Once again, the Court evoked

INTRODUCTION

the civil sphere's binary discourse to explain why it had felt compelled to act. To qualify as civil, a law must be reasonable; the intention of the electoral bonds scheme was "manifestly arbitrary," and therefore unconstitutional (Rajagopal 2024). Arbitrary power is anti-democratic because it cannot be rulebound; if it is not subject to deliberative reason, it is profane. Reporting that same day, the *Times of India* rhetorically deepened the Supreme Court's binary legal discourse, framing it in terms of the symbolic logic of purity and danger.

> [The Court] ruled that voters could not be kept in the *dark* about *huge donations* to political parties when money played a significant role in elections. The bench held that *secret* corporate funding of political parties, possibly for a quid pro quo, breached voters' *right to information*, adversely impacted [the] *purity* of *free* and *fair* elections and *polluted democracy* by disturbing [the] political *equality* [of] polls. (Mahapatra 2024)

The anti-democratic side of this symbolic logic establishes a profane semiotic sequence: huge donations = darkness = secrecy = pollution. On the other side of this equation, the *Times of India* lays out the semiosis of democracy = purity = information = free and fair = equality = voting.

The author of this electoral bond opinion was Chief Justice Dhananjaya Chandrachud, who had been appointed to his office in 2022, not by Prime Minister Modi but, instead, by a collegium of Justices, with preference given to seniority. During his six years as a Justice and three years as Court leader, Chandrachud persistently confronted, not only the Modi state, but, implicitly, the repressive culture of Hindutva. Describing dissent as "the safety valve of democracy," the Justice asserted that "political freedoms impose a restraining influence on the state by carving out an area in which the state shall not interfere"; in doing so, he argued, political freedoms "impose obligations on the state," requiring that "the state must ensure that conditions in which these freedoms [can] flourish are maintained" (in Bhatia 2019).

Chandrachud also wrote the lead opinion that, for the first time in Indian history, carved out a right to privacy, declaring unconstitutional Section 377 of the Indian Penal Code, which forbade "unnatural offenses," e.g., sexual activities that were deemed "against the order of nature." The "rights of discrete and insular minorities [who] face grave dangers of discrimination," the Justice insisted, are "as sacred as those conferred on other citizens" (Supreme Court of India 2017). Describing "sexual orientation [as] an essential attribute of privacy," he assigned to it a civil purity that should not stigmatized: "Discrimination against an individual on the basis of sexual orientation is deeply offensive to

25

THE INDIAN CIVIL SPHERE

the dignity and self-worth of the individual" (ibid.). Initiating a feminist extension of India's civil sphere, Chandrachud declared that sexual harassment in the workplace violated "the fundamental rights of a woman to equality . . . and to live with dignity" (Supreme Court of India 2020). In his widely reported P. D. Desai Memorial Lecture in Gujarat, the Justice declared that "the framers of the Constitution rejected the notion of a Hindu India and a Muslim," but "recognized only the Republic of India" (Chandrachud 2020). For democracy to flourish, there needs to be a universalizing discourse over and above particular religious beliefs, "a shared culture of values and commitment to the fundamental ideals of . . . individual and equal dignity" (ibid.).

The pushback against Hindu nationalism that so unexpectedly marked the outcome of the 2024 national elections demonstrated that Justice Chandrachud's rousing normative prescription was empirically descriptive as well. Despite Narendra Modi's boastful prediction that the BJP would win 400 parliamentary seats, the party's 240 seats fell well below a numerical majority, forcing it into a humbling coalition government with two secular regional parties. In vivid contrast, Rahul Gandhi emerged from the electoral struggle as a revivified collective representation of democratic India, performing so felicitously that Congress more than doubled the number of parliamentary seats from four years earlier. After the poll results were announced on June 5, Congress called a news conference, addressing the national citizen-audience via the communicative institutions of India's civil sphere. Waving a copy of the Constitution, Rahul Gandhi declared that "the people of India have saved the Constitution and democracy" (Chatterji 2024).[20] Indian democracy remains troubled, but its death has been highly exaggerated. The discourse and institutions of the India civil sphere are alive and in fair health, despite the swelling waves of backlash crashing against them.

* * * *

The powerful and variegated chapters that comprise the remainder of this book explore the complex, Janus-like condition of Indian democracy, making densely innovative applications of Civil Sphere Theory and revising it as well.

The first three chapters demonstrate, in vivid and often disturbing empirical detail, how civil repair and its discontents have contributed to the expansion of the civil sphere in the India of today. In chapter 1, Gorringe and Damodaran reconstruct frontlash and backlash in response to the Dalits' long march to civil incorporation in the southern Indian state of Tamil Nadu. Under newly expanded "scheduling," only members of the Dalit caste were allowed to compete for village council presiden-

INTRODUCTION

cies. This promise to significantly widen local civil spheres triggered a horrific, highly public murder of six Dalits – including the beheading of a recently elected council president – by infuriated, and threatened, members of the local ruling caste. Protests and fiery speeches by Dalit activists publicizing and protesting this flagrant denial of civil ideals effectively aroused public opinion, compelling regulatory institutions to levy material sanctions. Police arrested forty-four suspected perpetrators and, after a frustrating delay, seventeen of them were sentenced to life in prison. The historic triumph encouraged Dalits to aim higher, and they created a Dalit political party, the VCK, to contest continuing caste abuse electorally. In their first election, Dalit voters were so intimidated by upper-caste threats that they were unable to vote, with the result that VCK candidates failed to win a single council seat. Caste, not civil power, was translated into positions inside the state. But the VCK persisted, and its repression soon became an issue for communicative institutions. It was because the VCK maintained sacred civil commitments, "eschewing violence and seeking legal and electoral change," that journalists felt they "were unable to ignore" or "close their eyes" to the party's anti-civil treatment. Nourished by what soon became a more receptive milieu of public opinion, years of "struggle, lobbying, and campaigning" allowed the VCK eventually to win representation in the state, where they have become "a mainstay in the alliances of the parties that once sought to exclude them by force."

Tempering this inspiring account of how the civil sphere in southern India provided resources for the civil repair of caste exclusion, Gorringe and Damodaran briefly turn their attention to caste-instigated "honor killings," which are authorized by families when sons and daughters dare to couple with somebody from a lower caste. Concluding on a more upbeat note, Gorringe and Damodaran highlight how India's Supreme Court has recently declared honor killings to be a destructive intrusion into the national civil sphere. Describing them as a "catastrophic crisis for the rule of law," the Court insisted on the priority of civil obligations as against the more particularistic compulsions of caste and gender. "The *human* rights of a daughter, brother, sister or son," the Court declared, must not be "mortgaged to the so-called or so-understood honour of the *family* or *clan* or the *collective*" (italics added).

In chapter 2, Raju Chalwadi continues to explore the boundary tensions between gender, caste, and civil sphere, documenting how the Indian civil sphere rose up in indignation in the face of the murder of a lower-caste woman in Hathras, a town in the northern state of Uttar Pradesh. During the weeks she was treated for her grievous wounds, Chalwadi notes, the heinous attack simply did not register in the Indian collective

27

THE INDIAN CIVIL SPHERE

consciousness, either locally or nationally. Because it was not "news" for journalists, it did not become an "event" inside the civil sphere. To understand how it did eventually become "societalized," Chalwadi points to the explosion of local indignation, not over the murder itself, but over the refusal of Hathras police authorities to let the young woman's family take possession of her body in order to conduct last rites. Anger over what was conceived to be officials' "deeply atrocious and disrespectful" behavior not only triggered the arrest of four male suspects but an investigation by local journalists, who recorded and posted videos of the police cremation and broadcast interviews with villagers angrily denouncing it. With "the whole nation" watching, journalists framed the suffering of the victim's family as a violation of official responsibility, describing the police as "insensitive and ruthless." In civil sphere theory (CST) terms, the state and its agents had intervened directly into family and religion without civil sphere mediation, a mediation that would have demanded respect for religious freedom and individual rights. *The New Indian Express* editorialized against the corruption of office, describing "insensitive and blundering officials" as "prime examples" of everything "a bureaucrat and police officer should not be." India's leading national newspaper, *The Hindu*, commented that "the bleak image of a burning pyre illuminating a ghastly night while policemen stood guard will be forever etched in India's collective memory." A widely circulated letter with the signatures of 10,000 notables ranging from journalists to leaders of "civil society" groups, intellectuals, and artists condemned what they described as "blatant patriarchy and upper-caste dominance operating through sponsored violence."

In response to the swelling stream of collective representations testifying to the "utter injustice and deep humiliation" of the "forc[ed] cremation," regulatory institutions began to intervene. India's most important human rights institution, the NHRC, put Uttar Pradesh officials on notice, blasting them, on its official website, for "a serious violation of human rights." The state's High Court, attesting that the incident "has shocked our conscience," demanded that top state officials appear before the court to explain their misbehavior in a case that had "immense public importance." India's Supreme Court, describing the state's actions as "shocking" and "extraordinary," demanded that local officials provide the victim's family with legal representation and positively consider their request for witness protection. There were public rallies and marches, and a strike by sanitation workers from the same caste as the victim. Throughout these communicative and regulative interventions, the discursive reference was the discourse of civil society. "The binary of sacred (the constitution) and profane (caste) was used

INTRODUCTION

heavily by protestors," Chalwadi writes; "the state, police, and [local] ruling regime" were framed "in non-civil terms: as caste apologists . . . and Hindu fundamentalists."

As the model of societalization (Alexander 2018) predicts, such massive pollution of official misbehavior soon triggered powerful backlash. High caste leaders and government authorities committed to more Hindutva ideology lashed out. They physically blocked journalists from entering the city; accused their critics rather than local authorities of caste prejudice; suggested the young woman had actually been in a love relationship with the accused rapist or had been killed by her own family; and claimed the incident has been staged by "Islamic countries." The Uttar Pradesh state government hired a Mumbai public relations firm to circulate a "clarification note" to the national media and foreign correspondents stating the rape had never taken place. Despite these polarizing efforts, and the failure to achieve any significant institutional reform, Chalwadi argues that the Hathras movement had, in fact, achieved in its major goal. It brought the murderous injustice to the attention of a "larger audience," framing "it in a way to raise larger questions about caste and sexual violence." Societalization succeeded in "mobilizing a progressive population against the institution of caste that continues to threaten the expansion of the Indian civil sphere."

In chapter 3, Ramesh Bairy interrogates the clash between civil sphere and caste order from a uniquely individual, though not individualistic, point of view. His empirical inquiry is his own father, a Brahmin in his mid-eighties, whose life experience parallels the entirety of independent India's history. Bairy is interested in the micro inside the macro, the difficulties "the Brahmin" has in "*imagining* a civil sphere and practicing an ethic of solidarity." What he discovers in the course of his many hours of interview is that these difficulties emerged from the very nature of caste. He finds "a deep state of (irredeemable) instability" between the "thick(er) (in-blood) axis of solidarity of (caste) community and the thin(ner) invitation of (civil) association." The growing force of India's civil sphere poses to the Brahmin a fundamental challenge. In the traditional Hindu order, the Brahmin is "the divinity on earth who is a 'part apart' in all human affairs," a figure who, in order to maintain ritual purity, "must eschew association with not-Brahmin, let alone practice solidarity."

Bairy's father managed this tension by erecting a rigid boundary between civil and family spheres; outside the home, he accepted the impersonal tenets of the modern order, but inside the home he maintained the privileges of hierarchy. As a boy, his father had first encountered the "new language" of the "non-caste regulated world" in

THE INDIAN CIVIL SPHERE

school; he acknowledged that, in this world, "everybody was equal," and readily accepted the fact that a lower-caste schoolmate was "more intelligent" than himself. Given this radical separation between personal household and public civility, it was not surprising that establishing close friendships – the micro-foundation of wider solidarity – proved impossible. "There was simply no imagination of friendship," the father told his son, either in school, the occupational world, or in associational life. "It was definitionally impossible," Bairy explains, "to cultivate a sense of solidarity with any being outside the caste fold" or even within it, given the high walls surrounding the Brahmin self.

Bairy suggests that the same model of Brahminic isolation explains his father's quandary vis-à-vis the BJP and Modi, the first of which he endorsed ideologically, the second of which he loved. The old Brahmin's high caste status separates him from the BJP's support for a "Hindu Rashtra," a nationalist strategy that incorporates lower castes on the basis of shared religious identity. Bairy reaches an ambiguous conclusion. The "deeply unstable and unhappy state" of the contemporary Brahmin is the result of a "persona that has been made to stand for everything that impedes the arrival of an ethic of civility, the making of an unknown solidarity, and a universal morality." At the same time, the life of his father demonstrates that he made an earnest effort to "significantly [re-form] himself" – as he was "interpellated by and participate[d] in the anti-caste and anti-Brahmin discourse of his time."

The two chapters that follow these early explorations of the civil repair of caste hierarchy examine the twisting and turning path taken by the backlash against it. As they do so, they address one of the most vexed and muddled issues in contemporary Indian politics: whether or not the BJP's opening to lower-caste groups represents a genuine transformation of Hindutva.

In chapter 4, Suryakant Waghmore draws from his field research to suggest that, in recent years, Hindutva has become deeply committed, both in discourse and practice, to more open caste relations. In part, this has been driven by the logic of elections as a regulatory institution of the civil sphere; the BJP has been forced by the pragmatism of vote-seeking to develop policies and rhetoric that gave lower castes a place in party ideology and, in the process, access to offices in the state. At the same time, Waghmore shows, this opening up has also been a revision that is rooted, not only in pragmatism, but in the ideological nationalism that is at the heart of Hindutva as a backlash movement. In his study of Karnataka, the only state in southern India where the BJP was able to come to power, Waghmore observes the emergence of a "civil form of Hindu religion" that emphasizes "unity and equality" among co-religionists regardless of

INTRODUCTION

caste. Conceptualizing this as a "sublation" of Hindutva fundamentalism, Waghmore describes Tapas, an educational program established by a Hindutva philanthropic organization named Rashtrotthana; it tutors lower-caste children to enable them to score well on the exams that mediate entry into prestigious universities like India's Institutes of Technology. In Tapas, Waghmore finds, the Karnataka BJP had bent itself to "accommodating the impure," indeed to "transcending Brahminism." Yet, even as Waghmore testifies to how Hindutva "consistently re-invents itself" by "competing, learning, and coopting other civil solidarities in India's civil sphere," he concludes that this sublation remains anti-civil because it continues to pollute non-Hindu others, like Muslims, Christians, and tribal groups, and secular movements of criticism and civil repair. It is not enough, then, to create a Hindu "civil religion," in Bellah's sense. Expanding the Indian civil sphere, in a truly substantive manner, requires ongoing Hinduism to embrace the civil sphere as a secular or at least supra-religious space. In 2023, in the wake of Rahul Gandhi's Yatra, the Ahinda coalition wrested control of the Karnataka government from the BJP; Waghmore shows how it was a discourse about "justice and reason" that provided the cultural foundation for the winning coalition among Muslims, upper-caste liberals, and radical Ambedkarites.

In chapter 5, Ajay Gudavarthy explores the paradoxical rhetoric that has propelled the BJP to hegemony. Like Waghmore, he suggests that the BJP has been able to achieve power by performing culturally evocative ideological tropes that evoke the cross-caste solidarity upon which a civil sphere depends. Taking implicit issue with Waghmore, however, Gudavarthy suggests this is merely tactical, that it represents a simulacrum rather than an actual commitment to civil repair. Pointing to what he sees as the continuation of casteism, Gudavarthy argues that the BJP's discourse of "internal-civil-trust" is a surface ideology, one that is belied by a rhetoric of "external-uncivil-distrust" that lies just underneath. For the BJP strenuously "invokes an uncivil and retributive narrative of othering" that legitimates the "righteous lawlessness" of organized lynchings, not only of Muslims but also Dalits. Gudavarthy proceeds to deconstruct analyses of the "symbolic action" that has allowed such an objectively exclusionary program to be more persuasive than other, anti-BJP redistributive efforts that are more genuine. Here Gudavarthy draws from cultural sociology, a framework that is premised on the argument that the centrality of richly evocative symbolic tropes has not been displaced by the rationalizing and secularizing forces of modernity. He laments "the flattened and sanitized secular-constitutional discourses" that Congress has deployed to challenge the BJP's "authoritarian civil sphere," criticizing the political left for trying "to defend democracy

THE INDIAN CIVIL SPHERE

without a narrative or a story to tell." The BJP, by contrast, employs "memory and myth," drawing upon powerful symbolic forms buried deep inside the nation's collective unconscious that putatively demonstrate the superiority of ancient sacred Hindu ideas over those of modern secularity. In "seeming continuity with postcolonial critiques of 'Western Epistemology'," Gudavarthy observes, "right-wing decolonial discourse" highlights indigenous concepts about social harmony; converts unequal castes into a form of cultural diversity; and rhetorically idealizes "the world as a family" – all in the service of creating an "*imagination* of universality," a "majoritarian and monolithic imagination of the civil sphere" that is deployed to justify further segregation.

Among theorists who critically assess the path of contemporary India, Islam has too often been treated as a residual category, conceptualized only as an object of exclusion, for what it is not rather than for what it is. In chapter 6, Qudsiya Contractor provides a significant course correction. She demonstrates how, in striking contrast to the growing communalism of Hindutva politics, Muslims' increasing exclusion and marginalization has had the counterintuitive effect of submerging divisive doctrinal and class differences in a shared project of constructing a wider, more civil form of Muslim solidarity. Observing everyday life, religious festivals, and party-political organizing in an economically disadvantaged Islamic neighborhood in Mumbai, Contractor demonstrates how "civility is considered and performed as a public virtue." In the face of their growing cultural alienation from the Hindu Rashtra, which involves, as well, socioeconomic discrimination, there is a newly egalitarian caste to Islamic performances: scripts projecting civil solidarity translate progressive religious ideas – about ummah belongingness and stipulations that privileged Muslims must care for the poor – into a more politically oriented religious ethic. For example, during the annual mobilization and distribution of *zakat* (charity) during the month of *Ramzan*, what once were considered simply as pious acts of charity are now conceptualized "not only as religious obligations," but as "public expressions of community belonging [that] also reinforce civic solidarity." Contractor also suggests that the "spectacular nature of giving," its visibility as a very "public act of piety," stimulates "moral critiques about its very purpose," internally-oriented questions about the "dignity in the giving of alms" and externally-oriented questions that "illuminate the gap between what is given [as *zakat*] and what withheld by the Indian state." Thus, the leader of a popular Islamic political party "urged the audience to wake up and demand their rights, [declaring] 'this is a *jamhuuriyat* (democracy) and in a democracy if you don't get up yourself and demand your right no one is going to come and give to you'." Such political-actions-

INTRODUCTION

in-the-making, Contractor argues, represent a transition from Muslims as a counter-public to a vehicle for creating, and demanding, civil repair. Social solidarity is being "built on a shared commitment to an idealized future that is not just defined in Islamic terms (as the afterlife) but also is reflective of the aspirations of the Muslim poor in a civic sense," expressing the "hope of being part of something larger than themselves."

In their discussions of civil repair and backlash, the chapters discussed above point to the civil sphere's boundary relations, and conflicts with the non-civil spheres of religion, family, and state. In chapter 7, Kartikeya Saboo shifts focus by illuminating the boundary between civil sphere and markets. Since Marx, of course, this boundary has been a central focus for critical social theory, but Saboo's commitment to microfinancing institutions (MFIs) as vehicles for civil repair leads him reconsider such conventional understandings and, along the way, to rethink the relation between civil sphere and state. In critical theory, markets are conceived as destructive intrusions into the civil sphere, as efforts to substitute atomizing, competitive, exploitative relationships for trusting and solidaristic ones – in order to turn a profit. In CST terms, however (Alexander 2006: 205–9), the relations between civil and non-civil spheres are agnostic and open-ended; every non-civil sphere can be conceptualized theoretically, and has actually functioned historically, as also producing "facilitating inputs" for the more fulsome construction of civil spheres rather than erecting roadblocks against it. The recent historical transition away from state-directed to "neoliberal" approaches to poverty alleviation echoes the eighteenth-century movement from mercantilism to market logics, which was similarly legitimated in civil sphere terms (Appleby 1984); in the contemporary and earlier periods, the turn toward markets has been valorized as promoting freedom, independence, and reciprocal rather than coercive human relations.

This is precisely what Saboo and his banking colleagues believed when they increased the scale and uptake of MFIs in rural India. Rather than treating the poor farming women who were its primary beneficiaries as dependent, irrational, and incompetent, and thus reliant on patronage from the state, MFIs would create independent actors who could rationally calculate risks and make responsible decisions that would have the effect of lifting their families out of poverty and moving from marginality to mainstream. Before these expectations could be tested, local officials stepped in. Still deeply invested in exercising economic control over poverty alleviation, they deployed the profane, anti-civil side of civil society discourse to make private financing seem anti-democratic. First, the local DC (District Collector) rallied his influence over communicative institutions. He called a special press conference to denounce the MFIs

33

THE INDIAN CIVIL SPHERE

as a dangerous new anti-civil threat, accusing them of charging "exorbitant" interest rates; of putting "unbearable pressure" on borrowers to repay loans; and of aiming to dismantle the self-help organizations that already existed to aid the local poor. After the DC repeated his polluting performance to an audience of 1,500 local women affected – the accusations and the audience's warm responses were widely reported – local regulatory institutions stepped into the fray. Arguing that not repaying loans was a "human right," the DC initiated a lawsuit to prevent any further interest payments. The DC established a helpline for borrowers "facing harassment" from banks, and officials at the highest levels of the state, including the Chief Minister, organized a meeting to strategize how MFIs' activity could be stopped, and threatened to do so. Faced with degradation in the court of public opinion and threatened materially by states and courts, the private bank in question pulled the plug on its microfinancing enterprise. The Indian state's preemptive construction of market logic as inherently anti-civil made bank officials fearful of drawing any further attention. The result of this withdrawal from MFIs was to leave economic inputs to the civil sphere in control of the state.

It is perhaps fitting that in chapter 8, the final chapter of this book, Krishan Kumar provides historical ballast for the challenge to postcolonial theory that *The Indian Civil Sphere* represents (cf. note 1 above). Kumar criticizes thinkers, like Goody and Chatterjee, who condemn "civil society" as a "Western import" that constitutes an unwanted and unnecessary intrusion into Indian civilization. Despite its enormously rich culture and its extraordinary social vitality, Kumar insists, civil sphere discourse and institutions could not have emerged from within a self-contained Indian civilization. It was precisely the externality of the British Raj vis-à-vis traditional India, in Kumar's view, that allowed the colonizers to insert such a "foreign" substance as a civil sphere into the heart of its quickening modernizing life. The Mughal empire was much longer lasting than the British, but outside the realms of religious and esthetic culture, Kumar argues, it left little lasting imprint. While Islam was certainly a more consistently Axial religion than Hinduism, the Mughal rulers assimilated into Indian political and social life rather than imposing something external upon it. In sharp contrast, the British "liberal imperialism" that established control over the subcontinent – to "civilize" India after banishing the "merely" profit-seeking East India Company in the wake of the brutal Indian Mutiny – constituted the most highly developed, post-Axial society in the world. It had fostered the great scientific and democratic revolutions and created the first industrial capitalism; it was ordered by judge-made law rather than custom and ruled by elected representatives rather than aristocracy and kingship.

34

INTRODUCTION

It was in order to stabilize its dominion that British colonizers set out to transform India in their own image, creating a native ruling class that, in Thomas Macaulay's gob-smackingly arrogant words, would be "English in taste, in opinion, in morals, and in intellect." Yet, for "liberal imperialists" like Macaulay, the goal was always to prepare the colony to become independent of its colonizer, no matter how far into the future this might be. "Whenever it comes," Macaulay averred, "it will be the proudest day in English history." Only by being radically made over would India become capable of ruling itself. The gist of Kumar's argument is that this proposition turned out to be largely right. By 1882, some 1,100 appointees to the Indian civil service were graduates of British-founded universities. The leaders of India's independence movement were trained in the colonial metropole's elite public schools and universities, Jawaharlal Nehru, independent India's founding father, most prominently among them. In 2005, Oxford University awarded Manmohan Singh, another British-educated Indian prime minister, an honorary degree. In his acceptance speech, Singh fulsomely acknowledged the point at the heart of Kumar's chapter. "With the balance and perspective offered by the passage of time," Singh said, he was now able to underscore the "beneficial consequences" of "India's experience with Britain." Central among the consequences he enumerated, "our notions of the rule of law, of a Constitutional government, of a free press, of a professional civil service, of modern universities and research laboratories," were key institutions of India's democratizing civil sphere. "These are all elements which we still value and cherish," Singh declared, and "they have served our country exceedingly well." Those remarks were made twenty years ago. Let us hope that twenty years from now a future Indian Prime Minister will be able to say the same.

35

Civil Repair and Anti-Caste Movements

1

Caste, Incivility, and the Prospects of Civil Repair

Hugo Gorringe and Karthikeyan Damodaran

The effect of caste on the ethics of the Hindus is simply deplorable. Caste has killed public spirit. ... A Hindu's public is his caste. His responsibility is only to his caste. His loyalty is restricted only to his caste. Virtue has become caste-ridden, and morality has become caste-bound. There is no sympathy for the deserving. There is no appreciation of the meritorious. There is no charity to the needy. Suffering as such calls for no response. There is charity, but it begins with the caste and ends with the caste. There is sympathy, but not for men of other castes. (Ambedkar 1944 [1936])

Introduction: Caste, Covid-19, and Incivility

In his searing call for the *Annihilation of Caste*, B. R. Ambedkar – pre-eminent leader of Dalit (ex-Untouchable) struggles for equality, first Law Minister of India and Chairman of the Committee that drafted the Indian Constitution – highlighted the anti-civil effects of caste on social relations. In prioritizing belonging to the group and regulating contact with others, he argues, caste precludes the sense of fraternity or solidarity upon which democratic practice and the civil sphere (Alexander 2006) depend. In an echo of Dewey, under whom he studied, Ambedkar insisted that "Democracy is not merely a form of Government. It is primarily a mode of associated living, of conjoint communicated experience. It is essentially an attitude of respect and reverence towards fellowmen" (1944 [1936]). When India gained its independence and instituted universal suffrage it sought, overnight, to create a nation of equal citizens. Recent events offer insights into how far we are from achieving that goal.

THE INDIAN CIVIL SPHERE

In early 2020, India was hit by the global Covid-19 coronavirus pandemic. In a bid to control the spread of infection, places of work were locked down and transport disrupted. Bereft of employment and income, millions of migrant workers sought to return to their native villages to ride things out. Some initial research suggested that people were able to pull together against the common threat of the virus. Badri Narayan (2020) and his team found that "times of emergency as witnessed during the pandemic dilute caste rigidity in society – at least for that period of acute distress." Contra Ambedkar, civic virtues were on show as citizens helped each other out and recognized their common humanity.

> An OBC worker spoke about the acute danger they were facing. In times such as these, all migrant workers became people of one caste, which was the caste of sufferers (*Sab log woh samay ek jati ke ho gaye – dukhiyari jati ke*), he said. The worker said he was extremely thirsty, but had no water with him. "One sweeper from my locality travelling with me on the same train had some water left in his bottle. He offered the water to me. I drank it without thinking about caste purity and impurity." (Narayan 2020)

If this story foregrounds everyday practices of citizenship and civility, the reference to ignoring caste due to necessity is telling. Elsewhere in India, not even a global pandemic could erode caste feeling. Bharathi (2020) notes that numerous "instances of caste discrimination have been reported as a result of some linking the stigma associated with coronavirus to Dalit [ex-Untouchable] groups. *Evidence*, a Madurai-based NGO has recorded around 23 caste-related crimes during the lockdown period, including six murders and 3 (honor-related) caste killings in the state." Wallen (2020) likewise noted how "throughout history, Dalits have been subject to violence from higher-caste Hindus but the coronavirus pandemic and lockdown has seen the number of attacks surge, with the National Dalit Movement for Justice (NDMJ) reporting a 72 per cent increase in April and May compared with the same two months in 2019." Kathir, the founder leader of *Evidence*, captured the sense of despair and anguish he felt, in saying: "It's a shame that people are fine to die of coronavirus but won't let go of their casteism. Coronavirus is scanning the society. It's bringing out the worst in some people. Caste is even more dangerous than coronavirus" (Newsclick 2020).

As the quote at the head of the chapter shows, Ambedkar was all too aware of the inherent tensions between a social order built on caste and India's new democratic structures. As he stressed in the Constituent Assembly debates:

CASTE, INCIVILITY, AND THE PROSPECTS OF CIVIL REPAIR

In politics we will be recognizing the principle of one man, one vote and one value. In our social and economic life, we shall, by reason of our social and economic structure, continue to deny the principle of one man, one value. How long shall we continue to live this life of contradictions? How long shall we continue to deny equality in our social and economic life? If we continue to deny it for long, we will do so only by putting our political democracy in peril.[1]

Whilst the Constitution implemented affirmative action programs designed to offset caste-inequalities and rendered the practice of untouchability a punishable offence, Scheduled Castes – as Dalits are formally known – continue to lag behind other castes in socioeconomic indicators (Desai and Dubey 2011), and are still subject to violence, humiliation, exclusion, and discrimination on the basis of caste (Waghmore 2013; Gorringe 2017). Given this, and the fact that a recent national survey found that "more than a fourth of Indians say they continue to practise [untouchability] in some form in their homes" (Chishti 2014), it would be easy to echo activists in asserting that "nothing has changed." The fact that constitutional safeguards have been enacted, that Ambedkar has become a public icon, and that "only" one in four Indians practice discrimination in private, however, speaks to the possibilities for civil solidarity (at least in public). This chapter, accordingly, engages with the work of Ambedkar and Alexander to chart the strengthening of an Indian civil sphere and the possibilities for civil repair in a caste context.

The chapter begins by outlining and examining three paradigmatic cases of caste violence from south India. These violent instances of incivility were directed against efforts by Dalits to access democratic institutions and realize the civil promises of the Constitution. The first two cases focus on political representation and claim-making in local and national elections, while the third instance targets social integration through cross-caste marriage. These examples highlight the persistence of anti-civil values and practices in the "world's largest democracy," and remind us that the *de jure* abolition of untouchability does not automatically translate into its eradication in practice. For all the progressive legislation in place in India, this allows us to grasp how some have used the pandemic to reinforce caste boundaries. "Ideals don't just realize themselves," as Alexander (2006: 7) argues, they have to be fought for, so "in considering the dynamics of civil societies, social movements must be given pride of place." Having outlined the incidents and the official response, therefore, the chapter turns to the work of Dalit movements which highlight and condemn such atrocities, and examines their struggles to effect civil repair. We will see how they frame the effects of casteism in universalistic terms, and also consider the response of

41

dominant castes to their activism. Whilst Dalit movements have made some gains, eradicating caste requires a wholesale change in attitudes and culture. In closing, therefore, we briefly address the realm of cinema to see how representations of caste are beginning to change. Mainstream films are intricately tied up with politics in Tamil Nadu (Hardgrave 1979; Vaasanthi 2006) in ways that reinforce Alexander's point that "fictional media create long-lasting frames for democratizing and anti-civil processes alike" (2006: 76). Whilst the outbreak of violence during the lockdown suggests that casteism is rampant, we ask whether recent blockbusters point to a change in social attitudes, and close by considering the prospects for civil repair. First, though, to understand why civil repair is needed, we outline and analyze instances of caste violence.

Melavalavu Massacre:
Caste Morality and Movements for Change

The first example dates back to Gorringe's initial fieldwork in Tamil Nadu in the late 1990s. This was the high point of Dalit grassroots mobilization in the state. Frustrated at the slow pace of change, Dalit activists threatened to "hit back" and take the law into their own hands. Dalit assertion aroused the ire of dominant castes, who responded with a "new kind of violence" designed to keep Dalits in their place (Mendelsohn and Vicziany 1998). One of the main triggers for upper-caste anger was the State decision to extend reservations to the panchayat (local council) level, meaning that only Dalits could stand for the position of president in a number of villages. Whilst this top-down attempt was intended to promote social inclusion, the inversion of local hierarchies was too much for some dominant groups to stomach.

On June 30, 1997, the Panchayat President of Melavalavu – a small village in Madurai District, central Tamil Nadu which had recently been reserved – and several followers went to Madurai to meet district authorities to discuss caste harassment and discrimination that was preventing him, as a Dalit, from carrying out the duties of his office. On his return from the city, the bus in which he was traveling was waylaid in broad daylight and men wielding sickles and machetes dragged the Panchayat President, Murugesan, and several others off the bus. Six of them were murdered on the road, whilst two escaped across the fields. Later that day, another prominent Dalit was also murdered. Murugesan's head was cut off and cast into a nearby well, for daring to flout locally dominant caste assertions that no Dalit should contest from the village (Gorringe 2005). "There may be a Paraiyan [derogatory reference to member of the Paraiyar caste] as the President of this Republic," the murderers were said to have stated, "but we will not permit a Paraiyan to become our panchayat president" (speech by Thirumavalavan, leader of Dalit Panthers, June 1999, recorded by author). The reference here is to K. R. Narayanan who was then in office as the first Dalit President of India (a largely titular role). The message was clear: "we do not care what happens at the national level, or what the Constitution sets out, we rule this locality."

The Melavalavu murders illustrate how legal changes have failed to generate equal citizenship or cultivate a sense of constitutional morality amongst groups convinced of their superior standing and status (Vincentnathan 1996). Caste, as Ambedkar notes, is a form of graded inequality. It "is not merely a division of labour. *It is also a division of labourers*" (1944 [1936], emphasis in original). The dominant caste group in question here, the Thevars, lie just above Dalits in the status hierarchy. Under colonial rule they were described and persecuted as a Criminal Tribe, and it was only through concerted political mobilization that they succeeded in gaining sociopolitical power (Damodaran 2018a). Having just established themselves in politics and cultural representation as a martial caste of rulers (cf. Damodaran and Gorringe 2017), they were reluctant to cede authority to those below them and engaged in anti-civil violence to thwart Dalit assertion.

Ambedkar's fears about caste killing public spirit seemed to ring true as local media (populated by dominant castes) ignored the murders and English-language dailies offered short reports that blamed "caste clashes" for the violence (Gorringe 2005). Whilst this suggests the absence of a sphere premised on solidarity, there is a counter-tradition – encapsulated in the Constitution and in radical social movements – that points toward the institutionalization (albeit partial) of a civil sphere in India. In fact, in the early to mid-twentieth century, Tamil Nadu witnessed a movement led by the radical iconoclast Periyar, which saw the eradication of untouchability as central, campaigned for *samadharma* (equality), and forged a "deep horizontal comradeship" between members of different castes (Geetha and Rajadurai 2011). The principal political parties in the state all grew out of, and express allegiance to, the *Dravida Kazhagam* (Dravidian movement) – so called due to its emergence in the southern states that were said to have been populated by ethno-linguistic groups speaking Dravidian languages (ibid.). Although entry into politics has led to a deradicalization of Dravidian parties, this legacy means that challengers to the status quo have a rich narrative tradition of critique on which to draw. The way in which Dravidian parties used rhetoric, symbolism, and cinema to propagate their values and displace Congress

THE INDIAN CIVIL SPHERE

in the state also offers a template for radical actors. In his book on Tamil oratory and politics, Bate (2009: 5–6) thus notes the centrality of lyrical speeches in pure or refined (*cenmai*) Tamil for doing politics in Tamil Nadu.

If mass mobilization and protests by Dalit groups against the Melavalavu killings gained police attention, it was the ardent rhetoric of the eloquent and impassioned leader of the Dalit Panthers of India, Thirumavalavan, which enabled these marginal protestors to appeal to a wider civil sphere. The combination of protests and speeches in the register of Dravidian politics eventually compelled authorities to arrest the perpetrators. Despite the severity of the crime it was not till September – nearly three months later – that charges were filed (CSCCL n.d.). Even then, cases were not registered under the Scheduled Caste and Scheduled Tribe Prevention of Atrocities Act – which is non-bailable – meaning that most were able to avoid detention for years as the case progressed. By contrast, action was taken with alacrity against protesting Dalits, forty-one of whom were charged with damaging public property during a demonstration in Chennai in July,[2] in a clear attempt to delegitimize and discredit the protestors (Thirumavalavan 2004: 14).

These efforts were reinforced by the fact that Thirumavalavan at this time was best known for fiery rhetoric promising to fight back against caste oppression. As seen in the counter-cases and arrests mentioned above, the Dalit Panthers could be tainted with the label of "militants" and "extremists." Although Dalit activists portrayed themselves as upholding the Constitution and campaigning for equal rights, their claims were frequently dismissed as those of fringe actors. What we see in Melavalavu, thus, are the limits of legislation that lacks full cultural legitimacy (cf. Alexander 2006). Whilst Dalits throughout acted in accordance with the law, the dominant caste laid claim to moral superiority by virtue of their superior caste status and history. They also benefited from the marginalized nature of their adversaries. Police, lawyers, politicians, and justices were networked to the dominant castes, or scared to act against them (cf. Jeffrey 2001). Witnesses were threatened and the case had to be moved to a different High Court before convictions could be secured (Gorringe interview with Lajapathi Roy 2012). In an historic move, seventeen of the forty-four charge-sheeted in the case received life sentences. Advocate Lajapathi Roy noted how witnesses had to be housed in secure locations to avoid intimidation, and hailed this as a "landmark case" (ibid.),[3] which highlights the tussle between competing values, and reveals that the legal order retains some autonomy from caste.

Dalit movements have long legitimized their actions by reference to the Constitution and civic values, and the process of securing justice entailed a conscious recalibration of movement rhetoric. In a speech delivered on the second anniversary of the massacre, for example, Thirumavalavan cast Panchayat President Murugesan's actions in terms of civic duty: "'If you do compete we will behead you', they threatened. Even after such threats and scare-mongering, and with the sole objective of protecting the government-given rights to reservation and make them a reality, Murugesan did not bow to the pressure or the threats. 'Even if my head rolls, we will protect these political rights' he said, and competed in the government elections" (Speech, June 1999, recorded by author). Lacking favorable media coverage, this attempt at "translation" was limited to those Dalit activists who were present and to a handful of activists and NGOs. As with the Civil Rights Movement in the United States, whose success, Alexander (2006: 303) observes, "depended on its ability to establish a solidaristic relation with the broader, less racially distorted civil sphere, which drew its power from geographical regions outside the South," the Dalit movement sought solidaristic ties to a more autonomous layer of civil sphere outside the locality. In the run-up to the Fiftieth Anniversary of the Universal Declaration of Human Rights, thus, the Dalit Panthers insisted that "Dalit Rights are Human Rights" and reached out to the international advocacy group Human Rights Watch (HRW) (Bob 2007). The upshot was a path-breaking report from HRW in 1999 entitled *Broken People*, which catalogues a series of caste atrocities and abuses to an international audience and sought to place external pressure on the state to act on the provisions of the Constitution. Here as elsewhere, the "global civil sphere" was drawn on by local groups to bolster their actions and strengthen the contested but quite critical civil sphere in India. Despite this, the prominence afforded to the slogan "hit back" continued to legitimize police and higher caste repression, meaning that in 1999 the Panthers felt compelled to abandon their extra-institutional assertion and form a political party to underscore their democratic credentials. It is to their first foray in electoral politics that we now turn.

Votes and Violence: Caste and Chidambaram Constituency

In 1999, the newly formed *Viduthalai Chiruthaigal Katchi* (VCK; Liberation Panther Party) contested elections as part of a Third Front in Tamil Nadu. If their ability to form a party and their incorporation into an alliance with the more established *Tamil Maanila Congress* (Tamil State Congress) suggested a degree of recognition and acceptance (of assimilation in Alexander's terms), the run-up to the polls in Thirumavalavan's constituency of Chidambaram demonstrated the limited nature of this shift in public opinion. Unprecedented levels of violence were unleashed to ensure that his campaign did not succeed. Judging from representation in some news media, this was a robustly fought election. Rediff.net (1999) reported that: "Sporadic clashes between Dalits and Vanniyars and road blockades continued for the third day today near Chidambaram." The news emerging from eyewitness and independent accounts, however, tells a different story. Two of Gorringe's key respondents in 1999, Palani Kumar and Kamaraj, spoke of booths being seized, movement activists suffering severe violence, huts being burnt, and a partisan police force (Gorringe 2005: 303). An Independent Initiative report likewise found that "in most of the villages visited in Chidambaram constituency Dalit people had been threatened not to cast their vote on polling day."[4] "Polling agents belonging to the VCK coalition were attacked, huts were set ablaze and an *urkattupadu* (order by a caste panchayat) was imposed on Dalits in Anukkampattu ... stating that they should either vote for the PMK [the opposition, dominant Vanniyar caste-led Toiling People's Party] or abstain. Consequently no Dalits went out to vote. All the same, their votes were cast by other people" (Ravikumar 2009: 194). The regulative institution of elections, in other words, was badly abused and distorted by police and caste forces.

The VCK alliance failed to win a single seat, highlighting disparities in power and the successful "pollution" of the "Dalit-front." Their strategic decision to adopt the parliamentary path, however, was not without effect. Local journalists were unable to ignore the Lok Sabha elections or to close their eyes to what occurred on the ground. Unlike the English-language account above, the Tamil magazine *Nandan* reported that: "Though accusations came from both sides, burned houses and looted goods show that the downtrodden have suffered the most" (Sonamandan 1999: 13). By eschewing violence and seeking legal and electoral change, in other words, the VCK undermined efforts to sully them. Activists pointed to the violence to question whether India was a democracy, thus casting a spotlight on their opponents. Naresh Gupta, the Election Commissioner, insisted that "only if ballot boxes are seized or ballot papers are torn up will there be a re-poll in Chidambaram." "There is also a rule," the magazine reminded him, "that voters should not be threatened, and this regulation has been fully violated" (Sonamandan 1999: 14). If this foregrounds the relative cultural and institutional autonomy of the civil sphere, it also emphasizes the centrality of elections to the Indian civil sphere. In addressing "why Indians vote," Carswell and De Neve (2014: 1049) conclude that "people's passionate insistence that voting is the most fundamental right they have and their assertion that it is their personal duty to make use of it indicates a high awareness of voting as a medium of democratic assertion."

In appropriating the language and practices of democratic contestation, the Panthers were able to delegitimize those clinging to their dominance. "Mass media institutions respond to opinion," Alexander (2006: 5) notes, "but they also structure and change it." Faced with a scenario in which Dalits were abiding by the dearly held values of democratic participation in the face of caste aggression, local reporters chose to amplify their struggle. Twenty years have passed since this first foray into politics, and relentless struggle, lobbying, and campaigning mean that Thirumavalavan is now a mainstay in the alliances of the parties that once sought to exclude him by force. If this points to an increase in cross-caste solidarity, the question remains whether he has been accommodated in tokenistic fashion or whether his demands and concerns have been acted upon. In considering this question we turn, finally, to the third example of caste violence.

"Honor Killings": Policing Caste Boundaries

Nearly two decades after the Melavalavu massacre, on March 12, 2016, a young Tamil couple went shopping in the provincial town of Udumalaipettai. As they returned to their vehicle on the main street, six men armed with sickles approached on motorbikes. In an attack caught on CCTV, the culprits attacked the couple and left them for dead. The reason for the murderous assault was that the couple belonged to different castes. Shankar, the husband, hailed from a Dalit caste, whereas Kausalya, his wife, was a Thevar – a locally powerful (albeit ritually low-status) caste who saw the union as transgressing caste norms. Shankar succumbed to his injuries in the ambulance, but Kausalya survived, recovered, and not only stood firm in fighting a legal case against her parents who had ordered the attack, but has gone on to lead campaigns against caste violence (Jyoti 2017). Even within members of one family, it is clear, there may be competing value systems and commitments to civic solidarity. Significantly, in contrast to Kausalya's brave and principled stand, the institutions of political mediation were found wanting. The ruling party maintained a calculated silence in part, it would seem, for fear of alienating the strong Thevar vote-bank they depend upon. Equally culpably, the opposition leader M. K. Stalin, who was in a loose electoral alliance with the VCK at the time, failed to condemn the casteist murder outright – speaking merely of "law and order" problems in the state (Kumar 2016). In the face of such persistent and continued silencing of

THE INDIAN CIVIL SPHERE

their voices, we can follow Rao (2009: 185), in arguing that it is Dalit symbolic politics that places issues on the agenda and seeks to "expand the categories of who or what could be a political subject" – appealing to, and seeking to realize the promises of the Constitution.

We first need to explain the context within which murdering one's own child is conceivable. Violence against cross-caste marriages is articulated as a defense of family and caste "honor." As Abraham (2014: 58) argues, control of women's sexuality is "about maintaining privilege and power, or asserting caste pride." Indeed, George (2006: 37) notes that "individual honour is usually subsumed to family and religious or caste community honour." This understanding of "honor," as Welchman and Hossain (2005: 4) observe, is "vested in male (family and/or conjugal) control over women and specifically women's sexual conduct: actual, suspected or potential." This reflects the crucial role that female chastity plays in the construction of boundaries (cf. Yuval-Davis 1997). In a caste context, where male honor rests on their ability to control women's bodies (Welchman and Hossain 2005), female honor entails abiding by appropriate and sanctioned roles and codes of conduct (Still 2011). Kausalya, thus, was seen to have "dishonored" her family by choosing her own husband, more particularly by choosing a Dalit spouse. The driving force in this process is the collective humiliation attached to the failure by men to protect or control "their" women. Given the significance accorded to honor in Tamil society, such shame (*veka-kedu*) reduces one's standing in society to an almost sub-human level (Gorringe 2006).

The violence inflicted against cross-caste couples, thus, is referred to under the heading of "honor crimes" (*gourava kolaigal*): a misnomer that tacitly legitimizes the impulses behind such action.[5] Kumar (2016) illustrates how dominant caste leaders allege that Dalit men are deliberately "targeting their women" and shows how posts on social media routinely celebrate caste pride and exclusivity. In relation to the Udumalaipettai case, one post read:

> Every Thevar clan should teach their kids as they are growing up – We belong to an upper caste, we have an image in society, you have to protect that image until the end – parents should teach this to children. If after all that they go for an inter-caste marriage, there is nothing wrong in hacking both of them to pieces. Being Thevar is a matter of pride, to protect this is our duty. (in Kumar 2016)

Dalit leaders, by contrast, articulate the more universalistic and inclusive sentiment that "love is blind" and that people have the right to choose their own life-partners. "Our country got Independence," as Kausalya put it, "but we don't even have the freedom to love" (Jyoti 2017). In the face of naked casteism as seen above, Dalits have allied with rationalist and communist parties and worked through legal channels, operationalizing the (imperfect) institutions of the civil sphere in India to counter caste prejudice. Dalits in this context have the law on their side, but the idealistic and egalitarian commitments of India's civil sphere are consistently at odds with the anti-democratic institutions of caste which conspire to thwart the implementation of progressive legislation. Again we see the value of protest for civic repair here. Sustained Dalit pressure on politicians, the media, and the courts has served to alter attitudes – not least within the judiciary. In contrast to the judges in 1970, who refused to entertain the thought that landlords could be responsible for burning forty-four laborers to death (*Economic and Political Weekly* 1973), Yamunan (2018) reports on a landmark ruling by the country's Supreme Court which termed so-called "Honor Crimes" a "catastrophic crisis for the rule of law." Justice Mishra insisted that: "The human rights of a daughter, brother, sister or son are not mortgaged to the so-called or so-understood honour of the family or clan or the collective."

There is no guarantee, however, that such views are universally applied and numerous cases in which justice has been denied, or convicted killers have been freed, have meant that Dalit groups both call for specific legislation against "honor killings" (Viswanathan 2018) and tap into a global civil sphere that has sprung up around UN conventions on the eradication of racial discrimination (Bob 2007). The aim here is to shift the narratives around shame and honor away from the caste or family level and onto the national government. The hope of activists is that global scrutiny will strengthen the civil sphere in India – perfectly illustrated in the judgment above – and make it more likely that laws will be enforced. The difficulty lies in the question of cultural legitimacy. When perpetrators of caste violence openly articulate trenchant defenses of murderous attacks there is, as Alexander (2006: 289) argues, a need for "changes in communicative institutions, to new cultural understandings, and to alterations in face-to-face interactions." Whilst Dalit movements are key players in processes of civil repair – reporting and condemning atrocities, demanding the implementation of legislation, monitoring authorities, and articulating alternate visions – we need, therefore, to also subject dominant cultural texts to critical scrutiny. In the wake of Shankar's murder, therefore, Rajendran (2017) called for analysis of how "certain caste narratives have been created, sustained and glorified on the big screen." Civic repair, we contend, requires cultural scripts to be challenged and changed too.

Scripting Change?

As we have argued elsewhere (Damodaran and Gorringe 2017), there are close ties between politics and cinema in Tamil Nadu. Given how central films are to public consciousness and public discourse, "there is a need for analysis of the implicit caste norms and values carried in these films and the impact that they have" (Damodaran and Gorringe 2017). Following Srinivas and Kaali (1998: 212), it is clear that Tamil movies reinforce and replay patron–client relations and reproduce "caste power." The most popular films through the 1980s and 1990s shaped and reinforced the self-image and perceptions of the Thevar castes in the south, and what Srinivas and Kaali (1998: 222) term "the discursive hegemonies of caste society." Tamil cinema, in this sense, functioned as a non-civil sphere. "The hierarchies in these non-civil spheres," as Alexander (2006: 7) notes, "often interfere with the construction of the wider solidarity that is the *sine qua non* of civil life." Nowhere is this clearer than in the audience response to the 2004 blockbuster *Kaadhal* (Love, dir. Sakthivel 2004) – a film about a doomed romance between a couple of unspecified-caste youngsters who are, nevertheless, identifiable as a Thevar girl and a Dalit boy. When the transgressive love affair is discovered by the girl's family they thrash the boy mercilessly. The film concludes with the unhappy heroine, now married to a man of her own caste, observing her former love driven to insanity. At face value, this is a film that critiques caste violence and espouses humanitarian and civic virtues. Indeed, director Balaji Sakthivel has spoken about his intention to showcase the evils of casteism (Darshan 2019). Drawing on hegemonic narratives of caste valor and pride, however, local audiences interpreted the film as a corrective rather than a critique. Anand (2005) vividly captures how the representations on screen are transposed into the caste politics of everyday Tamil Nadu:

> [A] friend who watched Kaadhal in a Madurai cinema talked of how Thevars – the dominant "backward caste" of the southern districts – in the hall shouted aloud: "Fuckers, this will be your fate if you think you can get our girl." Dalits watching the movie in the southern districts were intimidated both by the depiction of the hero and by the participative enthusiasm of the Thevars among the audience. (Anand 2005)

The difficulty of forging an inclusive civil sphere is highlighted here. What is required is the creation of completely new scripts and social visions for a more open and democratic society. "Power conflicts," Alexander (2006: 233) reminds us, "are not simply about who gets what and how much.

They are about who will be what, and for how long. Representation is critical." Despite the assertion of Dalit movements in the state, it is only in the past decade that we have seen the introduction of a new set of symbolic categories that challenges caste dominance and offers an alternate and more inclusive imagining of society. It is, we contend, only with the arrival of directors like Pa. Ranjith that films have offered a Dalit-eye's view of everyday life (Damodaran and Gorringe 2020).[6] Ranjith's films *Madras* (2014), *Attakathi* (Cardboard Knife, 2012), *Kabali* (A Name, 2016), and *Kaala* (Black or Death, 2018) are not dramatically different to other Tamil films in terms of plotlines or style, but they showcase people and places hitherto denied the right to non-stigmatized representation. *Kabali* and *Kaala* stand out here in taking the most mainstream and iconic Tamil filmstar of all – Rajinikanth – and casting him as an assertive Dalit.

Did the message translate to the audience though? The caste politics of the films was widely discussed online, but curiously absent from many of the reviews which spoke of "gangster dramas" (Bose 2018). As Bose (2018) argues, however, "caste is not incidental to *Kaala*, it isn't a minor accompaniment to the plot. Dalit assertion is the bedrock of the movie, its strongest theme, the crux of its politics." We would say the same of *Kabali*, which opens with the protagonist reading a Dalit autobiography and features a low-caste hero who is conscious of the power of dressing, who knows the politics behind Gandhi shedding his clothes and Ambedkar donning a three-piece suit. Whilst the Dalithood of the hero is not spelled out explicitly, Dalit icons and arguments are given prominence in a way that has not occurred before. Indeed, the fact that Kabali and Kaala are portrayed as Tamils first and foremost perhaps amplifies the films' message. "Universalism is most offensive and indeed most radical," Manoharan (2016) notes, "when it is proposed by subalterns who wish to break particularist identities of their own selves and also of their erstwhile superiors. A Dalit speaking the language of complete Tamil liberation can unsettle the mechanism of caste far more than when his concern is with the specific welfare of his own caste." Alexander (2006: 289) maintains that "if the fragmented structures of CS are to be effectively changed, shifts in regulatory institutions must be related to changes in communicative institutions, to new cultural understandings." It is, we argue, precisely such understandings that are offered by the new films. As Bose (2018) optimistically notes: "The lack of a counter [to caste hegemony] from our education system, in even the so-called 'good schools' underscores why we need to generate more conversation around caste in popular culture. Our directors and stars could just do what our textbooks and teachers have failed to." Inspired by the assertion of

Dalit movements, Tamil films are now offering alternate scripts. Further research is needed to delineate the contours of this process, but the *potential* for such scripts to enhance civic repair is clear.

Conclusion: Dalit Struggles and the Possibilities for Social Repair

India, we are frequently told, is the world's largest democracy. Processes of cultural transformation, however, are clearly complex and contested. Whilst the Indian Constitution created a nation of equal citizens in 1950, that legislation has lacked the cultural legitimacy required to engender widespread change. The Constitution did contribute to the delegitimization of caste authority, with the result that caste norms are increasingly upheld through violent means. In this chapter we have charted how the incivilities of caste continue to erode the sense of fraternity and common citizenship that Ambedkar saw as the bedrock of a new nation. In the eyes of dominant castes, quite simply, Dalits remain polluted and marginal members of the polity. This explains why Thirumavalavan, the leader of the Liberation Panthers, used his maiden speech as an MP in the Lok Sabha in 2009 to insist that: "Without eradicating untouchability we cannot develop democracy" (Lok Sabha Debates 2009). Seventy years after independence, the fact that G. Mohan's film *Draupathi* which condones "honor killings" could be released (Shekhar 2020), and that a Dalit youth in Andhra Pradesh can be tonsured (a form of caste humiliation and abuse) *in a police station* (Nagaraja 2020), highlights the persistence of "hierarchical values" (Harriss 2012) and the continued lack of public spiritedness that Ambedkar saw as the hallmark of caste society.

The values and institutions of the civil sphere in India persist, but are far from hegemonic. Against this backdrop, Dalit movements and parties emerge as "cultural and social movements of civil repair" (Alexander 2001: 588). Whilst Dalit movements are frequently dismissed as engaged in "narrow identity politics," we have seen above how they draw on the civil criteria laid down in the Constitution to press for civic and political rights, to condemn casteist violence and to call for a more inclusive and tolerant society. When Dalit activists call out caste abuses in universal terms – 'if I am cut, do I not bleed' – they are laying down a claim to equal and solidary citizenship. "The Dalit movement," as Satyanarayana (2015) argues, "has been instrumental in establishing the fact that Dalits have been denied 'human status' and are not seen as 'proper citizens' and that caste is a mode of power in India." Following sustained mobilization, Ambedkar's words and image are now a common feature across

CASTE, INCIVILITY, AND THE PROSPECTS OF CIVIL REPAIR

India, carrying the promise of new values and modes of interaction premised on solidarity or fraternity rather than hierarchy. In eschewing violence and using legal and democratic means to demand an end to the incivilities of caste, Dalit movements have spearheaded processes of civil repair. Sudamani, state assistant secretary of the VCK affiliated Women's Liberation Movement (*Mahalir Viduthalai Iyyakam*), offers an insight into the changes that the movement has helped to bring about:

> I have been in the party for 25 years, but before that I too lacked awareness [*villipunnarvu*]. ... We are becoming aware since the advent of the party. Before then how many women suffered from casteist abuses? How many doused themselves in kerosene? Dominant caste people would use the women to sate their desires; there are so many women who have been abused in this way in a situation where they could not speak of it publicly. ... Now they have the ability to take up these issues and to protest and struggle to protect their honour. That is a huge *achievement* [in English]. (Interview August 2012)

Mobilization has empowered Dalits to resist caste abuses, has infused them with self-respect, and has animated legislative instruments that would not otherwise be enforced (cf. Carswell and De Neve 2015). They have, furthermore, had a knock-on impact in terms of cultural representations in influencing a new wave of cinema directors and writers. That the vision of a society free of caste remains utopian and radical, speaks to the fragility of civil sphere institutions and the unfinished project of civil repair. In continuing to highlight caste abuses, demand equal citizenship, and call for the implementation of the Constitution, Dalit movements are key components of the civil sphere. "Constitutional morality is not a natural sentiment," as Ambedkar noted in 1947, "it has to be cultivated."[7]

Acknowledgments

We first presented this chapter as a paper at a conference in Yale in 2021. We are indebted to the participants, and especially to Jeffrey Alexander and Suryakant Waghmore, for constructive comments that have helped to strengthen the paper. Huge thanks to Jane Fricker and Patti Phillips for editorial input.

2

The Indian Civil Sphere and the Question of Caste

The Case of the Hathras Movement
Raju Chalwadi

Introduction

On September 14, 2020, in rural northern India, a nineteen-year-old woman was gang-raped, tortured, and brutally assaulted. The victim belonged to the Valmiki community, one among thousands of caste groups in India who are known as Dalits (oppressed/crushed). The perpetrators, by comparison, were four dominant-caste men belonging to the Kshatriya/Thakur caste/community. Initially taken to the district hospital, the woman was immediately referred to a city hospital, where the police recorded her statement twice – over a period of eight days – during which she named the four rapists, all of whom lived in the same village as she did.

Only when her condition worsened, was she finally transferred to a state-run hospital in Delhi. But after a two-week battle for her life, she succumbed to her injuries on September 29, 2020, in the national capital. Following her rape and forced cremation, India witnessed a wave of protests, identified here as the "Hathras movement," in which people demanded justice and the arrest of the perpetrators, while raising questions about state/police violence against the victim and her family. The protests brought India's long unresolved caste question to the fore. In turn, parallel counter-movements arose, made up of state apologists and caste conservatives who sought to discredit the Hathras movement and frame the victim, her family, the protestors, and solidarity groups through anti-civil codes.

In the chapter that follows, I draw on civil sphere theory (CST) to offer insights into the nature of contemporary India's civil sphere. As a macro-framework, CST allows us to better understand the ongoing process of social change: more specifically, the plurality of discourses that operate during a social movement as well as how culturally specific binary codes are deployed to either elevate or pollute the discourse, people, or institutions in question (Alexander 2006). CST helps to shed light on the extent of civil expansion and contraction India witnessed following the Hathras movement. Using CST as a guide, I show how the Hathras movement resonated with three key elements associated with the civil sphere: communicative and regulative institutions and public opinion.

In this case study of the Hathras movement, I apply Alexander's (2018) concept of "societalization," which describes the process through which "problems become crises" (p. 1049). Societalization refers to how actors transform an event into a societal problem, taking it out of a specific domain and bringing it into the larger, available civil sphere to initiate the process of civil repair, with the expectation that "when sphere-specific problems become societalized, routine strains are carefully scrutinized, once lauded institutions ferociously criticized, elites threatened and punished, and far-reaching institutional reforms launched and sometimes achieved" (Alexander 2018: 1050). The societalization of the Hathras movement, however, has not been as successful in bringing about radical change due to the caste nature of Indian society; nevertheless, I argue, the movement has shown the presence of and possibilities for the Dalit in exerting civil power in the contemporary Indian civil sphere.

Dalits, India's Civil Sphere, and Anti-Caste Movements

Across the Indian subcontinent and India, in particular, the caste system continues to shape the life opportunities of individuals. The mention of caste and its "divine" origins is found in the sacred text of Hindus.[1] The caste system distributes status, morality, rights, and duties, among other things. In the twentieth century, social theorist B. R. Ambedkar (1979 [1916]) defined caste in India as "an artificial chopping off the population into fixed and definite units, each one prevented from fusing into another through the custom of endogamy" (p. 9). Caste groups have continued to be arranged hierarchically and assigned "ritual" status; however, one social group that remains outside of this hierarchically arranged system, and one of India's minorities, is the Dalits. Historically, Dalits have been non-Hindus (Roberts 2016), and they have resisted or, at least, quietly undermined their inclusion into the Hindu fold (Lee 2021). Nevertheless, Dalits have been treated as "untouchables" by Hindus and considered "ritually impure."

For centuries, there has been an absence of participation in public discourse and democratic culture for the majority of the Indian population. The Dalits, specifically, were excluded from both civil and non-civil life. They were denied public resources, such as roads, wells, ponds, and habitable lands for settlement, among other things. In many parts of India, for instance, in Kerala, Dalit women were not allowed to cover their upper bodies. Brahminical Hinduism legitimized the exclusion of "lower" caste groups and Dalits on religious grounds and branded them as "anti-civil" masses. Dalits, for instance, were seen as polluting agents and were assigned the polluted code of "untouchables."

As a consequence, the pure Hindus distorted India's civil sphere in terrible ways. Brahminical Hinduism thus constituted a destructive intrusion, blocking the creation of an Indian civil sphere. Access to communicative and regulatory institutions was denied to lower-caste groups, in general, and Dalits, in particular. For much of India's history, Dalits were forcefully restricted from entering the civil sphere. It was Hindus who participated in, shaped, and decided on the qualities needed to qualify as being a part of the civil sphere. The Dalits were framed as being non-civil and unclean: as untouchables, polluted, outcastes, docile, irrational, and other similar framings. Accordingly, within this context, the anti-caste movements, to use Alexander's (2018) term, "societalized" the caste question, in general, and the Dalit question, in particular.

The genealogy of critically questioning the institution of caste and its associated ideas about high/low human beings in the Indian subcontinent dates back to, at least, the time of the Buddha (see Omvedt 2012). This critical tradition became more institutionalized, organized into what are today called anti-caste movements (ACMs) or struggles; it began in the nineteenth century and included Jyotirao Phule, one of the founders of the modern ACM in western India. ACMs initiated the civil repair of caste and Hinduism, which framed Dalits in polluted terms, and, thus, a project was initiated to reconstruct the positive history and identity, and role of Dalits within India's civil sphere. ACMs are not only political mobilizations that raise questions about unequal power and representation, but, at their core, these movements aim for, to use B. R. Ambedkar's words, "[the] reclamation of human personality" (Keer 1954: 351) for the millions relegated to the margins of society and for a deep cultural transformation to expand India's civil sphere.

ACMs believe that the "annihilation of caste" is a necessary condition for expanding the civil sphere and removing everyday violence from social life in India. To establish domestic peace, caste must be tackled. ACMs thus imagine and aim to establish democracy devoid of caste. Like the civil rights and feminist movements, ACMs aspire to establish a new cultural foundation in a radical project to expand India's civil sphere. However, like any other movement that aims to reconstruct a civil life devoid of persecution, ACMs have only partially achieved their aims: caste-oppressed peoples, in general, and Dalits, in particular, have remained if not outside at least not fully within the civil sphere dominated by Hindus.

Rise of the Bharatiya Janata Party

India's liberal constitution came into effect in 1950 and envisioned a secular India, promising economic and social progress to all Indians. However, post-independence, the Indian National Congress ruled India, and, as Jaffrelot (2017) suggests, it "diluted the secular discourse of the state in a way that has given the Hindu-nationalist idiom a new legitimacy" (p. 53). The revival of Hindu nationalism, which began in the early 1990s, and the rise of the Bharatiya Janata Party (BJP), winning an absolute majority in 2014 and 2019, have deeply undermined India's secular premise. Progress made in expanding the civil sphere was undercut and, after 2014, was aggressively overtaken by upper-caste Hindus again. As Drèze (2020) writes, "the growth of Hindu nationalism can be seen as a revolt of the upper castes against the egalitarian demands of democracy."

In 2014, the BJP, a Hindu caste-conservative party, came to power in India with a commanding majority. Its candidate for prime minister was Narendra Modi, who was projected as a *"Vikas Purush"* (Man of Development) with the catchy slogan that he would usher in *"achhe din"* (good days) for Indians after coming to power. Indians across caste lines voted for Modi, as he promised social and economic mobility for all. However, atrocities against Dalits continued. For instance, a report sponsored by the United States Commission on International Religious Freedom says that since 2014, both Dalits and religious minority communities in India have experienced a dramatic increase in hate crimes, assaults, forced conversion, and social boycotts (Puniyani 2021).

A string of incidents made the civil sphere more violent for Dalits: the Una flogging case (2016), the institutional murder of Rohit Vemula (2016), the Saharanpur anti-Dalit riot (2017), and dilution of the Scheduled Caste/Scheduled Tribes (SC/ST Act) (2018). These events mobilized Dalits across the nation against the BJP government and framed the BJP-led government as one not committed to Dalit rights and welfare. In all the cases mentioned, Dalits felt betrayed, having experienced blatant discrimination from the state and society at large.

THE INDIAN CIVIL SPHERE

Thus, within this context, in late 2020, as Dalits continued to experience civil exclusion, the rape in Hathras district resulted in Dalit communities feeling humiliated and attacked.

Emergence of the Hathras Movement

After battling for her life for over two weeks, the Dalit woman died while receiving medical treatment on September 29 in Delhi. However, the case still needed to be taken seriously by communicative agents inside the civil sphere. For instance, David (2020), through her investigation of news reporting of the case, wrote in *Newslaundry* that "in the two weeks preceding the woman's death, there had been radio silence on the incident from two leading newspapers in the area. The Lucknow editions of the *Times of India* and the *Dainik Jagran* did not deem it newsworthy enough to carry in their pages, let alone the front page." Most Indian news channels, too, did not cover the case initially. How did the case become societalized? What led the communicative or regulatory institutions to take notice of it?

When the woman died in the hospital, her body was rushed by ambulance to her village by the state police. In the early hours of the next day, around 2:30 a.m., the police and state administrators committed a deeply atrocious and disrespectful act. The media were informed that the police and the state, not the family, would perform last rites over the body. Hearing this, the woman's family and relatives began demanding the body be returned to the family for last rites and requested that the body not be cremated at night. The police and state did not heed their requests. In news footage, the woman's family was seen begging the police to hand over the body to them and throwing themselves into an ambulance to stop the cremation (NDTV 2020). However, after state policemen formed a human chain to prevent people from coming near the vehicle and the victim's family and relatives were locked in their homes, the body was cremated.

Yet, somehow, journalists reached the village and, with their cameras, provided real-time live coverage of this deeply disturbing event. The whole nation witnessed the act of forced cremation, with police using petrol, live. Indians watched it on their televisions and mobile devices or saw the images in newspapers the next day. Furthermore, the family members, who were locked in their house, were not even allowed to see the face of the woman or perform last rites. Many interpreted the event as an act of deep religious profanation, while others saw it as a deeply anti-woman and anti-Dalit act, triggering feelings of outrage across the

THE QUESTION OF CASTE

nation. All told, this blatant act of injustice and heavy-handedness by the state societalized the case.

By airing the live event, the journalists and news channels crystallized public opinion and framed the victim's family in civil terms. The visuals of the helplessness of the victim's family and the treatment of the state shook the nation's consciousness. The footage disseminated by communicative agents framed the state and police in non-civil terms: insensitive, ruthless, anti-Dalit, and anti-women. The forceful cremation, utter injustice, and deep humiliation for the majority of progressive Indians sowed the seeds for the emergence of the Hathras movement, and "[t]he case started gaining nationwide momentum" (Ara 2020).

Beginning the next day, India's major regulatory institutions took notice of the case and started shaping the future discourse that largely framed the woman, her family, protestors, and solidarity groups in civil terms. India's apex institution for protecting human rights, the National Human Rights Commission (NHRC), a statutory public body, took *suo motu* cognizance of the case the very next day. The NHRC was established in compliance with the Paris Principles of Human Rights (1991) and is a watchdog for human rights in India. The NHRC sent notices about the case to the state's chief secretary and director general of police (*The Hindu* 2020a). In a statement uploaded on its website, it described the events as "very painful" and "a serious issue of violation of human rights" (NHRC 2020). Furthermore, the commission directed the state government to provide "proper police protection" to the deceased's family and the other members of the SC community in her village (NHRC 2020).

On the very same day, making a first judicial intervention, the Allahabad High Court in Uttar Pradesh also called out the state government over the handling of the case and the forceful cremation. The bench headed by Justices Rajan Roy and Jaspreet Singh said that the incident of forced cremation "has shocked our conscience," and they directed top state officials to appear before the court, describing the case as of "immense public importance" (Scroll 2020). The Supreme Court of India, the top regulatory institution in the judicial domain, hearing a petition seeking an investigation from the central investigation agency of India about the case, described the Hathras case as "shocking" and "extraordinary" and asked the Uttar Pradesh government whether it had a witness protection plan and whether the Hathras family had access to a lawyer (Scroll 2020).

However, the state was quick to intervene and promote its own version of the story. To save face, the Additional Director General of Police (ADGP [law and order]) of Uttar Pradesh state, Prashant Kumar, called a press conference and declared that, based on a forensic report conducted in Hathras, a rape *did not* take place and a traumatic neck injury caused the victim's death. Furthermore, he claimed that "some people twisted the matter to stir caste-based tension" (*Outlook India* 2020). Both of these "facts" were then repeated by the state over the coming weeks. Two weeks later, Justices Mithal and Roy, who headed another bench of the Allahabad High Court, asked the District Magistrate Praveen Laxkar, who gave permission for the forced cremation, "if he would have allowed his daughter to be cremated the same way?" (Abhishek and Sharma 2020).

Newspapers and television networks strongly condemned bureaucrats and unjust state actions. One of India's most widely read newspapers, particularly in the south, was highly critical of the two state officers, Prashant Kumar and Praveen Laxkar, for their role in spreading fake news about the victim not being raped and their part in the forced cremation. In its editorial pages, *The New Indian Express* (2020b) wrote: "These two insensitive and blundering officials are prime examples of what a bureaucrat and a police officer should not be." Consequently, there were demands from the woman's family, solidarity groups, and anti-caste activists to suspend the two officers immediately; however, the state did not do so. Furthermore, India's foremost national daily, *The Hindu*, commenting on the forced cremation in its editorial, opined that "the bleak image of a burning pyre illuminating a ghastly night while policemen stood guard will be forever etched in India's collective memory" (*The Hindu* 2020b).

Reportage of the issue was equally visible on television news channels, with the case and events that followed being discussed, debated, and aired for the month after. One television news channel, NDTV, during one of its prime-time shows, asked, "Why did the police do the cremation; is that justice? Why did they burn the body at midnight to settle the matter before morning? Was she a terrorist? What mental trauma her family could have got?" (NDTV 2020). Indeed, throughout the episode, NDTV came out clearly against the state and police, compared with the stance taken by most news channels.

Moreover, progressive politicians, civil society members, anti-caste activists, lawyers, and intellectuals created a discourse in favor of the deceased and her family during televised debates. For instance, in one such debate, Kiruba Munusamy, one of India's leading anti-caste lawyers, asked, "[S]he [the deceased woman] was in the hospital for fourteen days battling to survive; we sent *Nirbhaya*[2] abroad for treatment but we not even able to provide AIIMS bed for Hathras victim. . . . Why was the government not concerned about the health of a Dalit woman?" (*India*

THE QUESTION OF CASTE

Today 2020). The fact that the police and state did not take an active interest in the case and the state did not provide the woman with access to the best healthcare facility was broadcast loudly.

Moving to virtual space, Dalit Women Fight, a Twitter handle used to describe a community-led digital project founded to amplify the voice of Dalit women for justice, came up with an innovative and accessible way for social media users to register their anguish and complaints about the Hathras case. The site shared a link to a draft letter describing the complicit nature of police administration and upper-caste groups, followed by several demands for justice for the Hathras victim. The letter was addressed to the Uttar Pradesh government, the Supreme Court of India, the United Nations Special Rapporteur on Violence against Women, the Prime Minister of India, and the National Commission for Scheduled Caste. Concerned citizens could simply click the link, and an email would be sent to the above organizations (Dalit Women Fight 2020).

Similarly, a letter with approximately 10,000 signatories, ranging from journalists and civil society groups to filmmakers, demanded the resignation of the state's chief minister over his "indifferent attitude." The letter further stated that the Hathras case "is an example of blatant patriarchy and upper-caste dominance operating through sponsored violence" (*The New Indian Express* 2020a). Transnational solidarity came in the form of a joint statement signed by more than 1,800 representatives worldwide, including prominent personalities, academic journals, civil society organizations, and academic departments from various universities in the United States (Antipode Online 2020).

While regulatory institutions and communicative agents within the civil sphere were making important contributions toward building a civil discourse, on the ground, various progressive groups, especially Dalits, were actively mobilizing people and demanding justice for the victim. The first recorded large-scale protest that I could find took place in Uttar Pradesh's Hapur district and was led by the Valmikis on the very day after the police forcefully cremated the victim's body. Thousands of protestors walked through the streets chanting the slogan "Jai Bhim" (Long live Ambedkar) and demanding capital punishment for the rapists. Protestors were seen holding placards that read, "#Hang the Rapist and #No More BJP" (Rai 2020).

Most Valmikis in contemporary India, due to a lack of symbolic, economic, and cultural capital, continue to hold sanitation jobs. However, during the Hathras movement, they transformed these sites into a mode of protest. They registered their dissent and anger against the complicit nature and caste standing of the Indian state. For instance, Valmikis who were involved in sanitation labor in Uttar Pradesh's two districts undertook eight long protests in the form of a strike to show solidarity and demand justice for the victim and her family (Sabrang 2020). In Mumbai, Valmiki residents, especially those working as sanitation laborers, patient caretakers, lab assistants, cleaners and helpers in municipal hospitals and offices, organized protests or, at least, arranged formal gatherings to pay homage to the victim in association with Ambedkarite or working-class unions.

Though protests took place across India, one major protest took place at Delhi's Jantar Mantar and was called for by various civil society groups and attended by students, concerned citizens, and politicians from opposition parties. One of the left-leaning politicians present at the protest site, commenting on the lawlessness in Uttar Pradesh, suggested "a caste code [is] in operation, not the Constitution of India" (*The Wire* 2020a). The binary of sacred (the Constitution) and profane (caste) was used heavily by protestors to frame themselves as inside the civil code – rational, justice-oriented, law-abiding, and anti-caste people – whereas others now included the state, police, and ruling regime, framed in non-civil terms: as caste apologists, orthodox, and Hindu fundamentalists.

The organized nature of performances in the form of protests, sit-ins, and demonstrations ran parallel to the societalization that was happening from "above" (regulatory and communicative agents). Taken together, these actions helped to translate the case from a community-specific concern into a general concern about caste and the sexual violence that threatens the Indian civil sphere as a whole.

However, a week after the woman's death, the Chief Minister of Uttar Pradesh, Yogi Adityanath, in a meeting review about an upcoming by-election in the state, commented on the protests around the Hathras case, saying, "those who do not like the development . . . they want to incite caste and communal riots in the country and state and want to stop development." This statement was later followed by a series of first information reports (FIRs) being filed against protestors in the state. In total, nineteen FIRs were filed, as state administrators led by Yogi Adityanath sensed that an "international conspiracy" to defame the government was under way (*The Wire* 2020c).

In response to accusations of an international conspiracy, *Telegraph India*, one of the leading newspaper agencies, in one of its editorials, wrote a scathing comment:

> There it is – the "foreign hand" . . . This is the most imaginative defence to have been thought up to discredit the countrywide protests against administrative and police actions to suppress the realities of the alleged gang rape of a Dalit girl in Hathras by upper-caste men and her subsequent death. (*Telegraph India* 2020a)

The newspaper not only dismissed the accusation, calling it an "*imaginative* defence," but also stressed the fact, again, that a rape did occur, even though the state was still in denial, thereby questioning the intent behind the state's partisan act. Summing up the whole episode of unjust treatment meted out against the victim and her family through the state's biased approach, in another editorial, the *Telegraph* opined, "Institutional complicity in efforts to protect upper-caste criminals when the crimes are against Dalits was laid bare in the Hathras case in Uttar Pradesh" (*Telegraph India* 2020b).

The preceding discussion shows how regulatory and various communicative agents, together with the protestors, played a significant role in framing the Hathras movement in civil terms. The community in question, the Dalits, had very little representation in either regulatory or communicative institutions; however, both of these civil institutions played a critical role in societalizing the case, thereby expanding the boundaries of the existing civil sphere in the material sense. Alexander (2006) suggests that social movements can be seen as civil translators in that they translate the local and particular into the universal. Civil and regulative institutions regularly highlighted the caste of the woman and questioned the insensitive approach of the state. In doing so, caste and state violence were projected as destructive intrusions into the Indian civil sphere.

Specifically, the larger themes of caste patriarchy, state violence, and domination of the upper castes in the cultural and social sphere took center stage in prime-time shows on liberal or left-leaning news channels. Taken together, the role played by civil institutions and protests helped garner support from a larger audience, which translated into extended empathy and the development of civil feeling among Indians. Alexander (2018) writes that "journalism is a key communicative institution of the civil sphere" (p. 1053). In contemporary India, many media houses are owned by businessmen close to the current regime or, at the very least, are right-leaning. Nevertheless, many newspapers and television channels, as we saw earlier, did reconstruct the event in a civil manner.

In societalizing the case, both protestors and civil institutions highlighted the deep, systematic, and pervasive cultural and social hegemony of upper castes as part of their framing of the state in non-civil terms. But as Alexander (2018) forewarns, societalization also triggers a backlash. And in this case, the regulatory and communicative intervention quickly triggered a response. The caste-cultural elites and the state saw the societalization of the Hathras movement as one that framed them in polluting terms, thereby potentially eroding their power and legitimacy.

Hence, rather than expanding civil solidarity for justice, the counter-movements construed the solidarity discourse and protests as dangerous. The backlash resulted in attempts to "retake" the civil sphere and return it to its original position, where membership was limited and boundaries were guarded by caste powers. The narrative was turned upside down as the victim, her family, and protestors became increasingly framed as uncivil, and the perpetrators, the state, and the police were now civil. The resulting polarization blocked societalization, and is discussed in the following section on the counter-movement led by civil societies, upper-caste Hindus, Indian media, the Uttar Pradesh state, and the Indian government, which emerged and ran parallel to the Hathras movement.

The Backlash

The first signs of a counter-movement came from within the caste community of the four rapists. A day before the woman died, state police arrested the four accused men, owing to building public pressure. One civil society organization, namely Akhil Bharatiya Kshatriya Mahasabha (ABKM, All India Kshatriya Council), a body of Rajputs/Thakurs, came out in support of the four rapists. What's more, the ABKM hired a lawyer to defend the accused. The lawyer, A. P. Singh, was himself a Rajput and known to the nation for his previous misogynist remarks. The ABKM engaged in crowdfunding to pay A. P. Singh's fees and, in a press release, the president of the ABKM read a letter that said, "[T]hrough [the] Hathras case, the SC-ST community is being 'misused' to malign the upper caste society, adding that it has particularly hurt the Rajput community"[3] (*India Today* 2020; Sharma 2020).

The Rajput organization, by suggesting that the "SC/ST community" is being "misused," replicated age-old upper-caste patronizing behavior toward Dalits and projected Dalits as an agency-less community incapable of making decisions of their own. Furthermore, the letter stated that Singh would plead the case for the accused parties "to bring out the truth" – the "truth" being that the accused did not commit rape and were not guilty. The switching of codes from "guilty" to "not guilty" was indeed the primary aim of the wider counter-movement that ran parallel to the justice movement.

From day one, the whole village was turned into a fortress by the state authorities. This was done to stop the news media, civil society, opposition politicians, and concerned citizens from reaching out to the woman's family. The authorities in Hathras imposed Section 144 of the Indian Penal Code, which barred the assembly of more than four people in the village and surrounding areas. This happened during the first week of the protest. The village was completely sealed off from outsiders, and "the police announced that no politician or media person will be allowed to enter into the woman's village in Hathras" (Scroll 2020). However, the authorities' caste sympathies became clear when hundreds of upper-caste men were permitted to gather in the same village to support the four accused rapists (Scroll 2020) while a "curfew" was in place. The complicit nature of the police, authorities, and state government was visible and in action.

Seeing developments in India over the Hathras case, the United Nations expressed broader concern over cases of sexual violence in the country. The UN statement was lauded by both progressive and anti-caste circles in India and shared widely on social media. The Government of India, however, reacted sharply to the comments and dismissed UN concerns as merely "some unwarranted comments," further stating that "unnecessary comments by an external agency are best avoided" (*Hindustan Times* 2020). The government and, later, news media sympathetic to the government, began popularizing the idea that foreign agencies need not intervene in an "internal matter."

However, the case did receive considerable international media attention, as US- and UK-based news agencies covered the story widely. For instance, reporters for the *New York Times*, responding to the post by the Indian prime minister that the "strictest action" would be taken against the culprits, wrote "but justice is unlikely" as prosecution rates are low in sexual assault cases in India (Kumar and Schmall 2020). In order to save face and not be seen as a state that is a party to injustice, the Uttar Pradesh state government hired a Mumbai-based public relations firm, which circulated a "clarification note" to foreign correspondents in India and national media, stating that a rape did *not* take place in Hathras.

The note further claimed that the entire episode was created to push the "state into caste turmoil" and suggested that the Uttar Pradesh police would "now probe as to who was responsible for this mala fide campaign." In its analysis, the online news portal *The Wire* (2020b) wrote that "this particular mention in the press note should be read as a warning to domestic media houses which have reported the Hathras incident as a gang-rape . . . beside sending out a caution to foreign correspondents to stay away from it."

The fake news campaign began on day one, as seen earlier when Uttar Pradesh's police chief, based on a forensic report, claimed rape did not take place. This fake news, indeed, enjoyed mass support, especially among upper-caste Indians. Along with the rape denial, the idea that "tension" existed and a "riot" was being planned under the cover of protests, too, had a long career, shown in how these two ideas were spread through state-sympathetic media houses.

In the preceding section, we saw that the Hathras movement did receive media support from a few Hindi news channels but mainly from English-language left/liberal news outlets and newspapers. However, the majority of Indians are non-English speakers, and so vernacular media houses, especially Hindi ones, took the lead in supporting the state and upper-caste version of the "truth." One Hindi daily, *Dainik Jagran*, the highest circulating newspaper in India in Hindi, printed a story with a misleading headline ten days after the woman's death. In bold letters it read, "the woman was killed by her mother and brother," and only just above the headline in small font was it mentioned that this was an accusation made by the four men in the case (Rai 2020). Thus, newspapers, through strategies of headline placement, participated in supporting the fake news that a rape did not take place.

Another news portal, News 18 Hindi, distributed a story on October 10, 2020, with a headline that read, "Naxal connection in Hathras case." The portal claimed that a woman who was Naxalite was hatching a conspiracy in Uttar Pradesh and that the woman had been living with the victim's family between the time of the rape and the woman's death. The claim was based on "sources" from a special investigation agency (News 18 Hindi 2020b). However, news agency claims about the Dalit woman being killed by her family and a Naxalite woman living with them had no substance, nor did they prove correct.

Nevertheless, the major force behind the backlash came from Hindi news channels. Barring few, most news channels, both English and Hindi, were inclined toward the state's version of events, the opposite of what the victim's family, protestors, and regulatory institutions held to be "true." Television news channels aired shows and held debates that projected the victim, her family, protestors, and leaders from opposition parties in non-civil terms. The content of television news channels was pro-government and portrayed the police, the administration, and the state in positive terms.

Zee News, one of the most widely viewed Hindi news channels, played a crucial role in disseminating the state version to the Indian Hindi population. Zee News began covering the Hathras case by blaming the victim and her family. To take one example, in a prime-time show that aired on October 5, 2022, its anchor, Sudhir Chaudhary, claimed, based on "ground reporting," that the woman had had a "love affair" with the main accused, that the second accused was "trapped in the case," and that the two others accused were "not even present in the village" the day the rape took place. This account raised further doubts about the claim the woman had been raped (Zee News 2020). It was the same counter-narrative that the upper castes of the village endorsed, with its victim blaming and framing of the accused in civil terms. This version tarnished the woman who was raped, accusing her family of "faking the rape" and "trapping" the young Rajput boys, who were framed in civil terms: as innocent.

Aaj Tak, another widely watched Hindi news channel, also began covering the case with its own "ground reporting." In a series called "special coverage" and "ground report," the anchor of the channel went to the woman's village and asked mainly upper-caste residents questions that included "whether they wanted a CBI [Central Bureau of Investigation] inquiry into the case," "whether the four accused are not guilty," and, given the chief minister said that the caste angle had been brought in to create tension, "do you all think there is a conspiracy?" (Aaj Tak 2020). The reporter asked leading questions that reproduced a version of events that the upper castes, in general, and the ruling politicians from the upper castes, in particular, endorsed, including that the CBI inquiry should be a "non-partisan" investigation, designed to find out "if the accused are wrongfully framed."

Another Hindi news channel, Republic Bharat, promoted one of its prime-time shows with the headline "in the name of justice; big deal of congress exposed." The show replayed a phone-call recording between an alleged Congress supporter and the brother of the deceased woman. Based on the alleged clip, it was then suggested that Congress, the major opposition party in India, had "offered the family Rs. Fifty lakhs" to give statements against the state (Republic Bharat 2020). Additionally, Republic TV, the English version, in one its prime-time shows, categorized the whole incident in Hathras as a "fake story." The anchor suggested that the rape had not taken place and that the entire narrative set up by the family and solidarity groups had involved "fictional stories" (Vaishnav 2020).

A few news channels, such as News 18 Hindi, Zee UP, and Uttarakhand, aired a show that ran for days, discussing how the Hathras case was a planted story being run to defame Prime Minister Modi and Uttar Pradesh's chief minister. It was alleged that some "Islamic countries" and civil society groups, such as Amnesty International, were "funding the movement to create a caste and communal riot in the country." It was also claimed that in the United States, a riot was orchestrated under the banner of Black Lives Matter and that the same was planned for India. All these claims were based on a "secret report" and/or "intelligence report" submitted to the Uttar Pradesh government (News 18 Hindi

2020a, 2020b). Thus, the Indian mediascape was highly polarized during the peak of the movement.

The backlash was largely led by the Uttar Pradesh state and communicative agents who were caste apologists and close to the ruling political party. This counter-movement aimed at defaming the woman, her family, the protestors, and the opposition parties, with the resulting polarization, thus, blocking the societalization of the Hathras case and justice movement. A section of the media, as shown earlier, interpreted the solidarity movement as having ulterior motives. These counter-movements claimed to provide "a non-partisan" account of the event. However, its members were largely state apologists and regularly concocted stories in favor of the accused, including the narrative that the rape was a fake story and groups with ulterior motives were behind the growth of the Hathras movement in an attempt to create tension and malign the state and nation as a whole. The accused, the state, and upper-caste groups now became the victims, and the deceased woman, her family, solidarity groups, and civil society were the culprits.

Conclusion

A number of pertinent questions remain: What happened to the Hathras movement? Did it achieve its goal? Did the backlash movement succeed in discrediting the justice movement? And, finally, how did this movement and the counter-movement shape the civil sphere in India? The organized nature of the movement at a mass level no longer exists, and there seems to be a return to a steady state, away from the effervescence achieved at the height of the movement. Currently, the family is living under heavy state security, and the village, dominated by upper-caste Hindus, continues to boycott them. Furthermore, among the many "promises" that were made to the family, only one has been fulfilled, that being financial compensation. The family's demands to be relocated to an urban area and that a government job be provided for the woman's elder brother are still unmet, as the state is unwilling to provide any support to the family (Khan 2022; Mohan 2023b; Scroll 2022). In terms of the judicial outcome of the Hathras movement, at the time of writing, in March 2023, the special court in Hathras, where the trial occurred, pronounced its judgment. None of the four accused was found guilty of rape or murder. The court ordered the acquittal of three of the four men accused, and a life sentence was given to only the main accused. Even he was not found guilty of murder and rape but of "culpable homicide."

THE QUESTION OF CASTE

This judgment contradicted the charge sheet filed by India's CBI earlier, that had confirmed that the four culprits gang-raped and murdered the Hathras woman (Taskin 2023). As soon as the judgment was announced, the victim's sister-in-law, speaking to the media in anguish, questioned the caste nature of the state and judiciary and commented, "Thakurs have got the justice, not us" (Sirsiya 2023). The woman's brother said likewise: "This is all politics. Had this happened if we weren't Dalits and they weren't Thakurs?" (Taskin 2023). The family reiterated to the media that they would approach higher courts for justice, and the advocate representing them also said, "We will try to appeal this judgment before the high court" (Mohan 2023a). The belief in regulatory authorities continues to ignite hope for justice.

The public support gained at the height of the Hathras movement had, indeed, dominated the counter-movement. However, the discourse that emerged during the Hathras movement also brought to light the contradictory nature of the civil sphere (Alexander 2006). While, on the societal level, the woman and her family are yet to receive justice, regulatory interventions are indeed keeping hope alive. It could be argued that the goals set by the Hathras movement, such as bringing the case to the attention of a larger audience and framing it in a way to raise larger questions about caste and sexual violence, have been achieved. In other words, the Hathras movement may not have been able to make changes in the regulatory domain or bring immediate justice to the woman and her family, but it did achieve partial success by mobilizing a progressive population against the institution of caste that continues to threaten the expansion of the Indian civil sphere.

3

Can the Brahmin be Civil?

The Ambiguous Repair of Caste Privilege
Ramesh Bairy T. S.

Introduction

This chapter approaches civil sphere theory (CST) via the location (and reflections) of one individual caught up in and facing up to the normative demands of the civil sphere. If "[c]ivil spheres exist, not only in modern, but also in modernizing societies, and in other societies, some part of which strives to expand beyond solidarity of a primordial kind" (Alexander 2015: 173), it is imperative that sociological description be generated from diverse contexts and at distinct levels of its "existence."

Sifting through the now-burgeoning scholarship on CST, I am struck by the dearth of research on individuals and their life trajectories, leading me to ask what individuals do when faced with the ethical demands of solidarity. The value of "zooming in" is to provide textured accounts from which we can better appreciate and evaluate the central concerns of the ambition that undergirds Alexander's framework (2006). Indian sociology, on the other hand, has long been preoccupied by the problem of "the individual," posited most acutely vis-à-vis the question of caste. Presented in classic formulations (see Ambedkar 1944 [1936]; Dumont 1964, 1970; Marriott 1976), the epistemological and normative impossibility of the "individual" in a caste society is a problem that has driven sustained discussion (see, e.g., Beteille [1986] and Inden [1990] for theoretical critiques; and Freeman [1979] and Mines [1994] for contrarian empirical illustrations).

It is at the intersection of these two conversations that this chapter finds its coordinates. The material is based on an extended interview that I did with my father, a Brahmin man in his mid-eighties, coaxing him

CAN THE BRAHMIN BE CIVIL?

to offer an account of himself. I seek here to track the fortunes of the demands of solidarity and a universalizing moral order.

Caste – a system adjudicating the distribution of both symbolic and material resources to status groups and individuals – remains resilient in mainland India. It continues to be a central, though not the only, determinant of life chances in the Indian social order. Accordingly, the fortunes of the civil sphere in India crucially depend on squaring up the caste question – mediating its logics of separation and hierarchy. For reasons that I describe below, approaching this relationship through the "Brahmin subject" stages this theater, perhaps, most acutely. This chapter is about the continued difficulty for the Brahmin to practice civility (a cultural ethic that insistently seeks that individuals aspire to and frame their lifeworlds vis-à-vis solidarities beyond primordial networks), notwithstanding the continuous provocation and invitation to take on such a challenge. In order to heed the demands of a "secular" solidarity, which appears to be foundational for the making of the civil sphere, not all cultural structures and dispositions are favorably prepared and/or willing. Such differences are at once matters of legibility and legitimacy. We are told that all Axial religions contained greater propitious circumstances for the making of the civil sphere (see Alexander 2015; Bellah 2015; Khosrokhavar 2015). Yet, as I argue, the Brahminical order[1] has remained normatively closed to "harbor[ing] the potentiality for a civil sphere insofar as it promotes 'universal' messages that transcend particularistic belonging in the name of a 'god-inspired humanity'" (Khosrokhavar 2015: 166; cf. chapter 4).

The chapter begins with an outline of the normative positioning of the Brahmin – as both a "conceptual category" (see, e.g., Das 1982) and as an identity/empirical group – continuing in the second section with a discussion of the difficulties that the Brahmin faces in imagining a civic sphere and practicing an ethic of solidarity. I also seek to demonstrate the continued resonance of this "horizon of meaning" in the life of Brahmins today.

In the third section, I contextualize the life of this Brahmin man we are tracking and frame him within and vis-à-vis the trajectory of the Brahmin community over the last century, in what became the south Indian state of Karnataka. Through this particular life story, I seek to ask what is the condition of caste amidst the challenge to practice and make one's own "civic solidarity"? I argue that this opens up, at once, possibilities of status aggrandizement for the caste subject, as well as those of enervation and even atrophy. Under these conditions, the caste self finds itself in a deep state of (irredeemable) instability – a state that in an earlier book (Bairy 2010) I posited as an oscillation (even vacillation) between

71

the thick(er) (in-blood) axis of solidarity of (caste) community and the thin(ner) invitation of (civil) association. This description (and argument) is presented in terms of the constant (and consistent) back-and-forth between the specificities that mark our respondent's life and the general sociality of the Brahmin community of Karnataka.

The fourth section includes a few instances from my father's life that he himself framed as apposite and significant for a researcher interested in his engagement with the public and civic-ness. The instances are telling in their starkness, revealing the structural instability that the Brahmin subject inhabits and seeks to have a measure of. They are also significant in persuading us to see this instability as not merely an exclusive burden/ disposition of the Brahmin but of the life of caste sociality itself. In the concluding section, I offer some ways of thinking about Brahmins, the caste system, and the life of the civil sphere.

The (Categorical) Problem of the Brahmin

If cultural legibility and legitimacy of ideas and practices of solidarity (extending beyond one's primordial ties) is a necessary precondition for the formation of a civil sphere, then the Brahmin has a peculiar difficulty. I describe that difficulty in broad brushstrokes in this section.

Dumont (1970) argued that the caste system has no conceptual wherewithal to see humans as "individuals."[2] In the holistic society of caste India, it is impossible to imagine the individual. Accordingly, a body matters, is recognized as human, and is socially meaningful only after it answers the question, "what caste are you?" The spectrum of dharmasutras – legal codes – does not recognize "all-as-one" or its converse, "one-as-all." And the "social" is assembled only after bodies are stacked up in terms of caste locations. Ambedkar (1987: 97), comparing the Christian tradition (viz., Paul's exhorting, "Of one blood are all nations of men . . .; for yet are all one in Christ Jesus") with what he terms the "Hindu social order," points out:

> The Hindu social order is based on the doctrine that men are created from the different parts of the divinity. . . . The Brahmin is no brother to the Kshatriya because the former is born from the mouth of the divinity while the latter is from the arms. The Kshatriya is no brother to the Vaishya because the former is born from the arms and the latter from his thighs. As no one is a brother to the other, no one is the keeper of the other.
>
> The doctrine that the different classes were created from different parts of the divine body has generated the belief that it must be divine

will that they should remain separate and distinct. (Ambedkar 1987: 100)

It is under these conditions that the caste subject – most acutely, the Brahmin – finds it difficult to imagine oneself vis-à-vis others in a language of fraternity. The burden of this impossibility, which at once assumes urgent behavioral limits, is perhaps the gravest for the Brahmin. The problem for him, Esther Gallo felicitously poses, is one of addressing the demand to transform oneself "from devyam (gods) to manushyam (human beings)" (Gallo 2017: 4). The Brahmin in the caste world is positioned as the "bhoosura" – the divinity on earth – who had to be treated as a "part apart" in *all* human affairs. This was legislated in the burgeoning legal-code/*sastra* literature constructed through much of the first half of the first millennium in the Common Era. Though it is no one case that the normative and the performative neatly coincided, the ideal of Brahmin exceptionalism was, and remains, as we seek to illustrate, a hegemonic technology of self-making.

The sastras, by their very nature as enunciators of moral law codes, present the Brahmin's exceptionalism, primacy, and singularity as both total and incontrovertible. Brahmin, in this ideology, is singular for the social formation as a whole, whose singularity is to be protected and preserved by the wielder of political power (McClish 2009). But, as we know, legal codes are not happy guides for discerning social action. Accordingly, how to read this body of texts is a persistent question. In any case, this claim of/on behalf of the Brahmin has remained, at the very least, an enduring and powerful normative doctrinal position (Sathaye 2015).

For our purposes here, tracking the fortunes of a solidarity that might extend beyond the primordial, another feature of the Brahmin normative ideal, is significant. The householder/grhasta Brahmin bound by the ritual order enjoined upon a Brahmin man in the grhasta stage of life is the exemplar Brahmin self (see Heesterman 1988), and he needs no cultural/religious resources from the outside world to observe his ritual duties. Indeed, the (unregulated/able) outside is a perpetual source of anxiety about becoming polluted. And the Brahmin is not pure because he is Brahmin; he is pure because he continuously and anxiously remains in (or regains) a state of purity (Olivelle 1998).

The Brahmin, then, is structured through a stable mapping of subjectification in which he is, perforce, hailed to imagine himself as not only singular but also as one who must eschew association with the not-Brahmin,[3] let alone practice solidarity. This framing of Brahmin exceptionalism continues to cast its long shadow into the present, also

THE INDIAN CIVIL SPHERE

posing robust limits to the constitutional promise of working toward realizing the democratic, republican imaginary of "we, the people."

Yet, in seeking to make sense of the contemporary moment – via our respondent but placed firmly within the sociology of caste in Karnataka – I take seriously the possibility that Brahmin subjectification exhibits uncertainty, even vulnerability and incomprehension. Giving credence to the instability of Brahmin subject-making in the contemporary moment does not mean that I do not recognize and hold within the terms of my argument the dominance the Brahmin wields. That is to say, the recalibration of the contemporary caste question is not to render the Brahmin into a poignant romantic project. The hope is to offer a sociological description that is able to approach the Brahmin subject in an emergentist fashion – simultaneously dependent and autonomous, stable yet contradictory, assured yet anxious, dominant yet deeply discomfited. Thus, I suggest that the Brahmin self today – much like any caste subject today – is held together by a constant, if not consistent, oscillation between a deep and perhaps non-negotiable subjection to the demands that modern reconfiguration of the world entails and the still-robust structural disposition that the caste logic makes on turning away from demands of solidarity.

As the extant historical and sociological investigations of the Brahmin figure caught up in the sweeping and tumultuous conditions of colonial modernization have shown (see, e.g., Geetha and Rajadurai 1998), the Brahmins, like everyone else, made spirited negotiations with the new world, subjecting themselves to it even while subjecting that world to their discursive regime. It is to that fraught world that I turn now, where the Brahmin subject finds itself oscillating, sometimes securely and at other times helplessly, between community and association.

The Brahmin Subject amidst the Demands of Solidarity

Within Karnataka, in recent centuries, the attribution of the highest ritual status has translated into disproportionate access to important forms of capital for the Brahmins. Disproportionate in the sense that the Brahmin community makes up between only 3–4 percent of the region's population, but had by the early decades of the last century managed to occupy more than three-quarters of modern educational and occupational spaces; had become an overwhelmingly urban community, accessing the increasingly urban-oriented and desired opportunities; and had learned to speak the normative language of modernity, secularity, and meritocracy.

CAN THE BRAHMIN BE CIVIL?

Paradoxically, caste – as identification and axes of networks and solidarity – proved to be the most crucial modality for obtaining modern resources. Access to any education beyond the primary level was facilitated through entrenched Brahmin networks, and this early syncing of caste and access further consolidated individual life trajectories.[4] Accordingly, similar to the ways in which elites the world over deploy their ethnic, cultural, gendered, and class locations, to emerge as the voices of modern secularity and citizenship, the Brahmins in Karnataka (as in many other regions of caste India) likewise institute (and indeed recraft) their caste status and identity, but to speak in ways that ostensibly have nothing to do with their caste locations.

My father, born in 1939, in a village in Udupi, coastal Karnataka, largely replicates the Brahmin trajectory. Villages along the coast were mostly isolated, single landlord settlements (in his village the only landowner – his own – was Brahmin; the landlords were usually Brahmins and Bunts, the "dominant caste" of the region) with the farmhand families (almost always non-Brahmin) living clustered around the land. As late as the 1950s and 1960s, even primary schools remained few and far between. Yet, he went on to complete high school, which was located in a small town, some 11 kilometers away. His father took him away to Bengaluru, where, after working as a waiter in a small eatery for a couple of years, he landed a "permanent" central government job with the Railway Mail Service (RMS) when he was twenty-two years old. Even as this was among the most secure jobs, ensuring middle-class status and upward mobility, it was only one among many other opportunities available for a young man like him. He tells me how easy it was to secure a job in a bank at the time, another important avenue for Brahmin men.

Yet in a move perhaps unusual for his times, he left the government job to take a position as a salary clerk in a private industrial firm, MICO, the Indian arm of a major German multinational company, and worked there for thirty-two years until his retirement. He pointed to the better salary structure that MICO offered as the primary reason for his shift, despite the fact that it was a non-transferable job, unlike the one with the RMS.

Over the course of his employment, he and my mother were able to secure a stable middle-class existence, marked by owning a house in Bengaluru, getting their children educated, and assisting extended kin – most importantly, their younger siblings – to gain access to the city, modern education, and employment. His experience pretty neatly corresponds with Brahmin transformations over the last century; as a group, by the 1920s, the community dominated the ranks of urban, educated, and modern employment. Through the last 150 years, the general direction of state policy and the aspirational models that Brahmin families assumed dovetailed happily. Drawing disproportionately from welfarist measures of highly subsidized education, health, and real estate sectors, Brahmins were uniquely placed to take advantage of the opportunities and challenges the global economy presented from the 1980s onward.[5]

Yet Brahmin presence in the project of modernization has not equally enhanced the fortunes of the democratic civil sphere. If anything, as pointed out before, modern configurations actively enabled Brahmin entrenchment and consolidation of caste power. Although the modernization of a caste and the making of a democratic civil sphere are neither co-generative nor necessary for one another, as Alexander has repeatedly pointed out (e.g., Alexander 2006: ch. 18; 2019b), the Brahmin subject has, but inevitably, been insistently interpellated by the provocation, the invitation, and indeed the demand to look beyond the confines of the familiar/l, the primordial. Through a complex assembling, caste through the last century has been positioned as, perhaps, the most acute hurdle in realizing the goal of becoming a modern people, with the Brahmin presented as the creator, legitimator, and beneficiary of the caste system. Brahmins, because of both having anointed themselves the spokespeople for the nation-to-be and inhabiting the spaces of modern institutions, experience and enunciate great difficulty in being the bearers of two radically different ways of being human and associating with others and the world. It is to that deeply disconcerting negotiation that I turn in the rest of this chapter. I argue that we must remain discomfited by both the Brahmin's own narrative of heroic struggle to successfully represent the voice of the people and the anti-Brahmin/caste presentation of this space of Brahmin enunciation as an act of deception. The following section provides a sequence of events/utterances/ruminations from the interview, from which to weave together a description of the Brahmin negotiating this new world.

Incompatible Demands, Irredeemable Vacillation

"'Hello, Hello,' That is All"

When I told my father at the beginning of the interview that the chat was about his engagement in the non-kin, public, "civil" world, he took off without a pause or reflection, describing how in his childhood there were only two *gurutugalu* (identifications) – viz., *brahmana* and *abrahmana*. I was struck by this opening salvo, in that he instinctively recognized the connection between the problem of caste and the possibility of a public.

CAN THE BRAHMIN BE CIVIL?

Throughout the five-hour long interview, he deployed many terms – in Kannada but also in English – to signal the distinction between the Brahmin and the not-Brahmin.[6] When I pressed him, asking what he meant by *gurutugalu*, he explained:

> There were two identifiable *gurutugalu* – Brahmin and not-Brahmin. Brahmins alone were one class/stage. . . . Those who sit on top of the stage are different from those who sit down. The "others" – *itareyavaru* – recompensed/feted this identity that we possessed.

The word *itareyavaru* is a holdall term for everyone other than the Brahmins, buttressing their singularity vis-à-vis the rest, no matter high or low. His generation routinely uses *adu/avu* (Kannada words used to refer to the non-human – things and animals – but also, affectionately, children, including Brahmin children) to refer to the not-Brahmins.

Yet if early entry and overwhelming presence in modern secular education were what enabled Brahmin dominance and reproduction of their hubris, that very space also instituted a primary ground of instability to their sense of being singular. He readily admits that intelligence – as academic achievement – had little to do with one's caste. That is, the Brahmin who is "on stage" need not necessarily be more intelligent or predisposed to learning. He mentions Mahalinga, a Billava classmate, who used to always come first in exams, my father consistently placing second. A Billava teacher was also remembered for his teaching excellence.[7] This ready admission is unlike the Brahmin self-representation we are familiar with that makes an inherent connection between the Brahmin, intelligence, and merit (Bairy 2010; Fuller and Narasimhan 2014; Subramanian 2019). Likewise, talking about his own younger brothers and sister, he was very clear that they did not study well, not for lack of opportunities but owing to lack of interest. His siblings were born much later than he, and by the time they were school-going age, my father had secured his RMS job and the family had moved to Bengaluru, and there, as he points out, the issue was not one of school accessibility but of lack of "mind." My mother completed her tenth standard after marriage, which was a significant achievement. What is more, she was offered a government school teaching job, which she did not take up, since she was already burdened with familial caregiving. So, notwithstanding his confident proclamation about the lack of "mind," gendered hierarchy was clearly a crucial factor.[8]

The space of the school was, for my father and the Brahmins of his generation from the coastal villages, the first (forced) reckoning of the new language of a non-caste regulated world. It was here they came to recognize individuality and, thereby, the possibility of seeing everyone

- across castes – as the same and thus equal. In fact, he used the word *samaanaru* – that "in the school, everyone was *equal*." That said, he repeatedly emphasized that the separation between the space of the school and the home was clear and not to be breached.

> We were identified as Brahmins when home, but we mixed with everyone in school, everyone without distinction – whether Dalit or Bunt. But when I got back home, I remained Brahmin and he [Mahalinga] remained Billava.

When asked if he was "friends" with Mahalinga – they had for years walked miles to school and back, twice a day and on isolated forest tracks by themselves – my father readily offered a perspective:

> There used to be friendship. But once home, he used to maintain the distance. As they say, ours is a hierarchical society; but in school all rungs of the ladder were present and everyone was equal. Back in the village, Mahalinga never entered our house; [he] stood at a distance even from me.

Amongst the most striking aspects of the interview was his concern about the imaginary of friendship and his investment, or lack of, in it. He characterized the friendships that he developed all through his life in consistent ways. Some of the remarkable glosses were: "there was simply no imagination of 'friends'/'friendships'; it was merely 'hello, hello,' that is all"; "we were together but no friendships"; "I had thick friendships with no one at all." The unaffected way in which he described his associations with individuals from non-kin locations was stark, and the time and place of these associations ranged from his primary school days – spent in rural, unelectrified, forested isolated villages, indeed hamlets – to his work spaces and involvement in many public/civic initiatives, while living in a metropolitan city. He categorically averred that he had no "best friends," ever. While persuasive when he describes his particular circumstances – for instance, having to walk 11 kilometers each way to high school every day or being the eldest male child, having two jobs so that he could provide for not only his younger siblings but also other extended family who came to Bengaluru, leaving no time or leisure to forge friendships – there remained, nevertheless, a discernible pattern in his non-kin relationships in that the fortunes of friendship never arose.

Yet, despite his affective underinvestment in cultivating friendships, professional work life meant spending significant time away from the kin world. Here he did develop longstanding relationships (which, except for one, he refused to call friendships). But in those relationships, too,

I noticed, he sought out fellow Brahmins. Of course, the thickness of solidarity with work relationships was not at the same level as with kin, but, as has been long recognized, one central self-representation of caste groups is to see themselves as extended kin – in ideal, if not in real terms. In his long employment with MICO, he tells me that there had been just one friend, a fellow Brahmin. But it is perhaps not incidental that this friend worked with my father in the neighborhood Brahmin association as well as in the workplace. This brings me to the next register.

"Sandigdha Paristhiti"

Throughout my father's life, the defining distinction and absolute hierarchy between the spaces of the domestic/familial and the public/civic have remained assiduously guarded. His elder son's request to marry an office colleague, a Nair (the dominant caste of Kerala but whom the Brahmins look at as not-Brahmin) woman, remains the closest this familial space came to being attacked – a proposal which he instantly and unambiguously prohibited. The continued cultural and economic force with which endogamy is sustained is easily the most important modality for caste reproduction, and thus this marriage proposal, which sought to transgress caste, was put down swiftly. While this transgression that challenged the strong symbolic and visceral norms of purity and pollution was expectedly quashed, his authority to decide on such matters did not create so much as a mild flutter, and his son accepted the decision, marrying a couple of years later a Brahmin woman whom his parents chose. Also, what surely testifies to the banality and force of this distinction is the fact that the familial house in Bengaluru, to the extent possible, adheres to caste norms of regulating the traffic and behavior of not-Brahmin bodies. Even as class has increasingly intervened in who is admitted and how, the discomfort that alien bodies cause remains palpable. That it retains a great deal of affective value came to be described during the interview – a conversation that lasted many days and was conducted over many sittings. Sometime on the very first day, he told me that he would describe in detail a "situation of predicament/crisis" (*sandigdha paristhiti*) that he/his family experienced when their erstwhile Bunt tenant family came to visit many decades ago. Clearly, he had thought long and hard about it; it had continued to preoccupy him and he was visibly emotionally charged when he spoke about it in the last sitting. And the build-up, and the suspense, indicated the significance that he thought it held for a researcher, for he said, "this is at the heart of what you are interested in"! It was the heart indeed, though not in the ways in which he perhaps meant it to be.

THE INDIAN CIVIL SPHERE

Clearly the kin/caste-suffused world presented him with a clear dharma/order of prescriptions-proscriptions that made it definitionally impossible to cultivate a sense of solidarity with any being outside the caste fold. Yet the new order brought him in contact with a social-moral and demographic density that included individuals from diverse caste locations. The protocols of the two worlds were distinct, demanding radical and definitional reconfigurations and introducing instabilities to the self-making process, even while opening up moments of possibility to forge real radical solidarities across and beyond caste. Yet my father's life demonstrates the felicitous ways in which modern assembling of life and morals enabled – even normalized – reproduction of caste solidarity and, indeed, power, demonstrating how the mere arrival of a modern ethic and institutional corpus is not guaranteed to produce a civic solidarity geared toward democratization and justice.

The "crisis situation" that he delineated assembles a few interesting dimensions of this problem. What is crucial is the fact that this "crisis" event took place more than three decades ago. He has been bothered by it ever since and been thinking about how one must resolve such situations without available maps for legitimate/acceptable action. But, first, let's listen to him describe the event:

> Back in the village, we [the Brahmins] sit above, and they [the not-Brahmin] sit below. When we give them food, they clean the utensils themselves even to this day. They are not let to sit with us to eat, and, even we invite, they shy away from sitting along with us. Before the "reforms" [he means the Land Reforms Act, 1961, which was (unevenly) implemented securing the rights of the tenants] came, we were the only landlords in the village and the other three households (all not-Brahmin) were our tenants. We left the place, land reforms came, they became landowners, we settled in Bengaluru. They also became economically strong, education, too, increased. The son of the Bunt couple got into real estate business and became super-rich. But the earlier generation continued to be how they were. When the parents came to Bengaluru to visit him, the son brought them to our place. I was at the factory; my parents and my wife were home. The guests were all well-dressed.

At this point, his voice began to waver; he was clearly emotionally charged, trying to offer a description – to himself, too, it looked like – of the situation after all these decades. And he posed the key question this event brought up: "How to treat [using the English word] them now?" He continued:

> The guests were invited into the house. But they hesitated. Then they came inside. They were offered dosa on our own plates. After they

80

finished eating, if this was in the village, they are expected to wash their own plates. Here, neither they were comfortable finding themselves in this predicament nor did we know what to do. Finally, they left the dishes in a corner and left after seeking my parents' blessings.

This is what I consider a severe moment of predicament where neither they know what to do nor we. If the economy [he meant economic condition] improves or gets weakened . . . in the village, whatever one's economic position, he will not be let in. What is to be done? Even here in Bengaluru, when Rudrappa [a marginalized caste laborer, whom the family occasionally hired to bring down the coconuts from the trees in their compound], if he is given coffee, he himself washes and leaves the cup out [which we bring in and wash again]. The predicament is when [the] situation changes, neither of the classes have a sense of what is to be done.

What interests me here is how the anti-caste discourse – persistent most acutely in southern India for at least the last 150 years – setting up new horizons of meaning around ideas of equality, fraternity, and justice, and demanding to foster modern publics and an architecture of civility, was so absent in my father's sense of the world, leaving such an inarticulate trace in his life mapping. The emotionally charged ways in which he described this event left me convinced that this struggle is not (or, in any case, not merely) a problem of dominance or instrumental/strategic deployment of an argument, but a deeply moral one.

That moral struggle was rendered inordinately complex as he went on living his life, accumulating – not incrementally but as a tapestry – contradictory elements pulling him in many directions. Do note that, in his early working life with the RMS, he had to be away from the family, cooking and eating with his co-workers who, he says, were from different castes. Even now he eats in public restaurants (with the caste of the cook or the server being unknown), of course, as long as they are "pure veg"! And in the public, increasingly unregulatable world, Brahmins have for generations shared encounters with the not-Brahmin as similar and equal. Consequently, the normative demand to practice an ethic of solidarity, or "feeling for others" (Alexander 2006: 3), is neither far away nor safely resolved. But, the question is what reception the call is accorded. What does the Brahmin do? In the remaining discussion, I describe the contradictory inhabitation of the Brahmin subject in the civil sphere, seeking to show how destabilizing his experience is, how deeply unhappy it remains.

THE INDIAN CIVIL SPHERE

Jati as Association

Previously I described the modality of friendship, noting that even as my father's social world expanded, most of the people he remembered as significant in his life were/are Brahmins. Perhaps this was effortless for Brahmins of his generation, given the homogeneity of the middle-class spaces he assuredly became part of. It appears that, for him, as kin distance increased the emotional density decreased. This held true not only if the other person was not-Brahmin, but also amongst the Brahmins, as his thickest associations remained with those belonging to his specific *jati*.[9] For years, he was active in theater groups based out of his office and he was part of neighborhood Citizen Welfare Associations, one of which he was a founding member. These are familiar urban civic spaces. Yet even in those spaces, most of the acquaintances he recalls happened to be Brahmin. He was simultaneously taking part in neighborhood Brahmin caste associations, a couple in which he remained a core member, working hard to better their profile and reach. But, as if that was where his entire life trajectory was moving him toward, he has found a great sense of solidarity and comfort in the jati-specific association that he helped found a decade ago. This is the only (modern) associational space that he is now active in, where, as he told me, if he took the time and effort to do so he could establish how all of association members were related to one another, through either blood or marriage. Yet, this receding into the comforts of the kin group is a mirage, given the complex suturing of many worlds and many logics, all the time seeking to intrude into the (thick) community.

That it has become near impossible to contain this intrusion he realized in the most poignant way recently. After building the jati association from nothing, the small founding group that he was part of embarked on an ambitious project of reviving their own jati-specific *matha*/monastery. Claiming an unbroken history of more than 1,000 years, the matha by then was barely functioning. With the mobilized energy of the jati association behind them, the group decided to anoint a head and bolster the matha with monetary contributions from the community.[10]

After a couple of years of sustained work – primarily financial mobilization and finding a suitable candidate to head the matha – they anointed a head in 2006, to whom they submitted the money collected, which was close to 10 million rupees, a substantial sum. They also buttressed the management of the properties the matha possessed; so, all in all, they left the new head with a stable matha.

The first indication of disquiet came via information that a mendicant had come to reside in the matha and was beginning to take control of

CAN THE BRAHMIN BE CIVIL?

its affairs. By the time news reached the community association, that the head had signed a cheque worth a large sum to some unknown person who was clearly out to con the matha, there was panic. The association office bearers arrived at the matha and sought an explanation. The head, instead, questioned the locus standi of the association (and thereby of the jati) in the matter. In the extensive archival work that I have done, scouring the voluminous records pertaining to the mathas from the mid-nineteenth century on, there has not been a single instance where a matha head questioned the legitimacy of the community. The reasoning behind this unprecedented move – a move that brings to crisis the very structure of the matha – was simple. The head proclaimed that the matha, for thousands of years, has had heads from all caste communities, including the "Untouchables" and tribals, and that the institution has been sustained by all communities. Consequently, one caste cannot claim exclusive ownership of the matha, as it belongs to all Hindus. This ended with the association, as a body, cutting off all ties with the matha. The consensus among association leaders was that the head's response was the usurper's handiwork and its particular form owed its origins to the latter's active involvement in the Hindu Right.

This event is a radical remaking of the matha question in Karnataka – one that attempts to decouple the caste–matha equation and tether the hugely influential institution to the new Hindu formation. In terms of our considerations in this chapter, this remaking surely is an invitation for the Brahmin to shed his divine status to equalize himself with the larger fraternity of the Hindu population in order to exercise solidarity, even if that fraternity is instituted on othering other religious groups, particularly Muslims, in India. This, for my father, was deeply unsettling.

Thus, a Brahmin may strive to be ensconced and contained by the jati space and, thus, seek to remain a part apart, but the world within which such striving takes place renders such efforts impossible. Being a voluble supporter of the Hindu Right, my father has found it difficult to traverse this challenge. Even as he espouses many of the key tenets of the Hindu Right – most importantly, that India is a Hindu nation under attack from the foreign Islam and Muslims, and that secularism is a fancy word for Muslim "appeasement" – the invitation to become Hindu leaves him confounded. He would rather use the term "*sanatana dharma*" (as against the word "Hindu" which he knew was an Other-imposed identity); but the term's strong Brahminical overtones has rendered its usage within the Hindu Right rather limited. In such a context, the rationale provided by the matha struck at the very heart of the deeply unstable self-making that my father is assembling now.

THE INDIAN CIVIL SPHERE

The upper caste-led Hindu Right, through its life of nearly 150 years, has found the caste question to be the limit that it cannot transcend in realizing the project of Hindu supremacy. They have found it ideologically, even conceptually, difficult to present a stable category of the Hindu, as caste distinctions continue to offer the primary architecture, expression, and means of life-making for this population.

In a final snippet from the interview, I get to this instability that the ascendant Hindu Right presents to the Brahmin subject, bringing us full circle. If we were to position the ongoing, increasingly dominant presentation of a Hindu self as but the latest challenge the Brahmin has had to encounter over millennia, then perhaps we could better account for my father's articulation.

In the last many decades since the late 1980s, surely two axes that have provided anchors for our interlocutor's self-accounting have been Brahminical ideology and the project of constituting a Hindu Nation. But the two discourses do not converse peacefully with one another and, thus, require continual calibration, producing an unstable Brahmin subject. My father is greatly enthused by the recent successes of the Hindu Right, and proclaims repeatedly that he is an ardent supporter of Prime Minister Modi. He is animated, follows news diligently, volubly rationalizes the moves of the government, and is eager to put down any opposition. This is a far cry from even a decade ago when he – and the Brahmin community at large – had nothing but contempt for and anger against the state. He now believes that Modi is correcting grave historical wrongs and Brahmins are finally getting the respect and recognition they are due. Also, he sees the expansion of the BJP into marginalized caste groups as a vindication of what Brahmins had all along recognized – viz., the grave danger that Hinduism is in and the threat that Islam and Christianity represent. For instance, he proudly stated: "for decades, when the Brahmins voted for the BJP, you all mocked, calling it a Brahmin/ical party. Now why are the untouchables and sudras voting for BJP? When you recognized that Brahmin oppression and dominance is a fiction that politicians fed you with to deflect attention away from the great danger Hinduism was in, now you run to the Brahmins and 'their' party."

Yet, I detect a sense of worry and foreboding in him, a worry that primarily hovers around the cacophony of voices that the BJP has given space to. If anything, the recent unprecedented success of the party owes simply to the fact that it was able to garner a significantly large number of non-upper caste "Hindu" votes. My father is alert to the contradictory effects of democratization that the BJP has brought about. On the one hand, given that the Hindu Right is respectful of many key Brahminical principles, the Brahmin has now a renewed sense of confidence to speak qua Brahmin, something that he had carefully avoided or partialized or contained through the twentieth century. Public articulations against Brahmin social power by marginalized caste groups have quickly become unsayable or at least risky to air publicly. The BJP leaders continue to fete the Brahmin community, and the Brahminical ethic is increasingly presented as a timeless civilizational achievement. The former BJP government in Karnataka even started a Karnataka State Brahmin Development Board in 2019, with a seed grant of 200 million rupees; something that was unthinkable a few years ago. All this buoys his spirits. So much so that at one point, amidst one of those bitter conversations with me, he went as far as saying that "anti-nationals" like me must be imprisoned for opposing Modi. This strong sense of solidarity with the project of becoming Hindu that could allow him to make peace (rhetorically, at least) with putting his son in harm's way – that is, breaching the most immediate kin group – informs me of the success of the Hindu Right in mediating/backgrounding caste loyalties.

Yet, he is equally resolute in stating that Brahmin economic decay will not stop, no matter who comes to power. He is clear that the framing of caste groups as "Hindu" brings forth both the question of sameness – and thus equality – and of the diffusion and staking claim over what was hitherto the symbolic and material property exclusively in the possession of the Brahmin community. When such questions come up, as they did in the matha contestation, my father was very aware that the Right would not be able to protect Brahmin interests. In fact, during the stand-off between their matha and the community/association, the local Hindu Right organizations steadfastly refused to be drawn into it. Understandably, my father remains confused and in an arresting struggle to seek a stable ground of enunciation.

Conclusion

To return to the beginning, if the "civil sphere" is a social fact, then there is an ineluctability about it. The task that remains then is one of assembling sociological descriptions from diverse cultural locales and social agents caught up in its folds, strategizing and playing the game. Two specificities mark the context of caste sociality: first is the normative Brahminical social order, which is antithetical to seeking solidarity; and the second is the Brahmin, the drivers of this normative ideal, who have little wherewithal to participate in the modern civil sphere.

What is clear, however, is that, over the last century, notwithstanding the deeply unstable and unhappy state it leaves the Brahmin in, there has been a remarkable move toward democratization and a sustained challenge to Brahmin exceptionalism. And my father, the Brahmin, has remained alive to this and significantly re-formed himself, consistently recalibrating modes of self-enunciation and presentation, and he is, indeed, interpellated by and participates in the anti-caste and anti-Brahmin discourses of his time. But, this in and of itself is not a new observation for one familiar with caste studies. The question, really, is what is enabled conceptually by reading this narrative through the frame of the civil sphere?

I began by asking what encountering the problem of the civil sphere at the level of the individual entails and enables. The Brahmin that we heard from here renders at least one aspect of this problem of furthering the fortunes of democratic civil sphere stark: the "cultural structures" that Alexander (2006) repeatedly flags need tangible guides for individuals to take action and forge solidarity. This is perhaps more so in the Indian context. In India, the primary driver of democratization and the attendant far-reaching transformation in the present has remained the modern State – colonial and postcolonial. Perhaps the most important (passive revolutionary) measure in this period remains the policy of reservations/affirmative action that has forced a modicum of redistribution of capitals. Yet, when the State becomes the principal agent – deploying its legislative, ideological, and repressive apparatuses – in the making of a fraternity-from-above, the fortunes of the civil sphere perhaps remain diminished.

The Brahmin who finds himself in the thick of modernization has both mediated and been mediated by the anti-caste discourse in which, more than anything else, his own identity and persona is made to stand for everything that impedes the arrival of an ethic of civility, the making of an unknown solidarity, and a universal morality. This unparalleled positioning means that for the Brahmin to even participate in the civil sphere, he needs to stand outside his-self, critique his-self, and Other his-self. He cannot but engage with imaginaries and institutions of the civil sphere no matter how alienating the task is – alienating not only from the world that is being inexorably assembled but also from himself.

Like elites elsewhere, privatization of feelings of superiority/supremacy accompanied by public performance of acquiescence to civil order[11] is indeed a strategy the Brahmins adopt, with all its contradictions and stutters. Yet, I suggest, the binary of private–public might both be too easy and, perhaps, only defers the question: to what effect, for the subject and for the civil sphere itself? The Brahmin cannot but engage with imaginaries and institutions of the civil sphere, but at the cost of a stable sense of self and of being alienated not only from the world that is being inexorably assembled but also from his-self. What we come to stare at are the very terms of such a paradoxical life that will but be lived. Identarian exhortation (and exaltation) apart, it is in the living that the battles at the very heart of the invitation to belong to a civil sphere are encountered.

Acknowledgments

I am grateful to Jeffrey Alexander and Suryakant Waghmore for their kindness, generosity, and patience. The participants of the "The Civil Sphere in India Workshop" at Yale University, and Sharmila, Ratheesh, Cara, and Maithreyi gave me much to think about. Thanks for that.

4

Civil Sphere versus Civil Religion

Hindutva and its Multiple Opponents in Karnataka
Suryakant Waghmore

This chapter sets up an analytical exchange between Robert Bellah's *civil religion* and Jeffrey Alexander's *civil sphere* to explore the ideational basis of Hindu solidarity under Hindutva and the constructive civil challenges Hindutva faces from its opponents. I suggest that the dialectic between Hindutva and its opponents – progressive social movements within the civil sphere that advocate for individual rights and equality – contributes to processes of imagining, constructing, and building a universal solidarity that might exist beyond segmental and primordial loyalties, one which Hindutva seeks to construct along religious lines. Focusing on cultural and institutional change in the making of the civil sphere helps us move beyond the romantic celebration of community over individual in the study of Indian society.

The growing discourse and performance of individual equality rights, newly emergent non-primordial solidarities, and the collective conscience, though incipient, have indeed affected kinship and religiously based particularistic solidarities. The Indian civil sphere that emerged out of colonial rule produced movements for nationalism and independence (Gandhi/Congress) and gender and class equality, in addition to anti-caste movements, *adivasi* movements, and several other movements in the struggle for greater equality and unity beyond primordial solidarities. These progressive movements, which have only multiplied, generated a discourse of justice that celebrates freedom, equality, and inclusive solidarity.

Likewise, Hindutva aspires to build Hindu solidarity beyond caste; however, it is faced with increased fragmentation and individuation, along with newer and broader solidarities that are more universalistic in aspiration. In this chapter, I suggest that Hindutva, despite having taken progressive measures against caste inequality and having universal aspirations, represents an illiberal counter-revolution against the new collective morality and universalism stemming from India's exchange with colonial modernity and postcolonial democracy.

To provide context for the dialectics between Hindutva and its opponents, I discuss the foundational role of caste in Hinduism. I then theorize Hindu solidarity beyond caste loyalties under Hindutva as a process associated with the making of Hinduism as a civil religion. To do so, I draw on Robert Bellah's concept of civil religion, through which he showed that liberal democracy was rooted in Christianity. I suggest that non-Western democracies, too, might productively evoke a conscience both religious and secular to make meaning of changes in traditional subjectivities under modernity and democracy. Paradoxically, however, while Hindutva constructs Hinduism as a civil religion for Hindus, in everyday practice, it creates discursive Others: Western, Christian, and Muslim. Hindutva has its opponents in the vibrant civil sphere that produces broader universal solidarities, which have evolved over the last two centuries. I explore the actual workings of this dialectical process in the southern state of Karnataka, where Hindutva and, more recently, the Bharatiya Janata Party (BJP) have gained a firm foothold in the last three decades.

Civil Religion and Civil Sphere

Civil religion as framed by Robert Bellah (1967) offers much scope for analyzing the making of Hinduism as a civil religion under Hindutva, and the case of Hindutva also helps us understand the limits of the concept as imagined by Bellah. His idea of American civil religion referred to a set of beliefs, symbols, and rituals that exist alongside of and are, rather, clearly differentiated from the churches.

> The American civil religion was never anticlerical or militantly secular . . . it borrowed selectively from the religious tradition in such a way that the average American saw no conflict between the two. In this way, the civil religion was able to build up without any bitter struggle with the church powerful symbols of national solidarity and to mobilize deep levels of personal motivation for the attainment of national goals. (Bellah 1967: 13)

Religion could thus be mobilized for public goals and national purposes. In contrast, Hindutva has within it a reformist streak – whereas civil religion for Bellah (1967) need not impinge on private religion. Hindutva constructs Hinduism as a civil religion, while also consistently rewriting the meanings of Hinduism and its rituals, to incorporate and include impure castes, simultaneously, generating a feeling of Hindu pride that is anti-Muslim.

Civil religion draws on religious resources for public purposes and higher causes. One recent attempt to recover civil religion within the contemporary context was made by Philip Gorski (2010). For him, the enemies of civil religion lay in religious nationalism and liberal secularism, and so he calls for the rescue of civil religion, which could help to balance the competing demands of pluralism and solidarity. Excessive solidarity based on racial and national identities, he argues, leads to fragmentation, whereas civil religion could help bring together realism and hope, which, for Gorski, is a theological and civil virtue (2010). The primordial turn in civil religion under the Trump presidency is, therefore, *not* associated with civil religion as understood by Gorski (2021). He distinguishes Trumpism as Christianism from Christianity, as the former strips religious identity of its ethical content and transcendental reference (Gorski 2021). Both Bellah and Gorski lean toward positive readings of civil religion, with Gorski, in particular, carving out a space where religious nationalism and liberal secularism coexist.

Even Gandhian nationalism in the colonial era and Nehruvian socialism in the postcolonial period can be understood as civil religions, as they partly drew on religious resources – the former aggressively and the latter less so. In actual public life, however, there may be a wide spectrum of civil religions – from worthy causes to regressive social closure, symbols, and rituals (state and non-state) – used by opposing groups in competing forms for internal consolidation within particular ethnic or religious groups. In religiously plural democracies, civil religion may hold the illusory promise of equality for in-group members, and the civility of indifference and even violence for those outside the group.

For Bellah, civil religion, or secular faith, draws from the religious realm; however, he locates the root of virtues and morals in the sphere of politics, beyond private forms of religion. Yet we must exercise caution, as Bellah's concept of civil religion is based in Christianity and faces the challenge of applicability in non-Western societies. Still, his (2015) reliance on religion remains extraordinary, as, from his perspective, the civil sphere, too, originates in the religious realm.

If the ontological basis of religion is itself anti-civil, drawing civic foundations from religion for public purposes ends up being a complex, conflictual, and even a contradictory process, as will be shown in the case of Hindutva. It is here that Jeffrey Alexander's civil sphere theory (CST) provides us analytical recourse for understanding the limits of religion in the actual processes of the civil sphere. For Alexander (2006), the civil sphere is fully secular and largely independent from religious experience. Progressive and reformist processes in the religious realm may be the outcome of communicative actions undertaken in the civil sphere, pursued by various social movement actors and other institutions.

Alexander's CST is one of the more underutilized social theories in the study of Indian society and its polity. Alexander draws most rigorously from Durkheim to build a normative, neofunctionalist theory to help counter the economic reductionism of Marxist approaches and, simultaneously, dissuade us from the seductive culturalism of postcolonial theory. Civil sphere theory provides a way to better comprehend the processual nature of social change and the making of freedom and equality in a deeply hierarchical and unequal democracy such as India. Moving beyond civil society, civil sphere theory helps us delve into the dynamics of real civil societies. Unlike the civil religion of Bellah, the civil sphere is organized around its own cultural codes; it is fully secular, while it hosts the complementary nature of collective solidarity and individual autonomy.

By moving beyond the concept of civil society to that of civil sphere, we are able to account for politics, the economy, and non-civil solidarities, as well as civil and uncivil elements that coexist within the civil sphere. The question then becomes how actors succeed or fail in mobilizing the inclusionary potential of the civil sphere, through successful performances that align themselves within the positive binaries of the civil code, while at the same time polluting their adversaries and competing narratives of the good society. The cause of justice is thereby advanced or hindered through the mechanics of successful performances. In the course of this chapter, I suggest that Hindutva represents a civil religion, whose mechanics are not fully captured by the concept of the civil sphere as theorized by Alexander. Nevertheless, Hindutva is part of the civil sphere. And as we will later see, the civil religion of Hindutva advances the cause of Hindu recognition and representation and, simultaneously, discredits non-Hindu ideas and subjects as being lower or anti-nationals.

CST places non-primordial solidarity at its heart, as religion, family, politics, and markets only create chasms in society. In turn, civil change and repair depend on civil solidarities, which themselves have inclusive and exclusionary dimensions organized along the binary codes of liberty and repression. Social movements mobilize solidarity and the moral obligation to act, and can revolve around multiple progressive or regressive concerns. Though civil sphere theory may seem utopian in its assumption of universal and non-primordial solidarities, in practice it is a pragmatic approach that acknowledges the challenges involved in achieving such solidarities in real and complex conditions of varied democracies. The civil sphere is, therefore, rooted in often unrecognized cultural structures of secular faith; it produces its own enemies and informs us of the inclusive potential of modern society, along with the challenges in achieving it.

Although imagining Hinduism as a civil religion presents ontological challenges, as I will discuss later, Bellah's concept of civil religion did not readily apply within the US context, either. He seemed to attribute the shortcomings or polluted parts of the civil sphere (racial domination, militarism, fundamentalism) to forces outside of "civil religion" and underemphasized the role of the liberal-*cum*-republican secular themes as vital regulators of American democracy. Alexander, on the other hand, reconstructs the liberal-*cum*-republican secular discourse in his civil sphere theory in the model of the binary "discourse of civil society" (Alexander 2006).

Caste and Hindu Habits of Heart

Does caste affect the possibility of producing a civil religion from Hinduism? Caste is foundational to Hinduism in many ways. Caste and Hinduism are necessarily consubstantial observes Claveyrolas (2023). If Hinduism lacks a universal salvation philosophy of solidarity, and may seem more like a collection of castes that occasionally unite for political and ritual purposes, how does one construct civil religion from Hinduism?

Culturally, the Hindu worldview ends where the hierarchical universe of *varnashrama dharma* ends and the cosmos is itself imagined through the hierarchical ontology of *varnas*. De Tocqueville suggests that Islam represented an aristocratic civil religion and Hinduism was an uncivil religion – a religion of superstition and inequality (Kelly 1995). Historically, however, caste and Brahmanism have been challenged in Indic cultures, and, therefore, Robert Bellah (2011) attributes the Axial age in India to Buddhism as against the particularism of Brahmanism:

> The ethical universalism that had emerged in Buddhism and the edicts of Aśoka, therefore, did not die, but lived on in tension with Brahmanic particularism in subsequent Indian history. Indeed, Aśoka's *Dhamma*, together with Buddhism, which so clearly influenced it, acted as a continuing axial challenge of ethical universalism to the archaic heritage of Brahmanic particularism, such that later Indic civilization, perhaps more than most post-axial civilizations, was an uneasy compromise between axial and archaic cultural strands. (p. 559)

The dialectic between archaic and Axial cultural strands continues in the present age. Bellah's quest for ethical universalism and the "uneasy compromise" he points to above brings him closer to Bhimrao Ramji

CIVIL SPHERE VERSUS CIVIL RELIGION

Ambedkar (1936) on caste and Brahmanism. The Upanishads, for Bellah like Ambedkar, mark the incipient tide of the Axial age beyond the varna order, making Buddhism, indeed, a radical achievement. For Bellah, "Written by and for Brahmins, Manu's *Dharmaśāstra* is first of all a kind of handbook for proper Brahmin behavior but secondly it is concerned with how kingship relates to dharma and more specifically to the Brahmins" (Bellah 2011: 553).

Caste, thus, constructs Hindu habits of heart that are compromised, and they affect the formation of civil religion. A modern and free individual beyond caste is almost impossible, and broader civic solidarity, based on equality beyond religion and caste hierarchy, is seen as anathema. The incipient liberalism under British colonialism posed the biggest challenge to caste and Hindu habits of heart. Anti-caste movements that grew during colonial times and anti-caste discourses now constitute major movements that mobilize around Phule–Ambedkarite ideology. These discourses have led to formation of an imagined *Bahujan* collective solidarity of the impure majority (Waghmore 2013). Left and other liberal movements have also entered the arena, promoting anti-caste ideas and politics. Caste is, thus, at the receiving end of progressive ideas and material changes. States with strong anti-caste movements are less likely to have households practicing untouchability – Gujarat has over 30 percent of households reporting the practice of untouchability, whereas Maharashtra has fewer than five (Thorat and Joshi 2020).

Under the influence of Buddhism, Islam, Bhakti movements, and colonial rule, late Hinduism became at once pre-Axial, Axial, and even post-Axial. These cultural influences and political conditions underpinning Hindutva, in the right conjuncture (competing with the Indian National Congress Party and India's economic development), allow for a more civil-incorporative perspective. I refer to this incorporative spirit of Hindu unity and equality that Hindutva has evoked and mobilized for more than a century as the making of Hinduism as a civil religion. Hindutva has historically pursued a nationalist critique of caste and, thus, been part of the Hindu modernizing/reform process. While anti-caste ideologues such as Jyotirao Phule and B. R. Ambedkar insisted on the limits of civic spirit in Hinduism, pure-caste Hindu reformers disagreed and remained hopeful of Hindu reform. Contemporary forms of accommodation that incorporate "impure" castes in Hindutva's ideology building thus unravel the possibilities of constructing Hinduism as a civil religion.

Hindutva – Hinduism as a Civil Religion

At an event meant to celebrate Sant Ravidas Jayanti (his birthday) in February 2023 in Mumbai, Mohan Bhagwat, the *Sarsanghchalak* (Chief) of Rashtriya Swayamsevak Sangh (RSS),[1] once again emphasized that caste was "bad" and even went on to recognize that priests (Brahmins) were responsible for the creation of caste, and not God. In the same speech, he called for refraining from religious conversion to other religions in search of equality. Ravidas had himself been an anti-caste untouchable and saint in the medieval period, and Mohan Bhagwat was now addressing participants who were largely outcastes.

Bhagwat's anti-caste appeal for Hindu nationalism was met with immediate outcry from none other than the Shankaracharya[2] of Puri. The Shankaracharya was quick to condemn Bhagwat for his misguided attempt and he emphasized that caste and *varnashrama dharma* were a gift from Brahmins to India, something that the West should be taught to emulate. This clash of ideas between the Shankaracharya and Sarsanghchalak of RSS brings to mind the distinction between Hindutva and Hinduism that well-known postcolonial scholar Ashis Nandy (1991) identified. While Nandy hoped for an end to Hindutva at the hands of Hinduism, the former has not only survived but also grown in leaps and bounds.

Hindu nationalists have since engaged with the problem of Hindu disunity caused by caste and anti-caste movements by resorting to the discourse and politics of Hindu unity and humanism across castes. Ritualistic solidarity has, thus, been turned into political solidarity. New cultural codes are worked out through nationalist Hindutva, which emphasizes Hindu identity instead of particularistic caste codes (Andersen and Damle 2019). Purity is now evoked in terms of nationalist pride, where the Hindus are considered natural bearers of patriotism and others have to continually face tests of authenticity and purification. Hindutva seeks to actively unite the divided and hierarchically ordered castes, under the rubric of Hindu unity. The fear of the "Other" (Muslims and Christians) mainly dominates the repertoires of such mobilization, along with the protection of cows and localized communal conflicts. A sustained cultural and economic intervention with marginal groups like *adivasis* (indigenous tribes), too, has been another important strategy (Froerer 2010). While gaining votes and the trust of marginal groups is the motivation, Hindutva increasingly seeks to deepen social unity across castes, advocating an ethic of equality and solidarity at the same time. Hinduism is imagined as a civil religion in this politics of Hindutva

CIVIL SPHERE VERSUS CIVIL RELIGION

transcending the particularism of caste. But does the ideational basis of Hinduism that is rooted in hierarchy and inequality facilitate or obstruct the making of Hindu solidarity beyond caste?

Robert Bellah (1967) is not confident of traditional religions and their ability to unite societies, instead, placing faith in *civil religion* to achieve harmony and solidarity. The RSS and BJP, however, challenge secularist nationalism, firstly, through *strategies of ideology building*, where a diverse set of socio-religious practices was grouped under the rubric of Hindu nationalism (Jaffrelot 2007). Secondly, Hindu nationalism draws on older reserves of religious nationalism (as against modern nationalism) that were central to most forms of Indian nationalism (Van der Veer 1994). And finally, Hindu nationalism emerged out of the longest and most successful trajectory of democracy in India – it has succeeded in mobilizing and bringing Hindu consciousness to the fore in public arenas and electoral politics (Hansen 1999).

The alternative civil society that the RSS constructs (ibid.) feeds off, albeit selectively, other progressive left and liberal civil currents in order to evolve dynamically and continually consolidate Hinduism as a civil religion. Civil religion here, unlike what Gorski (2010) and Bellah (1967) would assume, is based on ideology building, older forms of religious nationalism, and association with the successful trajectory of democracy in India. I therefore suggest that civil religion need not be opposed to religious nationalism and the making of civil religion may itself be a political process – Ambedkar's conversion to Buddhism and his construction of Buddhism suitable for compassionate social democracy is a case in point (Fuchs 2001). Competition and even conflict may, thus, ensue in the civil sphere, claiming the best of civility and civil religion between and within competing ethnic and religious groups. We see the same transition presently in the move from Gandhian Hinduism as civil religion to the more aggressive nationalist Hinduism of Hindutva.

Drawing from Alexander (2006), we could suggest that Hindutva is also a binary discourse – the binary in Hindutva being primordially defined from the very beginning against non-Hindus. The ideational basis of traditional Hinduism (purity and pollution) provides cultural resources for Hindutva for the othering of non-Hindus, especially Muslims. As we will see in the following sections, the nationalist Hinduism of Hindutva claims to be more tolerant and inclusive and, thus, more civil than any other religious communities (Muslims and Christians), while simultaneously pursuing aggressive politics of exclusion against non-Hindus.

Hindutva and Sublated Hinduism in Karnataka

Karnataka is the only state in south India where the BJP has had a notable presence and power. It is known for its anti-caste progressive movements and leaders – the twelfth-century Bhakti saint Basaveshwara being the foremost. Interestingly, followers of Basaveshwara (Lingayatism) in north Karnataka are also major supporters of BJP in the present day. Whereas Vokkaligas, the other dominant caste with a prominent presence in south Karnataka, have a regional political party named *Janata Dal Secular* (JDS), which occasionally forms an alliance with the BJP and Congress based on the numbers it secures in regional elections.

Hindutva thrives through its social (RSS) and political (BJP) organizations in Karnataka, as is the case in the rest of India. While RSS has a much longer presence in Karnataka, the last two decades have seen a massive rise in the popularity of the BJP, evident in its electoral success. Anti-Muslim discursive practices play a central role in the mobilization of Hindutva, which operate through a network of organizations affiliated with the RSS.

In early 2022, Mr. Janta,[3] a former member of the legislative council (MLC) from the BJP in Karnataka, attacked the Congress party for its "love" of Muslims. Muslims he said are the (biological) parents of Congress and the Gandhi family that leads Congress. He went on to say that those who have two children (Hindus) pay taxes and those with ten children (Muslims) reap the benefits of state welfare, despite research showing that the birth rate amongst Muslims, too, was declining in Karnataka. This former leader himself had five children, was from a caste listed as backward, and had only tenth-grade education. I had the opportunity to work under him in 2002, when he was appointed regional chairman of a rural development and funding agency with the central government, where I worked as a development sector professional. Power had switched hands in Delhi from the Congress to the BJP by then and as the BJP took over the regional committee, with this leader as chairperson, other RSS members joined the committee. With this change, the recitation of Sanskrit prayer was introduced at the beginning and close of quarterly meetings. During the same period, NGOs funded by our agency complained about receiving phone calls from the chair's office demanding a cut for the developmental grants they received. Not all of them paid, but a cultural shift had become clear – spiritual purification and economic corruption went hand-in-hand.

When I worked with Janta, he had not yet been promoted to MLC status. But following his appointment as chair, he bought a new white

Ambassador car (symbol of governmental power then), which read in front, *Chairman XXXX Agency*. The only difference from previous officials was that this leader tried to learn Sanskrit prayers, despite his non-Brahmin upbringing, and he also specialized in the art of anti-Muslim discourse central to Hindutva, while carrying on a tradition of state-corruption. He claimed to be pursuing a higher and sacral form of politics as opposed to Congress. Although he was later accused of being involved in land scams, he went on to be nominated to the State Legislative Council and was even leading the BJP in Karnataka. The BJP was thus a site of inclusive Hindutva for impure and non-dominant caste politicians and simultaneously a normalizing apparatus for a new Hindu conscience and sacral politics.

During its last term in Karnataka, ending in May 2023, the BJP passed significant regional laws symbolizing Hindu power, which included a ban on the slaughter of cows, a hijab ban in schools, and anti-conversion laws. These laws provide civic credentials to the anti-Muslim and anti-Christian sentiment that RSS had generated through its social movement.

Unlike RSS, the BJP does not best represent the collective conscience of Hindutva, as party politics involves pragmatic compromises. RSS on the other hand is cadre based and Brahmins control most leadership positions. Politics is assigned an impure status in RSS, since it affects the idea of seva and sacrifice. Another member of the XXXX agency was also a full-time RSS *brahmachari* worker (*pracharak*) from Kerala. He was in his mid-forties then, a non-corrupt but ideologically committed worker. And he offered me a job due to my "professional" approach. Over the past years, NGOs run by RSS have become richer and professional. While the relationship between BJP and RSS is not always harmonious, a senior worker within the RSS in Bengaluru, whom I interviewed in 2019, commented on the corrupt nature of politics, "Guruji [Golwalkar] used to always say politics is like the bathroom and if you enter there's always a strong possibility that you will slip and fall." Slipping and falling implied losing your morals and ethics and falling into the (impure) world of corruption, seduced by power. BJP works based on the pragmatic needs of politics and non-Brahmins therefore dominate BJP. Though the BJP may seem like a compromised or corrupt form of politics, its state control provides easy access to state resources and power for RSS. Amongst the RSS-affiliated organizations in Karnataka that benefited due to the BJP's control of federal resources in 2018 was Rashtrotthana Parishat (Waghmore 2022).

In the following section I explore the politics and processes of inclusion and broad-basing in Hindutva by focusing on Tapas, a recent and important educational initiative of Rashtrotthana Parishat. Tapas is an initiative in higher school education targeted toward brilliant but economically disadvantaged boys aspiring to study engineering at IITs (the most prestigious engineering colleges in India). Tapas aims to counter the marketization of education by providing quality education, residence, and coaching to the most meritorious among those students living in poverty, to enable them to compete without disadvantage in the screening exams for IITs – India's Joint Entrance Examination (JEE). Based on findings from structured and unstructured interviews and group discussions I had with key leaders, volunteers of Rashtrotthana, and alumni and students of Tapas, I will argue that Hindutva consistently reinvents itself, while competing, learning, and coopting other civil solidarities in India's civil sphere (Alexander 2006).

Sublated Hinduism: From Hinduism of Caste to Hinduism as a Civil Religion

Presently, Rashtrotthana runs several projects that, broadly, cover health, education, livelihood, and culture, with religious nationalism being the ideological force behind all its initiatives. While Rashtrotthana began as a movement in the 1960s to produce literature for Hindu awareness and unity, over the years, it has emerged as a major social, educational, and cultural organization in Karnataka. This has been achieved with significant support from successive governments, corporate and individual donations, and the ideological commitment of RSS workers. In Bengaluru alone, Rashtrotthana has two major English-medium schools (of the twenty-five schools in Karnataka most are Kannada-medium schools), a major blood bank and thalassemia day care and dialysis center,[4] a *goshala* (shelter for indigenous cows), the Yogic Sciences and Research Institute, and a well-equipped publishing house, which publishes books and booklets on important Hindu personalities[5] who embodied the ethic of sacrifice for the nation.

The impressive infrastructure is mobilized through donations. Rashtrotthana is a comparatively small player as compared to the Lingayat and Vokkaliga networks in Karnataka. However, it seeks to compete with several other institutions and market forces that are believed to undermine Hindu tradition and culture. Rashtrotthana counters its marginal position through repertoire and strategies that weave together a discourse of economic justice, the recovery of Hindu heritage, and compassionate and sacrificial ethics – broadly framing and consolidating Hinduism as a civil religion. To illustrate, below I discuss the case of Tapas.

IITs are considered premier institutes of engineering education in India, and admission to them is sought by the new and old middle

CIVIL SPHERE VERSUS CIVIL RELIGION

classes. Admission to the undergraduate programs is through the national competitive JEE. Success in this exam, however, is more a function of coaching, and coaching companies charge anywhere between 4 to 6 lakh rupees annually. Coaching begins as early as seventh or eighth grade and is well beyond what families with limited means and income can afford. In discussions, the workers and founders of Tapas maintained that the Tapas project is aimed at reaching the most meritorious low-income students in Karnataka and making coaching available to them.

The term "Tapas" draws from "*tapasya*,"[6] and its mission statement was decided upon to be in keeping with the NGO discourse of "reaching the unreached." Founders emphasize the need to provide quality education to the poorest individuals, irrespective of caste and religious considerations. It is worth noting, however, that only one Muslim student has studied at Tapas. The idea was borrowed from Super 30, an educational coaching program for economically disadvantaged students run by Anand Kumar in Bihar. Super 30 is known for its exceptional success, and Anand Kumar has received several national and international awards. There was even a Bollywood movie made about him. Funds were mobilized from IT workers in the Bay Area in California to support Tapas, while Rashtrotthana used the infrastructure available at its Thanisandra campus in Bengaluru. An arrangement was negotiated with the leadership of a coaching company, BASE (Be Ahead with Sustained Excellence), to provide free coaching to students selected by Tapas. BASE agreed to provide free coaching as part of their corporate social responsibility (CSR) activity; they also helped Rashtrotthana hold statewide entrance exams to select the best students among the economically deprived.

Built into the Tapas program is also an assumption that students from disadvantaged backgrounds could better preserve culture and contribute to nation-building, as opposed to well-off students who study at IITs, most of whom leave the country. Leaders believed that quality education should be made available to all free of cost, and education at Rashtrotthana was in accordance with UNESCO's ideal of rooting education in culture, and so the *Panchamukhi Shikshana*[7] of ancient *Gurukul* form.

Besides education, "culture" is also taught to the students at Tapas. Khudeshvany (aged 20) experienced and came to understand a new form of Hinduism at Tapas. His parents run a provision store and live in a rented house in Bengaluru. He could not get admission to any of the IITs and now studies computer science at PES Mandya. Even so, he continues to carry the spirit of Hindu unity and equality with him. Influenced by the ideological and cultural education he gained at Tapas, he is critical of caste divisions and conflict in Karnataka. Khudeshvany is a Vannikula Kshatriya, a caste that is listed as OBC (Other Backward Classes) in Karnataka. Besides receiving coaching for the IIT-JEE, Tapas introduced Khudeshvany to the "greatness of Indian *sanskriti*" (culture) that had been "lost" over the years, making India "insignificant" as a world power. The projection of the past, though invented, does not make this invention less effective; rather, the invented version is tailored to present-day needs and sensibilities.

"Outside there is caste," said Khudeshvany, "something that we need to counter." He distinguishes the popular Hindu religion outside from the civil form of Hindu religion he learned at Tapas. This Hinduism is different from the one he grew up with at home. While the two forms share most rituals and festivals, the earlier form of Hinduism was without consciousness for him. "Our calendar is *Panchanga*, *sanskriti* [culture] is the right path and the main motto of *shakhas* [branches of RSS are referred to *shakhas*] was unity," shared Khudeshvany. The making of a (non-caste) Hindu self and its unity with the Hindu nation (past and present) points to a new form of sublated Hindu consciousness, tied to neither caste nor individualist orientations. Such Hindu consciousness also counters the alienation that caste may bring, especially for castes considered marginal and lower. Khudeshvany hopes to become active in politics and correct the wrongs.

> What B.R. Ambedkar had thought and what are we doing? Politics is selfish. Politicians have ignored drought. Only Narendra Modi is working for 18 hours. We need youth force [but] they are distracted. [We need to] fill patriotism in each of them. I will work for 5–6 years in IT and join politics.[8]

Khudeshvany's nationalist Hinduism is not purely Brahminic; the RSS is being strategic in allowing some de-Brahminization as part of the project of building Hinduism as civil religion. Khudeshvany, for instance, did not like the food much at Tapas; he is fond of meat (but not beef), something that was not allowed during his two years of residence at Tapas. Occasionally when he stepped out to meet his parents, he would enjoy his favorite meals. Living at Tapas for two years did not alter his dietary preferences, and also the workers of Rashtrotthana did not insist on vegetarianism outside of Tapas.

In the everyday functioning of Rashtrotthana, and more particularly Tapas, the hierarchy of caste is replaced with the hierarchy of respect, seniority, and submission to authority within the movement and the historical narratives on which it is based. None of the current students from marginal castes, whom I spoke with or those students my assistants interviewed, complained of discrimination along caste lines. This is decidedly different from popular Hinduism. Such a version of inclusion is, indeed, not egalitarianism; it is, rather, an alternative version of hierarchy that promises a reversal of the embedded estrangement of non-pure castes in popular Hinduism.

This new Hinduism is a form of sublated Hinduism. Sublation in Hegelian dialectics is both negation and preservation of an earlier form, and it is neither synthesis nor irony (Palm 2009). Gowtham R, a first-year student at Tapas, shared that "'Singing *Vande Mataram*[9] makes me feel very patriotic and happy. It makes a shiver run down my body. I feel immense source of happiness and pride when I sing it. I am so happy to be here in Tapas because it helps me love my country more than I could till now." The transformation of Hinduism into a civil religion through Hindutva discourses is, thus, part of the dialectics within Hinduism.

As suggested earlier, the citizenship discourse and anti-caste politics in Phule–Ambedkarite movements frame caste-based Hinduism as one opposed to the freedom and citizenship rights of marginalized groups, and this discourse has now spread from southwest to northwest India. The making of Hinduism into a civil religion in Hindutva discourse is, thus, a necessity both for local politics and global cosmopolitan claims. Rashtrotthana is religious but not absolutely Brahmanic. It is this effort of transgressing Brahmanism that renders Rashtrotthana a civil form – that is, universalistic and incorporative. Still, Hindutva is also a binary discourse – the binary being primordially defined from the very beginning against non-Hindus.[10]

Thus, the BJP and RSS's cultivation and circulation of anti-Muslim and anti-Christian discourse is crucial to the making of Hinduism as a civil religion under Hindutva. Mughal invasion, demolition of temples, slaughter of cows, conversion out of Hinduism, and more recently *Love Jihad*[11] are all framed as dangers that pollute Hindu religion and democracy. Pro-Hindu laws such as the ban on hijabs and cow slaughter as well as the Citizenship Amendment Act are various forms for mobilizing a passionate Hindu solidarity beyond caste.

Hindutva in Karnataka operates as a "sacred form" that is constructed through the help of symbols and discourses relating to issues of "liberating" Hindu and the rejuvenation of Hindu institutions such as *seva* (Bhattacharjee 2019). These processes and the politics of Hindutva do not go unchallenged, however. Hindutva has multiple opponents in Karnataka. In the following section I engage with the liberal solidarities in the civil sphere that contradict the civil religion that Hindutva seeks to construct.

THE INDIAN CIVIL SPHERE

Civil Sphere versus Civil Religion

Robert Bellah's civil religion draws only from the religious realm. He argues that the religions of great civilizations, including India, produced a civil sphere, and thus the civil sphere for Bellah predates secularism and modernity by ages (Bellah 2015). Bellah's suspicion of secular discourse is exaggerated however. While we need some kind of sacrality that draws not only from the discourse of civil sphere but also from divine discourse, especially in deeply religious societies like India, the cultural current of a civil sphere is much more than civil religion. The case of Hinduism and associated civil religion poses a major challenge to Bellah's reliance on secular religion as being deeply rooted in religion. Bellah might have been able to defend the concept of civil religion in the US, but it actually has limited compatibility in India. Movements that continue to challenge Hindutva have not relied on the discourse of religion alone.

In December 2019, Ramchandra Guha, a renowned Gandhian and liberal "high caste" historian, was briefly detained in Bengaluru (capital of Karnataka) for participating in a protest against the Citizenship Amendment Act (CAA). When arrested, Guha was holding a placard with an image of B. R. Ambedkar, the architect of India's Constitution, and a message that read, "CAA against Constitution." In the protests against the Act, the symbols of the Constitution and Ambedkar had suddenly gained universal currency, whereas the Constitution and rule of law had generally been evoked by ex-untouchable groups to escape the tyranny of village dominants (Waghmore 2013). In these actions, there was recognition of the Constitution as an important mode of civil regulation (Alexander 2006). And like the above-mentioned protests by privileged liberal and leftist groups against the CAA, Karnataka also had several protest groups that cut across caste and religion, and who resorted to constitutionalism in their protest against the CAA. There was a momentary alliance between Muslims, upper-caste liberals, and Ambedkarite and Ahinda[12] groups, a coalition further described as an alliance against fascist repression that resulted from Hindu nationalists coming to power.

A major counter-force to the nationalist Hinduism of Hindutva in Karnataka has come from non-Brahmin mass movements from below that have aligned with Congress, which helped the party regain power in Karnataka in May 2023. Congress had resorted to anti-caste Bahujanist discourse in its mobilization, a radical departure from its earlier ideological stance. Besides the increasing corruption under the BJP, it was Rahul Gandhi's (great grandson of Nehru) walk across Karnataka and then the whole country to Unite India (*Bharat Jodo*) against Hindutva "politics of hate" that is said to have helped Congress. However, the Ahinda groups, who voted in large numbers in favor of Congress and their universal welfare promises, also galvanized support. Siddaramaiah came to be the Chief Minister again. And though the right-wing radicals of the BJP described Siddaramaiah as a radical leftist, he was more of an anti-caste liberal centrist with proximity to Phule–Ambedkarite ideology. Ahinda solidarity worked well and Siddaramaiah has partly delivered on his liberal and welfarist promises upon winning the elections.

Against Cow Nationalism: Republican Solidarity from Below

The cow is considered holy in Brahmanic texts and popular Hinduism in much of northern India, and the killing of a cow is equal to the murder of a Brahmin – both signify God's actual presence on earth. The economic mobility of middle and lower castes over the last few decades, along with sanskritization (and modernization) processes, has led to the rise of vegetarianism or non-beef-eating meatarian culture amongst non-Brahmin castes and even outcastes who were known to traditionally consume beef. Thus, against the ideas of anti-caste movements there has been a parallel and overwhelming effort amongst the impure but mobile masses to integrate within the pure Hindu universe, by adapting to the ideas, discourses, and symbols of an accommodative Hindu universe. Such accommodation of the impure is also based on the othering of Muslims as outsiders, as "beef-eaters," and the new untouchables (Waghmore and Contractor 2015).

The cow is considered holy in Congress's discourse too, especially in north India, and both the BJP and Congress occasionally draw from Mohandas Gandhi's ideas on vegetarianism and the sacrality of the cow. While Congress increasingly distances itself from radical cow politics in the contemporary context, the party has historically played a role in the cow's sacralization. Cow worship is, therefore, not alien to Congress either, and the protection of cows was even made part of the Constitution of India under the Directive Principles of State Policy (DPSP). While there was a demand from Hindus (Brahmin) within Congress to add cow protection to the section on Fundamental Rights, Ambedkar salvaged the civil nature of the Constitution by emphasizing scientific reasons for cow protection – such as the need to protect indigenous species of cattle (Gundimeda 2023).

Siddaramaiah is, perhaps, amongst the very few CMs in India who speaks openly against the excesses of Hindutva, including the violence caused by cow vigilantes. He also openly confesses his liking for beef.

THE INDIAN CIVIL SPHERE

Once Congress regained power, everyday manifestations of cow-related violence, or what Ferry (2018) calls cow terrorism, have been reduced in Karnataka. K. Venkatesh, a Vokkaliga minister in Siddaramaiah's cabinet even asked, "What was wrong in slaughtering a cow when other animals like buffaloes can be slaughtered?" K. Venkatesh is a close confidant of Siddaramaiah and a member of the newly elected legislative assembly in the state of Karnataka. Venkatesh was one of the 135-winning Members of the Legislative Assembly (MLAs) from the Indian National Congress (INC), which overturned the fortunes of the ruling BJP in May 2023. He challenged the civil religion of Hindutva and, thereby, the sacrality of the cow by resorting to discourses of justice and reason. For cow vigilantes, the protection of cows is justified, even to the extent that the occasional lynching and murder of cow traders or beef-eaters (mostly Muslims) is seen as immanent in the politics of Hindutva.

Another important social and political leader within the Ahinda social coalition is Satish Jarkiholi from Belgavi, north Karnataka. He is known for his Buddha–Basava–Ambedkar ideology and the Manava Bandhutva Vedike (Human Solidarity Forum) that he leads. For the last two decades, Satish Jarkiholi has mobilized ideas and the masses, going beyond Hindutva ideology and the dominant caste politics of Vokkaligas and Lingayats. Like Mr. Janta, Satish Jarkiholi has not had higher education and he, too, has studied only up to twelfth grade. Over the last decade, however, Satish Jarkiholi, besides being a wealthy and powerful politician, has earned status as a critical intellectual in Karnataka, by regularly challenging the politics of Hindutva. Jarkiholi is from the Valmiki caste[13] and that makes him a powerful player from the lower order.

Satish enjoys massive support amongst Dalits, Muslims, and lower Shudras (especially from the Kurubas, the caste that Siddaramaiah belongs to). His forum Manava Bandhutva Vedike has been critical of Hindutva, posing the ideology of Buddha–Basava–Ambedkar to challenge both Hindutva and the Hinduism of caste and superstition. For instance, he intentionally files for election nomination during what is considered an inauspicious time in astrology and holds massive annual awareness rallies of Manava Bandhutva Vedike in graveyards. Cremation and graveyard grounds are considered to be the most impure places according to Hindu tradition. What's more, these rallies are held on December 6, marking the anniversary of Ambedkar's death.

In May 2023, when Satish Jarkiholi took oath as cabinet minister, invoking Buddha, Basava, and Ambedkar, instead of God, the crowd cheered. He has been vocal about the ills of cow-worship, having gone as far as supporting a minor anti-caste group in 2014, the *Karnataka Praja Vedike*, when they held a beef party on government premises. Supporters of Hindutva and BJP purified the government office immediately afterwards with the ritualistic cow-urine ceremony. Around that time, in 2015, I interviewed Satish Jarkiholi in Belgaum, during which he shared his ideology:

> Buddha, Basava and Ambedkar are the *mahapurush* (great men) we need to follow. Education and reason will help us challenge Brahmanism in this country. I urge our people to give up superstition. Hinduism is full of superstition and inequality; it keeps us away from education and empowerment. We need to take Buddha, Basava, and Ambedkar to every home in Karnataka.[14]

The axial age that Bellah (2011) attributes to Buddhism and its (compromised) continuance in *bhakti* currents has been reconstructed by activists and politicians like Satish Jarkiholi for the contemporary era, to challenge Hindutva so as to form a broader humanistic solidarity that is not based on othering Muslims or romanticizing the "great past" of Hindus and Hinduism. Jarkiholi and Siddaramaiah's politics intersect, however, with the liberal civil sphere and a constitutionalism that focuses on individual rights and, simultaneously, urges the poorest people to contribute less to (Hindu) temples and invest more in children's education. Here, reason is evoked against the hierarchical and superstitious rituals of Hinduism. Such criticism of Brahmanism has not been part of Congress's discursive practices in north India and the party has increasingly become accommodative of these ideational changes in Karnataka under new leaders like Siddaramaiah and Satish Jarkiholi. Congress in Karnataka accommodates these discourses because its major support comes from non-dominant castes (Lingayats and Vokkaligas) and non-Brahmin solidarity.[15]

Lingayatism – Post-Hindu Civil Religion

Another major form of civil solidarity within Hinduism that has emerged in Karnataka is the claim to a different religion by groups within the Lingayat sect. As mentioned earlier, followers of Basava/Veersaivism are called Lingayats. After the rise of enumerative politics and majoritarianism in colonial times, Veersaivism came to be considered part of Hindu religion. Despite its anti-caste credentials it became more of a sect within Hinduism (McCormack 1963). While there has been a long-pending demand amongst Lingayats for recognizing Lingayatism as a religion, separate and distinct from Hinduism, this demand has become stronger in the last few years and could also be a counter-result of Hindutva's politics. Some intellectuals and religious leaders within the sect claim that

THE INDIAN CIVIL SPHERE

Lingayatism is a contra-Hindu religious ideology, one that is grounded in equality and not hierarchy – a claim that was supported by Ahinda leaders and Congress alike but seen by the BJP and RSS as dividing Hindus. These same religious leaders of Lingayats regularly participate in Ahinda rallies and support programs organized by anti-caste groups.

Concluding Remarks

The civil sphere in Karnataka comprises various social and political movements that took root under colonial governance and were consolidated through an independent India. These movements have diverged and fragmented while giving rise to newer solidarities from above and below. Solidarities that are liberal and anti-caste, collectively, pose a major challenge to the primordial politics of Hindutva. Yet individualism and individual rights alone do not define the discourse of these countermovements in the civil sphere nor are they void of religious sentiments. Instead, a solidarity that involves collective obligations is defined in a civil, not primordial way. Individual rights and civil solidarity go hand in hand – liberalism is not the only democratic tradition that has contributed to the culture of the civil sphere, and republicanism, which is much more group-oriented, has always been a critical force (Alexander 2006).

Robert Bellah's framework of civil religion allows us to understand how Hindutva's religious basis and reformist streak produce a sublated Hinduism. We also gain insight into the limits of such civil religion, as it continues to draw on the regressive, particularistic, and primordial ideas that are central to Hinduism. Despite its universal claims and incorporative possibilities beyond caste, Hindutva generates hubris and superiority amongst pure-caste Hindus and their followers, while normalizing anti-Muslim sentiment and violence. A study of the dialectic between civil religion and the civil sphere informs us of how actors succeed or fail in mobilizing the inclusionary potential of the civil sphere through successful performances, which align them within the positive binaries of the civil code, polluting at the same time their adversaries and their respective narratives of the good society. In turn, Hindutva is framed by its adversaries as repressive and polluting. The Constitution, Buddha, Basava, and Ambedkar serve as plural and critical symbols of resistance even for Congress as it departs from its Nehruvian socialist past in the current context and contemporary moment.

5

The Authoritarian Civil Sphere, Populism, and Secular Sectarianism

Ajay Gudavarthy

Civil sphere theory describes a space of normative, universal solidarity that is beyond particularistic identities, a form of solidarity that is broader than "those created by physical co-presence, emotional attachment, repeated interaction, resource exchange, and political or religious homophily" (Kivisto and Sciortino 2019: 268). The civil sphere is an "imagined community of equals" and a universalizing force of civil solidarity, which provides the ground for advancing claims of mutual recognition through culturally embedded structures, present as cultural/ civil codes. Cultural sociologist Zygmunt Bauman (2001) has referred to community as the fantasy of sitting around a cozy fireplace – a paradise lost – that can never be fully realized in real time.[1] Similarly, the civil sphere is an endemic fantasy that cannot ever be fully realized but which continues to inform political mobilization and democracy, institutions and also everyday practices. Its presence can be felt in the universal promise of citizenship, the nostalgia of civilizational ethos, or the insidious emotional attachment of nationalism.

Even as these ideals offer universal inclusion, in the real-time workings of institutionalization they remain exclusionary. The ongoing dialectic of inclusion–exclusion produces ethical dilemmas, between institutionalized ethical values and the real-time backsliding that takes place, only to find another afterlife in the push for greater inclusion. While civil sphere theory (CST) privileges the universal-normative, it refuses to take a moral position that would privilege the abstract ideal over real-time conflicts and backsliding. It prefers to see the formation of the civil sphere as a process without a direction or guarantees. In this sense, CST is foundational in accepting an innate drive toward the normative-universal and anti-foundational in accepting the lack of guarantees in realizing it and not assuming a linear zeitgeist.

Critical theorist Axel Honneth points out that CST, in order to make this shift, gets confounded in inextricable conceptual dilemmas where, "On the one hand, Alexander does not think we can bridge the gap between practical politics and social analysis by doubling down on the 'universality' of norms that remain ineluctably tied to particular cultural interpretations and historical configurations of power. On the other hand, we must also avoid succumbing to the opposite extreme, which would deprive historically situated normativity of any context-transcending validity" (Honneth 2015: 87). It is a classic case of theory being normative, and the empirical world being messy. CST is normative to the extent that it privileges solidarity, but it does so in a way that remains sensitive and open to how and why backsliding takes place. In this sense it is both normative and analytical.

Civil sphere theory, in essence, presents a challenge to received modes of understanding power, foregrounding power relations as being porous and fluid. Power is not reproduced by creating "governable subjects," but it is interrogated by citizens as actors in their everyday negotiations. CST takes the difficult entry point of making sense of an open-ended process that is simultaneously normative and empirical, which is what, perhaps, allows us to explore some of its propositions in varied historical and spatial locations.

Civil solidarity, in its more universalist and not merely primordial form, is intrinsic to human societies, just as conflict is. In turn, the civil sphere is both the means and end and an irreducibly incomplete ideal in all societies. CST argues that domination can take more structural forms, but civility needs to be lived, is social, and part of an active subjectivity and imagination (Alexander 2006). It is, therefore, necessarily based on underlying cultural structures. Enabling subjectivity is created by means of "civil repair," creating "emotional and psychological identification" (Alexander 2014a) between socially differentiated groups. CST advocates for a distinct discourse of moral universalism, over and above the elements of universalizability that exist in non-civil spheres such as the economy (for instance, its dependence on cooperation) or law (its standardized applicability).

For the civil sphere to actualize itself in complex and socially differentiated societies requires a degree of secularization based on performance, even as it draws resources from religion, education, and other non-civil spheres. Though the universality of the civil sphere can be segmented and segregated, and almost always combined with and in non-civil discourses and practices, it still holds the potential of becoming global, cutting across national boundaries. In this sense, salvation is at the heart of the civil sphere and it remains "relatively autonomous" of material conditions and social structures.

CST, therefore, cannot be reduced to the rational discourse of a Habermasian public sphere; instead, what is intrinsic to it is "politics as performance" through cultural codes, clearly reflected in the current populist upsurge. From this perspective, populism is best approached and understood through the subjective meanings that social actors ascribe to what constitutes the civil and anti-civil codes at a given point in time. It is about analyzing the process for what it is, including the micro-dynamics of ethics and emotions that are not "merely" received experiences but are also evaluative in nature (Sayer 2005).

Finally, social movements and democratic institutions remain potent instruments for realizing civil solidarity in real time (Alexander 2006). In other words, everyday feelings, sensibilities, and emotions take an institutional form to become sustainable and create a concrete reality out of an imagined ideal. Social movements are seen as manifestations of "culture structures," pushing against a reading of culture as abstract moralism or equating it with conservatism. CST provides an alternative way of analyzing the labyrinth of ideals, strategies, and interests.[2] Transcendental justice is understood as neither linear nor additive; it is instead nebulous and contingent. The quest for justice is a "driving motor" of history but does not guarantee us the passage from "pre-history" (*à la* Marx) to global civil society. In this respect, CST differs by attempting to make utopian imagination itself a driving force, independent of other modes and intrinsic and irrespective of historical renderings – imagination, not the "banality of materiality," drives human action.

In this chapter I focus on the current populist-authoritarian impasse in India to argue that it has a heady mix of all key propositions of CST, including culture, universal solidarity, performance, civilizational codes, going global, and social movements for civil repair. Here, right-wing populist-authoritarianism has "appropriated" latent tropes of transcendental justice and civil solidarity, while, in a relational sense, secular-constitutionally oriented social movements/discourses have been assumed to be more sectarian. The current populist-authoritarian regime in India reflects key elements within CST. The populist regime speaks of motivations not rationality, universal civil solidarity not narrow interests; it speaks of civilizational continuity and not the rupture of modernity; it lays emphasis on myths and mythologies for meaning-making; it is embedded in "politics as performance" and not "banality of materiality"; it privileges democracy as lived and experiential and not merely driven by structures; it speaks of *samrasta* (harmony or solidarity) and not exclusively about equality or material interests; it mobilizes on underlying civil codes of good and evil, and civil and uncivil, and sacred and profane. It speaks of undoing "historical injury" (for instance, invoking the memory of cultural trauma of Partition in 1947) and creating a new kind of "psychological and emotional identification" – civil repair – among the various social units within Hindus; it speaks of cultural nationalism that relates to culture structures as against "mere" emphasis on legality and institutions. It speaks of *vasudaivika kutumbakam* (world as one family) even if it realizes that practical imperatives may create hurdles; and, finally, it refuses to reduce culture to conservatism and emphatically attempts to include uncivil (divisive/communal) practices as given cultural practices into the hegemonic civil sphere through alternative discourses of anti-elitism and decolonization. In effect, populist mobilization attempts to blur the very distinction between the civil and the uncivil.

The current regime in India has given rise to an authoritarian civil sphere through a hegemonic discourse that claims a normative universality, while remaining exclusionary and hierarchical. What in CST allows us to critique the conceit in performance and recover the civility hidden in the underlying cultural codes? How might we "wedge open" the real-time effects and outcomes of exclusion and discrimination (especially against the Muslims and the Dalits), yet explain the popular consent the regime continues to enjoy because it places emphasis on universal solidarity? The next section will lay out the possible similarities between the propositions of CST and the workings of the authoritarian civil sphere in contemporary India.

Populism and Civil Solidarity

Populist-authoritarianism in India is building populist internal-civil-trust by claiming to produce an "authentic people" (Hindu national identity), ostensibly cutting across particularistic identities of caste, class, language, and ethnicity, while at the same time creating external-uncivil-conflict by excluding religious minorities and all others whose politics differ from those of the current regime.[3] Populist mobilization runs across many axes. It invokes the civil as universal, although a constrained version of the universal-normative as being Hindu, and, finally, it explicitly invokes uncivil and retributive narratives of "othering."

This mobilization is civil-populist to the extent that it invokes culture, civil codes, civilizational ethos, and shared values, but is uncivil-authoritarian in its use of force, exclusion, violation of laws, sectarianism, and enforcement of "righteous lawlessness" (for instance, organized mob lynching of Muslims and Dalits). The civil sphere is imbricated in deep-seated cultural codes, exposing the "shallowness" of (modern) secular and institutional practices. In the current populist-authoritarian context, the civil sphere refers to a harmonious community of nation and civilization, while secular pronouncements that also speak of inclusion, minority rights, and equality before the law are by default perceived to be sectarian, a social privilege, elitist, and about narrow interests, mainly because they are not grounded in cultural structures. Culture here is seen as values, memory, and myths indispensable for everyday meaning-making.

The civil sphere of populist-authoritarianism is inclusive of uncivil practices, para-legal modalities, and extra-institutional mobilization that "breaches the civil order," and it has a "family resemblance" to the "radicalism" that civility otherwise unfairly misrecognizes to keep out underprivileged social groups from gaining desired mobility (Stack 2019). It is working at the brink of what postcolonial scholar Partha Chatterjee (2004) refers to as "political society," which is constituted by subaltern social groups, such as the peasants, urban poor, migrants, among others. Such mobilization works as popular or "folk politics" with the "creative power of the community," as against the institutional niceties, sanitized procedures, liberal rationality, and constitutionalism that appeal to the urban and English-speaking middle classes. The latter belong to "civil society," while the former to "political society." Populist-authoritarianism's strategies as "folk politics" are sieved through cultural codes and, therefore, received as authentic *sans* instrumental reasoning. It allows for modern-rational discourses of secular-progressive politics to come across as part of an "instrumental rationality" that lacks the affective/communicative dimension.

What we are witnessing is a potential conflict between the "constitutional morality" identified with social elites in the civil society (that includes the caste Hindus, upper classes, and economic elites) and the populist reality of a potentially inclusive but authoritarian civil sphere. This civil sphere is populist, rooted in culture and the rhetoric of local idiom, anti-institutionalism, and "emotional and psychological identification" between various social units (castes/jatis) of the majority religious community, but it excludes religious minorities and its political opponents through these very processes that thereby also produce authoritarianism. As scholars have reminded us, "CST is agnostic on the outcomes of civil performances" (Kivisto and Sciortino 2015a: 7). However, CST is useful in its self-understanding that "civil repair" is necessary to "wedge open" the populist civilizational-inclusive ethos from its exclusionary-authoritarian trends, a space that has to be built from the same binary civil codes (pure/impure; civil/uncivil; good/evil; sacred/profane) and has to effectively resignify cultural codes and processes through effective performance. Civil repair as counter-mobilization has to invoke memory, myths, and mythologies for effective meaning-making and not

THE INDIAN CIVIL SPHERE

slide back into exclusive dependence on rationality, reason, evidence, and data without a narrative or a story to tell. In other words, the current authoritarian civil sphere has been built and imagined by plugging into the right kind of civil codes, performance, myths, and narrativization. It resonates with a certain kind of civilizational ethos – what historian Romila Thapar refers to as "collective subconscious" – about solidarity (Thapar 2020).

A recent report by the Pew Research Center, New York, titled *Religion in India: Tolerance and Segregation*, provides us some interesting clues into how popular imagination (collective subconscious) and underlying cultural codes (civilizational codes) about solidarity and commonality work in India. Among its many findings is the observation that 66 percent of Hindus see themselves as very different from Muslims, a sentiment that most (64 percent) Muslims echo. The report concludes that Indians "simultaneously express enthusiasm for religious tolerance and a consistent preference for keeping their religious communities in segregated spheres – they live together separately." Segregation, here, refers to avoiding common neighborhoods and resisting religious inter-marriage. It seems that Indians find it challenging to separate legitimate anxieties about recognition from popular prejudices. At least some part of prejudice is integral to how communities construct and self-represent themselves.

In the survey, the majority of respondents felt that diversity is beneficial to India. It records that nearly two-thirds (65 percent) of Hindus who voted for the Bharatiya Janata Party (BJP) in 2019 felt that being Hindu and speaking Hindi are crucial to be truly Indian. The same cohort also felt that religious diversity benefits India, compared with about half (47 percent) of other Hindus, who voted for non-BJP parties in 2019, and who do not think India benefits from diversity. However, the flattened and sanitized secular-constitutional discourses that put a premium on the separation of religion from politics and argue for citizenship as a legal identity are unable to make sense of or speak to such paradoxical modes of meaning-making. They are also singularly unhelpful in making sense of the continuum between diversity and difference on the one hand and recognition and prejudice on the other. The Pew survey found that Hindus tend to see their religious identity and Indian national identity as closely intertwined: nearly two-thirds of Hindus (64 percent) say it is "very important" to be Hindu to be "truly" Indian. It found that "for many Hindus, there is no contradiction between valuing religious diversity (at least in principle) and feeling that Hindus are somehow more authentically Indian than fellow citizens who follow other religions."

Regarding Indian Muslims, the report notes, "Today, India's Muslims almost unanimously say they are very proud to be Indian (95%) and

112

express great enthusiasm for Indian culture: 85% agree with the statement that Indian people are not perfect, but Indian culture is superior to others." This certainly points to the underlying commonality of ethics that cuts across religious communities, whether one is Hindu or Muslim. For instance, the report observes, "Muslims in India are just as likely as Hindus to say they believe in karma (77% each) and 54% of Indian Christians share this view."[4] One could, perhaps, add caste as the indigenous (Indic) contribution to Islam and Christianity. The findings also, perhaps, emphasize the trust Muslims continue to have in Indian democracy and public reasoning, as evidenced by their unfailing participation in elections and the faith the community puts in the regulatory legal system, despite all its limitations. Prime Minister Narendra Modi himself said that there is no homegrown terrorism in India, and most of it gets exported to India from across the border.[5] That is, a sense of belonging is reflected in the shared cultural beliefs (such as the belief in and practice of karma) of Hindus and Muslims and the active participation of the latter in electoral processes.[6]

One could possibly argue that the current populist-authoritarian regime understands the continuities that overlie the underlying segregation in the society and is attempting to produce *hierarchical solidarities with polarized differences*. Sociologist Ashis Nandy (2002) made an intriguing observation that religious harmony in the southern state of Kerala exists because communities mutually dislike each other. He says, "Every community thinks that they are the best and have negative comments about the other community. They also know that the other community also thinks the same about themselves. But people are accustomed to living with differences."[7] What such "negative dialectics" allow for is a "way of life" with self-contradictory belief systems. The everyday normativity that sociologist Andrew Sayer (2005) refers to as "lay normativity" is fluid, discontinuous, and explicitly self-contradictory, but this does not necessarily preclude ideas and practices of commonality and tolerance. What is sequestered at one level imagines a commonality at another, or rather acceptance of commonality is dependent on the assurance of segregation. Diversity is celebrated as an abstract ideal, while segregation is practiced in the social reality. The promise of civility is contingent on the practice of incivility.

The current authoritarian civil sphere in India resonates with this reality. It builds an abstract imagination of universal solidarity but creates or continues to support existing exclusions and segregation in the concrete. What this in effect builds is a commonality or solidarity or fraternity that is hierarchical. The promise of universal inclusion does not preclude exclusion but, more importantly, this is not perceived or experienced as a

THE INDIAN CIVIL SPHERE

paradox or self-contradictory in popular imagination, as reflected in the survey. The current authoritarian civil sphere is built around political slogans of *sab ka saath, sab ka vikas* (universal inclusion and development), *saafniyat, sahivikas* (clean intention, ethical development), and ideals of *samrastha* (harmony/solidarity) and *vasudaivika kutumbakam* (world as one family). Such imagination, ironically, only seems to further justify the need to protect segregated living and propel anxieties that consent to organized violence against religious minorities and all other social groups constructed as uncivil, anti-national, and evil.

The idea of fraternity in current populist-authoritarianism is a wish to preserve social differences but as polarization – not diversity – with Hindu identity as the sole basis of unity. In preserving the differences, it does not make efforts to bring communities together but builds on differences as prejudices. In the regime's understanding, every difference has a latent prejudice. As noted earlier, where to draw the lines between difference and diversity and recognition and prejudice is unclear. The current populist-authoritarianism collapses the two boundaries. It is intriguing that even as the regime harps on about nationalism, it actually thrives on regionalism and localism.[8] By mobilizing the local in a "conflictual unity," it strengthens the national/center and other dominant forms. For instance, it supports the formation of smaller states for better governance and decentralization for more participation, but deploys these processes, in effect, to create a stronger center and greater centralization of decision-making processes. Similarly, it mobilizes smaller sects among the Dalits and the Other Backward Classes (OBCs) by providing them with more political representation against the more dominant sects/subcastes within the Dalits and the OBCs. In this way, consent is gained as it breaks the patron–client relation between the dominant and weaker subcastes within the Dalits and the OBCs. But that also weakens consolidated Dalit or OBC resistance against the domination and exclusion by the dominant-caste Hindus. And it eventually works toward the consolidation and reification of the power of the dominant-caste Hindus.[9]

Meanwhile, the secular-progressives emphasize secular/civil solidarity but through an either/or discourse that assumes a linear progression and cannot address a social reality – a Hindu way of life – in which continuities and commonalities exist alongside segregation and prejudice. For instance, processes of modernization and secularization have attempted to erode, loosen, and erase primordial/ascriptive identities or attempt a separation of religion and politics, or separate culture from institutions. Secular notions of civility thereby come across as a "borrowed" worldview: "western," elitist, and sectarian. Interrogating the hegemonic-authoritarian civil sphere may require a more dialectical approach: one acknowledging that uncivil prejudices as well as the possibility of civil solidarity exist across communities, without always equating all of culture with traditionalism or conservatism. Culture, ethics, and emotions need to be framed as not only being deeply experiential but also evaluative.[10] As CST rightly suggests, collectives are sense-making and share goals through culturally based performances in complex and socially differentiated societies.[11]

Populist-authoritarianism has managed to articulate the complexity of socially differentiated societies by allowing for speech-acts that could potentially carry not only multiple meanings but also explicitly self-contradictory ones.[12] This, however, does not preclude its potential to create shared meaning as an "overlapping consensus."[13] Conflict itself becomes a mark of generative commonality, and social hierarchies, exclusions, and polarized differences are offered a hermeneutic turn and interpreted through the discourses of civilization and culture as an effort toward effective decolonization. Prejudice and discrimination imbrued in everyday practices are allowed a more lateral and neutralized representation of lived cultural practices that has a seemingly visible continuity with postcolonial critiques of "western epistemologies," "imperialism of categories," and the project of "provincializing Europe" (Rudolph and Rudolph 2008; Kaviraj 2010; Chakrabarty 2007 respectively).

Dualism against Duality

One of the definitive changes in the move for uncivil practices and identities to be recognized as civil has been the shift from "annihilation of caste" (title of a famous tract by B. R. Ambedkar) to "secularizing caste" and "politicization of caste" (Rudolph and Rudolph 2008). The process of identifying vertical exclusion and hierarchical discrimination was supplanted by an idea of moderate inclusion through accommodation within the known registers of the hegemonic civil sphere.[14] This, however, did not happen through what CST identifies as "duality," where a group dominated or mistreated in a non-civil sphere, or even inside a civil sphere institution has a position of duality: They are oppressed, on the one hand, and promised equal treatment and autonomy, on the other. They can use this duality to protest and create social movement.[15] Moderate inclusion was instead "accommodated" through a form of dualism where a caste with specified lower status in the caste order remains discriminated against yet attached to the caste system because they are also in receipt of benefits over those below them in the pecking order. Ambedkar refers to this as "graded inequalities." Differing from the idea of duality in CST, based on slavery and racism as examples of inequality, the duality within "graded inequalities" sub-divides the sufferers and the exploited themselves along an unequal matrix of burden and benefits. Those who suffer discrimination also benefit from the power to discriminate. It is only the Brahmins who are absolute beneficiaries at one end and Ati-Shudras who are absolute sufferers at the other. In such "absent presence" there is no promise of equality through duality but complexly differentiated ways of justifying inequalities through a reiteration of karma, merit, and social Darwinism. The same set of justifications also benefits the sufferers. The difference between the expectations of duality and the actual workings of dualism in India clearly demonstrates an operative logic that, perhaps, cannot be captured within the limits of CST. The workings of dualism also impact the subjectivity of those excluded and produce strategies that are driven by intangible socio-psychological imperatives.

The processes of *sanskritization* (mobility through emulation of higher castes) were explicitly challenged at certain points through radical anti-caste politics, which meant searching for an alternative kind of civility and throwing a challenge to verticality, hierarchy, and exclusion in all its forms. It also alongside emphasized lateral solidarity cutting across castes. For instance, organizations such as the Dalit Panthers in the 1970s argued that all the dispossessed, irrespective of their caste of birth, would count as Dalits. Their efforts are an example of how vertical exclusion was challenged by forging lateral solidarity. Such an expansive understanding of anti-caste politics transmuted after taking an identitarian turn around the 1990s into a form of accommodation within the given vertical structure that understood cross-caste solidarity as a form of patronage.[16] The emphasis shifted with the identitarian turn in anti-caste politics, a shift toward exclusive "lived experiences," where Dalits alone could speak for the Dalits for both epistemic and ethical purposes.[17]

Such decentering of solidarity was also accompanied by a more lateral imagination of caste, essentially, as community and culture and less as a system of prejudice and discrimination. Postcolonial scholarship's interventions interpreted it as a different way of "doing politics," outside the conventional ways of challenging structures, and they had a crucial impact on the contours of anti-caste politics. Thus, postcolonial scholarship reinterpreted caste as community and discrimination (at least a part of it) as culture. Following Foucauldian theoretical interventions through the process of subjectivation, norms and cultural rules were sought to be seen not only as being hegemonic but also conditions for inhabiting norms to refashion resistance as disruption.[18] Here, citizens come across as "actors" and not merely as subjects of the workings of "power-knowledge" systems (Alexander 2011b).[19] However, the problematic relation between difference and discrimination/prejudice continues to plague public debates in India, which also mark the difference of approach in duality, as against dualism.

It was within such a context that populist-authoritarianism under the current regime emerged through the combined "strategy" of enculturing difference and prejudice with an effective discourse of decolonization. The discourse of the ruling regime began with a critique of concepts of human rights, liberty, and then equality, to be replaced by "indigenous" concepts such as *samrastha* (social harmony). It was solidarity without equality, and not equality as solidarity as CST suggests. They found sanction for such an interpretation in ancient texts such as *Bhagavad Gita* (not *Manusmriti* that was widely critiqued by anti-caste champions for justifying social inequalities and the varna order) and mythologies such as *Ramyana* and *Mahabharata*. *Samrastha* is an oblique reference to harmony through segregation based on castes and the varna system. Right-wing decolonial discourse is an invitation to reinterpret *varnashrama dharma* as an alternative "way of life" and culture. It was about preserving diversity as differences in castes, their lifestyles, and food habits. And it was a lateral interpretation of a vertical imagination of the civil sphere. Suryakant Waghmore aptly refers to it as "Hindu cosmopolitanism," meaning "a degree of caste closure as an ideal ethic for urban cosmopolitanism and is partially based on the remnants of the ideology of caste hierarchy" (Waghmore and Gorringe 2020: 21). Lower-end castes, through dualism, remain attached without an explicit promise of overcoming exclusion or discrimination and caught up in a process where a cosmopolitan ethic approves of caste closure, which also gets reflected in the way opportunities for mobility, spaces of mutuality, and dense social interactions get closed. In other words, uncivil "caste closure" in the concrete is reinterpreted as civil inclusion by forging a "common" idea of culture, community, and civilization by the populist-authoritarians, but in consonance with earlier shifts in the anti-caste struggles and discursive interventions by a postcolonial discourse.

However, an inherent critique within analyses such as Hindu cosmopolitanism is its social critique of the political supplanting of aspects of politics that influence the social.[20] The dialectical interface between the political and the social allows us to explore further how the excluded subaltern castes themselves reproduced the dominant tropes, with implications that followed from working within the norms of the hegemonic civil sphere. It was not about "duality" in the CST sense, of working on the promise of universal autonomy and inclusion, but of gaining a sense of inclusion (as a psychological imperative) by excluding those who were weaker in social and economic terms – which is what I refer to as secular sectarianism (Gudavarthy 2019).

Secular sectarianism infused deradicalized incivility – incivility that was not transformative – at the lower end of the society and found performative justification for interpreting closure and exclusion as culture and Hindu cosmopolitanism at the higher end. Populist-authoritarianism emerged and found strength in its ability to appeal to both ends of the society marked by "graded inequalities."[21] It mobilized deradicalized incivility of the subaltern castes against religious minorities, allowing them through civil performance a sense of unification with the larger Hindu collective/civil sphere. Populist-authoritarianism further consolidated and reiterated hierarchical solidarity by allowing for dominant-caste Hindu (discriminatory) cultural practices to be interpreted as representative of the normative-universal. It coincided with both the identitarian turn of the anti-caste politics, which ceased to articulate a solidarity that cut across castes, as in all those dispossessed, and the postcolonial interpretation of caste as community.

Populist-authoritarianism successfully combined the decolonization project that provided it performative legitimacy in articulating underlying civilizational cultural codes with a critique of Western modernity, while justifying the practice of authoritarian exclusions. For instance, in a recent document (Dutta 2022) on "India as a Democracy" prepared by the Policy Planning and Research Division of the Ministry of External Affairs (MEA), after the downgrade of Indian democracy by global watchdog institutions for curtailing media freedom, and for human rights violation, among other such issues, the Ministry reasserted the "Indian Way" on democracy. The document invoked the idea of a distinct "civilizational ethos," arguing "India is a deeply pluralistic society, intuitively an international society." The term *vasudaivika kutumbakam* (the world as a family) is deeply entrenched in Indian thinking, the document states. Describing Indian democracy as a "human institution," the MEA attempts to place its practice in the "civilizational context" tracing it to "panchayats in Ramyana" and "Shanti Parva in Mahabharata." It argues, very much along the lines of CST, that democracy is lived and not about institutions and, thereby, actively recognizes "politics as performance" grounded in cultural structures. Connecting to cultural structures becomes a justification to run down "western" concepts/discourses that inform the democratic institutional imagination, including rights discourse. In effect, authoritarian practices find civil-cultural justification. The latter is projected as a matter of interpretation and not of practice, a matter of indignity and not exclusion, and a matter of culture and not discrimination.

118

THE AUTHORITARIAN CIVIL SPHERE

The same type of interpretative narrative that CST (and also cultural sociology) places at the heart of its understanding was invoked in recent campaigns for vegetarianism. It deployed both ancient practices and modern rational knowledge to justify vigorous campaigns for vegetarianism that included prohibiting public displays of meat. The Municipal Corporation of Delhi in its proposal to ban displays of meat argued, "It has been seen that non-vegetarian food items are displayed publicly by restaurant owners. . . . By doing so, there is danger of contamination to non-vegetarian food items. It also hurts the sentiments of the vegetarian public."[22] The campaign for vegetarianism is again an attempt to impose the dietary habits of a minority – caste-Hindus – over the majority – Bahujans.

Further, consider the instance of a recent advertisement in news dailies that invited applicants to buy apartments meant exclusively for the Brahmins in the southern city of Bangalore. Although there was some protest against this, the move was defended as a way of creating living conditions and an environment with which they were familiar. In fact, food habits and vegetarianism were offered as legitimate reasons for segregation that are not necessarily discriminatory toward meat eaters. In ancient India, Brahmins lived in exclusive agraharas at the heart of the village, where non-Brahmins were not allowed to enter. As I noted, vegetarianism is also being pushed through new rational-scientific evidence on its health benefits, for example in combating the Covid-19 pandemic. The phenomenon of mob lynchings against Dalits and Muslims has overtly to do with consuming beef and covertly with pushing a dominant narrative for vegetarianism. As part of the current government's Swatch Bharat Mission (Clean India Mission), public displays of meat are being prohibited in many places. The emphasis on "commonality" within the civil sphere is couched in deep-seated cultural practices, modern/rational justifications, and multiple significations of health, hygiene, and ecology.

Secular Sectarianism and "Civil Repair"

We have so far identified how the current populist-authoritarian regime has forged deep links to cultural structures for effective symbolic communication and to construct ideas of Hindu-civility.[23] Further, we attempted to delineate how the imagination of the normative-universal is tied in its workings to a system of dualism, as against the notion of duality in CST. This allows for a separation between abstract imagination and concrete processes without them converging and, instead, works in a self-contradictory manner where the imagination of universality ironically

119

THE INDIAN CIVIL SPHERE

justifies further segregation and, on occasions, even organized violence. It is in such a context that there is an impending need for civil repair, but, as elaborated, mobilizations for civil repair, too, seem to get caught inextricably in the dominant logic of an authoritarian civil sphere.

Secular (civil/profane/political) narratives in popular imagination have come to be received as being narrow and sectarian because they do not connect to the cultural structures, and their constructs of civility are seen to obstruct the mobility of the excluded. Further, the practice of secularism as the preservation of distinct identities, separation of religion and politics, and as the abstract project of citizenship has only managed to socially ghettoize groups. It obfuscated civility as dense social interactions and, instead, addressed the question of difference through distance between cultural groups in order to preserve their autonomy and distinct claims.[24] This is, however, what I refer to as secular sectarianism – inclusive-civil-secular discourse that produces sectarianism.

To overcome the condition of subalternity, marginalized and excluded social groups use the secular rubric as a form of ethical civil repair to demand justice against inequality, but one that does not question the unevenness of "graded inequalities" within marginalized groups. The impact on the political landscape of India and its social movements was a proliferation of intra-subaltern conflicts.[25] In "divided societies" with caste as a ladder-like structure, graded exclusions operate through being both "unequal and uneven" (Gudavarthy 2019). Questioning inequality vis-à-vis the dominant castes does not guarantee solidarity – psychological and emotional identification – against unevenness within marginalized groups. This partly explains the split between an admiration for diversity in the abstract as against the practice of segregation and prejudice in the concrete. The admiration for abstract ideals of diversity and equality works to advance one's own demands, but they fail to deter the divisiveness in the concrete.[26] Secular and constitutional democratic ideals, thereby, remain abstract, failing to find immediate articulation in the concrete. This also, therefore, explains why populist-authoritarianism in India does not reject secularism and constitutionalism, because abstract claims to civil solidarity do not disturb uncivil exclusions in the concrete. It works its way through democracy and its privileging of public opinion and electoral imperatives and pretty much identifies its own workings with progressive/inclusive ideals in the abstract while institutionalizing exclusionary practices in the concrete. It perceives no direct conflict with abstract ideals of universal inclusion, although invoking it does not translate into concrete strategies for social inclusion.

The split between the abstract-normative-universal and concrete-sectarianism creates a template for mobilizations of civil repair to become tame replicas of the prevalent logic of exclusions. It is, therefore, possible to see in popular imagination the current authoritarian civil sphere as a continuity of earlier versions of liberal and social democratic mobilizations enshrined in "Nehruvian consensus." The authoritarian civil sphere marks a *non-disruptive change*. It is producing a majoritarian and a monolithic imagination of the civil sphere as the new normative-universal working through not against the earlier democratic-discursive articulations. Social movements working toward civil repair are struggling to unhitch strategies and discourses they are familiar with from their appropriation by the current populist-authoritarianism. However, the civil repair they are attempting through earlier registers is going unnoticed in popular imagination. It is failing to provide motivation and its performance looks inauthentic or inappropriate. Their symbolic communication is attempting to performatively produce solidarity without being grounded in cultural structures.

In order to explain the failure of civil repair to create "emotional and psychological identification" between differentially located social groups I will refer to the endemic split between political representation and social power in India. Gandhi designed anti-colonial mobilization through a split between the political strategies used against the colonial/outside rule and social tactics used against cultural/inside hierarchies. The former was based on strategies of non-cooperation and civil disobedience, while the latter was about building a consensus and accommodation. Against the British, he pursued a boycott of foreign cloth and violation of tax laws; against caste, class, and gendered discrimination, he offered the concepts of trusteeship (propertied as the trustees of the poor) and "constructive work," including cleaning of public toilets (equating caste-based discrimination with the idea of filth and mental-manual distinctions). He envisaged "change without conflict," "materialism with moralism," modernity with spiritualism, and a nation with village republics (Frankel 1978). He attempted to change social hierarchies without breaking the collective sense, commonality, and mutual solidarity "innate" to culture and community. Gandhi, effectively, proposed a "third way" – a "gradual revolution" – between the individualism of the liberal-capitalist methods and the collective-etatism of the communist kind.

His vision of social transformation in post-independence India was a way out without directly challenging the social structure. For instance, with regard to the "woman question" he politicized women's role within the family and brought women into the public realm to join the anti-colonial movement. Regarding the boycott of foreign cloth, he said its success was dependent on women since they decided who wears what at

THE INDIAN CIVIL SPHERE

home. Similarly, he declared women to be greater *satyagrahis* (as moral exemplars) since they were abodes of patience, love, and compassion. In continuation of his "consensus" building mode of bringing change, Gandhi envisaged changes in social structure through greater representation for those marginalized, which would gradually dissolve the social conservatism, discrimination, and distance between social/cultural groups without direct conflict. This vision was the guiding force for the constitution-making process. Indian constitutionalist expert Granville Austin argues that what was unique about the constitution-making process was its emphasis on "consensus" and "accommodation" (Austin 1999a [1966]).

What this translated into over a period of time in post-independence Indian politics was greater political representation for subaltern castes, classes, and religious groups. They could deploy what Partha Chatterjee (2004) refers to as the "creative power of community" through vote-bank politics influencing electoral outcomes. Demographic imagination and numerical majority became significant in propelling the process of laying claim to political power. Ambedkar, too, noted the significance of political power in order to forge social change. Both during the colonial period and post-independence, India had elaborate debates on representation, from first-past-the-post, to proportional representation, to separate electorates, and reserved constituencies. However, what this split between political representation and social power resulted in was a flexible process of political inclusion and a somewhat stagnant social structuration. It helped pave the way to Dalit-Bahujan political formations such as the Bahujan Samaj Party (BSP), who came to power in large states like Uttar Pradesh in the north, but it meant very little in terms of its impact on social and cultural practices. Social justice was reduced to political representation, and representation was divested from its connections to issues related to social power. Thus, the "politics of presence" of Dalits, OBCs, and Muslims did not guarantee active mobilization against social exclusion.[27]

It is this split between political representation and social hierarchy that the current populist-authoritarianism further builds on. They carried forward the logic of representation that was imagined to offset the inequalities between the dominant castes and the "lower" castes, into the realm of "unevenness" between the subaltern castes. They mobilized those castes that were at a disadvantage because of unevenness within the marginalized sections and broke the patronage of the "dominant" castes within the marginalized and backward castes. They mobilized those social groups that were in a numerical minority and provided them with political representation.[28] This somewhat "radical" subversion of the process of political representation, however, did not mean a challenge to the social superiority of the dominant castes.

The cultural and ritual hierarchy of the higher castes coexisted with subversive expansion of political representation into subcastes within the Dalits and backward classes/castes. It broke the possibility of "emotional and psychological identification" between the subaltern castes and further strengthened the social superiority of the dominant castes by directly fashioning campaigns such as for vegetarianism. The expansion of representation to weaker and smaller castes has lent greater performative legitimacy to the current populist-authoritarian regime, even as they are managing to socially and culturally further undermine caste groups but also make them feel empowered, by ascribing a common Hindu identity based on a common civilizational ethos. The effectiveness of the sense of belonging to a common Hindu identity/lifeworld is built and dependent on the secular sectarianism of subaltern groups and progressive/secular political formations.

The civil repair now being attempted by progressive political formations is through appeals to abstract ideals of secularism and constitutionalism. They remain exclusively political (civil disobedience), while the authoritarian civil sphere is based on cultural structures and the popular/Gandhian imagination of "change without conflict." For instance, recent protests by Muslims against the National Register of Citizenship (NRC) and Citizenship Amendment Act (CAA) called out to "save the constitution" and "save democracy and secularism." These appeals lack grounding in cultural structures; they lack performative power and continue to work within the limits of secular sectarianism. There is an impending need to rework secular sectarianism in order to breach the authoritarian civil sphere.

There is, however, a possibility that the fault lines between the civil and uncivil could be redrawn from within the interstices of the convergence between secular sectarianism and populist-authoritarianism as well as the continued imperatives of civil repair, as CST reminds us. Recent protests by farmers in India brought together a large number of social demands that cut across castes and classes. They foregrounded the issues of development models, inflation, unemployment, monopoly capitalism, media control, misuse of regulatory institutions, and violations of law, use of force and intimidation, among many other such issues. Farmers' protests led by rich peasantry and upper social echelons organized *maha panchayats* that promised greater inclusion for Dalits, yielding more space for women's leadership, and public apologies to Muslims for communal riots and organized violence. Social activists on the margins have been articulating their demands for a common school system in order to provide equal opportunities to all castes and address the problem of social prejudices. There are new voices among the Dalit-Bahujans that speak beyond the registers of narrow identitarian language; identity politics is coming to be recognized more as a template for articulating the demands of a tiny (educated) group of social "elites" within the Dalit-Bahujans. All of this aims at notions of civility beyond secular sectarian logic and civil solidarity beyond the limits of populist-authoritarianism. As CST suggests, solidarity as a "driving motor" will find an afterlife that will require combining social demands with cultural structures. This remains a possibility in light of what looks like a durable "civil" order established by populist-authoritarians who seem to understand underlying cultural codes and the possibility of blurring neat distinctions between the civil and uncivil in popular politics.

The Macro Framework

6

Building Solidarity, Attempting Civil Repair

Pious Altruism and Muslim Politics in Post-Babri Mumbai
Qudsiya Contractor

The premise of civil sphere theory is that societies are neither governed by power alone nor fueled only by the pursuit of self-interest (Alexander 2006: 3). Feelings for others matter and are structured by the boundaries of solidarity. How solidarity is structured, how far it extends, what it is composed of – these are critical issues for every social order and especially those that aim at the good life. Alexander (2006) proposes that solidarity is possible because people are oriented not only to the here and now but also to the ideal, to the transcendent, and to what they hope will be the everlasting. He argues that "justice depends on solidarity and on the feeling of being connected to others and part of something larger than ourselves – a whole that imposes obligations and allows us to share convictions, feelings, and cognitions, giving us a chance for meaningful participation and respecting our individual personalities, even as we feel we are all in the same boat" (p. 13). His is a highly optimistic view of how a social order can be transformed for a better future – one I argue is a useful lens for looking at Muslim society and politics in India today.

The spread of new religious movements and the articulations between religion, politics, globalization, and neoliberalism have prompted analyses of the shifting geographic and social boundaries between religious and secular institutions, practices, and discourses in recent decades. The rise and popularity of Hindu nationalism in the broader realm of public culture and public space in much of urban India, where the anxieties of modernity seem most palpable, raise questions about the growing salience of religion in contemporary times (Deshpande 1998; Hansen 1999, 2001; Rajagopal 2001). In postcolonial Mumbai, Hindu nationalism seems to be omnipresent in public culture – public spaces where individuals and communities imagine, respect, and recognize themselves through political discourse, commercial and cultural expression, and representations of state and civic organizations (Hansen 1999: 4). The demolition of the sixteenth-century Babri mosque in the north Indian town of Ayodhya by Hindu nationalists in December 1992 was a landmark in the communalization of politics and public culture in the country (Van der Veer 1994; Hansen 1999; Rajagopal 2001). The secular and cosmopolitan image of Bombay (as it was known then) changed considerably after communal violence ravaged the city from 1992 to 1993, in the aftermath of the mosque's demolition (Hansen 2001). Middle-class neighborhoods, in particular, preferred to maintain social homogeneity (Falzon 2004), while poor neighborhoods experienced an exodus of Muslim residents, who chose to move to predominantly Muslim areas (Chatterji and Mehta 2007). The demolition of the mosque and its violent aftermath came to symbolically and materially represent social suffering, contributing to a cultural construction of collective trauma connecting the city's Muslims (Alexander 2004, 2012).

In Mumbai, a history of labor migration and spatial segregation as a consequence of communal violence has made slum neighborhoods diverse in terms of linguistic, regional, and doctrinal backgrounds yet increasingly homogeneous in terms of religious identity.[1] In one such predominantly Muslim slum where I conducted fieldwork,[2] mosques had a humble beginning, constructed through *zakat*[3] donations. However, mosques were eventually used not only for prayers but also as centers for the distribution of water during acute shortages, shelter during times of communal violence, or as venues for community meetings, addressing housing scarcity or devising strategies to counter state slum-demolition drives. These traditional bastions of Islamic authority have been used in unconventional ways to address the urban experience of Muslims living in urban poverty. In their responding to everyday concerns of economic deprivation, sociopolitical marginalization, and, in the process, a loss of spiritual self-confidence (Geertz 1971) they reimagine Islam and reconstruct a Muslim urban identity in newer positive ways as an emotional resource. Public expressions of Islam through acts of charity, the construction and maintenance of places of worship, and the "public" observation of days of religious significance not only mark this particular Muslim neighborhood as a religio-cultural space, distinct from the rest of the city, but also seek to forge a civic solidarity rooted in ethics and fraternity that can transcend neighborhood boundaries. Muslim slum dwellers use religious practice and imagination to continually rework the urban spaces they occupy, while these spaces form essential locations for pious self-reflection – addressing questions of what it is to be a good Muslim and constructing one's Muslim identity within a local context

BUILDING SOLIDARITY, ATTEMPTING CIVIL REPAIR

yet influenced by transcendental traditions of Islam. These improvised religious idioms respond to local contexts of poverty, sociopolitical marginalization, and religious-based discrimination by linking individuals to the larger community and to a shared narrative about the nature of the world (Orsi 1999). I argue that these processes of building solidarity are not exclusively religious but rather form the bedrock of civic participation, where civility is considered and performed as a public virtue essential for not only democratic integration but also social criticism. Hence, religion is one of the many influences in the lives of the Muslim poor, and their engagement with religion is shaped as much by their personal circumstances as by the political, economic, and social conditions they find themselves in.

During the last two decades of the twentieth century, Indian politics witnessed a dramatic increase in political action and debate around issues of culture and identity, exemplified – but not monopolized – by the rise of Hindu nationalism (Zavos et al. 2004). Such debates reflect not just the rise of the Hindu Right parties and their ability to mobilize people around issues of culture, but also attempts by their opponents to coopt the same cultural symbolism in order to defeat them politically (Jaffrelot 2003b; Michelutti 2008). In the case of Muslim politics in India, the growing salience of culture and identity has shifted attention away from civilizational threats to Islam as a basis for political action toward growing cultural alienation and socioeconomic discrimination as a basis for ideological transformation of political agendas and a forging of civic solidarity. For instance, the ideological transformation or moderation of Indian Islamists, members of the *Jama'at-e-Islami Hind* (Islamic congregation of India), was brought about by the growing dissonance between its earlier radical agenda and the political subjectivity of the Muslim public in the context of a secular democracy (Ahmad 2009). While at the neighborhood level in Mumbai, the separation of the realm of politics from the supposedly non-political realm of culture, where communities tend to be represented as static, seems rather unstable in the light of new political assertiveness among "low-status" Muslims, who continue to challenge the hierarchical divide between "pure" culture and "low" politics (Hansen 2000).

This chapter examines social criticism, debate, and action within two contexts – one during the mobilization and annual distribution of *zakat* in the month of *Ramzan*[4] and the other at neighborhood-level debates about the future of Muslim politics, set in motion with the entry of a regional political party making inroads to capture a Muslim voting base. I look at how acts of pious altruism are used to build civic solidarity in the present context and how, by considering *zakat* not only as a religious

129

obligation but also as a means for addressing socioeconomic deprivation within the Muslim community, networks are created that transcend spatial boundaries. These networks, I argue, are a means to turn personal acts of piety into more than public expressions of community belonging; they also reinforce civic solidarity, creating new possibilities for imagining and practicing Islam that combine its traditional markers with the modern sensibilities of its subjects. Pious altruism in this context brings together the religious and civil spheres in that the moral basis behind the act of charity combines with the modern relevance of the secular needs of the Muslim poor. I engage with Alexander's (2006) thesis on the civil sphere, to argue that this sphere relies on religious solidarity, even among those who are not directly known but are recognized and respected through an acknowledgment of the common experience of being a religious minority with a history of violent persecution and faced with pronounced social exclusion in the present. The parameters of this sphere are contested and extended in relation to other spheres of civility that define what the state recognizes as marginalized communities. Deliberations on the future of Muslim politics in political rallies, at street corners, or tea stalls within the neighborhood reveal how the ideals of institutional secularism may not necessarily be in sync with the messiness of urban life. Lived realities often create ruptures within communities and continuities across social groups. Hence, Muslim politics are perpetually riddled with the problems of maintaining a balance between pursuing community interests within the parameters of institutional secularism and the pursuit of constitutional justice.

Muslims and the Civil Sphere in India

The quest for a political identity among Indian Muslims is a product of the breakdown of an old political system, extensive economic change, disruption of small groups, migration to cities, and the development of a new social stratum (Metcalf 1982; Burke and Lapidus 1988; Pernau 2013). Before the consolidation of the British Raj, the Mughal empire contained a heterogeneous Indian population. The empire was officially Muslim, but the dominant elite included a Hindu aristocracy and cultivated a syncretic cultural style that drew heavily on Indian symbols. The Muslim subject population did not have an empire or an Indian identity but was divided into numerous small groups organized around lineages (*biraderi*) and ethnic or caste communities (*jamatbandi*), as well as Sufi *turuq* and other forms of religious organization. The dissolution of the Mughal empire entirely disrupted the old system of society and opened the way for a century-long struggle to define new forms of Muslim political organization (Lapidus 1988: 7–8).

The modernizing project of the secular colonial state had a strong influence on modern religion in Indian society, creating a conducive environment for religious movements to flourish, who continue to play an important role in the modern public sphere (Van der Veer 2002). A diversity of Islamic reform movements, such as those originating in Aligarh, Nadwah, and Deoband in north India, and East Bengal, proliferated in the context of political loss, responding to the need to sustain high forms of Muslim culture and end un-Islamic practices – thereby increasing competition between Muslims and non-Muslims in both the economic and political spheres (Metcalf 1982). The *ulama*, the traditional religious leadership, chose a strategy of turning within, with the sole concern of preserving religious heritage through instruction in authentic religious practice and belief, while using both new institutional forms and modern technologies (Metcalf 1982; Zaman 2002). Religious renewal in the context of reform movements marked a change in old ways and a move toward newer interpretations of tradition and its place in the transformation of the self and the modern world (Robinson 2008). The adoption of modernity as an idea among Muslim intellectuals, such as those involved in the Aligarh movement in the nineteenth century, provided intellectual and political foundations for Muslim movements that produced Islam as a new historical entity, designating a moral community that transcended the particularity of royal, clerical, or mystical authority (Devji 2007). Just as the Aligarh movement was able to think about a collectively ethical way of being Muslim, one without an organic relationship to traditional institutions of authority, *Jama'at-e-Islami*, an Islamist movement founded in 1941, transformed its ideological stance from being an intellectual to a political movement (Masud 2000). As early examples of Islamic counter-publics, these modernist Muslim movements uncoupled religio-ethics from traditional institutions of authority while evolving from intellectual to political movements. The trajectory of *Jama'at-e-Islami* was influenced by a context in which the colonial state began to deeply affect individual and collective lives (Ahmad 2008). On the other hand, working-class Muslims and those considered low-status became more involved in public displays of religiosity, infusing it with a greater martial spirit that transcended social groups, and who were later stereotyped as bigots and fanatics (Masselos 1982; Pandey 1983; Gooptu 2001; Green 2019).

In Bombay, the shift in social and political power was highly localized, reflected in the social organization of space (Masselos 1976, 1982). The public presence of a diversity of Muslim groups across linguistic

THE INDIAN CIVIL SPHERE

and ethnic identities was reflected in the changing public displays of religiosity during *Muharram*[5] processions and *urs*[6] of Sufi saints. The involvement of elite Muslim groups extended beyond religious domains, through the patronage of religious institutions, into the city's public life, with engagement ranging from politics, public charities, to the literary arts (Khan 2019; Ranganathan 2019). Industrialization, migration, growing urban density as well as the declining economic and political power of Muslim groups radically shaped the way public customs forged neighborhood and community boundaries (Masselos 1982; Green 2019). Islam in Bombay responded to both the industrial change the city had endured and the implications this change had on the city's social organization (Green 2011). Colonial prohibition of political gatherings was also circumvented with the use of a religious festival to publicly disseminate views against the ills of society, including the excesses of colonial governance, providing a space for public dissent where communal forces began to crystallize, particularly along the antagonistic axis of Hindu–Muslim (Kaur 2003).[7] However, communal identities became salient not only during conflict, but also through affirmative actions. The founding of *Anjuman-e-Islam*, an Anglo-Urdu educational institution, addressed the need for education among Muslims, catering to the desire to keep Urdu as a language for Muslims alongside English, as they were losing out to other social groups in British and Christian missionary run institutions in the city (Noorani 1969; Dobbin 1972).

On a larger level, Islamic paradigms resting on key Islamic concepts of *umma* (community) and *ijma* (consensus), deeply rooted in Islamic history, had a major influence on the development of Muslim representative politics in late colonial India (Shaikh 1989). These paradigms were grounded in the normative prescriptions of a religious tradition that privileged the community over the individual and recognized the consensus of the moral community as intrinsically superior to the rules of arithmetical democracy that were believed to sustain the political community (Shaikh 1989). This Islamic discourse, shared among sections of *ashraf* Muslims, who became vital mediators in articulating an alternative "ideology of representation," stood in sharp contrast to the "law of numbers," a term associated with colonial liberal-democratic representation. This debate also formed the basis for considerations of cultural autonomy through minority safeguards, reflecting the concerns of Muslim political representatives regarding the submergence of a distinct cultural identity in independent India (Bajpai 2000). Although the discourse was heavily informed by the dominant assumptions of Islamic and Indo-Muslim thought, it was neither intransigent nor static. Although it stressed the primacy of the community, its definition was open to debate, and though it placed a premium on communal consensus, the mechanisms of consensus were often contested (Shaikh 1989). The use of Islamic symbols and their presumed universal appeal also suggested a disparity with the factionalized social structure of the Muslim population. A legacy of sharp class cleavage between *ashrafs* and lower-class corporate groups in Kanpur, north India, as well as the lack of a historical cultural basis for Muslim unity in Bombay, precipitated the need for a nation-wide Muslim identity. The formation of an Indian Muslim identity was, thus, not a monolithic process at all, but one full of variety in its very localized expressions. The need for a public structure for fragmented Muslim communities led to attachments to subcontinent-wide Muslim symbols, although their use in political action in India has been riddled with many challenges (Freitag 1988). At the center of many of these processes was an engagement with the changing contours of Muslim identity, influenced by larger concerns of what ideological and political foundations the new postcolonial state would be built on and how the latter would meet the aspirations of India's diverse polity (Reetz 2006). Transition from an older type of plural segmentary society toward a new national political identity, mediated by symbols divorced from political actualities, has nonetheless generated an Indian Muslim consciousness (Lapidus 1988). Bringing together communal symbols for the needs of political action has been a challenge for Muslims in the Indian context.

In the following sections, I return to the working-class Muslim neighborhood to look at how historical processes shaped the present contestations around the future of Muslim politics, as well as what it means to be a Muslim, by not just privileging Islam but emphasizing the actual world that Muslims live in (Osella and Soares 2010). But first, I begin by addressing how the blurred boundaries between religion and politics have meant the reinterpretation of Islamic values of egalitarianism.

Pious Altruism as Social Solidarity

Zakat is one of the five pillars of Islam around which Muslim spirituality and devotional life revolve. It is a social obligation rooted in the belief that since everything one possesses belongs to God, people living in poverty have a share in one's possessions and income and have a right to claim a portion of it. Unlike *sadaqah* or voluntary charity, *zakat* is not a matter of conscience: it is a duty and an obligation that must be fulfilled (Rahman 1983). *Zakat* has important social implications for the community, even though its most specific definition and realization is religious and focused on the individual and God. Historically, *zakat* has been one means to sustain poor members of the community in need, providing a mechanism for collecting and redistributing wealth, obliging Muslims to acknowledge responsibility for other members of their confessional group. *Zakat* was intended to translate belief (*iman*) into action and good deeds, which play a fundamental role in the Muslim community (Singer 2008). The distribution of *zakat* during *Ramzan* is a common annual occurrence in the slum neighborhood where I conducted fieldwork and is a key element of community building. Charitable donations are distributed through networks, starting from the financially better off within the locality to the city's wealthy Muslim elite. These philanthropic networks exist as part of mosques, Islamic reform movements, labor employment, business transactions, and philanthropic institutions. This echoes a larger trend with Islamic charity being on the rise, given the declining socioeconomic condition of Indian Muslims, and a new moral economy supplanting the decline of Muslim welfare institutions and endowments (*waqf*). Individual cash donations within *zakat*-fundraising networks are fast becoming the norm, as the financial lifeblood of associational networks spanning vast distances across India (Taylor 2018). *Zakat* distribution in the slum involves a network of volunteers across sects, *zat/biradari* groups, and doctrinal affiliations that extend far beyond its geographical boundaries. *Zakat* is collected from individuals, employers, family members, businesses, and institutions, while local volunteers are involved in the smooth distribution to worthy recipients identified from within the locality. *Zakat* could be offered in the form of groceries, school supplies, clothes, health check-ups, and medicines, or even free professional training for people who dropped out of school. Pious altruism becomes a form of social action where the core ethical tenets of Islam are reimagined and mobilized through interactions between donors, intermediaries, and recipients, extending moral horizons beyond the divine. It is a form of altruism motivated by a range of factors that are hard to disentangle. Islamic volunteerism in this context is motivated as much by piety and humanitarian impulses as it is by the socioeconomic alienation and political marginalization of Muslims in a city with a history of communal strife.

One such volunteer engaged in the collection and distribution of *zakat* donations is Mr. Mehboob Shah, a scrap dealer, and he belongs to the *Fakir biradari*, followers of the Sufi cult of *Zinda Shah Madar*, who also have lower social status in the descent-based hierarchy unique to South Asia (Ahmed 1973). Each year during *Ramzan* he volunteers to help out with *zakat* distributions to those living in poverty in his neighborhood for *sawab*.[8] He is part of a group of volunteers who approach wealthy Muslims for *zakat* donations and organize their distribution. Mehboob

BUILDING SOLIDARITY, ATTEMPTING CIVIL REPAIR

understands this form of religious volunteerism as not only a service to God but also his social responsibility, one ensuring that the Muslim elite remember their religious and societal obligation to the poor by participating in a moral economy of compassion. Mobilization of *zakat* donations as a religious obligation combines humanitarian impulses and political sensibilities, which seek to address the declining socioeconomic status of a large section of the city's Muslims. The impetus behind philanthropy and volunteerism is hence multilayered, combining religious and secular motivations (Deeb 2011; Mittermaier 2014; Osella 2018). Furthermore, pious philanthropy during *Ramzan* provides an opportunity to build networks across social hierarchies within the Muslim community, an important aspect in forging civic solidarity. During one of my conversations with Mr. Shah, he talked about religious and secular motivations in the collection and distribution of *zakat*:

> M: During *Ramzan*, you should see how this entire room is filled with rations (food grains) – rice, wheat, sugar, and clothes. We identify the poor, make a chart to plan the distribution, give them coupons, write down their names in a register, make *potlas* [packets], and then distribute the items. Several of us come together to volunteer during Ramzan. Adil Bhai [a Rajput, belonging to a warrior caste] started doing this here because he has some education and he hangs out [*uthna baithna*] with good people, educated people. He would get *zakat* donations from them and we would then help him distribute it to the poor in our neighborhood.
>
> Q: Whom do you get the donations from?
>
> M: There is a circuit. There are a few individuals in the locality to whom *Allahtala* [God] has given enough to be able to give to others. Then they tell their friends to donate and then there are also some wealthy employers like Jalaluddin and Imtiaz. We go to them and tell them we are planning to organize distribution of alms in our locality during Ramzan; they then ask us to distribute 500 kilograms of rice and wheat or a hundred items of clothing for women and children on their behalf. All of this is done voluntarily every year.
>
> Q: How many families are you able to reach out to?
>
> M: At least 750 families, that is the number we reached last year; I have it all on the register [gets up to bring the register]. We first go to homes to distribute coupons, and then when they come to collect, they give us the coupons and then we hand out the packets and write down their names.

As Mehboob recollects, with a hint of pride, the donations he is able to gather from the city's well-to-do Muslims for *zakat* distribution among the poor, he associates pious volunteerism not with religiosity or social privilege but with education and a sense of social responsibility. The

THE INDIAN CIVIL SPHERE

keeping of records and issuing of coupons or receipts serve as material rituals of symbolic community that combine modern modes of accounting with the spiritual (Taylor 2018). Receiving and giving in the context of poverty creates possibilities for imagining inclusion and belonging in the wider Muslim community, contingent on the mutuality of social proximity and the pleasure of fulfilling God's will (Osella and Widger 2018). However, the motivations for obtaining *sawab* are driven less by the possibility of maximizing reward for oneself and more by the way that rewards are distributed through moral networks. Moral merit and blessings are not seen as values to be maximized but as qualities whose exchange, circulation, and distribution define the social, that is, the connections that bind persons to one another (Anderson 2018).

During my fieldwork, I had an opportunity to witness what *zakat* distribution looks like during *Ramzan*, an activity which seemed to create a space for social critique. Yasmin Khan, a *sayed* (a social group that claims direct lineage from the Prophet and, hence, has higher social status), is an independent women's rights activist who has been actively involved in addressing several social issues in the slum, in association with local NGOs, political parties, and human rights groups. She was in her late thirties when I met her, a mother of two teenage daughters. She was volunteering for *zakat* distribution in her neighborhood, through donations received from a city businessman, and explained that there had been a long queue of women standing waiting since morning for the truck transporting the *zakat* to arrive. Yasmin complained about how bad the situation was: in spite of the fact that the amount of food grains they were to distribute was hardly enough to last a household for a week, women had been standing in the rain for a long time. Soon we reached the location where a long queue of women was standing along the road, huddled in the rain, drenched. There was still no sign of the truck at 4:00 p.m., which was supposed to have been there at shortly after noon time. Yasmin was among four or five volunteers meant to oversee the distribution of food grains to women who had been given numbered coupons a day earlier. A total of 600 coupons were distributed. The truck full of individual white polythene bags containing rice, dal, and wheat, and plastic bottles of oil finally arrived around 4:30 p.m. and stopped close to the mosque across the road. The volunteers got busy making arrangements for the distribution. Smaller groups of five women at a time were asked to come forward, and each time this was done, the queue was thrown into disarray. As the distribution proceeded, volunteers made sure the flow of traffic on the road remained smooth, while a crowd of onlookers stood watching the spectacle. Volunteers had made a human chain, holding hands to prevent women from crowding the truck. Despite

BUILDING SOLIDARITY, ATTEMPTING CIVIL REPAIR

this, one woman was pushed out from her place in the queue. With a coupon clutched in her hand, her face distorted in anger, she started shouting at the volunteers, "Do you think you are doing us a favor by giving us food grains? What is the point of giving us coupons? I have been standing in line since morning, my clothes are all wet (*Meharbani kar rahe hain kya anaaj de ke? Number le kar kya fayda. Subha se line main khade hain baarish main sab kapde geelay hogaye*)." After standing there for a couple of minutes, she walked away without a bag of grain.

Public acts of pious philanthropy, such as the one described above, define the social by connecting members across social boundaries in a moral network of social accountability enabled by divine obligation. Through the interactions between donors and recipients, the core ethical tenets of Islam are mobilized and reimagined. The spectacular nature of giving renders it a public act of piety that makes it vulnerable to moral critiques about its very purpose, as was evident from the woman who walked away without receiving *zakat*, raising questions about dignity in the giving of alms. Giving creates the possibility of critique that illuminates the gap between what is given and what withheld by the Indian state. Forms of philanthropy can be instrumentalized as a means of criticism, to reveal the deficits of the state in addressing the needs of disaster survivors, or survivors of communal violence. The unwillingness of the state to provide care is brought to public attention through giving as a manner of criticism, captured by the concept of "partonomic philanthropy," which indicates that the part we give is an indication of the whole that is not given (Banerjee and Copeman 2018). Pious philanthropy is disenchanting, as its mobilization is grounded in liberal ideas of justice and equity, while simultaneously re-enchanting, as it reimagines the moral and divine as grounded in the everyday. Although the motivation for altruism might originate from a notion of service to God, it is not always possible to differentiate between religious and secular motivations behind giving and receiving (Deeb 2011; Mittermaier 2014; Osella 2018). Yasmin's experiences in organizing *zakat* distribution point to a similar paradox of giving as a criticism of what has not been given. *Zakat* donations are never enough to address the material needs of urban Muslims living in poverty, yet those who participate in the public act of pious philanthropy illuminate the state's inability to address socioeconomic deficits alongside the former's divine motivations. In other instances, personal practices of piety take public forms and carry public meaning by signaling membership in a community of the modern pious, demonstrating both individual morality and the new political presence of marginalized communities (Deeb 2011). Pious philanthropy serves as a site for exchange, circulation, and distribution of moral and

THE INDIAN CIVIL SPHERE

ethical values that connects the individual to the social. However, as embodied and discursive practices of piety convey a sense of visibility of religion and the perceived newness of authenticated Islam, they also expose contestations over the details, definitions, praxis, and boundaries of both personal and public religiosities.

Universalizing the Language of Civil Justice?

In 2014, Asaduddin Owaisi, a lawyer and the leader of the All India Majlis-e-Ittehadul Muslimeen (AIMIM or also colloquially referred to as MIM[9]), a Hyderabad based political party, visited a slum in the suburbs of the city. He began his speech by addressing the concerns of secular parties about his focusing on only Muslims, justifying it by quoting census statistics that indicated the number of Muslims living in poverty was increasing, while their representation in government jobs was not in proportion to their share of the population. He went on to say that Muslim representation in jails was disproportionately high, as was the history of communal violence while secular and Hindu Right parties were in office. He argued his focus on Muslim marginalization was not meant to incite communal hatred, as was alleged. After clarifying his stance, he commented on living conditions in the slum and urged the audience to wake up and demand their rights, "this is a *jamhuuriyat* (democracy) and in a democracy if you don't get up yourself and demand your right no one is going to come and give it to you. Isn't this true?", which was followed by cheering from the audience. Since it was the eve of *Bakri Eid*,[10] he appealed to the crowd to sacrifice their time and sweat and to vote for him, as he was not a leader but a soldier for their cause. He appealed to Dalits to vote, too, using the slogan "Jai Bhim, Jai MIM,"[11] which was again met with cheers. Muslim identification was used here in an attempt to forge a collective spirit, by stringing together a common experience of marginalization and political alienation, a strategy often found effective in Indian political culture. The fact that the gathered crowd responded to his claim to uphold secularism suggests that a new generation of Muslim voters was beginning to connect with such identifications, in the context dominated by Hindu right-wing discourse, in contrast to an earlier tendency to downplay their Muslim identity and align with secular liberal parties.

Within a year, welcome posters in English announced the arrival of Asaduddin Owaisi and his brother, Akbaruddin Owaisi, to a health camp organized by the AIMIM in the neighborhood. The atmosphere was effervescent, as music played in the background and streets were dec-

138

BUILDING SOLIDARITY, ATTEMPTING CIVIL REPAIR

orated with green paper bunting, while local groups of young volunteers, recognizable by their badges, were busy managing a growing crowd of onlookers, by keeping them off the roads to maintain smooth traffic flow. The Samajwadi Party (SP), the main political contender in the locality, had also put posters up in the area and even organized a rally in another part of the city in response to competition from AIMIM. Many SP supporters I had spoken to earlier expressed apprehension about the arrival of a "new" party in the area, "their team is full of emotional (*jazbaati*) young people," said one. It was risky to be openly emotional about one's religious (Muslim) identity he added, "some things should be said where they are appropriate, we should use only when they are necessary." The area has been the stronghold of SP, who had won the legislative assembly elections in 2009 based on a promise of bringing a steady water supply, an essential amenity that the neighborhood has been notoriously deprived of. SP was seen by many in the area as a political party able to overcome bureaucratic instruments of exclusion that prevented slum-dwelling Muslims from accessing public services (Contractor 2012). Yet water was just one among the many concerns of the area. The word around the locality was that AIMIM rallies were major crowd pullers, as just a banner or an announcement would suffice to get people to gather at a venue; there was no need for even a podium to be set up.

Closer to the venue policemen stood overlooking the crowd slowly gathering. As a vehicle with party leaders (a black SUV decorated with flowers) approached, the volunteers and police worked together to ensure that there were no interruptions. The volunteers formed a human chain to make way for vehicles and to keep people from getting too close to Akbaruddin Owaisi. There was excitement in the air, yet the crowd remained silent until Mr. Owaisi arrived at the venue. Women stood at the windows of their homes watching, while people stood on the sides of the road and some on elevated platforms to get a glimpse of Mr. Owaisi. The Owaisi brothers had asked for the health camp to be organized to make sure it was accessible to Dalit areas for greater participation, although there were very few Dalits around. Youth gathered at the venue taking pictures with their mobile phones and began shouting slogans, "Look, look who is here. The lion is here, the lion is here," referring to Mr. Owaisi, "*Allah hu akbar*" (God is great) and "*upar chchatri niche sayaa, bhaag Modi Akbar ayaa*" (An umbrella above and shade below, run Modi Akbar is here). Javed, a party worker I met, later told me that there is a perception among supporters that no one comes back empty handed when they go to visit the Owaisi brothers: "many people have done things for the community, but no one has the promise that they have." Akbaruddin Owaisi, who is known for his fiery speeches, did

THE INDIAN CIVIL SPHERE

not make any this time but silently inaugurated the health camp that was attended by women in large numbers. As Mr. Owaisi was about to leave, some supporters shouted out, laughing, "Say something Akbar bhai (*kuch to bolo akbar bhai*)."

Doctors from the tertiary-care hospital in Hyderabad were volunteering at the health camp and making referrals to local municipal hospitals whenever needed. Nearly 4,000 people attended the health camp, and the party workers seemed very satisfied with the success of the event.

Despite its popularity, the entry of MIM set in motion debates about the nature and future of Muslim politics, highlighting both aspirations and apprehensions. For Mr. Rehman, a fifty-five-year-old municipal school teacher and social worker, religious identity could not be a basis for politics in a secular democracy: politics had to be based on an ideology or a set of morals that everyone agreed upon beyond one's community membership: "Politics should be on the basis of ideology or morals. But just having a political party with Muslims we can't achieve any progress in this country. In fact, we will end up creating a dent on the majority Hindu community. If we have a common agenda of peace, humanity, justice, equality, the safety of women, and freedom from crime, we will have to take everyone together (*sabko saath lekar chalna hoga*). We cannot go too far with a political party just for Muslims." Firdaus Khan, a twenty-nine-year-old member of the AIMIM, and a science graduate who runs a construction business and is involved in voluntary work, was very aware of the criticisms circulating within the neighborhood and beyond: "Even the Samajwadi Party faced similar criticisms when it started to gain popularity after 1992–93. They won a sympathy vote from Muslims. They started off by doing good work but look where they are now. They treat this locality as a vote bank. Abu Azmi is among the wealthiest MLAs [Members of the Legislative Assembly] but his constituency is among the poorest. Looking around it doesn't feel that we are living in the twenty first century. We are not saying that MIM [referring to it by its colloquial abbreviation] should be a Muslim party, we have also taken Dalits with us." He spoke at length about the lack of education and health facilities in the area and the rising drug abuse among youth. The lack of state facilities has cast a web of patronage that continues to keep slum dwellers dependent on the goodwill of a handful of Muslim politicians. He explained to me that AIMIM is trying to create an image of Muslim politics distinct from the plebian assertion that was characteristic of the Samajwadi Party in the 1990s, by not engaging in muscular politics but by focusing on legal provisions and constitutional rights. Hence, a discourse of cultural difference is not all that can be relied on for Muslim representation in politics to be successful, but, rather, the use of a moral vocabulary of justice within a liberal secular framework of democracy and equality. Everyday contestations and debates about what constitutes good politics remind us that urban Muslims living in poverty are not simply passive recipients of change but are also actors in its making (Bayat 1997). Such an engagement with formal institutions of democracy also marks a departure from the more conservative responses to violence and political alienation, such as the series of bomb blasts orchestrated by Dawood Ibrahim, a gangster from Mumbai, following communal violence in 1992–3 or in early forms of radical jihadism.

The distinctiveness of Muslim politics may then be said to lie, rather, in the specific, if evolving, values, symbols, ideas, and traditions that constitute "Islam." These include notions of social justice and communal solidarity that have been inspired by the founding texts of Islam, such as the Quran and the sayings (*hadith*) of the Prophet. They may also include a sense of obligation to authority that has been informed as much by social practice as by Quranic injunction, the practices of mystical orders (*tariqas*), and the established schools of Islamic law. Hence, Muslim politics constitute the field on which an intricate pattern of cooperation and contest over form, practice, and interpretation takes place (Eickelman and Piscatori 1996: 21).

As one cannot assume that urban Muslims living in poverty inevitably live according to a fixed normative code or that Islamic influences are invariable – religion may not be the only guiding principle or unique foundation for Muslim identity and political practice. There is a need to recognize that Muslim politics are not monolithic but, like politics in all civilizations, plural (Eickelman 1992). This suggests that contemporary ways of being Muslim involve the complex politics of Muslim self-fashioning, including debates about religious practice, the nature of the state, citizenship, and efforts to simply be in the current historical conjuncture (Osella and Soares 2010). Based on his study of a majority Muslim society like Indonesia, Hefner (2000) suggests that democratic consolidation will require not only a civil society of independent associations (although these are important too) but also a public culture of equality, justice, and universal citizenship. In other words, though a civil society and civic culture are required to make democracy work, by themselves they are still not enough. A healthy civil society requires a civilized state. In the case of Muslim politics in India, the civil aspects of Islam can never be fully realized in Hefner's terms because the influence of Islamic ideas and practices of civility are dwindling within the public sphere with the rise and popularity of Hindutva. The only source of civility then is the state. Unfortunately, how civic solidarity is largely understood is also shaped by the terms set by the state, where group differentiation and cultural difference are not identified as sources of democratic representation but of separatism. In order to better understand how solidarity is forged, it may help to focus our attention on how the ideals and values that formal institutions and processes uphold are realized in informal spaces. The critical question then is not what kinds of social, cultural, economic, and political resources are available, but, rather, how they can be mobilized to transition from being a counter-public to sites of civil repair. The exclusion of large categories of people from membership within civil society and the construction of their otherness in terms of civil incompetence essentializes them as a matter of democratic self-protection. It is no wonder that dominated groups have struggled for not only power but also cultural reclassification (Alexander 2002). Civil repair draws on a commitment to the moral principles on which the civil community is based, inspired by the universalistic ideals of a democratic solidarity. Belief in the aspirational ideals of the civil sphere works as a source of strength and ultimately courage to engage in civil repair. Social contexts play an important role as well, as seen here – it is the moral content of religious teachings rather than religious affiliations per se that may be a relevant motivating factor (Tognato 2020).

Conclusions

In this chapter, I have tried to show how social solidarity within a predominantly Muslim slum neighborhood is forged through a reinterpretation of traditions that reinforce an egalitarian ethos in the context of increasing socioeconomic marginalization of large sections of the urban Muslim population. Universal civil elements in the practices of Islam are being reinterpreted in newer ways to address the present, while social solidarity is, simultaneously, built on a shared commitment to an idealized future that is not just defined in Islamic terms (as the afterlife) but also is reflective of the aspirations of the Muslim poor in a civic sense. The processes of building solidarity are, then, not exclusively religious but, rather, form the bedrock of civic participation, where civility is considered and performed as a public virtue, essential not just for social criticism but also democratic integration. Drawing on civic and religious resources requires that we not only look inwards as a community, but also outward to acknowledge and address other forms of marginalization and the communities affected by it. Hence, religion is but one of many influences in the lives of urban Muslims living in poverty, and as much as their engagement with religion is shaped by their personal circumstances, they, in turn, are shaped by the political, economic, and social conditions they find themselves in. Solidarity-building processes are not necessarily geared toward building a counter-public but are, rather, an attempt at civil repair, with the hope of being part of something larger than themselves.

7

Financial Inclusion

Private Interventions in the Civil Sphere
Kartikeya Saboo

Anxious to reconcile extant contradictions between the empirical and the normative in mid-twentieth-century liberal philosophy, late critical theory, and the social sciences in general, Alexander (2006) posits a sphere of imagining and enactment, morally and ethically concerned with justice, and immersed in the concrete, a sociological sphere informed by a deeply moral philosophy. The theory of the civil sphere (CST) is informed by a dynamic moral universalism, multiculturalism, solidarity, and inclusion.

Alexander argues that this "sphere of solidarity" (2006: 193) be an object of study itself, recognizing both the actual existence and heuristic demarcation of institutions, actors, movements, processes, subjectivities, symbols, and discourses. A central postulate is the presence of binary codes in the civil sphere, which have positive and negative valences: inclusion–exclusion, good–bad, liberal–illiberal, sacred–profane. The civil sphere is, ideally, the place for the blooming of the sacred and positive ends of binary codes, but may also reduce solidarity, "pollute" identities as profane, and allow privilege in other spheres to become criteria of hierarchy and exclusion.

Analytically, the study of motives, relations, and institutions that come to represent consensus on the common good belongs within the civil sphere. Boundaries of the civil sphere seek expansion via recognition of new identities and positions legitimized as civil (e.g., the hitherto unrecognized rights of LGBTQ individuals). The civil sphere seeks incorporation, the inclusion of those previously marginalized or obstructed from empowered membership (e.g., the materially deprived, hindered from full participation due to the lack of economic opportunities and concomitant investments in their health and education). Historically, the modes of incorporation have differed (multiculturalism is the latest), depending on which groups, formations, and identities are being gathered into the civil sphere. Also salient to CST is the idea of civil repair, the reparative and restorative processes that proceed before and along with different modes of incorporation to realize and expand the civil sphere.

Culture, civil translation, and social movements are essential to understanding the analytical framework of CST. The civil sphere generates cultural codes of solidarity. Therefore, apprehending solidarity – its codes, discourses, and expansion; its influence on preconceptual commitments in non-civil spheres; appeals made on its behalf – requires a perspectival broadening. Attention to culture enables this openness.[1] Using Geertzian thick description as its style, CST integrates flesh-and-blood interpretivism from the hermeneutic intervention, taking seriously ideas of meaning, experience, and symbolism (Geertz 1973).

Civil Translation. The concerns of other spheres – market/economy, polity, religion, and private relations – are and can be translated through the discourse of the civil sphere, having implications for solidarity. Thus, boundary relations between the civil sphere and other spheres can be investigated to tease out their implications for inclusion.

Social Movements. The symbolic charge and dramatic potential of performance to alter the representational order and expand the symbolic universe of public discourse is central to CST. Thus, social movements instigate the expansion of solidarity and purification of hitherto stigmatized claims, identities, and positions. That said, CST has also been fruitfully applied to the study of organizational structures other than social movements (Egholm 2019), the latter of which I do in this chapter focusing on a private financial institution.

In sum, binary codes, their empirical signifieds, symbols and cultural structures and social institutions of the public sphere, communicative and regulatory institutions, other analytically independent spheres (Kivisto and Sciortino 2015a), boundary relations between spheres, solidarity and reciprocity (and their opposites), and civil repair are part of the CST framework. CST seeks social justice, expansion, and inclusion. Thus, the civil sphere emerges as both a *theory* and a *project* grounded in and immanent from "the strong program in cultural sociology" and its proponents' position on the autonomy of culture (Alexander and Smith 2003; Alexander 2011a).[2]

As with any model, the analytical rubber must hit the road. Alexander performs his own argument by viewing the civil rights struggle, the feminist movement, and antisemitism through the lens of CST. While debate continues about the analytic and theoretical foundations of the framework (Alexander 2015; Kivisto and Sciortino 2015a), a busy research

THE INDIAN CIVIL SPHERE

agenda has been fostered under the aegis of CST, including volumes on regional applications (Alexander and Tognato 2018b; Alexander et al. 2019a, 2019b) and topical volumes, addressing themes such as populism (Alexander et al. 2020), the importance of narrative and dramatic performance in the phenomenon of Barack Obama (Alexander 2010; Alexander and Jaworsky 2014), the 2016 US Presidential elections (Mast and Alexander 2018),[3] the exclusionary and oppressive dimensions of values (Alexander 2013), and critique and commentary (Kivisto and Sciortino 2015b).

Background – Exotic Finance for Exotic Locales

In 2001, I helped design a derivatives-based product that would insure farmers who owned plots of land the size of a large US suburban backyard against weather-related risks of crop failure. I was part of a small team working in a private bank, investigating barriers to financial access for the poor. We conceived of financial services for the poorest individuals as including credit, savings, insurance, and derivatives.[4] To develop the business model, I consulted with others in the bank's insurance, credit, legal, and risk departments, and with development experts (including the International Finance Corporation, part of the World Bank group) and nonprofit organizations countrywide. In my first encounter with derivatives, these financial instruments did not seem like "financial weapons of mass destruction" or "time bombs . . . for the economic system" (Buffett 2002: 14, 16), as they were characterized elsewhere.

Our work followed in the wake of the neoliberalization of India's economy through structural adjustment programs (SAPs) that made debt and aid conditional on economic liberalization, and the concomitant shift toward market-based solutions to poverty in the development sector. Established discourses about the government's role in the economy and public welfare (poverty alleviation) became unstable. Boundary relations were in flux, as the economy was expected to hew closer to the free market conception of Western capitalism. The period of "*License Raj*" – bureaucratic control of economic activity – was being ushered out. The state's new role was to deepen property relations, aggressively deregulate sectors of economic activity, actively step out of the market, and link the economy intimately to international markets. Under SAPs, the state was expected to deregulate measures historically put in place to protect the national economy from volatility in global markets. Instead, new policies were enacted to encourage Foreign Direct Investment (FDI) and reduce checks and controls on business activity.

146

A parallel discourse emerged in the development sector. Grant funding for poverty-alleviation programs was deemed unsustainable. Instead, microcredit – small loans to groups of low-income borrowers who guaranteed each other – emerged as a tool of poverty alleviation. Aid agencies, nonprofits, and state governments sought deeper involvement in this nascent finance sector.

In this contribution to *The Indian Civil Sphere*, I tell the story of a market-based civil repair initiative, one that promised large-scale financial inclusion, before a public, political, and regulatory reckoning curtailed it. This project intersected with the (politicized) regulatory environment and political dynamics of economic development. I begin by outlining the movement of the idea from the boardroom and corporate offices to the neighborhoods experiencing rural and urban poverty, and then discuss the impacts, responses, and fallouts.[5]

This chapter unites a number of strands within CST– civil repair and translation, borderlines and boundary relations, and discourses/meanings that "generate" the civil sphere – offering the following contributions:

1. I show that civil translation can involve depth over expansion. The protagonists of this initiative implanted and submerged civil motives by translating them into the language of exchange and profit (also reversing the direction of translatability). Depth also came from phenomenal "thickness," deepening the lines between civil and other spheres, albeit briefly.[6]
2. The study uncovers borderline heuristics within a postcolonial setting. Actors and institutions straddle or even lie "schizophrenically" planted *within* multiple spheres. I effect this conceptualization of borders and relations as "interstitial thickness," following Tognato's discussion of thick institutional spaces and overlaps in boundary exchanges (2018: 150–3).
3. The financially excluded become a "site" when we interpret the discourses and meanings the signifier "poor" evokes. Both our success and failure at generating new significations about the poor (we succeeded internally by translating them into a business proposition and failed externally when others appropriated the civility of the signifier) instantiated the performative instability of civil discourse (Tognato 2018).
4. Finally, I offer a civil sphere theorization of microfinance.

Methodology

My narrative and analysis are based on dialogue with bank departments (e.g., risk, legal, structured finance), and our team's internal discussions and working papers. The crisis event is reconstructed from the reports of local bank staff (especially their translations of newspaper articles), conversations with stakeholders (microfinance institution CEOs and employees, bankers), and my own observations. An interpretation of my intimate engagement in the events, this account also represents an "expiation ritual," of work that feels like a lifetime ago.

The Universalizing Discourse of Market Salvation

Based in India, the bank was listed on the New York Stock Exchange and had international investors, so principal–agent debates from the United States influenced decision-making. The top management official who created our team held a US doctorate. He fervently (or uncritically) believed in the power of markets and exchange and wanted to create future clients who benefited from models for better health, basic education, and financial access. The initiative to provide financial services to the poor was stimulated by the work of leading US management scholars (Porter and Kramer 1999). In philanthropy, or "socially responsible investment," "adding value" via a market-based approach to social problems was the litmus test for decision-making. However, this globalization of US market-managerial discourse was not confined to business philanthropy; similar rhetoric was proliferating in the development sector.

Why would a private bank do business with the poor? Technically, the question was how could management justify it to shareholders?[7] We claimed a "double bottom line": profit in the present (and brand image if we wanted it, which the management did not), and future clients for other bank products (investment, retail finance, mortgages, credit cards). This recalled a conception of the corporation as a stakeholder in the community (Dodd 1932), which has been supplanted by the shareholder primacy norm over the last five decades.[8] The proposition was a happy combination of market and civil motives: profit-making purified of any "unprofitable charity," through a new economic institution – microfinance – which was conceived with civil motives. Inevitably, our work would bleed into other spheres, raising questions of boundary demarcations, relations, and exchanges.

Boundary Lines and Constructing the Poor

Compared with rationalized Euro-American economies, the Indian economic sphere is porous. Postcolonial economies are dense with actors

PRIVATE INTERVENTIONS IN THE CIVIL SPHERE

and motivations that extend beyond profit-making. The state defines and regulates the economy and is also an active participant. Neoliberal logics have become increasingly dominant, and market-managerial language has permeated the discourse of development and policymaking since the implementation of SAPs in the 1990s. Still, capitalist development remains uneven, and India's democracy and economy cannot be neatly read through the bourgeois-democratic lens of "advanced" liberal democracies (Rose 1996). The continued relevance of developmentalism belies neoliberal optimism about the market solving problems of capital allocation and distribution.[9] This complexity of the ongoing history of capitalism in India indexes a difficulty in separating spheres (not just civil, non-civil, anti-civil, but also economy, politics, religion, and civil) empirically and heuristically.[10] Further, "civil" cultural logics inform the discursive formats *within* the economic sphere and permeated this case.[11]

The translation of privileged accumulation by elites into control of civil society discourse and institutions is not the only barrier to solidarity. Boundary definition and boundary relations are dynamic.[12] The poor are an *object* of this amorphous complexity, an *exemplar* of the stakes of defining the discourse, a *source* of flexible and new meanings, and a *terrain* of boundary relations and contests.

The poor are a "site," for politicians, government, nonprofits, businesses, scholars, activists, movements, mass media; and they are a "stage" on which these actors "perform the poor," professing to speak for them. The middle-class mainstream is an occasionally interested audience. The civil sphere and other spheres intersect, intertwine, overlap, mix, collaborate, and contest over the discourse of the poor, which is also a discourse *on* the poor that virtually "constructs" the poor. Compared with US constructions, where meanings are couched (and opposed) in metaphors of individual responsibility, personal autonomy/deficiency, and moral virtue/failure, the poor in India are seen, rather, as unfortunate victims, objects of sympathy, and the reservoir of human dignity. Nevertheless, they are also objects of blame, and I encountered many who shrugged their shoulders at why the poor could not change their condition. However, the civil sphere framework – as far as it concerns the materially deprived, but also more broadly in terms of conceptions of the person – in India is not based on an individualistic and atomized Euro-American conception of the person; rather, it begins with concern for the downtrodden and invests them with affirming meanings and virtues lost in the pursuit of self-interest by others elsewhere in society.

Accordingly, much is invested in poverty, not all of it in alleviation;

civil repair is "big business" for social and symbolic entrepreneurs, both as an artifact of history and a product of ongoing exclusions.[13] Barriers to financial participation and economic inclusion, while recognized as social problems with economic roots, are not always seen to restrict the inclusive scope of the civil sphere. One gets a tacit sense that there are limits to alleviating poverty and financial exclusion. The poor qua poor are a significant constituency, with actors in civil and non-civil spheres invested in their "maintenance." Many actors and sectors compete to dominate the discourse on the poor, with the state (non-civil) and political parties (civil, but variously polluted) especially keen to control the meanings that emanate from this discourse, and the empirical referent they index and interpret.

The proliferation of NGOs in the 1990s was new and disruptive; now a market actor, they posed a novel threat to this discursive contest. Unintended or not, large-scale financial empowerment of the poor threatened boundary relations (market–civil–non-civil) and created anxiety about the relative position of these actors toward the poor and each other.

Microfinance

Microfinancial services may be viewed as those financial services that enable the poor (and those vulnerable to poverty) to reduce their vulnerability and participate in the economic growth process ...

These services would include:

  i. Banking and investment services
 ii. Insurance including life, disability, health, and assets
iii. Finance including credit, equity, and leasing
 iv. Derivatives

(Ananth et al. 2002: 22–3)

Microfinance – the concept, the sector, the organizations – broadly originates in the work of Mohammad Yunus, who lent money to groups of women in Bangladesh, who, in turn, guaranteed each other in lieu of collateral. Although savings were recognized as critical, credit was the main offering due to regulatory restrictions (Rutherford 2000). Multi-issue nonprofits and microcredit-only organizations used grant funds to make loans, although some sourced bank credit. Like other development-sector initiatives, committed individuals started organizations and sought recognition from aid agencies to reach scale and stabilize operations.

PRIVATE INTERVENTIONS IN THE CIVIL SPHERE

Locally known as non-governmental organizations (NGOs or non-profits), the NGO sector boomed with economic liberalization (late 1980s–early 1990s). Many states in India went from having a few NGOs to hundreds almost overnight. In one view, they emerged from failed social movements (Petras 1999). Certainly, the growth of the sector reflected the exhaustion of socialist ideology and wider changes in the geopolitical order. Nonprofits created social change through projects and local demonstrations of possibility. However, the problem in a nation-state of this size remained one of scale.

We at the bank were a small group with two approaches in creative tension. Trained in community and NGO-centered development and social welfare administration, I joined colleagues from the Institute of Rural Management, Anand, a storied institution known for its success with cooperative business structures. Our group, thus, comprised a "closet activist" on one hand, and two technical-solutions-oriented managerial professionals passionate about alleviating poverty on the other.

Constructing the Poor, Redux – Office Cubicle, Village, Slum

You take a loan, repay it, you take another. This proposition appealed to me in its austerity. Critical as I had become of development discourse (Ferguson 1990; Sachs 1992; Escobar 1995; Hart 2001), creating access for excluded clients (not "beneficiaries") in a relationship based on exchange was oddly liberating. The atomistic, impersonal nature of a relationship based on debt and its repayment seemed strangely dignified. It allayed anxieties about framing the poor as deficient, depoliticizing poverty by isolating it from structures that perpetuated marginalization, by distributing enlightened knowledge to tell the poor what to do, and then wringing our hands in despair when things did not change.

So, if not mobilization for total emancipation, this would do. Quietly, in our small circle, we dreamt of demonstrating that the poor were resilient, imaginative, risk-taking, entrepreneurial, and represented the future. This perspective was internal to our team and informed our energy; inside the hard-nosed, profit-oriented decision-making structures of the bank, we had to convince them strictly in terms of products, risk, growth, and profitability.[14]

We conceived of the poor as creditworthy customers entitled to financial inclusion and as future clients of all financial services. The primary clients of microfinancing services were poor women. Accordingly, they became economic actors facing three types of problems that hindered their

151

empowered participation in the economy: generating a surplus, keeping it safe, and making it productive; mitigating vulnerability; and managing risk, which stood between survival and growth strategies (Ananth et al. 2002). So financial services for the poor included basic banking (savings and credit), risk-mitigation (insurance and derivatives-based products), and value-adding/added products (investment and long-term finance). The ultimate vision was to create large financial portfolios for sale on the secondary market.[15]

Historically, the local moneylender filled this gap in access and was vilified as usurious and exploitative. Yet, the moneylender was essential, a source of credit where others were unavailable. Our aim was to provide this informal economic institution with competition to trigger adjustments in the terms and conditions of service beneficial to clients. We hoped that competition would facilitate civil output – "to keep the moneylender honest," said the top management official who created our team. This approach to the rural–urban financial ecology was at odds with approaches that imagined a financial utopia in which the "evil moneylender" was extinct.

Over ten months, we conducted extensive field- and desk-based research on microfinance all over the country. We met with NGO leaders and their communities, commercial organizations providing financial services, officers of state-owned banks, and international development professionals and consultants. We sought insight into the innovations and constraints within organizations (civil sphere NGOs, and market-based non-bank finance companies or NBFCs) to formulate a role for a large financial institution in facilitating scale.[16] Sometimes civil sphere and market activities inside the same organization were internally divided. Often, NBFCs evolved from NGOs, with the recognition that grants for lending created a distorted combination of charity and finance, unlikely to produce sustainability and scale.

The microfinance institution (MFI) specialized in social mobilization to create civil infrastructure (animating and organizing borrowers) and manage small-in-size and high-in-number transactions: groups of women meeting weekly, repaying loans in fifty small installments.[17] The MFI needed reliable and potentially large-scale lending funds to grow operations. Banks had a strong capital base and mobilized savings and investments from retail and corporate clients. At the same time, banks needed cost-effective infrastructure (not bank branches) that was readily accessible to clients. Although larger banks were already engaged in lending to NGO/MFIs, it was nowhere near the scale required to serve demand. Our innovation was to create two structures that enabled MFIs and banks to partner at scale.[18]

152

"So, you want to create a structure to offer small loans, without collateral, to urban and rural poor women?" Our meeting with the managing director of our bank was brief. Presented with the ideas and a scale that would be large in terms of client numbers, but miniscule in terms of capital allocation vis-à-vis the overall business of the bank, he was sanguine. "How computerized are these partners [MFIs]?" was the only question he asked. He deemed the project a "no brainer."

"So, you want to create a structure to offer small loans, without collateral, to urban and rural poor women?!" In our conversations with other teams at the lower levels of the bank's management hierarchy, each of these propositions – small loans, no collateral, remote areas, poor women – was met with incredulity. Colleagues in risk management openly laughed at first. In these, and other interactions with the internal structures, we occasionally took recourse to the executive authority of our top management official. Whether convinced by our arguments or not, the legal team had to make this work. Presciently, one of the skeptics noted, "elections, the poor... how do these MFIs manage political risk?"

The legal team faced unique challenges, as they aimed to protect the bank from unanticipated outcomes in the field (apart from the usual default risk, inherent to all lending). Designing a legal agreement posed a humorous quandary that indexed the disconnect between the corporate office and the dirt patches of borrower group meetings; after much wrangling, they drafted a loan document only one page long, to be cost effective for the MFI. It was the shortest loan agreement ever designed in the bank.

Acclaimed as a breakthrough in the sector, the model reached 1.2 million clients inside of eighteen months. Other banks adopted the model, which was emulated elsewhere with global variations. Regulatory changes – minor in the larger national picture but vital for us – were an acknowledgment that bank-lending within this structure was indebted to social mobilization and seemed to confirm that the approach was sound. Perhaps there would be a groundswell of civil repair, breaking a fundamental barrier to empowered market participation.[19]

The State: Regulator, Participant, Actor

In a nation of over 1 billion souls, with about 40 percent living below the official poverty line at the turn of the century, the state redistributes capital, regulates the economy, and competes in markets. Colonial administrative priorities left a lopsided economy and contracted industrial capacity when India achieved sovereignty in 1947. The market was envisioned as much a site for economic redress as it was for exchange and resource allocation. Accordingly, the post-independence state set economic priorities through five-year plans.[20] State-owned enterprises were, and remain, significant market players in the twenty-first century. With the aforementioned liberalization of investment and ownership controls since 1991, some state-owned businesses divested to become privately owned; in 2001, we were a decade into the state's relative retreat from market activity.

The Reserve Bank of India (RBI) is the banking regulator and lender of last resort. Owner of the largest public bank, it is also a participant. The redistributive actions of the state took place through poverty alleviation programs run by local government, and some of these programs included microcredit. This competitive density and the rapid growth of MFIs created conditions for a state–political party–civil society conflict.

The local government ran a World Bank-funded program in the province where the ensuing conflict unfolded and where the state's roles, sphere borderlines, and untenably undefined boundary relations came into relief. Thus, it was apt that a powerful government functionary inaugurated the public drama. Other players, including politicians, heads of poverty alleviation programs, police, and government functionaries, soon took positions. Everyone wanted to "embody the same ideal codes" in this contest over the poor.

The Symbolic Appropriation of International Women's Day, March 2006

Two large MFIs were bracing for disruption after expanding to a new district (county). There were informal exchanges with the district collector (DC). The DC is the most powerful local bureaucrat, effectively sovereign in their control over the district. Apparently, coincidental and prefaced with an interest in "learning more about your work," the details of what transpired in his conversations with MFIs are limited. It was a conversation composed of hints and allusions, but both MFI CEOs agreed that the DC did not appear assuaged by the information and details we presented about our operations. Then, at the end of the financial year (March), a series of events unfolded.

Local newspapers were primed by the DC in a news conference, where he made the following claims:

PRIVATE INTERVENTIONS IN THE CIVIL SPHERE

1. MFIs are actively dismantling Self Help Groups (SHGs) organized by government agencies and disrupting their dynamics in remote rural areas.
2. MFIs are charging exorbitant interest rates on loans to poor clients.
3. MFIs are putting unbearable pressure on borrowers to recover loans.

The DC concluded by suggesting he was considering legal action, and borrowers had a "human right" to stop repaying MFI loans. Another speech and legal action followed.

On the eve of International Women's Day, the DC exhorted microfinance clients of his district to stop repaying loans given by non-state agencies, accusing them of charging usurious rates and exploiting the poor. It was a dramatic performance attended by 1,500 women, including SHG members, women's federations linked with political parties, women working for the state-run poverty alleviation program, and local *anganwadi* (rural day care center) teachers. He concluded with a flourish, calling the local police chief to the stage, and announcing a newly created Helpline for borrowers "facing harassment" from MFIs.[21]

Three days later police arrested staff and seized records from fifty branches of the two MFIs. Government officials visited villages and slums to collect complaints about MFI procedures. First information reports (FIRs) were filed with police, naming MFI employees.

In an email exchange, one bank officer observed, "We may need to do PR [public relations] work with government officials to avoid problems in the future." Microfinance was about to "go mainstream," drawing wider public attention. Having discreetly achieved much, it was time for a public reckoning.

Local news media were keen to report sensational stories of social injustice. Readers – who knew little about the clients of MFIs, much less about microfinance – were treated to dramatic accounts of usurious interest rates and coercive practices. One lurid front-page story claimed that the MFI approach amounted to "we support you when you need money. . . and you must pay even if you die." Other reports claimed that a woman suffocated while hiding from MFI staff in an iron drum, another died by suicide, and a third burnt herself alive after being harassed to repay. MFIs were alleged to have caused nearly fifty suicides. Some local media owners also owned finance companies, creating conflicts of interest inside of these communicative institutions.

The reportage was riven with basic misunderstandings about microfinance. For instance, one middle-class interviewee found objectionable the provision of loans for consumption (healthcare, wedding expenses, household goods), saying "loans are given for wasteful personal needs or to purchase home appliances." However, health expenses that might prevent days of lost labor were, in fact, productive expenditures for the poor. In addition, the judgment that a poor person using microfinancing to buy a home appliance is being wasteful was ironic, given the booming market for retail finance of household goods targeted at the middle class, whom this interviewee was part of. Similar confusions arose about joint guarantee in lieu of collateral. "MFIs create peer pressure on the group member who has not paid the installment through other members in the same group," which is essentially an accurate statement about the structure of joint liability integral to microfinance methodology, but was being depicted as horrific coercion. Interest rates were presented as usurious without contextualization, ignoring the cost of provision, comparative moneylender rates, lack of access to mainstream banks, and other factors that necessitated this innovation in the first place. We shook our heads: to a mainstream audience, microfinance was being vilified for being microfinance!

Other machineries clicked into gear. The State Level Bankers Committee headed by the Chief Minister (CM), the US Governor equivalent, together with the state Finance Minister, the Minister of Rural Development, other senior legislators, representatives of the RBI, and leaders from public and private banks, organized a meeting. Privately, the CM appeared to be non-partisan, criticizing MFIs but expressing concern about bankers: "they [MFIs] have become worse than moneylenders. MFIs borrow from banks at 15 per cent and, in turn, charge high interest rates to their clients. So, banks get hurt and SHGs [the typical clients of state-run programs financed by government-owned banks] get hurt." News coverage began to draw a clearer line against the living standards of MFI CEOs, these "servants of the poor," who were (it seemed) hypocrites because they owned cars and houses.

Reports claimed that members of the state legislative assembly (MLAs) were set to make a presentation to the CM about MFI activities. The local Member of Parliament (MP) raised the issue in parliament. Bankers and MFI leaders knew that *Panchayati Raj* (village self-governance council) elections were imminent and politicians might encourage clients to not repay loans. Although there was one local political party that indicated support for MFIs, in the main, collaboration with political parties made everyone – bankers, MFI leaders, employees – skittish. Staff and leaders were advised to avoid any meetings with politicians.

The CM announced an inquiry committee. This was an imprimatur of sorts; any newsworthy scandal requiring intervention from legislators achieves a cynical legitimacy once a call to form a committee is issued.

PRIVATE INTERVENTIONS IN THE CIVIL SPHERE

Microfinance, I noted bitterly to my colleagues, had finally "made it big," achieving mainstream notoriety.

The private bank and partner MFIs took a different path, given the risk of massive losses and the aura of scandal around MFIs – this new institutional form that was not well known and apparently doing bad things to poor people in obscure places. Leaders from MFIs, microfinance associations, and affected banks met in late March 2006. They decided to establish dialog with the authorities, i.e., the state government, the national government, and the RBI. Inviting a comparative "public audit" of MFI operations and state-run microcredit programs was mooted. Preparing a code of conduct for MFIs, and one for banks, was proposed. And finally, interviews and advertisements to improve public understanding of microfinance were discussed. There was a sense that media relations were somewhat of a lost cause: banks did not want more publicity, and MFIs that had not yet drawn attention preferred to avoid the spotlight. Similar content, for *both* the authorities and the media, was drafted at this meeting.[22]

Banks and MFIs had to tread carefully, lest the issue become more politicized. Rather than contest the DC's arbitrary use of power, the network association of MFIs focused on regulatory scope. They asked the RBI to ratify that the local Moneylending Act invoked to justify police action did not apply to MFIs. MFIs urged government officials to visit and assess operations, in a demonstration of transparency. Backdoor conversations ensued at multiple angles and levels (state and federal, amongst the affected MFIs, partner banks, and individuals with local influence). Banks supported the MFIs' request for regulatory clarification; one finally arrived in mid-2006.

The worst of the crisis was over by early 2007. Lasting damage, however, had already been done. Banks suspended their partnerships to take stock, MFI operations constricted as cashflows declined, and borrowers engaged in rational choice (those with many installments stopped repayment, those with a few installments were keen to repay and borrow again).

Discourses, Meanings (and their Absence)

In retrospect, the political risk associated with creating large-scale financial access seems inevitable. Our team at the bank underestimated MFIs and their clients' appetite for growth when we removed liquidity and capital constraints. Anxious to appear apolitical, banks never seized control of the discourse and meanings that emerged in public consciousness,

THE INDIAN CIVIL SPHERE

and MFIs lacked the power (perhaps the inclination) to transform into a social mobilization.

The polemic over who "truly" served the poor – private banks and MFIs, or state-run programs and public sector banks – was tilted in favor of public agencies, especially when juxtaposed with urban, "tech savvy" and "profit-hungry" private banks and MFIs. Banks did not respond, fearing politically tinged attention. As a consequence, the DC, local administration, and political players appropriated the stage. As for my bank, stupendous as the growth in microfinance was, it remained a miniscule portion of the total business; it was expedient to exit rather than seek voice and more attention.

This innovation, which was a facilitating input that could one day expand the inclusiveness and solidarity of the civil sphere, created a sense of threat for some state, economic, and civil sphere elites, in a crisis that became *societalized* (Alexander 2018, 2019a; also see Lee 2019) through the DC's speech and police actions. Societalization was the moment of chance, when a social problem from a non-civil sphere might come to "be evaluated according to the more solidaristic and democratic perspectives of the civil sphere" (Alexander and Tognato 2018a: 2). However, it was aborted. The language of the "social whole" (p. 2) was seized by those who straddled multiple spheres: the DC formally belonged in the regulative structure, but self-consciously performed the persona of a politician, a social mobilizer, and even symbolically appropriated the discourse of women's empowerment (on International Women's Day) by framing microfinance as a form of women's oppression. Politicians, media, and competitors also usurped the language and terrain to advance their own interests in the name of the poor.

The moment had provided an opening to generate symbols and meanings that could expand inclusion and the scope of solidarity. However, and this might be a constitutive limitation for a market institution, the intra-institutional elite of the private bank never publicized a discourse that could claim the language of the social whole. They operated within the institutional logic and language of clients, growth, and profits. The bank was not interested in entering "the public life of the civil sphere" (Alexander 2006: 231). Neither fighting over extant cultural codes, nor willing to struggle over the germs of a new code, no compromise formation emerged, and state and civil sphere elites joined in the backlash. As alluded to above, they were not so much interested in the exclusionary potential of the civil sphere as in maintaining the poor in their current position – nominally already in the civil sphere – so others could speak on their behalf.[23] The possibility of civic competence was not allowed to enter the discourse. The clients of microfinance remained largely silent:

158

PRIVATE INTERVENTIONS IN THE CIVIL SPHERE

they were never offered the alternative of a dramatic, moral, idealistic, and passionate vision of emancipation and inclusion to rally behind. Politicized state bureaucrats, state development agencies, regulatory institutions, and media became protagonists, with MFIs and banks taking a reactive stance.

Considerations through the Lens of CST

The Concrete Context

CST's applicability to phenomena other than social movements and public struggles for social justice has been argued (Egholm 2019). Originating in a business corporation, this case study demonstrates a similar applicability.

Depth vs. Expansion

The analytic value of this civil translation – this applies to the bank I worked at but also MFIs in their very design – is that the universalizing, inclusive, and solidarity-promoting potentials of civil translation may not present only as expansion. Rather, civil motives can embed themselves in market institutions and promote *deep* possibilities for civil repair. No doubt the scuttling of the initiative precisely when it was going mainstream needs consideration. However, even making the innovation possible in a bank – after decades of leaving the poor to the moneylender and informal finance – was historic. It is a cruel irony that *existing civil discourse* was used to vilify our partner institutions as anti-civil and sideline the meanings and significations we generated about the poor. Given their design and objectives, it should be no surprise that neither the bank nor MFIs tackled this contradiction. Perhaps it was always bound to end this way.

Boundaries and Phenomenal Thickness

To view corporate action, public impact, state response, state and bureaucracy realpolitik via CST complicates the task of separating the "civil" from non-civil spheres and institutions where these actions, discourses, and imaginations live. One need only look at the multiple roles of the state, or the variety of organizational forms in microfinance. The civil sphere as an analytic is, therefore, "fashioned" through a reflexive accounting of events in other spheres, driven by multi-sphere actors. This also implies that boundaries between spheres – already more difficult to define in a postcolonial context as compared to a Euro-American one as discussed above – will have to be defined retrospectively. Perhaps the borderlines can be read from the effects. Non-civil sphere discourses and enactments (institutional infrastructures and cultural structures of other spheres), and new networks and infrastructures created in microfinance relate to CST in their "fallouts." Belonging to economic-financial, private, and government sectors, the actors, their discourses, and enactments produced new impacts and articulations, and new civil imaginings. New crevices and margins emerged as institutions intersected *in the same sphere*.[24] The reader closing this hermeneutic circle will decide if the descriptions I offered render and evoke this phenomenal, interstitial thickness (more below).

Translations, Discourses, Meanings

This project attempted civil repair, with unrealized expansive aspirations. The possibilities it generated emanated from a silent core: the vision of empowered financial participants positioned sustainably in an expanded civil sphere remained a hidden discourse, translated into the roles offered "on stage" – the logic of profit for a private market actor; problem-solving for the growth ambitions of grassroots MFIs; and in turn, formatted into the prevailing laws and regulation. Maybe we hoped that growth would enable others to generate new codes and meanings about the poor (Politicians? The State? Regulators? A social movement? A cluster of communicative actors?). As it turned out, this hidden discourse fell silent in the face of societalization. Once the mainstream took notice, others occupied the stage as "real" representatives of the poor to maintain existing boundary relations. *The failure to perform lasting civil translation, then, became moot.*

Civil sphere logic, translated into market language, created collaborations between banks and MFIs and boundary exchanges with institutions and players from political and economic spheres. Nonprofits or profit-making in organizational form, MFIs had a civil mission: to prove the poor were profitable as clients and self-reliant members of the civil sphere. These aspirations and organizational forms speak further to what I am calling the constitutive "interstitial thickness" of motives, relations, and institutions.

Not only does the developmental state operate in many spheres, but CST reveals that an interstitial thickness emerges from its multiple roles *in the same sphere*. It is an open question whether our attention to this phenomenal thickness, my characterization of it as creating interstices, other studies from Latin America and East Asia, and theoretical observations such as those of Villegas (2023) have yet accreted to a change or expansion of the basic CST framework. Another question is whether this is analytically and empirically applicable to only postcolonial societies. I conclude with a theorization of microfinance in CST terms.

Microfinance as a "New Institution" of CST

In 2006, Mohammad Yunus and his Grameen Bank received the Nobel Peace Prize. The timing was apt given the neoliberal turn globally, the general exhaustion of anti-capitalist ideologies and praxis, and the surging rhetoric of market-based solutions to social problems.

Microfinance, this voluntary, non-state institution, emerged to ameliorate financial exclusion, itself a barrier to inclusion in the civil sphere. Perhaps microfinance institutions were a harbinger of new institutional forms, motives, and relations (lender–client, MFI–bank, loan–expenditure) that could be conceived in a civil mode, translated into market logic, and realized using social (civil) mobilizational and organizational capacities. This constitutive overlap – emerging in one sphere while informed by transcendent ideals of another – does something other than straddle spheres. It awaits a neologism.

In the interim, facing "a new possible," other players, other spheres, and other institutions took a hand. It remains to be seen if this enabling input, which created civil depth in a market institution by spawning internal interstitial relations, produced energies and a discourse that might one day "alter the representational order" (Kivisto and Sciortino 2015a: 21).

8

The British Raj and its Legacy for Democracy and Civil Society in India
Krishan Kumar

We had known the hordes of Moghals and Pathans who invaded India, but we had known them as human races, with their own religions and customs, likes and dislikes, – we had never known them as a nation . . . But this time [with the British] we had to deal, not with kings, not with human races, but with a nation, – we, who are no nation ourselves.
Rabindranath Tagore, *Nationalism* (1917: 19)

Every previous ruling class, whether it had originally come from outside or was indigenous, had accepted the structural unity of India's social and economic life and had tried to fit into it. It had become Indianised and had struck roots in the soil of the country. The new [British] rulers were entirely different, with their base elsewhere, and between them and the average Indian there was a vast and unbridgeable gulf – a difference in tradition, in outlook, in income, and ways of living.
Jawaharlal Nehru, *The Discovery of India* (2010 [1946]: 328–9)

[British] imperialism brought its own negation: the Gospels and democracy, intellectual criticism and nationalism. . . . Imperialism introduced modernity to India, and with it the criticism of its own regime.
Octavio Paz, *In Light of India* (1997: 76, 102)

British Rule and the Transformation of Indian Society

India has been ruled by foreigners – if by that we mean non-Hindus – for much of its recent history. Muslim rulers occupy much of that history. Starting with the Arab conquest of Sind in the eighth century, it continued with Turkic rule under the loosely integrated Delhi Sultanate of the thirteenth and fourteenth centuries. But it was the Mongols – "Mughals" – who more firmly took over the reins of power in India, establishing

THE BRITISH RAJ AND ITS LEGACY FOR DEMOCRACY AND CIVIL SOCIETY

from the early sixteenth century a centralized Muslim empire that effectively lasted for 200 years (though they were not formally deposed until 1857).

Their successors were the British, who, starting in the mid-eighteenth century, also ruled for about 200 years, not leaving until 1948. "Modern history" therefore, for India, means primarily rule by foreigners.[1] But Mughal and British rule had very different effects on India. The Mughal legacy has been primarily in religion and culture. In India today the 200 million Muslims (14 percent of the population) attest to the religious impact; the cultural impact is best seen in architecture, in such magnificent monuments as the Taj Mahal in Agra and the Red Fort in Delhi, and in the Persianate influence in art, language, and literature (Schimmel 2004; Robinson 2007; Dale 2010).

These are of course vital aspects of Indian life. Islam, and Muslims, are clearly an integral part of India, past and present. The current attempt by India's ruling party, the Bharatiya Janata Party (BJP), to turn India into a purely Hindu state flies in the face of India's history (Schoch and Jaffrelot 2021: 406–44). History books for schoolchildren are rewritten to redact the Muslim presence, or to make it appear wholly alien and destructive of "traditional" Hindu civilization. A whole history of plurality and diversity is discounted in favor of presenting Hinduism – or Hindutva – as the "essential" India.

But so far as politics and the elements of civil society are concerned, the Muslim legacy is far less evident. The Mughal empire was an "early-modern" empire, one where many of the characteristic features of modernity were absent or undeveloped. This was almost as true of Europe as it was of the East, which lacked the feudal traditions that in Europe contained the germs of representative institutions. Only with the eighteenth-century European Enlightenment, and the American and French Revolutions, did the significant contours of political modernity appear; only with the British Industrial Revolution did the dynamic industrial form of capitalism take root, expanding to encompass and transform the globe.

In both of these developments the British played a central role. Their impact on India was bound to be correspondingly greater than that of the Mughals. Jawaharlal Nehru's verdict on Muslim rule seems accepted by most historians: Muslim rule "did not vitally affect the essential continuity of Indian life. The invaders who came from the north-west, like so many of their predecessors in more ancient times, became absorbed into India and part of her life. Their dynasties became Indian dynasties and there was a good deal of racial fusion by intermarriage. A deliberate effort was made, apart from a few exceptions, not to interfere with the

163

THE INDIAN CIVIL SPHERE

ways and customs of the people. They looked to India as their home country and had no other affiliations" (Nehru 2010 [1946]: 254; see also Richards 1995; Mukhia 2004).

The British, as both Nehru and Tagore – quoted in the epigraphs to this chapter – observed, were different (see also Naipaul 1968: 211). They did not merge with the native population; and they brought radically different traditions and attitudes to India. After an early period of "co-habitation," in which the British tried to come to terms with Indian culture and work through Indian (mostly Mughal) institutions, they embarked on a vigorous attempt to remake Indian politics and society along the lines that were developing powerfully in British society itself. Under the impress of Utilitarianism and "philosophic radicalism," and guided by such works as James Mill's immensely influential *History of India* (1818), Governor-Generals such as Lord Cornwallis (1786–93), Richard Wellesley (1798–1805), Lord Bentinck (1828–35), and Lord Dalhousie (1846–56) sought to put British rule in India on an entirely new footing (Stokes 1959; Bayly 1990: 76–89; Metcalf 1997: 28–65). The aim was "the flowering on Indian soil of those institutions which defined Britain's own society and civilization," among which were private property, the rule of law, the liberty of the individual, and Western forms of knowledge and education (Metcalf 1997: 35). Macaulay's famous "Minute on Indian Education" (1835), which sought to create a class of Indians "English in taste, in opinions, in morals, and in intellect," was all of a piece with this "civilizing mission" (Macaulay 2003 [1835]: 237). There were ebbs and flows in this endeavor throughout the nineteenth century – "Westernizing" impulses being countered by "Orientalizing" ones, self-conscious efforts at Anglicization being met by reassertions and in many ways reinventions of "traditional" institutions and practices – but the net effect was clearly one that brought about decisive and wide-ranging changes in Indian politics and society as India was inserted in the system of British-led global capitalism and its attendant ideologies (Moore 1999; Washbrook 1999).

Democracy, in the formal sense, did not come to Britain itself until the late nineteenth and early twentieth centuries, so one should not expect to hear much discussion of it in relation to India. What could be and was debated, however, was what we might call the infrastructure of democracy, the practices and institutions of civil society. Jeffrey Alexander has re-theorized this old concept as the "civil sphere," a sphere distinguished from both market and the state, and from other social spheres such as the family, as a "solidary sphere" concerned with the realization of universalistic norms of justice, and with practices of "civility, criticism, and mutual respect" (2006: 31). If we add to this the role of social

164

THE BRITISH RAJ AND ITS LEGACY FOR DEMOCRACY AND CIVIL SOCIETY

movements – emphasized by Alexander – in pressing for the realization of these goals, then India under the British Raj can undoubtedly be regarded as an arena in which struggles for the attainment of a functioning civil sphere palpably took place.

To the criticism of such as Jack Goody and Partha Chatterjee that the concept of civil society is a Western import, with imperial overtones, and therefore unsuitable for Indian traditions and aspirations, Suryakant Waghmore rightly argues that the origins of the concept in the West should not be an impediment to its applicability to Indian conditions and strivings.[2] The fact that Christianity originated in the Middle East does not make its principles inapplicable in other parts of the world. With reference to the still persisting problem of caste, which has created "a form of public in India which is exclusionary and based on status privileges," Waghmore emphasizes "civil society and democratic civility as they hold the promise of equality irrespective of status privileges in public spaces" (Waghmore 2013: xx–xxi, 5; see also Chatterjee 2001; Goody 2001).

Even more pertinent to our present purposes is Waghmore's claim that "civil society as a realm of political freedom in India emerged during the colonial period." He notes that "before the colonial interpolation of civil society, India had non-liberal forms of pluralism," but with "the widening scope of citizenship, these groups reconstituted themselves as political agents." These included crucially lower-caste groups, especially those exposed to Western education through Christian missionaries, and stimulated also by the growth of the press, military recruitment, and the development of cities. All of these resulted from changes initiated by the British. "What is important to note here is that the newly emerging realm of civil society, under an alien and partially secular colonial state, created a buzz of political activity in the public sphere with the formation of associations around identities and socio-religious issues. Civil society did not necessarily emerge in contradiction to the state; rather it was promoted by the colonial state at times to disaggregate the society and discipline its subjects" (Waghmore 2013: 7–16).

This seems the right emphasis. The British did not consciously set about to bring civil society – let alone democracy – in being in India. But the imperatives of rule, the need to get their worldwide empire – of which India was a nodal point – into some sort of rational order, led them to embark on a series of reforms that resulted in the transformation of Indian society. Among the changes were ones that brought into being – haltingly and not necessarily comfortably, from the British point of view – institutions that socialized and educated a wide variety of groups into new forms of politics and public engagement. Eventually these were to lead to the demand that the British leave India. When they did – with

165

THE INDIAN CIVIL SPHERE

what seems in retrospect unseemly haste – they left behind a legacy that constituted the substance of modern Indian politics. If, as some think, democracy and civil society are imperiled in today's India, the weapons to counter the threats, as well as to some extent the character of the threats themselves, nearly all derive from the armory built up by the British in their 200-year rule.

The British Raj: The Making of Modern India

For nearly 200 years, from Robert Clive's victory at Plassey in 1757 to the British departure in 1947, India was ruled by a people who over the course of the nineteenth century rose to become the most powerful nation in the world, building an empire that by 1920 occupied a quarter of the earth's land surface and incorporated a quarter of the world's population. A good part of the empire's population lay in India, and British India – the British Raj – was indeed "the jewel in the crown" of the British monarch.

It was inevitable that, in the wake of independence, Indians would focus on the British legacy – what the British had done in and to India, whether it was on the whole for the good or bad. The Mughal period was less discussed, except to some extent its final years when the Mughals were being displaced by the British – and so the Mughals as much as the Hindus could be seen as victims of the British.

Moreover, the British Raj was also undeniably a foreign regime, more so than its predecessors the Mughals, who could call upon a centuries-old Muslim presence in India. That perspective of "the stranger" might account for the well-known fact that in the eighteenth and nineteenth centuries there was considerable interest among British administrators, military personnel, and scholars in studying and investigating Indian society with a view to governing it better (Keay 1988; Cohn 1996: 16–56; Metcalf 1997: 9–27). Sir William Jones, with his pioneering work on Sanskrit, is the most celebrated, but there were many other, lesser-known, figures, such as Mountstuart Elphinstone, the scholar-administrator, whose magisterial *History of India: The Hindu and Mahometan Periods*, first published in 1839, is still much admired and drawn upon today. Warren Hastings himself founded the Bengal Asiatic Society, which, under Jones's presidency, became a forum for wide-ranging scholarly debates about India's past and its culture. Hastings' purpose was explicitly to get the British to understand the country they were ruling, and so fit their rule to its customs and traditions (Cohn 1996: 45). Nehru, whose *Discovery of India* bitterly attacked British rule, nevertheless conceded

THE BRITISH RAJ AND ITS LEGACY FOR DEMOCRACY AND CIVIL SOCIETY

that "to Jones, and to many other European scholars, India owes a deep debt of gratitude" (Nehru 2010 [1946]: 345–6).

Sir John Malcolm, who spent many years in the 1820s as an administrator in central India, urged that Indian opinion could be won over "by the consideration we show to their habits, institutions and religions," and that it was particularly important to learn the Indian languages (in Cohn 1996: 41–2). This was a view that was later roundly countered by Thomas Babington Macaulay, with his dismissal of the value of Indian languages and literature, and the need for all educated Indians to learn English so as to become "interpreters between us and the millions we govern" (Macaulay 2003 [1835]: 238). Malcolm and Macaulay represented what we might call the two poles of British views and policies about India: accommodation or assimilation, learning to live with and rule through "traditional" Indian civilization, or transforming India on a European model, "modernizing" it such that it would eventually acquire the capacity to rule itself (Washbrook 1999: 395–9). We should not forget that for "liberal imperialists" such as Macaulay the goal was always – however indefinitely in the future – Indian independence. "Whether such a day will ever come," said Macaulay, "I know not. But never will I attempt to avert or retard it. Whenever it comes, it will be the proudest day in English history" (in Metcalf 1997: 34).

British concern for the preservation of India's heritage continued in the later nineteenth century, under the powerful patronage among others of Lord Curzon, Viceroy from 1898 to 1905. Curzon made Britain's very alienness a source of strength. "A race like our own, who are themselves foreigners, are in a sense better fitted to guard, with a dispassionate and impartial zeal, the relics of different ages and of sometimes antagonistic beliefs, than might be the descendants of the warring races or the votaries of rival creed" (in Sengupta 2013: 180; see also Metcalf 1997: 153–5). But that concern did not inhibit the radical diffusion among Indian elites, following the Macaulay model, of English education and culture, nor the increasing impact of British institutions and practices. It might be true, as Thomas Metcalf argues, that the idea of Indian "difference" – its essentially Asiatic character, seen as timeless or frozen since an early efflorescence – increasingly, especially after the 1857 Mutiny, came to mark British ideologies of rule. But Metcalf himself shows the strong persistence of the liberal ideal throughout the period of British rule, culminating in the Montagu–Chelmsford Reforms of 1919, the Irwin Declaration of 1929, and the 1935 Government of India Act. "The transfer of power on 15 August 1947 was . . . the only outcome that could be anticipated from the ideals that sustained the Montagu–Chelmsford scheme" (Metcalf 1997: 230).

167

THE INDIAN CIVIL SPHERE

In the end, whatever the respect shown to Indian traditions – many of which the British can be said to have invented as much as preserved – the encounter between Britain and India was transformative. It could not have been otherwise. Britain in the nineteenth century was the world's most dynamic power, experiencing massive economic and social changes. Its empire straddled the world, carrying the effects of those changes to all corners of the globe. India, at the time of the British conquest, was politically weak and riven with internal conflicts as the Mughal empire succumbed to invasion and endemic crises. The British, as self-proclaimed successors to the Mughals, re-unified the country and set about ordering it in accordance with British ideas of law, administration, and good government. There was little to stand in their way. What might hold them back, what might slow the pace of change and check the extent of reform would come not from native opposition but from disagreements and conflicts within the ruling order itself.

The India of today, in its political, economic, institutional, and even to a good extent cultural form, is British India. The British in the nineteenth century changed it at all levels. They attacked *sati* and *thagi*. They discovered, reified, and made central the "village community" as the most basic organ of local life. They codified and systematized the Indian languages, organizing them according to the requirements of British rule. They gave India a usable history, based on the "comparative method," which saw India "as a kind of living museum of the European past" (Cohn 1996: 78). They surveyed, described, and collected Indian art and architecture, forming the categories bequeathed to Indian scholars. They classified the population into essentialized "religious communities" – Hindu, Muslim, Sikh – and made them the basis of separate electorates in successive measures of Indian representation at local and provincial levels from the late nineteenth to the early twentieth centuries. The British did not, as some have claimed, invent the caste system, but they gave it a fixity and a coherence generally lacking in the looser understandings of the traditional system (Dirks 2001: 18; see also Bayly 1999; Inden 2000: 49–84).

Culturally, there was English schooling, at home and abroad, for India's elites. The language of instruction in all elite schools and in all higher educational institutions was English. The English public school was the model for a number of outstanding private schools, such as the Doon School in Dehradun and St. Columba's in Delhi, while Oxbridge provided the model for the top colleges and universities, such as St. Stephen's in Delhi (1881). Earlier, in 1857, the British founded universities in Calcutta, Bombay, and Madras – "a turning point towards the modern mode of collaboration" – whose graduates by 1882 accounted for some 1,100 appointments to government service (Moore 1999: 431). Teaching staff – many of them in the early days British – in these institutions had nearly all received their education in England, often at English public schools and Oxbridge. Wealthy and established Indian families might choose to send their sons directly to England for education. The first President of an independent India, Jawaharlal Nehru, educated at Rugby School and Trinity College, Cambridge, was a typical product of this practice. Doctors and lawyers too – Mohandas Gandhi among the latter – might also complete their training in England.

The English spread their mania for sport – again, mainly the ones developed at the English public schools. But cricket became a truly national game in India, affecting all levels of society (cricket, says the sociologist Ashis Nandy, is "an Indian game accidentally discovered by the English"). It seems fairly clear today that even if all other traces of the English legacy were to disappear in India, cricket would remain, so popular has it become, and so lucrative a business. Indian cricketing heroes share the limelight, and the headlines, with Bollywood actors and actresses.

Even Indian nationalism, when it came, carried a heavy British stamp. The Indian National Congress, which was to be the main bearer of Indian nationalism until independence, held its first meeting in 1885. Its main organizer and for many years its general-secretary and principal spokesman was a Scot, Allan Octavian Hume, son of a famous reformer and Radical member of the British Parliament. A. O. Hume, who had himself served as Secretary of Agriculture in the Bengal government, was joined in launching the Indian National Congress by two other former British members of the Indian Civil Service, the Englishmen George Yule (first president of the Congress) and the Scot William Wedderburn. Later Annie Besant, the English theosophist and champion of Indian Home Rule, became the first female – and fifth British – president of the Indian Congress (Paz 1997: 107).

The Indians who joined them in establishing the Congress party were all educated Anglophones, steeped in British and European culture. They drew on British political ideas and British political traditions in arguing the case for greater participation by Indians in Indian affairs. "The Western context of learning carried the assumption of India's advance towards constitutionalism and the enjoyment of civil rights" (Moore 1999: 431; see also Seal 1968). Until the First World War, and specifically the Amritsar massacre of 1919 which galvanized Indian opinion, most Indian nationalists – including Tagore and Gandhi – argued for Indian self-rule *within* the British empire (rather like Irish nationalists until the First World War). The model was the Dominion status acquired by the white colonies, Canada, Australia, New Zealand, South Africa.

Some scholars have argued for the native roots of Indian nationalism (e.g., Chatterjee 1993); but whatever native – mainly Hindu, Muslims felt increasingly shut out – elements there may have been, there can be no question that the form and a good deal of the content of Indian nationalism drew on European models, and specifically British ideas.

Anglicization à la Macaulay of course affected mainly the upper levels of Indian society, the professionals and educators, the scholars and writers, the bureaucrats and military men who played so large a part in running the British Raj. But it penetrated sufficiently into lower levels of society – for instance among the legions of clerks and secretaries who staffed the civil service organizations, and among village school teachers and village leaders – as to constitute a profound reshaping of Indian society (Cohn 1996: 21; James 1998: 645).

Something similar had occurred with Mughal rule, but there were two significant differences. One was that in the wake of Mughal rule, there were, and are, millions of practicing Muslims in India. Christianity under the British made few converts, and the British themselves did not settle in large numbers. When the British withdrew, they left behind plenty of evidence, material and cultural, of their 200-year presence, but they themselves were not there.

The other significant difference is one of temporality. India had had foreign rule for nearly a thousand years. The Mughals, and the earlier Muslim rulers, had to some extent fused with the native Hindus. The British did not fuse. They remained acutely conscious of their difference from Indians, and from native Hindu culture (Muslim culture, especially at the courtly level such as practiced at Hyderabad or Lucknow, was more attractive to them). This was partly due to different civilizational traditions; but it was also due to the point in time at which the two civilizations encountered each other. India was by no means some unchanging, "traditional," society, sunk in "Oriental Despotism"; but by the eighteenth and nineteenth centuries Britain was leading the way in becoming a dynamic modern society to a degree and extent that India was not. It was an encounter between unequals, and the outcome was clear by the second half of the nineteenth century.

The British were not just the latest conquerors, such that their impress on contemporary India was likely to be the strongest. They were also modern in a way that the Mughals had not been, and British modernity was therefore bound to be something of a template for Indian modernity once the British had left. And so it has proved. The English language remains dominant among educated Indians, not least because any native rivals, such as Hindi, stir up regional animosities. British parliamentary institutions and the British party system are the hallmarks

THE BRITISH RAJ AND ITS LEGACY FOR DEMOCRACY AND CIVIL SOCIETY

of Indian democracy today. The British system of justice, perhaps the most admired aspect of British rule, is the Indian system of justice. The Indian educational system, with outstanding institutions at every level, is a clear product of the British, especially English, educational system, and English remains the preferred language of instruction. "Hinglish," a variant form of English, is commonly spoken, in families and among friends.

The Tharoor Indictment

How should we assess this British legacy? Its presence is undeniable, but has it been for the good or the bad? Is Indian democracy, or Indian civil society, the better for it? These questions have been debated for a century, with inconclusive results. A spirited defense of British rule, shortly after Indian independence, was made by the Bengali intellectual Nirad C. Chaudhuri, in his *Autobiography of an Unknown Indian*, dedicated to the British empire and containing the ringing declaration that "all that was good and living within us was made, shaped and quickened by . . . British rule" (Chaudhuri 1951: 1).[3]

Chaudhuri remains distinctly in the minority, at least among recent Indian writers. Currently probably the most popular and widely-discussed account of the effects of British rule is that of the veteran UN official, writer, and Congress MP Shashi Tharoor's *Inglorious Empire: What the British Did to India* (2017). Tharoor had already tried out his arguments in a debate at the Oxford Union in 2015, on the motion "Britain Owes Reparations to Her Former Colonies." Having handsomely won the debate, Tharoor was inspired to turn his speech into a full-length book (published within a year of the debate).

Calling Chaudhuri a "notorious Anglophile," and his *Autobiography* "cringe-worthy," Tharoor in his own account lambasts the British for the devastation they have wrought on Indian society. He attacks on all fronts, economic, political, cultural. The British destroyed India's thriving textile industry, in order to flood India with cheap machine-made Manchester cottons. Their vaunted claim to have been the first to "unify" India politically can be questioned: India was substantially unified under the great Mauryan emperor Ashoka, and in any case has for long had a "sacred geography" – of "mountains, forests, rivers, hilltop shrines linked with tracks of pilgrimages" – that has given it an enduring sense of identity and unity (Tharoor 2017: 38).

Political institutions had been built up by the Mughals and the Marathas, and these could have been the building blocks of "a modern

THE INDIAN CIVIL SPHERE

constitutional monarchy" in India. But the British dismantled existing political institutions and stirred up "communal division" in the interests of their own continuing rule. Moreover, for the same reasons they shored up the political power of the "feudal" princes, giving them a new lease of life when their influence was waning. Tharoor also regards the various measures to increase Indian representation in government as window-dressing, not leading to any real empowerment of Indians, as real power remained in the hands of the Viceroy and the British Parliament (2017: 68–9).

Tharoor rejects the view of British historian the late Christopher Bayly (2012), that Britain helped liberal democracy take root in India by institutionalizing it through colleges and universities, newspapers, and colonial law courts. He accepts that "it must be acknowledged that it was the British who first established newspapers in India, which had been unknown before colonial rule," and that this allowed for a good deal of critical discussion of British policies (2017: 82). But he contends that a series of repressive acts – such as the Vernacular Press Act of 1878, and even more drastically the Rowlatt Act of 1919 – limited free expression, and led often to the arrest and imprisonment of journalists and editors. He seems to suggest that such a legacy might underlie the clamp-down on public opinion imposed by Indira Gandhi during the period of Emergency Rule (1975–7), since Mrs. Gandhi relied on legal powers inherited from the British. But he need only to turn to other democracies, such as those of Britain, France, and the United States, to find many other similar moments of the restriction of freedom of speech and writing, usually for the same reasons adduced by Mrs. Gandhi. "States of exception" are common in all democracies; on this score India may be said on the whole to have fared very well since independence. So far only Mrs. Gandhi has invoked emergency powers.

And what of Britain's vaunted parliamentary system? Was this not a boon to Indian democracy, one of the most precious legacies of British rule? Not so, says Tharoor. It is not only subject to many faults – as we can see in its operation in Britain and elsewhere today – but it was from the start a foreign import that was alien to Indian traditions. "The parliamentary system has not merely outlived any good it could do; it was from the start unsuited to Indian conditions and is primarily responsible for many of the nation's principal political ills" (Tharoor 2017: 87). What alternatives might be proposed remain shadowy; there are certainly few viable precedents in India's past, Hindu or Mogul. As in Western democracies, the parliamentary system in India might be thought, to adapt Winston Churchill, the least worst system, the one most capable of saving Indian democracy from its faults.

172

As for Britain's mission of bringing law to "lesser breeds without it," in Kipling's terms, Tharoor is equally skeptical. The British imposed their codes of law, and their legal system, on "an older and more complex civilization with its own legal culture." This involved "coercion and cruelty," and the reshaping of Indian "civil society" in a manner designed to help the British maintain their rule rather than to bring justice to Indians (2017: 93). When Lord Ripon attempted, through the Ilbert Bill of 1883, to allow Indian judges to hear cases involving Europeans, there was a massive racist outcry among the British, leading to a very watered down version of the Bill.

But Tharoor might have pointed out that it was the intense controversy aroused by the Ilbert Bill – "the most momentous clash of ideologies in British India" (Metcalf 1997: 203) – that led directly to the founding of the Indian National Congress and the movement for (eventual) national independence. The initiative was a reaction, led by English officials (as we have seen), to the opposition shown by those British who refused to acknowledge what was regarded by many as the most fundamental justification of the British imperial mission: equality before the law. It was this that had been promised in Queen Victoria's Proclamation of 1858, when she declared that "all shall alike enjoy the equal and impartial protection of the Law." The Bill's supporters – who included the Viceroy Lord Ripon and most of the senior members of the Indian government – knew that a cardinal principle of British rule was at stake (Moore 1999: 433). That they had in the end to accept a compromise showed that the liberal vision for India was still a long way from being realized; but it was that very vision that made it possible for the struggle to be taken forward by, among others, the British-trained lawyer Mohandas Gandhi.

Assessing the British Legacy

Tharoor's account is by no means new. It follows closely, though less temperately, the view of the British Raj and its impact on India in Nehru's canonical *The Discovery of India*, first published in 1946; and it is preceded by several recent studies of the Raj that make substantially the same case against the British (e.g. Chakravarty 1991; Wilson 2016).[4] Moreover, though not necessarily with the detail that Tharoor gives, many works by current postcolonial authors offer the same indictment of British rule, as a representative example of the oppression of European colonial rule in general (e.g., Andrews 2021).

What makes Tharoor a suitable focus for our discussion is his status as a public figure and the fact that his book has attracted much attention

THE INDIAN CIVIL SPHERE

in India and elsewhere; it also states in direct and popular form what more scholarly accounts tend to put guardedly and with many qualifications.

The terms of the indictment of British rule have been endlessly debated, and no doubt will continue to be so, since they lend themselves to such a variety of interpretations and so complex a calculus of measurement.[5] But in respect of the effect of British rule on the current functioning of Indian democracy and civil society one thing ought surely to stand out. That is that the very disputes and debates, the concepts and practices, that are discussed occur within the framework of the political legacy handed down by the British. So much of the apparatus of Indian democracy and civil society is the product of British rule that it makes it hard to find standards of judgment outside it. The Indian parliamentary system, the electoral and party system, the bureaucratic organization, the military system, the educational system, the wide variety of newspapers, even the broadcasting system – modeled on the BBC – all were either set up by the British or based on their practices. Even the special treatment of the "Untouchables," the Dalits at the base of the caste system, was pioneered by the British, in the 1935 Government of India Act. More generally the constitution adopted by the Constituent Assembly after independence was "but a revised version of that introduced by the 1935 Government of India Act," including the emergency powers that could be called upon by the center, and which were put to such draconian effect by Indira Gandhi in 1975–7 (Keay 2004: 519).

One can of course discuss the operations of Indian democracy today – how fair or efficient it is, how stable, how representative of the vast diversity of communities across the subcontinent? Most observers have been impressed by the fact that, compared with many postcolonial societies, not least its neighbor, Pakistan, Indian democracy has been remarkably resilient and long-lasting. Only the years of Mrs. Gandhi's "Emergency Decrees" have spoilt what has otherwise been a largely unblemished record. This by itself has to be seen as a testimony to the British legacy, given that Indian democracy is largely an extension of British democracy (its republican constitution notwithstanding). Indian democracy has the faults of British democracy – as of all democracies – but also its strengths, including respect for the rule of law, acceptance of electoral outcomes, and a powerful Lower House, the Lok Sabha, with a long tradition of informed parliamentary debate. India is particularly well-served by a flourishing free press, with a variety of opinions vigorously expressed, much of it at the local level in the vernacular; while the national, English-language, newspapers and magazines have a standard of writing and report-

THE BRITISH RAJ AND ITS LEGACY FOR DEMOCRACY AND CIVIL SOCIETY

ing that stands comparison with their counterparts anywhere in the world.[6]

In one area, that concerning communal identities, Tharoor and others are right to see that British policies of *divide et impera* sharpened and deepened, even if they did not create, the bitter divisions that led to the tragedy of the 1948 Partition, and the communal massacres that attended it. In the wake of the 1857 Mutiny, where the British found Hindus and Muslims united against them, the British sought to divide the communities and give them a sense of separate identity. As a counterweight to the Indian National Congress, seen as a vehicle for Hindu aspirations (which it certainly was not in its early days), the British sponsored the formation of the rival Muslim League. Indian nationalists regarded Lord Curzon's attempt to partition Bengal in 1905 as an attempt to create a Muslim-majority province in the east, and so vigorously – and, in the end, successfully – resisted it. From the Morley–Minto reforms of 1909 to the Government of India Act in 1935, the British designed electorates that were divided by religion (in addition, in 1935, to recognizing the "Untouchables" as a separate constituency).

The Mughals had sought to fuse Muslim and Hindu cultures and identities; the British pushed them apart. There was no thought of a separate Muslim-majority state until the early 1940s; but the ground had been prepared by British policies going back well into the nineteenth century. If the government of Narendra Modi and the BJP have exploited Hindu–Muslim differences to an extreme and dangerous degree, the British must carry some of the blame for their deliberate accentuation of those differences.

There is no warrant, therefore, for seeing the British legacy as wholly beneficial, and indeed, even those who think that in general India benefited from British rule tend to hedge their assessment with severe qualifications (e.g., Ferguson 2004: 216–18; Biggar 2023). But Lawrence James is right to say, with reference not just to India but also Pakistan and Bangladesh, that in good measure "these countries are what they are now because they were once governed by Britain and brought directly into contact with British ideas, values, learning and technology" (1998: 644). Gandhi and Nehru, no less than Muslim nationalist Jinnah, fought the British with tools and ideas derived from their British education and extensive experience of British life.

A remarkable testimony to this legacy was pronounced by the former Indian Prime Minister, Dr. Manmohan Singh, in his acceptance speech at the award of an Honorary Doctorate from Oxford University on July 8, 2005. Dr. Singh was no uncritical apologist for British rule. But he felt impelled to offer a tribute to what had been gained from it.

175

Today, with the balance and perspective offered by the passage of time and the benefit of hindsight, it is possible for an Indian Prime Minister to assert that India's experience with Britain had its beneficial consequences too. Our notions of the rule of law, of a Constitutional government, of a free press, of a professional civil service, of modern universities and research laboratories have all been fashioned in the crucible where an age-old civilization met the dominant Empire of the day. These are all elements which we still value and cherish. Our judiciary, our legal system, our bureaucracy and our police are all great institutions, derived from British-Indian administration and they have served our country exceedingly well. (cf., though more guardedly, Sen 2021)

Speaking of "the idea of India enshrined in our Constitution," Manmohan Singh discerns ancient Indian roots. But, he says, "it is undeniable that the founding fathers of our Republic were also greatly influenced by the ideas associated with the age of enlightenment in Europe," and that "our Constitution remains a testimony to the enduring interplay between what is essentially Indian and what is very British in our intellectual heritage." He goes on to say that "of all the legacies of the Raj, none is more important than the English language and the modern school system. That is, of course, if you leave out cricket!" (Singh 2005).

The novelist V. S. Naipaul, who had a complicated relation to India, the land of his ancestors, in the last of his trilogy of books on India also thought that one of the enduring legacies of British rule was that it gave India a sense of unity and an idea of its national self.

The British peace after the 1857 Mutiny can be seen as a kind of luck. It was a time of intellectual recruitment. . . . In the 130 or so years since the Mutiny – the last 90 years of British rule and the first 40 years of independence begin increasingly to appear as part of the same historical period – the idea of freedom has gone everywhere in India. . . . People everywhere have ideas now of who they are and what they owe themselves. . . . There was in India now what didn't exist 200 years before: a central will, a central intellect, a national idea. (Naipaul 1991: 517–18)

"The Independence of 1947 was the triumph of British ideas and institutions ... without the British," says another astute observer, Octavio Paz (1997: 53). Indian nationalism, and the very idea of India, developed through an intense engagement with Western ideas, filtered through the British educational system – whether in India or Britain. Here one encounters the familiar feature of the imperial creation of nationalism, "imperial ethnicities," in John Darwin's formulation, a process which worked "not by promoting a 'tame' indigeneity, but by subsuming local sources of meaning in a new supra-local identity" (Darwin 2013: 150; see also Kumar 2021: 72–93). For these ethnicities – "Hindu,"

THE BRITISH RAJ AND ITS LEGACY FOR DEMOCRACY AND CIVIL SOCIETY

"Muslim," "Sikh," or pan-Indian – empire provided not merely the arena for greater opportunities and mobility but also the resources for constructing oppositional identities. It was an education in nationhood. "The Indians who became increasingly drawn into the process of transformation of their own traditions and modes of thought were ... far from passive. In the long run the authoritative control that the British tried to exercise over the new social and material technologies was taken over by Indians and put to purposes which led to the ultimate erosion of British authority" (Cohn 1996: 56).

Indian democracy and civil society today, in both their strength and weaknesses, are substantially British creations. That does not diminish the importance in them of Hindu, Muslim, and other pre-British elements, nor the active participation of Indians in the construction of the civil sphere – impossible to imagine without Gandhi, for example. It is simply a statement of a rather obvious fact, that the British took over India when they themselves were revolutionizing their own society, and when they had the power to apply in India – and in some cases try out almost for the first time – ideas and practices that they themselves were still working through at home (Stokes 1959; Viswanathan 1990). In the process they transformed Indian society to an extent that had not even been attempted, let alone achieved, by previous conquerors. It is as futile to deny that as it is irrelevant to praise or blame it.

Empire has been a fact of world history; India has been drawn into that history for more than 600 years. The British were the latest and, so far, the last conquerors. But they were different from previous conquerors. Even as they tried to insulate their own people from the effects of their Indian environment, and however concerned to preserve many of the artistic and other cultural remembrances of India's past, they systematically set about reordering the society that they ruled in accordance with British ideas of law, justice, administration, and education. They also set in train economic changes that began the still-continuing process of industrialization and modernization. In doing so they brought into being modern Indian society. That is what most Indians inhabit today; it is there, and in the terms with which it was constructed, that the struggles for democracy and civil society go on today.

Commentary: India and the Civil Horizons of Political Community

Trevor Stack

My longstanding concern has been with the exercise of political authority, and specifically on how and when the governed engage and are engaged in the exercise of authority over them, to the extent they are considered *members* of a polity, which is how I understand political community. To study political community requires keen attention to who or what exercises political authority, and over whom, and to the myriad ways in which those subject to political authority are variously invoked and involved in its exercise – complicating any attempt to sort authority's exercise into simple binaries like "democratic" and "authoritarian" (Stack and Luminiello 2022).

The present volume gives rich accounts of how political authority is exercised in India, and of how those subject to political authority are engaged in its exercise over them: in ways that vary not only between citizens and non-citizens but between diverse categories of citizen, and which shift over time. Historically, the epigraph chosen by Kumar reminds us that nation was only the latest version of political community in India:

> We had known the hordes of Moghals and Pathans who invaded India, but we had known them as human races, with their own religions and customs, likes and dislikes, – we had never known them as a nation. ... But this time [with the British] we had to deal, not with kings, not with human races, but with a nation, – we, who are no nation ourselves. (Tagore 1917: 19)

Nation brought with it the status of citizenship by which those living within national borders were classified as Indian, giving them a stake in the authority exercised over them by the new Indian state. As Holston (2009) indicates for Brazil, citizenship was always subject to numerous

INDIA AND THE CIVIL HORIZONS OF POLITICAL COMMUNITY

qualifications and distinctions, and these were never static. Caste and religion cut across Indian citizenship, as seen in the recent Citizenship Amendment Act, which privileged Hindus over Muslims as candidates for naturalization. Further, as Gudavarthy indicates, the current government builds its political authority through decentralization and disrupting established client networks by privileging other groups, reworking political community in the process:

> It is intriguing that even as the [Modi[regime harps on about nationalism, it actually thrives on regionalism and localism. By mobilizing the local in a "conflictual unity," it strengthens the national/center and other dominant forms. For instance, it supports the formation of smaller states for better governance, and decentralization for more participation but deploys these processes, in effect, to create a stronger center and greater centralization of decision-making processes. Similarly, it mobilizes smaller sects among the Dalits and the Other Backward Classes (OBCs) by providing them with more political representation against the more dominant sects/subcastes within the Dalits and the OBCs. In this way, consent is gained as it breaks the patron–client relation between the dominant and weaker subcastes within the Dalits and the OBCs. But that also weakens consolidated Dalit or OBC resistance against the domination and exclusion by the dominant-caste Hindus. (p. 114)

Moreover, several authors cite Partha Chatterjee's older argument (2004) that only middle-class Indians embody the kind of political community that he dubs "civil society," as individual citizens making claims via established legal channels and institutions. Chatterjee uses the term "political society" to make the contrast with how subaltern groups engage with government, positioning themselves as "targets" for financial aid or making moral claims for recognition or as representatives of their respective subcastes. These are profoundly different textures of political community, ways of being invoked and involved in the business of governing. Yet the authors demonstrate, as others have, that Chatterjee's distinction is overdrawn, since subaltern groups do make claims consistent with what he dubs civil society, including by appealing to the Supreme Court. Further, Modi's regime has engaged subaltern groups in a new nationalism that changes the political claims open to them and, in the process, the political claims made by and on them.

I have long found civil sphere theory (CST) useful for enriching our understanding of political community – it helps us to apprehend political community's *civil horizons*. CST (in my reading) draws our attention to discourses of moral civilization, which hold up standards of proper conduct and mutual treatment, understood to bind actors deemed civilized, even if they differ and conflict in every other way. States, for example,

179

commonly claim that the standards of conduct they demand of citizens are not sui generis but reflect widely accepted civilizational norms. Citizens may pitch their expectations of states, and of each other, in similar terms. Further, states and citizens alike may call for treatment of non-citizens as civilized beings, for example, as political refugees. Conversely, they may distinguish between more and less civil citizens – this is one way in which citizens are differentiated. Thus, the civil horizons of political community *stretch beyond but also cut across political community*, as they shape the relationship between those who govern and the governed. International human rights norms are an obvious example; another is the discourse of social welfare that gelled in the 1940s.

Political community's civil horizons may *find a footing in the institutions* through which political authority is exercised. CST's strong claim is that civil discourse can affect sphere differentiation, opening spheres in which civil values have traction, as opposed to the values of other spheres, such as market, politics, or religion. Civil spheres may even function as *master spheres* to the extent that other spheres, even as they are subject to other values, are expected to remain within civil limits, and by setting and policing the boundaries between spheres – what practices can be deemed religious, for example, and what freedom that affords (Stack et al. 2015). Civil spheres operate as master spheres when, for example, civil discourse has traction in courts and the media, and where prestigious texts like constitutions can be drawn on to articulate civil values and determine how they are to apply across spheres. Alexander gives the US and UK examples of financial misconduct arising from inadequate government regulation or of judicial scrutiny of media misconduct as in the phone hacking scandal (Alexander 2018). Civil repair is, moreover, the process through which those deemed uncivil come to be recognized as civil and worthy of treatment as such – Alexander's best-known example is that of African-Americans through the Civil Rights struggle (Alexander 2006).

I have said that the lens of political community helps to complicate simple dichotomies like democratic and authoritarian, or indeed subject and citizen. The examples I have given reflect Alexander's emphasis: democracy thrives when underpinned by a particular civilizational vision, one that values the inherent equality of each person, whatever other differences. However, Alexander acknowledges that civil discourses are also deployed, for example, to stigmatize Jews or Catholics as uncivil, or denigrating immigrants as ungrateful and unruly. Others have shown that civility has in modern times served to justify capitalist and imperialist expansion and has been harnessed by states to discipline and repress (Fitzgerald 2007). Authoritarian states have also sometimes harnessed

INDIA AND THE CIVIL HORIZONS OF POLITICAL COMMUNITY

discourses of moral civilization, insisting that they embody accepted standards of civil conduct, alongside or instead of claims to embody the will of gods or peoples. More broadly, Alexander also accepts that the codes of liberal democracy are only one set of civilizational discourse in the contemporary world – for example, Palmer (2019) treats Confucianism as civil discourse in China.

India is an extraordinary case for considering the civil horizons of political community, and this book offers rich material for doing so.

Most authors across the CST literature have looked for dynamics comparable to the US processes that Alexander described in *The Civil Sphere* (2006). The comparison is easier with constitutional democracies like South Korea than it is with China, for example. Constitutions typically evoke a civilizational frontier for political community, and those with a grievance can appeal to that horizon. They do so especially when political institutions including constitutional courts give traction to their grievances, which typically happens after sympathetic attention from prestigious media, and often following protest which – even if radical – comes to be seen as constitutional.

However, authors across the CST literature have also found differences in how this basic structure plays out. These differences in cases often reflect profound differences in the constitutions themselves, in the institutions that offer recourse, in access to those institutions by those subject to political authority, and in regulations and attitudes concerning the kinds of protest that are acceptable. For example, I compare Alexander's case of the US Civil Rights Movement to the Mexican Zapatistas, who eschewed their Maoist origins to stage an armed rebellion that was – nevertheless – garlanded by national and international civil society, and which led eventually to a constitutional reform respecting indigenous rights (Stack 2019). An obvious difference is that, in the Mexican context, it came to be dignified as a civil struggle.

This book includes several cases – especially in the opening chapters by Gorringe and Damodaran and by Chalwadi – in which Indian actors appeal to powerful Indian institutions like the Supreme Court, often with the Constitution in their hand, and with the support of some media. They demonstrate how, for example, Indian politicians are chastised by the media articulating public opinion, and how local dominant castes get their come-uppance: for example, as Chalwadi recounts, when a young inter-caste couple are attacked with machetes and this is then vindicated publicly by caste champions. Just as public lynching in the post-Reconstruction US South, such acts reflect how political community in these contexts is the preserve of certain sectors, and deeply hierarchical. And yet, for example:

181

THE INDIAN CIVIL SPHERE

Though protests took place across India, one major protest took place at Delhi's Jantar Mantar and was called for by various civil society groups and attended by students, concerned citizens, and politicians from opposition parties. One of the left-leaning politicians present at the protest site, commenting on the lawlessness in Uttar Pradesh, suggested "a caste code [is] in operation, not the Constitution of India" (*The Wire* 2020a). The binary of sacred (the Constitution) and profane (caste) was used heavily by protestors to frame themselves as inside the civil code – rational, justice-oriented, law-abiding, and anti-caste people – whereas others now included the state, police, and ruling regime, framed in non-civil terms: as caste apologists, orthodox, and Hindu fundamentalists. (p. 62)

This example reflects the basic structure of civil sphere dynamics outlined in *The Civil Sphere*, and it is comparable as such with Alexander's US cases.

By seeking examples comparable to the US cases, however, the authors may risk overemphasizing the frequency and traction of such protests, including whether – as Alexander insists for the US – they lead to civil repair, that is, wrongs being perceived as such and righted, allowing constitutional values to triumph. This requires those values to take priority preferably through powerful institutions, that is, through what Alexander terms a civil sphere, setting effective limits for other spheres, including the political one thus inflecting political community – again, how the governed are engaged in the governing, for example as voters. Chatterjee (2004) insists, by contrast, that the subaltern only rarely has access to the recourse typical of "civil society," notably by having their claims to their constitutional rights as citizens taken up and upheld by institutions from established media to the courts and Congress.[1]

India's Constitutional Horizons – Beyond Authenticity

Kumar stresses that India's constitutional framework is itself far from sui generis. Together with other frameworks around the world, it descends from the British tradition with its civilizational horizons:

The aim was "the flowering on Indian soil of those institutions which defined Britain's own society and civilization," among which were private property, the rule of law, the liberty of the individual, and Western forms of knowledge and education (Metcalf 1997: 35). Macaulay's famous "Minute on Indian Education" (1835), which sought to create a class of Indians "English in taste, in opinions, in morals, and in intel-

INDIA AND THE CIVIL HORIZONS OF POLITICAL COMMUNITY

lect," was all of a piece with this "civilizing mission" (Macaulay 2003 [1835]: 237). (p. 164)

Those civil discourses were not static in Britain and they shifted through the years of British rule, and all the more so after independence. Nevertheless, Kumar concludes:

> So much of the apparatus of Indian democracy and civil society is the product of British rule that it makes it hard to find standards of judgment outside it. The Indian parliamentary system, the electoral and party system, the bureaucratic organization, the military system, the educational system, the wide variety of newspapers, even the broadcasting system – modeled on the BBC – all were either set up by the British or based on their practices. Even the special treatment of the "Untouchables," the Dalits at the base of the caste system, was pioneered by the British, in the 1935 Government of India Act. More generally the constitution adopted by the Constituent Assembly after independence was "but a revised version of that introduced by the 1935 Government of India Act . . . (Keay 2004: 519). (p. 174)

Otherwise put, the Indian state has inherited much of the civil horizon bequeathed by the British, to the extent that – for Kumar – it is difficult to stand outside of that horizon.

Wary of that legacy, other authors have argued that political community in India needs decolonizing, and Chatterjee's account can be read in that vein. In colonial times, few Indian subjects were considered fully civil in British terms, able to engage and be engaged by the institutions of British rule. Chatterjee argues that Indian constitutionalism remains the preserve of a relative elite which he terms "civil society." Several authors of the present book appear similarly critical of the scope of Indian constitutionalism. Gudavarthy notes, though, that postcolonial and Marxist critiques have since been reworked by Modi's government to undermine the autonomy of India's liberal democratic institutions, and to rework the fabric of political community, as discussed below.

The volume might have benefited from a more nuanced account of India's constitutional horizons. In *India: Political Ideas and the Making of a Democratic Discourse*, Mahajan (2013) has cautioned against looking for authenticity, whether British or Indian, in India's constitutional framework. Instead, she points to the complex historical processes by which political community is gestated. To begin with, Mahajan observes of the 1948 Constituent Assembly that performatively it gave rise to a powerful myth – all India's "communities" were engaged in drafting the Constitution – which still motivates commitment to the Indian

183

THE INDIAN CIVIL SPHERE

state by an extraordinary range of political actors. Further, Mahajan demonstrates how, against the staggeringly diverse background of post-independence India, such concepts as equality, freedom, and religion were refracted through India's constitutional debates, and in the process given new life and form. Mahajan recounts, for example, how spokesmen for India's Hindu majority agreed to minority recognition because they saw accommodating diversity as a hallmark of Hinduism, and diversity came to be accepted as a marker of the Indian nation.[2] Otherwise put, political community's civil horizons were imagined as hybrid from the start.

Tolerance for Diversity, Sphere Differentiation, and Civility at a Distance

Mahajan also describes how the Constituent Assembly gave rise to a distinction between cultural and political spheres, which has marked Indian political community ever since. In the political sphere, citizens were expected to engage as individuals; difference between communities was accommodated in the cultural sphere, as tolerance for diversity.

Several authors in this book bear out Mahajan's concern that caste remained an axis, even in the political sphere, in post-independence India.[3] For example, Gorringe and Damodaran maintain:

> Whilst the Indian Constitution created a nation of equal citizens in 1950, that legislation has lacked the cultural legitimacy required to engender widespread change. The Constitution did contribute to the delegitimization of caste authority, with the result that caste norms are increasingly upheld through violent means. In this chapter we have charted how the incivilities of caste continue to erode the sense of fraternity and common citizenship that Ambedkar saw as the bedrock of a new nation. In the eyes of dominant castes, quite simply, Dalits remain polluted and marginal members of the polity. This explains why Thirumavalavan, the leader of the Liberation Panthers, used his maiden speech as an MP in the Lok Sabha in 2009 to insist that: "Without eradicating untouchability we cannot develop democracy" (Lok Sabha Debates 2009). (p. 52)

Further, the political sphere has been dominated by endless disputes over minority recognition. Reading Mahajan's account of difference in India is exhausting:

> [N]o community could be unambiguously identified as the majority, not even the Hindus. Within the Hindus, the lower castes, which had been segregated and discriminated against for centuries, could not be

184

categorized with the rest as a majority. They were perhaps the most vulnerable and marginalized group in society. The situation became even more complicated after the linguistic reorganization of states. Now, even among the dominant Hindu castes, Bengali-speaking Hindus have become a minority in the state of Tamil Nadu and Telugu-speaking Hindus a minority in other states. (2013: 119)

Gudavarthy recounts how "mezzanine elites" have emerged to champion their castes or subcastes, yet in the process generating new intra-caste hierarchies:

To overcome the condition of subalternity, marginalized and excluded social groups use the secular rubric as an ethical civil repair to demand justice against inequality, but one that does not question the unevenness of "graded inequalities" within marginalized groups. The impact on the political landscape of India and its social movements was a proliferation of intra-subaltern conflicts. . . . Questioning inequality vis-à-vis the dominant castes does not guarantee solidarity – psychological and emotional identification – against unevenness within marginalized groups. This partly explains the split between an admiration for diversity in the abstract as against the practice of segregation and prejudice in the concrete. (p. 120)

On this latter note, Gudavarthy cites a recent Pew Research Center report that 66 percent of Hindus view themselves as being very different from Muslims, while 64 percent of Muslims similarly see themselves as very different from Hindus. The report concludes that Indians "simultaneously express enthusiasm for religious tolerance and a consistent preference for keeping their religious communities in segregated spheres – *they live together separately* [my emphasis]."

Civility at a distance is not unique to India's civil code – far from it. In Europe, the fault lines are similarly religious, whether Protestant and Catholic or more recently Christian and Muslim.

Most authors in the book acknowledge that Modi's government has significantly reworked the texture of political community and its civil horizons.

Hindutva: Reimagining Political Community and its Civil Horizons

Some authors in the book apply CST only to what Chatterjee dubs "civil society." Others are prepared to consider Hindutva as a species of civil discourse with its own civil sphere dynamics. This is provocative because the term "civil" might appear to confer legitimacy on Modi's

THE INDIAN CIVIL SPHERE

authoritarian politics. However, I use the term "civil" more neutrally than other CST authors, and I believe my account of CST can be usefully applied to the Hindutva project.

I have mentioned that tolerance of diversity was accepted by Hindu delegates in 1948 because they viewed it as consistent with Hindu civilization. Champions of Hindutva now disparage secular civil society as alien – Gudavarthy observes that "Secular notions of civility thereby come across as a 'borrowed' worldview: 'western,' elitist and, sectarian." However, several authors in the book observe that Hindutva incorporates elements of the constitutional tradition.

Waghmore maintains that Hindutva is best understood as a civil religion, following Bellah, rather than as a fully-fledged civil sphere. For Waghmore, only a secularist civil sphere offers the opportunity for Muslims to be recognized as fully civil subjects. It can be objected that India's secular civil sphere did little more than Hindutva to afford full citizenship to Muslims, much less to eradicate caste. That is, sphere differentiation between politics and religion has hardly been emancipatory in India. Neither is it clear that religions are necessarily more exclusive and hierarchical than secularism.[4]

Modi has built his political authority on a vision of Hindu civilization, by which the Indian state is the natural locus of Hindutva. This should not surprise us. Alexander in *The Civil Sphere* was right to insist that the US civil sphere was not *merely* a creature of state. However, states do adopt and adapt civilizational horizons, shaping how they engage with citizens and non-citizens – hence the idea of the "welfare state," for example (Alexander et al. 2019a). Hindutva is a nationalist discourse, but it is a nationalism with strong civilizational overtones. An example is Modi's speech to the G20 summit in 2023:

> As the "Mother of Democracy," our belief in dialogue and democratic principles has been unwavering since time immemorial. Our global conduct is rooted in the fundamental principle of "Vasudhaiva Kutumbakam," which means "world is one family." (Modi 2023)

Modi's vision may mask imperial ambitions, of course, as did British constitutionalism.

At the same time, Hindutva does not simply serve Modi's state-building project, and CST helps us to grasp this. Although Hindutva has become associated with Modi's presidency for the BJP, it was developed originally by the RSS movement. As Waghmore explains, RSS members often take up anti-political stances including to disparage BJP politicians.[5] Waghmore's account of the Tapas school in Karnataka is also revealing. On the one hand, the Tapas school displays the dynamic nature of the

Hindutva civil vision, including how it aspires to transcend caste, once considered axiomatic to Hinduism. Yet the school is not a state organ nor does it simply ape Hindutva politics. Modi's state project and the Tapas school project are elements of a broader refashioning of civil horizons impacting on spheres and their diffferentation, including but not only the political sphere.

As all civilizational discourse, including those of liberal democracy, Hindutva projects what I term a civil *persona*, against which others can be measured and found wanting, leading to some citizens and non-citizens being considered more civil than others.[6] Whether or not Hindutva is more hierarchical than, for example, US civil discourse, it is certainly no less; it is inclusive on one level and yet deeply exclusive and hierarchical on another. Waghmore (2019) describes Hindutva as a kind of "Hindu Cosmopolitanism [where] a degree of caste closure [is] an ideal ethic for urban cosmopolitanism" (p. 381). His suspicion is that Hindutva's caste closure – even as it draws on anti-caste and postcolonial elements – allows caste hierarchy to reproduce itself in the shadows.

Responding to Hindutva: Restore Civil Society or Seek New Civil Horizons?

As mentioned, most of the authors share misgivings about Hindutva, and other aspects of Modi's government. Some see Hindutva as anti-Muslim – this is why Waghmore dubs Hindutva a civil religion as opposed to civil sphere. Others consider that Hindutva provides cover for caste discrimination, especially in local contexts, even as it claims to transcend caste. Still others are concerned that Modi's government mobilizes Hindutva to instill majoritarian rule that undermines democracy.

Gudavarthy doubts, however, that "civil society" holds the remedy for Hindutva's ills:

> The civil repair now being attempted by progressive political formations is through appeals to abstract ideals of secularism and constitutionalism. They remain exclusively political (civil disobedience), while the authoritarian civil sphere is based on cultural structures and the popular/ Gandhian imagination of "change without conflict." For instance, recent protests by Muslims against the National Register of Citizenship (NRC) and Citizenship Amendment Act (CAA) carried out campaigns to "save the constitution" and "save democracy and secularism." These appeals lack grounding in cultural structures; they lack performative power and continue to work within the limits of secular sectarianism.

THE INDIAN CIVIL SPHERE

> There is an impending need to rework secular sectarianism in order to breach the authoritarian civil sphere. (p. 123)

Gudavarthy's concerns are multiple. To begin with, the protests lack the performativity that has, for example, characterized Modi's own interventions, and which CST has drawn attention to. He is also concerned that "civil society" – as represented by the NRC and CAA protests – lacks the popular resonance achieved by Hindutva. Gudavarthy worries that "secular sectarianism" obstructs the kind of solidarity across political community achieved by Modi's mobilizing of Hindutva. Finally, he is concerned that the protests fail to challenge the sphere differentiation characteristic of post-independence India, especially between politics and religion, politics and culture. All this makes "civil society" too easy a target for Modi's government and powerful movements like RSS.

Gudavarthy appears to seek a new politics capable of rivaling the powerful civil sphere dynamics of the Hindutva project. Gudavarthy is not ready, we infer, to abandon altogether the constitutional horizon to which, as the authors demonstrate, many subalterns do continue to appeal. However, just as Hindutva adopted many elements from "civil society," Gudavarthy seems prepared to take inspiration from Hindutva: for example, from Modi's performative ability to engage wide sectors of Indian society, building on many years of the RSS movement; from the way Hindutva has looked to unsettle the established sphere boundaries between politics and religion or politics and culture; and from the way that Hindutva transcends the logic of "secular sectarianism," overcoming persistent social and political blockages.

In the process, I suggest, Gudavarthy demonstrates, with the other authors, how CST can help us to reflect on how the governed engage and are engaged in the exercise of political authority, which is how I understand political community. CST draws our attention to political community's civil horizons, which stretch beyond but also cut across political community, holding up expectations of conduct, treatment, and care, which some – whether citizens or non-citizens – are felt to meet and deserve more than others. Some of the instances cited by authors bear comparison to civil sphere dynamics described elsewhere, including in the US, while – as Kumar insists – the constitutional forms were largely inherited from the British empire. Several authors point to the limited access and traction of the liberal civil sphere, echoing Chatterjee's famous distinction between "civil society" and the "political society" strategies by which most subalterns look to engage political authority. Waghmore and Gudavarthy signal how CST can also be applied to grasp the Hindutva project, which strives to rework political community by projecting new civil horizons, those of a transcendent Hinduism. Indeed, Gudavarthy draws on CST to begin to imagine what *other* politics – beyond Indian liberal democracy *and* Hindutva even if drawing on both – might better address ongoing challenges such as segregation and invidious hierarchy, including by seeking to articulate new civil horizons. In the process, they open pathways for CST to make good on its own ambition to develop an account of moral civilization that transcends the liberal democracy within which it was first developed.

Commentary: Leveraging the Heuristic Potential of the Indian Civil Sphere

Carlo Tognato

In 2018, BBC News Mundo drew readers' attention to a graph about inequality published by the OECD. There, Colombia featured as a country where poor people may take eleven generations to come out of poverty, that is, the equivalent of 330 years (Redacción BBC News Mundo 2018). Climbing the social ladder tends to be particularly difficult across the Global South, to the point where local observers occasionally draw parallels between social strata in their respective societies and Indian castes. Even in the North, commentators sometimes find it useful to metaphorically invoke Indian social reality. Take, for example, Italy, which has often been criticized at home and abroad for its petrified political-administrative class and its paralyzed society. In 2007, a best-selling book (Stella and Rizzo 2007) referred to this class as "the caste" and drew the attention of the Italian public to its privileges, its impermeability, and its lack of accountability (Reuters 2013; Bianchi 2017). Since then, references to "the caste" have punctuated the Italian public sphere, and denouncing it has made the fortunes of many rising populist politicians. Others, like Becker (2022), have invoked the idea of "caste" to make sense of the enduring civil exclusion of migrant workers even after decades of residence in Germany.

Given such metaphoric references to "caste" across the Global South, and occasionally even in the North, as an anchor for civil imagination in the struggles against exclusion, a book about the Indian civil sphere should not only be appealing to an audience of India specialists. Civil struggles against the Indian caste system may also speak to civil actors from other societal contexts, including those who might consider non-civil shortcuts in the pursuit of their civil goals. In fact, if Indian civil actors can fruitfully leverage the cultural and institutional mechanisms of the civil sphere in the pursuit of broader inclusion, then elsewhere,

LEVERAGING THE HEURISTIC POTENTIAL OF THE INDIAN CIVIL SPHERE

as well, those very same mechanisms should still work, since social differences may not be as petrified there as they are in the Indian caste system.

That said, metaphoric references to "caste" in the civil struggles outside India inevitably underplay the dramatic specificity of life in real caste systems and the sheer magnitude of the challenges that Indian civil actors face on the ground. At a time when in the West liberal democracy is under threat and self-complacency is a much more common commodity than civil courage, the endurance of Indian civil actors may provide a yardstick against which people around the world may measure their grit and ultimately draw inspiration from.

Since the publication of its foundational work (Alexander 2006), civil sphere theory has provided a useful framework that contributes to pinning down the meaning-making practices by which people go about broadening the horizon of inclusion within their own societies. Though the theoretical aspiration of civil sphere theory was to provide a lens that would help interpret such dynamics at all latitudes, its initial empirical focus was on the US and Europe. Since 2016, though, Jeffrey Alexander and a broad group of scholars from all over the world set out on a journey to deprovincialize the theory. This effort resulted in the publication of two books with a geographical focus outside the North – one on Latin America (Alexander and Tognato 2018b) and the other one on East Asia (Alexander et al. 2019b). *The Indian Civil Sphere* broadens the geographical reach of civil sphere theory and adds an important next leg of this intellectual journey.

This book features various chapters that underscore the continuity between the Indian civil sphere and the civil sphere in other societies.

In chapter 1 – "Caste, Incivility, and the Prospects for Civil Repair" – Hugo Gorringe and Karthikeyan Damodaran emphasize the importance of the institutions of the civil sphere – the law, the courts, elections, the media, and social movements – in relation to three cases. The three include the broadening of the horizon of inclusion of Dalits in India in relation to societal responses to the Covid-19 pandemic; the exercise of violence by members of upper castes seeking to quash the rise of Dalits to power in political elections; and honor killings of Dalits who dare marry women from upper castes. The authors underscore how important it is that social movements move past non-civil rhetoric, adopt civil discourse, and seek to project their civil credentials before local, national, and transnational audiences in order to persuade them of the deservingness of their civil claims. Gorringe and Damodaran also insist on the need for civil actors to strategically exploit the cracks within the state and family structures and wedge them open to channel their civil demands. Finally, they offer a rare contribution in the civil sphere literature to the analysis of the role of cinema in shaping Indian civil imagination.

In chapter 2 – "The Indian Civil Sphere and the Question of Caste: The Case of the Hathras Movement" – Raju Chalwadi builds on Alexander's idea of societalization (Alexander 2018) and addresses the crucial role that anti-caste civil movements play as engines of societalization in generalizing solidarity across profound cultural divides. The Hathras movement, he shows, emerged out of the public outrage that ensued when local authorities sought to shield from prosecution higher-caste perpetrators of the gang rape of a Dalit woman. The case not only shook the pillars of the civil community that the Indian Constitution had contributed to formalizing, but also offended the religious sensibilities of those Hindus who had not fully bought into the civil ideals that underpin the Constitution. Like most of the civil sphere literature, Chalwadi also insists on the fact that civil progress is never linear. Thus, forward advances may always give way to backlashes in a never-ending cycle of push and pull.

Along the transition out of the caste system, a broad spectrum of outcomes is always possible, some of which may turn out to be much less expansive than many civil advocates would hope for. Chapters 4 and 5 focus exactly on such cases as they address the state of Indian politics, particularly under Prime Minister Modi. In particular, in chapter 4 – "Civil Sphere versus Civil Religion: Hindutva and its Multiple Opponents in Karnataka" – Suryakant Waghmore discusses how Hinduism may be twisted into a nationalist civil religion that may help transcend the particularism of caste by replacing the hierarchy of caste with "the hierarchy of respect, seniority, and submission to authority" within the Hindutva movement (p. 100), though this is at the expense of Muslims and Christians. In the most recent civil sphere literature, there have been rare attempts to look at boundary exchanges between religion and the civil sphere. Arteaga Botello (2020), in particular, looked at the way Christianism provided a useful facilitating input into the civil agency of an internationally renowned group of Mexican volunteers who, over the past three decades, have assisted Central American migrants along their journey through Mexico to the US border. In this book, Waghmore goes beyond that and further elaborates on the differences between Bellah's idea of civil religion (Bellah 2015) and Alexander's treatment of religion within civil sphere theory.

In chapter 5 – "The Authoritarian Civil Sphere, Populism, and Secular Sectarianism" – Ajay Gudavarthy also discusses how the civil sphere may be leveraged for less expansive purposes by supplanting "vertical exclusion and hierarchical discrimination" with "moderate inclusion through accommodation within the known registers of the hegemonic civil sphere" (p. 115). In addition, Gudavarthy sets the stage for a timely discussion of one unintended effect of Indian postcolonial scholarship. This might be worth paying attention to, particularly in other regions such as Latin America. The agenda of postcolonial scholars could itself be viewed as a thread in the larger civil quest for the inclusion of entire segments of Indian society, whose voice had never been heard and whose history had never been written. And yet, Gudavarthy remarks, the emphasis by postcolonial scholars on caste "as community and culture" and "less as a system of prejudice and discrimination" has inadvertently provided a useful resource for conservative political movements such as Prime Minister Modi's. These, in fact, have managed to recast civil solidarity in a restrictive fashion by combining the "'strategy' of enculturing difference and prejudice with an effective discourse of decolonization" (p. 117).

In chapter 8 – "The British Raj and its Legacy for Democracy and Civil Society in India" – Krishan Kumar provides a useful complement to Gudavarthy's latest discussion point by addressing the broader historical development of the Indian civil sphere and by unpacking the role that British rule played in it. In particular, Kumar notes that British rule did not only have a greater transformational effect on Indian society than Mughal rule. Most importantly, it also channeled fundamental ideals and institutions of the civil sphere into Indian society, such as the Indian parliamentary system, the electoral and party system, a broad spectrum of newspapers, the broadcasting system, and the Constitution:

> Indian democracy has the faults of British democracy – as of all democracies – but also its strengths, including respect for the rule of law, acceptance of electoral outcomes, and a powerful Lower House, the Lok Sabha, with a long tradition of informed parliamentary debate. India is particularly well-served by a flourishing free press, with a variety of opinions vigorously expressed, much of it at the local level in the vernacular; while the national, English-language, newspapers and magazines have a standard of writing and reporting that stands comparison with their counterparts anywhere in the world. (pp. 174–175)

Two chapters in the book do not directly address caste in India, or at most do so only tangentially. And yet, their focus on boundary relations between the civil sphere and other spheres is crucial in the analysis of any civil transition out of the caste system. In chapter 6 – "Building Solidarity, Attempting Civil Repair: Pious Altruism and Muslim Politics in Post-Babri Mumbai" – Qudsiya Contractor elaborates on the facilitating inputs of religion into the civil sphere as she dwells on the way Muslim religious networks may sustain processes of solidarity building.

These, she adds, may ultimately "form the bedrock of civic participation, where civility is considered and performed as a public virtue, essential not just for social criticism but also democratic integration" (p. 142). Again, this chapter reveals a sense of continuity with the earlier mentioned piece by Arteaga Botello (2020) on Mexico.

In chapter 7 – "Financial Inclusion: Private Interest in the Civil Sphere" – Kartikeya Saboo does not specifically address caste, either. His discussion, in fact, addresses how civil motives are internally translated into market discourse within an Indian financial institution for the purpose of expanding access to credit for the poorest individuals. However, his analysis adds a very welcome nuance to the analysis of boundary relations between spheres by zooming into one specific institutional space where the civil sphere and the market come to overlap. There, Saboo shows how the civil logic may be grafted onto the market logic in the pursuit of civil repair and how, in return, a facilitating input from the market into the civil sphere may be paradoxically hijacked and neutralized within the latter.

Thus far, some of the chapters show a clear continuity between the Indian civil sphere and the civil spheres of other countries as well as with prior contributions to the civil sphere literature. Other chapters, in turn, sculpt new edges around the analysis of boundary relations. Chapter 3, on the other hand, differentiates itself more markedly with respect to the existing literature in the field. In "Can the Brahmin be Civil? The Ambiguous Repair of Caste Privilege," Ramesh Bairy redirects our gaze onto how subjectivities readjust and recompose as people attempt to exit caste and enter a civil community. He does so by granting readers access to the intimate dialogue between two Brahmins – his father and himself – the latter having completely bought into civil ideals and the former still being caught in a sort of limbo between the two worlds. Bairy shows that breaching particularistic identities and opening them up to the universalism of civil identities is anything but a linear process. This is why, he warns, as civil actors seek to push their agendas, they must be cognizant of the need to insert themselves and play into the oscillations between the "privatization of feelings of superiority/supremacy" and the "public performance of acquiescence to civil order" (p. 86).

The fact that the contributions included in this book bear witness to the continuity between the Indian civil sphere and the civil spheres that scholars have studied both in the North and across the Global South is a vindication that the theory provides a useful lens to capture civil dynamics even in a society like India where certain social practices may fundamentally defy civil ideals. Against this background, future contributions to the field coming from India may be better positioned to leverage the full heuristic potential that caste might have on the front of theory development. Let us unpack this point with reference to one possible front of advancement.

Civil sphere theory suggests that social divides across society have a chance to be bridged and solidarity may be generalized across them when people on all sides get to credibly translate their demands in civil terms. As a general bridging mechanism, the civil sphere literature has found that civil translation applies across many societies and at all latitudes. Still, scholars in the field have rarely sought to ascertain whether the depth and breadth of such divides might qualitatively affect the way civil translation is deployed. Caste involves the deepest tear one can possibly imagine in the civil fabric of society. If one seeks to attain a more nuanced understanding of civil translation, and if any qualitative differentiation in translation manifests itself as divides vary in depth and breadth, then such differentiation should pop up where the gulf across divides is largest and deepest. Zooming all the way in to capture the micro-mechanics of civil translation over caste might therefore serve this very purpose. One way to approach this matter might be by delving straight into the cultural and organizational dynamics that unfold right in the sites where non-civil claims may be recast in civil terms. In this book, Saboo positions his analysis at a level at which a more granular analysis of such processes may be possible. Egholm (2019), in turn, offers useful insights into the organizational dimension that underlies such translation processes, as she explores how Alexander's idea of translation may converge with Callon's and Latour's. And Tognato (2011) zooms further down as he sets out to bring into focus how sociocultural divides may be bridged even before civil translation might kick in, thereby shedding light over the continuum of discursive and performative strategies between an absence of translation and the practice of civil translation.

In conclusion, civil sphere theory appears to be capable of interpreting civil dynamics even in contexts where civil ideals face their toughest challenges, such as within the Indian caste system. This sets the stage to further use the heuristic potential of the Indian civil sphere to sharpen the theory and provide fresh insights to analysts around the world wherever metaphoric references to the Indian caste system are used to stir civil imagination in the pursuit of more inclusive societies.

Conclusion

Two Antagonistic Visions of India's National Identity

Peter Kivisto and Giuseppe Sciortino

The contributors to this inquiry into the Indian civil sphere have written their respective chapters during an especially fraught moment in the historical trajectory of democracy in India. As two non-Indian scholars who claim no expertise in Indian society, we looked carefully at the chapters assembled herein for clues regarding the authors' assessments of the relative robustness or weakness of the nation's civil sphere. We also listened intently to informal conversations that transpired during our "The Civil Sphere in India Workshop" that was held at Yale University in October 2022. These discussions proved to be more revelatory of the emotional responses of the participants to the nation's authoritarian turn during the past decade than is always evident in the written pages before readers.

We also looked to the assessments of scholars and journalists who have tried to make sense of the project set in motion by the Bharatiya Janata Party (BJP) under the leadership of Narendra Modi. Shortly after his electoral victory in 2014 that launched his first term as Prime Minister, perceptive students of authoritarianism such as Alfred Stepan (2015) spoke of the lurking "majoritarian danger." Modi's political agenda entailed the promotion of Hindu nationalism in reshaping national identity and an assertive neoliberal version of economic development. Some observers thought (or hoped) that the latter would temper the former, but as he moved into his second term in 2019 and consolidated power, the die was cast as Hindu nationalism is tangibly transforming the nation into a majoritarian state (Chatterji et al. 2019). While electoral vibrancy has been maintained, Modi's India is increasingly promoting an illiberal form of democracy (Varshney 2019) with a high threshold for tolerating violence directed at Muslims, other religious minorities, and political opponents (Roy 2023). Illiberal democracy is an unstable regime type.

CONCLUSION

In the transformation of a liberal to an illiberal democracy, the tendency of the trajectory is toward authoritarianism. Such an outcome is not inevitable. To the extent that the civil sphere is sufficiently robust and independent, the rehabilitation of liberal democracy is also a possibility.

In the lead up to the 2024 general election, assessments of efforts to undermine civil power in a complex pluralist society have often turned exceedingly dark. Thus, the journalist Debasish Roy Chowdhury (2022) has argued that "Modi's India is where global democracy dies," while a year later he contended that "Modi is pushing India to the brink" (Chowdhury 2023). Economist Ashoka Mody (2023) proclaims that "India is broken." *New York Times* columnist Lydia Polgreen (2023: A18) describes India as "jettisoning freedom and tolerance." Chowdhury and Australian political theorist John Keane (2021) argue that democracy is being killed as India makes its "passage to despotism." In his thick descriptive account of the ethnic democracy promoted by Hindu nationalism, Christophe Jaffrelot (2021: 349–405) sees in the current regime "the making of an authoritarian vigilante state."

To put these assessments into comparative perspective, an examination of widely utilized indices of democracy are divided about where precisely to locate India on the authoritarian–democracy spectrum. Whereas Freedom House, which focuses on civil and political rights, describes India as "partly free" and The Economist Intelligence Unit's Democracy Index locates India in the middle of the pack of flawed democracies, the V-Dem Institute (2023) contends that India is no longer a democracy, but rather should be defined as an "electoral autocracy."

In what follows, we turn to civil sphere theory (CST) to offer insights into the Indian civil sphere that can speak to both the reality of the existential threat to Indian democracy and the potential for its revival. To understand the present requires locating it in relation to the historical trajectory of the modern Indian state since independence. India has remained – with the exception of Indira Gandhi's imposition of a "state of emergency" in 1975 that was in effect for eighteen months – a democratic polity, despite enormous odds against it. India's democracy has been described as "improbable" (Varshney 2014, 2022) and "surprising" (Khosla 2020) – the consensus view among political philosophers and political scientists, in the words of Robert Dahl (1989: 253), being that it was "a leading contemporary exception to democratic theory."

The idea of India being an exception had to do with modernization theorists' understanding of the prerequisites for democracy: a literate, educated citizenry and a society with a sufficiently developed economy to insure a substantial and secure middle class along with a relatively small segment of the population living in poverty. Added to this were assump-

THE INDIAN CIVIL SPHERE

tions about the necessity of a shared national language and the absence of religious sectarianism. None of this applied to India in 1947. Only 17 percent of the population was literate and estimates of the poverty rate range between 70 percent and 80 percent. The persistence of caste (the subject of several chapters herein) insured that poverty was of the exceedingly durable and extreme variety. The country was economically underdeveloped and predominantly rural. Although Hindi was chosen as the nation's official language, there were an additional twenty-one languages designated as scheduled languages. Finally, religious conflict between the Hindu majority and Muslim minority led to the cultural trauma that resulted in Partition (Alexander 2012). In short, India would appear from the perspective of this mode of theorizing to offer less than hospitable soil for the blossoming of democracy.

And yet a democracy emerged, and it proved to have staying power. Early in *The Civil Sphere*, Jeffrey Alexander (2006: 37) approvingly quotes John Dewey: "Democracy is more than a form of government. It is primarily a mode of associated living, of conjoint communicated experience." It is a normative choice, a commitment that can only become instantiated and have staying power if it becomes embedded in and sustained by key regulative and communitive institutions. As Hugo Gorringe and Karthikeyan Damodaran point out, this view was shared by Bhimrao Ramji Ambedkar – a student of Dewey and the chair of India's constitutional draft committee. It was a normative choice, but why this choice – that is the question. In attempting to answer this question, we will turn to the recent argument made by political scientist Ashutosh Varshney in a collection devoted to examining "democracy in hard places." He argues that the longevity has been determined primarily by "*elite choices*" rather than deterministic structural variables (Varshney 2022: 36). Those choices, of course, began at the beginning and here we inquire into how a journey down a democratic path came to pass, and what the opposition to this path presented as an alternative.

Beginning in the 1920s, an emerging elite arose to challenge both British rule and the incumbent elites committed to protecting landlords, taking political form in the Congress party. This was the cadre out of which leadership roles were assumed by Gandhi, Ambedkar, and Nehru – all educated in the colonial metropole where the political values (but not the political reality) they encountered constituted a challenge to *Homo hierarchicus* (Dumont 1970) and an embrace of *Homo aequalis*. In this, as Krishan Kumar perceptively notes in his chapter, while the British had no intention of advancing civil society or democracy in India, the lessons the emerging elite took from their educational sojourns made them committed democrats, and, as he writes, they "fought the British

198

with tools and ideas derived from their British education and extensive experience of British life." Simultaneously, their attacks on landlordism from the late 1930s to independence set the stage for land reform policies – policies that were ultimately stymied when landlords entered into the ranks of the Congress party at the local and state levels. Linked to this and related efforts to overcome the nation's economic disparities and move it in a more egalitarian way, the indignities of the caste system were also challenged (Varshney 2022: 47–52).

The chapters in this book devoted to contemporary challenges to caste are case studies in attempts at civil repair. And as they reveal, such efforts to replace the vertical social order of caste with a horizontal social order that would establish a civic culture central to the functioning of democracy has made advances, but caste power remains potent. The quest for repair can be seen as embedded in the nation's founding, where its leaders made clear that their intention was to construct a new nation of citizens rather than subjects, an aspiration explicitly codified in the ratification of the Indian Constitution in 1950.

The Civil Code and Democratic Constitutions

In the chapter in *The Civil Sphere* on "the civil force of law," Alexander devoted a short section to the function of democratic constitutions, writing that they

> perhaps provide the clearest example of how law can function as a regulative institution of civil society vis-à-vis noncivil activities. This is because constitutions are fabricated documents, self-consciously designed to articulate general principles to establish moral frameworks that will guide the subsequent individual and institutional life of entire communities. . . . In democratic societies, constitutions aim to regulate governing and lawmaking in such a manner that they contribute to solidarity of a civil kind. (Alexander 2006: 164)

He goes on to observe that, as with other regulative institutions, constitutions "would be unnecessary if civil societies were not binary in their normative codes." As such, they can be seen as expressions of wariness "about others that mark the dark side of civil discourse; indeed, they are institutions for keeping that dark side under control" (Alexander 2006: 165).

India's Constituent Assembly appointed Ambedkar to chair the committee charged with drafting a constitution. In its three years of deliberations, it crafted a democratic constitution for a nation that had never experienced democracy. Making liberal use of the 1935 Government of India

THE INDIAN CIVIL SPHERE

Act and borrowing from other constitutions, the committee hammered out the longest constitution in the world. Its preamble asserted that India was a "sovereign socialist secular democratic republic" committed to "social, economic, and political justice," and echoing the values of the French Revolution, "liberty, equality, and fraternity." It instituted universal franchise at its founding for creating what Madhav Khosla (2020: 3) describes as a "democratic citizen." To accomplish this ambition, the Constitution was constructed on three pillars: codification of the rule of law, the centralization of state authority, and defining the individual rather than the group as the basis of political representation. In terms of codification, the authors thought it necessary to explicate in detail such things as the specific roles and limitations of legislative, judicial, and administrative bodies as well as the civic, political, and social rights of citizens. In terms of centralization, the Assembly rejected Gandhi's wish to create a nation where power resided in village republics (Moore 1966: 374). The collective judgment was that argued by Ambedkar and Nehru, which viewed villages as tradition-bound, provincial, and communal. Finally, the commitment to the centrality of the citizen as individual was intended to provide a constitutional basis for challenging religious sectarianism and caste.

Three other features of the Constitution are noteworthy. First, a form of federalism was established on linguistic rather than religious grounds in which major linguistic groups were granted states in which they could use their respective language as the official language of the state. Varshney (2022: 50) contends that this did not mean that India should be seen as what Arend Lijphart (1977) called a "consociational" rather than a liberal democracy – which would have been true if federalism was based on religion. Second, a form of affirmative action was instituted mandating proportional representation in legislatures and government bureaucracies for Dalits and tribals. The logic of this decision, advanced powerfully by Ambedkar, was, in Khosla's (2020: 124) words, "for individual liberty to be realized, the stubborn practices of superior groups needed to end." Finally, the Constitution was more than a rule-of-law roadmap. It was also intended to be a textbook, "a pedagogical apparatus that can bring into being . . . the people as free citizens" (Khosla 2020: 136). It sought to shape a new mode of solidarity predicated on the universalistic aspirations and the moral codes of a liberal democratic social order (Alexander 2006: 48–50).

The first election after the passage of the Constitution saw the size of the electorate rise from 30 million in 1946 to 173 million – the largest election in the history of the world. For the next quarter of a century the nation functioned reasonably well as an electoral democracy, though

200

it faltered in becoming a robust liberal democracy. Nonetheless, comparatively speaking India was in a small group of developing nations that succeeded in sustaining democracy over several decades.

That track record was undermined in 1975 when Prime Minister Indira Gandhi, having had her reelection bid overturned by the High Court due to campaign finance violations, invoked Article 352 of the Indian Constitution. This provision, inherited from British rule, allowed the head of state to declare an emergency if "a grave emergency exists whereby the security of India is threatened by internal disturbances." For eighteen months, Indian democracy had succumbed to dictatorship (Jaffrelot and Anil 2021: 1–20; Varshney 2022: 56–8). Thousands were jailed, the mass media were censored, the political opposition suppressed, and elections were cancelled. Gandhi's son Sanjay pressed further, creating hit lists of the political opposition, which were defined as enemies rather than legitimate opponents. If Congress prior to 1975 had been committed to the civil values shaping the Constitution, Gandhi's personal interests trumped that commitment. For its part, the judiciary proved an ineffective challenge to the emergency, which ended democracy, but was nevertheless constitutional. The political opposition, according to Jaffrelot and Anil (2021: 19), "oscillated between resistance and capitulation, proving utterly incapable of sustained and effective mobilization," and they quote approvingly a commentator who wrote of the press, "When you were merely asked to bend, you chose to crawl."

In January 1977 the state of emergency ended. New elections were called, political prisoners were released, press freedoms were restored, and citizens regained their basic civil and political rights. Gandhi ran for reelection, was defeated, and accepted the electoral results. This election spelled a turning point in modern India's history, it being the first time that Congress did not prevail electorally, setting up competitive elections at the national level. Gandhi's decision to re-establish democracy may have been shaped in part by international pressure, and she may have assumed that her electoral prospects were good, but long-time student of India Myron Weiner (1989) contended that the main reason was that Gandhi lacked a rationale for perpetuating the dictatorship. Framed in CST terms, she operated within and did not abandon the discursive contours of the civil culture code that at its inception sought to define the nation as a pluralistic, secular, liberal democracy, which among other things accepted the legitimacy of political opponents.

As the case studies in this collection vividly illustrate, there is a wide gulf between ideal and reality. The Indian civil sphere has been described as a paradox, for the vibrancy of communicative institutions and the role of the judiciary and rule-of-law have coexisted with high levels of political violence, corruption, and state dysfunction. Congress from its inception called for a social democracy addressing the basic material needs of people to make it possible for them to thrive. Two decades into the twenty-first century, despite demonstrable improvements in living standards, inequalities continue to mar the nation. Caste persists not only within the Hindu community, but in other religious groups as well. Civil repair occurs, but it confronts formidable challenges. This is evident not only in India, but in the diasporic community, where anti-caste activism has taken on a transnational character. A recent lawsuit filed by a Dalit working for Cisco Systems in California, accusing two Brahmin supervisors of caste discrimination, has led to legislative proposals to add disadvantaged castes to anti-discrimination laws (Kurien 2022). California was poised in the late summer of 2023 to become the first state in the US to pass such legislation, but in the end Gov. Gavin Newsom vetoed the Bill.

The Uncivil Code of Hindu Nationalism

One of the lessons deriving from the network of scholars involved in the CST project (Kivisto and Sciortino 2023) is that the universalistic aspirations of the civil code compete with parochial, hierarchical codes, some but not all of which are deeply rooted in a nation's history. For example, in Latin America, one finds the democratic code competing with a patrimonial code in Mexico, clientelism in Brazil, and the codes of the hacienda and revolutionary militancy in Colombia (Arteaga Botello and Arzuaga Magnoni 2018; Tognato 2018). In explorations into the civil sphere in East Asia, David Palmer (2019) describes three moral codes in China: the blue, yellow, and red. The blue represents the imported Western values of liberal democracy, while the yellow reflects the traditional Confucian code, and the red derives from China's (also imported) twentieth-century revolutionary tradition.

Similarly, the civil code that took form in India during the three decades preceding independence was from the beginning challenged by an uncivil ethnonationalist code articulated by early Hindu nationalist movement ideologues and activists. V. D. Savarkar's 1923 book, *Hindutva: Who is a Hindu?* constitutes the Ur-text of the exclusionary version of national identity shaping right-wing populism in contemporary India (Andersen 1972). Central to his argument is an effort to locate the true or authentic Indian in a mythic past that stressed race, language, and sacred territory: the descendants of the sons of the soil, the Vedic fathers; speaking the mother of all languages, Sanskrit; in a land circumscribed by the holy

CONCLUSION

rivers (Chatterji et al. 2019: 3). For Savarkar, religion was depicted as a "secondary attribute of culture" (Jaffrelot 2021: 13). It does, however, play a particularly important role politically in drawing the boundaries of ethnonational identity (Leidig 2020: 220).

Movement leaders were keenly interested in Italian fascism's militarization of society, and at the founding of the Rashtriya Swayamsevak Sangh (RSS) in 1925, it adopted Mussolini's paramilitary cells, developing a network of shakhas. It was conceived as the mechanism for recruiting new members to the cause, who were expected to take part in regimens of physical exercise, paramilitary drills, and educational classes focused on Hindutva dogma (Leidig 2020: 222). Although that dogma was defined by Brahmins, in order to build a mass movement, recruitment efforts were undertaken by downplaying caste. Christophe Jaffrelot (2021: 14–15) writes, "The shakhas are the framework for social and psychological reform on which the Hindu nation is supposed to be built, in the form of 'a brotherhood of saffron,' the color of Hinduism."

The rise of Nazi Germany influenced a racialist turn in Hindutva ideology, reflected in particular in the writings of another RSS leader, M. S. Golwalkar, who argued that being a Hindu was rooted in race, from which culture emerged. Like other prominent Hindu nationalists, he drew inspiration from Nazi Germany's Jewish policies, seeing them as a model for dealing with India's "Muslim problem" (Leidig 2020: 222–3). Given the history of Muslims in India and the fact that they constituted the largest minority, they were the primary group deemed to be Other. Anxieties about Muslims as an internal danger were exacerbated by concerns that they had allies in the Muslim-majority nations of the Middle East. But they were not the only Other. Christians were deemed outsiders because it was claimed that their missionary activities were designed to undermine Hindu identity. These two world religions were depicted as inherently foreign, and thus their adherents had, in Golwalkar's words, two options: they could "lose their separate identity to merge in the Hindu race, or stay in the country, wholly subordinated to the Hindu Nation, claiming nothing, deserving no privileges, far less any preferential treatment – not even citizen's rights" (quoted in Leidig 2020: 223).

As with their Italian and German counterparts, the RSS and similar ethnonationalist organizations in India condemned communism. A backward-looking worldview seeking to retrieve a lost golden age found Marxism's desire to create a radiant future free from the burden of history to be anathema. It was also opposed to the liberal democratic vision promoted in particular by Congress – one predicated on the creation of an independent India that accepted, rather than sought to eliminate, diversity. Not surprisingly, RSS was not part of the independence struggle, but

203

THE INDIAN CIVIL SPHERE

it was an active participant in the violence surrounding Partition. The propensity to resort to violence – "saffron terror" – has been a through line in its performative repertoire from its founding to the present. This led a Congress-dominated political system to periodically intervene by repressing RSS leaders and rank-and-file activists.

RSS persisted in its efforts to advance a majoritarian counter-version of national identity to that articulated in the Constitution, one that equated being an Indian with being a Hindu. It constructed a network of political and civil society organizations. This included a political party, the Bharatiya Jana Sangh (BJS), founded in 1951. Its xenophobic ideology was necessarily held in check in order to avoid being repressed by the state. This required a difficult balancing act, projecting on the one hand a public persona of a moderate form of patriotic nationalism, while on the other finding ways to continue to mobilize its militant members (Leidig 2020: 229). RSS was the umbrella for the Sangh Parivar, affiliated organizations with distinct purposes, including paramilitary groups, youth organizations, charitable NGOs, trade unions, farmers' unions, and student organizations (Leidig 2020: 228). In the aftermath of the restoration of democracy in 1977 and the rise of challengers to Congress at the national level, the effort to bring Hindutva into the center of Indian politics gained steam.

The Bharatiya Janata Party (BJP) and the Future of Democracy

Launched in 1980, the BJP was an attempt to repackage the BJS, which had never managed to shake off its extremist image. The BJP sought to promote the Hindutva project in moderate terms more acceptable to a larger swathe of the electorate. Jaffrelot (2021: 23) observes that, "From the very start, the Hindu nationalist movement has been borne by the upper castes due to the social conservatism it promotes," with Brahman values at its core. Upper caste, middle-class Indians had retreated from the electoral arena during the period of Congress hegemony, but with the creation of the BJS, this sector set in motion a "conservative revolution" that amounted to the "revenge of the elite" (Jaffrelot 2021: 5). When the leadership of the party was assumed by Narendra Modi, himself not a member of an upper caste, but an RSS member since he was eight years old, the fortunes of the party grew. Confined initially to electoral successes at the local and state levels, in 2014 he became the nation's Prime Minister and has dominated Indian politics since then – reflected in his subsequent victory in 2019.

204

CONCLUSION

The BJP, the largest political party in the world, fits the pattern of a populist radical political party (Leidig and Mudde 2023). Its success can be attributed to two strategies that Modi has pursued. On the one hand, though shaped by elite interests, it brought into its fold lower-caste supporters, in part by appealing to the neo-middle class, playing effectively to their desire for upward mobility and their insecurities (Jaffrelot 2021: 70). Caste hierarchy is not attacked, but rather the focus shifts from caste to class, thus protecting rather than seeking to eradicate caste. The electoral appeal of Modi is due to his ability to link the rhetoric of national security to Hindu nationalism. The second strategy involves his pursuit of economic development by embracing neoliberalism. Many who were wary of his adherence to Hindutva nonetheless chose to support him because they saw him as potentially instilling a dynamism and model for economic growth that would make India a force to be reckoned with on the global stage, a nation that could compete on equal terms with China.

With its 2019 electoral victory, the BJP shifted in a more markedly authoritarian direction. Rather than seeing opposition parties as legitimate opponents, they are vilified as enemies. The BJP has been explicit in its goal of creating a Congress-free India (Jaffrelot 2021: 349). It has passed legislation designed to permit the government to target "universities, media, and NGOs as enemy groups that can be considered the 'corrupt elite' alongside the Congress Party" (Leidig and Mudde 2023: 369). At the same time, vigilante groups, operating with the tacit permission of the Modi government, have intensified violent attacks on perceived civil society enemies. Attacks on Muslims, including lynching for what the perpetrators call "cow protection" and the prevention of "love jihad," have seen a dramatic increase since Modi took power.

Authoritarians, like CST theorists, understand the significance of communicative and regulatory institutions for functioning democracies, but they differ insofar as the autocrats' playbook calls for undermining both. The Modi government has been quite successful in weakening the media. According to Reporters Without Borders, India's World Press Freedom ranking is 161 out of 180, a twenty-place drop since 2014 (Travelli et al. 2023: A7). It has similarly cracked down on academics. It has also inflicted damage on the judiciary. Rather than attempting to rewrite the Constitution (unlike many other autocrats), Modi has taken advantage of its illiberal features. According to Saraphin Dhanani (2023: 2), "the Modi government has deftly deconstructed the scaffolding of the judiciary" and for its part the judiciary has proven to be, for matters of self-interest, complicit. The result is that constitutional principles have been attacked while political opponents have been criminalized (Sundar

2023: 134), a vivid example of what legal scholar David Landau (2013) describes as "abusive constitutionalism."

After nearly a decade in office, it is clear that under Modi, the BJP's project to replace the democratic civil code with the uncivil code of Hindutva is well under way. However, the democratic civil sphere persists. Democracy has not been jettisoned. Electoral politics offers a crucial vehicle for challenging authoritarianism, and, as the results of the 2024 election suggest, the Modi government is vulnerable on several fronts. First, the perpetuation of caste threatens to undermine the Hindu unity it seeks. Second, the BJP's embrace of neoliberalism exacerbates inequalities and makes possible a new iteration of crony capitalism and corruption – thus serving as a potential impetus for calls for civil repair. To the extent that Modi, who pitched his political rise on economic development, fails to deliver, voters may look elsewhere. Third, the federal system – which has been threatened by Modi – can serve as a bulwark against a centralized authoritarian state. Several of the states not under BJP control are economic powerhouses, which may serve as a brake on authoritarian policies. Fourth, as India seeks the spotlight on the international stage, the government's actions will be increasingly scrutinized by a global civil sphere. Such factors have led economist Pranab Bardhan (2022: 25) to conclude that "India may not be socialist or secular soon, but a complete obliteration of its already highly flawed democracy is somewhat less likely, as the country lurches on past its 75th anniversary, into the future." To which, CST would add that the character of Indian democracy will be determined in the agonistic struggle under way between frontlash and backlash forces (Alexander 2019b) – those seeking to realize Ambedkar's vision of an inclusive, liberal democracy versus those intent on undermining it.

Notes

Introduction:
The Indian Civil Sphere between Vitality and Suppression

1 As the preceding section has implied, this Introduction, and this book more broadly, challenge central tenets of postcolonial theory (e.g., Go 2016). From the perspective of the democratic project, it is dangerous and reductive to suggest that Western social theory can be comprehended merely as the translation of the material and cultural hegemonies of European colonialism into intellectual terms. From the Greeks onward, social theory has manifest an imminent criticism of the particular historical structures within which it has been embedded. Like other, more religious versions of "Axial" culture (Eisenstadt 1982; Bellah 2011), theory has a universalizing dimension that has allowed it to be *relatively* free-floating. Alongside the frequent legitimations that individual thinkers gave to colonial projects, the universalizing categories embedded in their ideas deeply inspired so-called indigenous anti-colonial intellectuals, providing the democratic integuments within which post-colonies framed their idealistic, emancipatory visions. As an alternative to what she condemns as the particularism and essentialism of postcolonial theory, the Indian political theorist Gurpreet Mahajan suggests that a Gadamerian "fusion of horizons" more accurately describes the relation between Indian and Western thought, a perspective that "prompts one to examine the way ideas, no matter where they come from, enter into public discourse and shape the political imagination of the people" (Mahajan 2013: 6). Pointing to "the fact that the social and political leadership in modern India has operated implicitly with this self-understanding," she argues, "makes this standpoint even more compelling" (Mahajan 2013: 7).

> Throughout the struggle for freedom ... concepts such as liberty and equality, state and bureaucracy, were used, unconstrained by anxiety about their origin. The leadership invoked these concepts to think about their own social and political situation and aspirations, and in doing so imbued them with new meanings. ... British rule in India had not only yielded the experience of political subjugation, it had engendered an intense encounter with another world-view – one that brought in

207

NOTES TO PP. 6–8

the language of equality and rights [that] challenged the socio-cultural practices and the ways of thinking that were prevalent in Indian society at that time. ... During the struggle for independence and in the Constituent Assembly [the leaders] used concepts and terms that were – and continue to be – a part of the modern democratic imaginary. (ibid.)

Waghmore's empirical studies of Indian anti-caste movements crystallize this philosophical perspective in a sociological way. "The colonial imposition of civil society," he asserts, "served as a political space of freedom and self-realization for Dalits" (Waghmore 2013: 202). Noting "the lack of this autonomous space or a civil sphere for collective mobilization ... in pre-colonial India," he argues that, in the intellectual vocabulary of pre-colonial India, there existed "no concept" of either "civil society" or "citizenship" (Waghmore 2013: 7). In other words, civil sphere theory is (contra Hammer 2020) anything but a colonizing project.

2 The more radical founding fathers were acutely aware of this tension. B. R. Ambedkar, the Dalit intellectual and political leader who studied with John Dewey while earning a doctorate at Columbia University, was a key figure in the drafting of India's Constitution. On November 25, 1949, he made his final speech to India's Constituent Assembly:

On the 26th January 1950, we are going to enter a life of contradictions. In politics we will have equality and in social and economic life we will have inequality. In politics we will be recognizing the principle of one man, one vote, one value. In our social and economic life we shall, by reason of our social and economic structure, continue to deny the principle of one man, one value. How long shall we continue to live this life of contradictions? How long shall we continue to deny equality in our social and economic life? If we continue to deny it for long, we do so only by putting our democracy in peril. (Corbridge and Harriss 2000: 34)

A similar anxiety drove Jawaharlal Nehru to initiate the series of "Five Year Plans" as blueprints for state driven industrialization (Brown 2003: 223–43).

3 I draw this point from an unpublished paper by my co-editor Suryakant Waghmore.

4 Collins' study of the papers of Dalit leaders supports this perspective. Challenging Chatterjee's claim that class conflict in "political society" took precedence over "civil society," Collins concludes that Dalit "organisers neither prioritised collective demands in violation of existing laws nor embraced political activity that eschewed civic norms; rather, they submitted written appeals through formal institutional channels that advocated the delivery of fundamental rights and the realisation of normative values they associated with democratic citizenship. In effect, [they] lobbied state officials to discharge their professional duties and fulfil their mandate to Dalit citizens, seeking to remedy specific grievances and redress instances of discrimination" (Collins 2017: 241).

5 For a revealing discussion of BAMCEF's effort to create cross-caste solidarities that, discursively and institutionally, constituted a kind of civil sphere in miniature, see Vivek Kumar (2024).

6 Just as the broader theoretical framework that informs this book represents a

NOTES TO P. 11

challenge to postcolonial theory, so does the sociological framework informing the empirical reconstructions in this section challenge the "subaltern studies" approach to anti-caste social movements. By insisting that "subaltern resistance constitutes an autonomous domain," Alf Gunvald Nilsen argues, subaltern studies "fails to appreciate how subaltern groups have appropriated the institutions, discourse, and governmental technologies" of the societies in which they struggle (Nilsen 2017: 15). Opposing the neo-Marxist, zero sum presuppositions of subaltern theory, Nilsen suggests there is "a far larger and more integrated contact surface between the politics and culture of elites and subalterns" (Nilsen 2017: 45). This contact surface, I suggest, is constituted by the discourses and institutions of the civil sphere.

7 Bellah put the broader social and political implications of this succinctly: "American civil religion was never anticlerical or militantly secular . . . it borrowed selectively from the religious tradition in such a way that the average American saw no conflict between the two. In this way, the civil religion was able to build up without any bitter struggle with the church powerful symbols of national solidarity and to mobilize deep levels of personal motivation for the attainment of national goals" (Bellah 1967: 13). (See Waghmore, chapter 4 in this book, for an analysis of the implications – for understanding contemporary India – of this quotation and Bellah's project of civil religion more generally.) In the present chapter, I am contrasting the religious embeddedness of emerging Western democracy with the emergence of democracy in India. Yet, there are similarities as well. The tension between religion and democracy in India parallels the bitter struggle between religion and civil sphere in France, which implicitly provided Bellah's contrast with the American case. The French version of the Enlightenment in eighteenth-century France, and the 1789 revolution inspired by it, sought to abolish Christianity. When Rousseau conceptualized a "civil religion" for the first time, in *The Social Contract* (1762), he envisioned it as a replacement for organized theocratic religion, not as something complementary to it. The short-lived French revolutionary state replaced the church with its own secular dogma and rites. In the backlash against the French Revolution, the ideology was not only Monarchist but also Catholic, the latter fueling a revulsion for democracy that undermined support, not only for the First and Second Republics but also for the Third. In contrast to the UK and the US, in France pro-Nazi anti-democratic movements flourished during the 1920s, helping to neutralize the resistance to Hitler's invasion at the end of the next decade and legitimating Petain's collaborationist "Vichy" government, which so readily accommodated Hitler's request to send tens of thousands of French Jews to extermination camps.

8 This issue of the relation between democratic discourse and metaphysics defines a central issue in political and moral philosophy. It was central, for example, to the philosophical evolution of the thought of John Rawls, the most important democratic theorist of the twentieth century. In his *Theory of Justice* (1971), John Rawls laid out a "contract" theory of an inclusive democracy that was abstract, universalizing, and rationality-imputing. In *Political Liberalism* (1993), he responded to his more historical and culturally inclined critics by acknowledging – in a manner that his German counterpart Jürgen Habermas never could – that such a system of self-generating civil repair could actually only work – in the real social world – if it were anchored inside an already-existing value system rooted in time and place.

209

NOTES TO PP. 11–21

For the American case, Rawls pointed to the legacy of secular republicanism and radical Protestantism.

9 While Hinduism was vastly preponderant in the Indian subcontinent, there existed some minoritarian religious strands that were more egalitarian, like Sikhism and Buddhism (Aloysius 1998), to the latter of which Ambedkar converted late in his life.

10 For the contrast between progressive and tragic narratives in constructing collective identity, especially in working through cultural trauma, see Eyerman (2001) and Alexander (2003b). Salman Rushdie's brilliant novel *Midnight's Children* (Rushdie 2006 [1981]) manages the aesthetic feat of intertwining both these narratives, creating characters and subplots that crystallize the multifarious plurality of India's cultural identities. At once manically ecstatic and tragically despairing, the story resolutely refuses to give up the new nation's myth of origins; Rushdie's principal protagonist, Saleem Sinai, is born on the stroke of midnight, August 15, 1947.

11 While the emergence of the Hindutva-related Bharatiya Jana Sangh (BJS) party in 1951 might present counter-evidence, its dismal fate suggests the opposite. Over the course of its four decades of existence, the BJS failed to generate significant electoral traction vis-à-vis Congress, particularly on the national level (Graham 1990). As Kothari noted in his seminal article, non-Congress parties – whether religious, Communist, tribal, or linguistic – could, even at their most successful, "only function effectively at the local and regional levels" (Kothari 1964: 1165). Mostly they functioned as fragmented "parties of pressure" that affected shifting coalitions inside the Congress itself. See Jaffrelot's observation, drawing from Kothari, that BJS was "caught in a vice by the 'Congress System'" (Jaffrelot 2021: 18). The BJS could enter into government only by dissolving itself. Yet, even after it had "merg[ed] with the coalition of anti-Congress forces that came together in the Janata Party" in the late 1970s, in the aftermath of the Emergency, ex-Janata members were soon ousted for their outspoken religious extremism (Jaffrelot 2021: 19). The BJP was born from the ashes.

12 While the radio show is one-way in the sense that Modi reads from a prepared script, his listeners, at his request, provide inputs into the script. See, for example, the announcement and solicitation posted on All India Radio News in late November, 2021:

> Prime Minister Narendra Modi will share his thoughts with the people of the country and abroad in the "Mann Ki Bat" programme on Akashvani on the 29th of this month. It will be the 114th episode of the monthly radio programme. People can submit their ideas and suggestions for the programme through the toll free number 1800-11-7800. People can also ... follow the link received in SMS to directly give their suggestions to the Prime Minister. People can also share their input online via the Narendra Modi App ... Suggestions for the upcoming episode will be accepted till the 27th of this month. (www.newsonair.gov.in/?s=MAnn%2BBAat)

13 Biswas observes that "giant posters of Mr. Modi promoting these schemes as his personal 'guarantees' dominate the landscape" in India today (Biswas 2024).

NOTES TO PP. 21–23

14 This, of course, points to the difference between the ideologies of right-wing conservativism and right-wing populism, the latter being distinctive, from Mussolini and Hitler onward, for intertwining primordial and anti-democratic sentiments with a positive orientation to the "social" question, i.e., by incorporating less privileged groups. Thus, the German Nazi party's ideology of "National Socialism."

15 Modi's personal popularity is unprecedented in the post-Nehru period. While his preternatural performative abilities are central, the background cultural scripts that he references go beyond Hindutva-inspired nationalism. Of real significance, for example, is "the phenomenon of guru-ship [that] has been a classic and enduring theme within South Asian scholarship" (Copeman and Ikegame 2012: 1), wherein the mystical, and often mystified, master–disciple relationship at the core of religious worship becomes transferred into the putatively secular political domain. Price and Ruud have written perceptively about the subcontinent's "lordly" style of leadership, how perceptions of "a benevolent person of expansive agency form a major element of allegiance to lordly leadership," either in "the glamorous and generous mode of monarchs or in the spiritual efficacy and knowledge of gurus" (Price and Ruud 2010: xxv). Another background script that Modi performatively draws upon is the almost visceral, patriotic/nationalist excitement among many Indians at the prospect of their nation's entry into the heady world of the "great game," an ascension facilitated, not only by India's cutting edge digital capitalism, but by its geopolitical centrality in the exploding struggle between capitalist democracies and a rising China.

16 In addition to the backlog of court cases, this aggressive strategy also relies on a "loophole" in India's otherwise democratic constitutional foundation, namely the legality of temporally-limited preventive detention without trial, which Krishan (2019) has laconically described as "a unique and interesting provision of the Indian Constitution according to which any person can be arrested without even actually violating any law of the land." Passed only one month after the 1950 ratification of India's Constitution, in the midst of what was experienced as destabilizing domestic and foreign threats, the "Preventive Detention Act" allowed a person to "be arrested and detained if his freedom would endanger security of the country, the foreign relations, public interests or otherwise necessary for the country" (ibid.). Despite its being subject to such severe criticism that elected governments were twice moved to formally abolish it, the provision's quasi-constitutional status has allowed it to remain in continuous use.

17 In the following, I draw from the participant and observer accounts in Pushparaj Deshpande and Ruchira Chaturvedi (2024) as well as from a Zoom interview with Deshpande and Chaturvedi themselves.

18 The event was covered by NDTV, at that time one of India's major purveyors of independent journalism. Following is an excerpt from this television coverage:

> Soon after Rahul Gandhi arrived at the public meeting at the end of the day's march the showers started but [he] chose to continue his speech. [The] Congress leader ... said nothing can deter the Bharat Jodo Yatra which is aimed at stopping hatred and violence spread by the BJP-RSS. ... Heat, storm, or cold can't stop this yatra. This river-like yatra will

211

NOTES TO PP. 23–44

carry on from Kanyakumari to Kashmir and in this river you will not see things like hate or violence. There will only be love and brotherhood as this is India's history and DNA. (NDTV 2022)

19 "Last year, I spent 145 days walking across the land I call home. I started at the edge of the sea and walked through heat, dust and rain, through forests, towns and hills, until I reached the soft snow of my beloved Kashmir. Many people along the way asked me: why are you doing this? Even today they ask: why? What were you looking for? What did you find? I wanted to find the thing I loved. The thing for which I was ready to give up everything, including my life. . . . Within a few days, the pain arrived. My old knee injury, one that hours of physiotherapy had banished, was back. . . . We would start walking in the darkness before dawn. Almost immediately, the pain would begin [and] it would follow me everywhere I went, waiting for me to stop. [But] every time I would think about stopping, every time I considered giving up, someone would come and gift me the energy to continue. Once it was a lovely little girl with a beautiful letter, another time an old lady with some banana chips, then a man who suddenly ran up and hugged me. . . It was as if a silent energy kept helping me, and like fireflies in a dark forest, it was everywhere. . . . The object of my love had suddenly revealed herself. My beloved Bharat Mata was not a land. It wasn't a set of ideas. It wasn't a particular culture, history or religion. Neither was it the case that people had been assigned. India was the voice of every single Indian, no matter how weak or strong. . . . How simple it had turned out to be. I had been looking in the river for that which could be found in the sea" (Gandhi 2023).

20 "The election result that has come today is the result of the people," Congress president Mallikarjun Kharge declared at the news conference, explaining that the civil sphere had spoken and was now placing new representatives into the Indian state: "This is the victory of the people and democracy. We humbly accept the public opinion in the elections of the 18th Lok Sabha. . . . The BJP has sought votes on one person and one face, but now it is clear that the mandate has gone against Narendra Modi. This is a huge defeat for them morally and politically. They have suffered a huge loss from a moral point of view" (Chatterji 2024). In its dissection of the election, *The Hindu* suggested Rahul Gandhi had been "pivotal": "He has galvanized the grassroot organizations of the party courtesy [of] his Gharat Jodo Yatra [which] brought Gandhi into direct contact with the masses [and] laid the foundation of the Congress' campaign" (ibid.).

Chapter 1: Caste, Incivility, and the Prospects of Civil Repair

1 See the debates in full here: https://www.constitutionofindia.net/consti tution_assembly_debates/volume/11/1949-11-25

2 If this speaks to the weakness, and partial caste capture, of civil sphere institutions, it is clear that some regulatory bodies adhere to the civil moral framework articulated by the Dravidian movement and enshrined in the Constitution. All charges against the protesting Dalits, thus, were ultimately dismissed in 2004.

NOTES TO PP. 44–72

3 Even this landmark case was diluted in 2019, with the premature release of the convicts in the case. Unsurprisingly, "Dalit activists and legal experts also said the premature release of these persons would send a wrong signal to other dangerous anti-social elements" (Rajasekaran 2019).
4 "Independent Initiative is a public interest organisation headed by Justice V.R. Krishna Iyer, Former Supreme Court Judge" (Independent Initiative Report, September 1999: 1). This organization monitored the poll process in Perambalur and Chidambaram, and the findings of their teams give credence to allegations that the contest in Chidambaram was neither free nor fair.
5 In an effort to flag these issues, Dalit writers and intellectuals have started using the term *aanava kolaigal* (Murders of Arrogance) and *Saathi Thimir Kolaigal* (Murders of Caste Arrogance) and even the English print media which had earlier addressed these killings as "honour killings" have started to use "(dis)honour killings" in a move marking the increasing pollution of such crimes in the public sphere.
6 Though Dalits featured in mainstream cinema, they have either been portrayed as submissive and the butt of jokes (Damodaran and Gorringe 2017), or have been subject to Gandhian style paternalism.
7 The Constituent Assembly debates may be read in full here: http://164.100 .47.194/Loksabha/Debates/Result_Nw_15.aspx?dbsl=144&ser=&smode=

Chapter 2: The Indian Civil Sphere and the Question of Caste: The Case of the Hathras Movement

1 Kumar (2014) writes that "the origin of Hindu social order is traced from the sacred text of Hindus – the *Rigveda*. The tenth chapter (91st hymn) of this text reveals that there are four groups better known as Varna" (p. 36).
2 In 2012, a woman was raped in Delhi. The government took quick action and sent her for treatment abroad. The argument here is that the woman (Nirbhaya) was an upper caste woman, so the state acted quickly, whereas in this case, the woman was a Dalit woman, so the state did not take the case seriously. For more commentary readers can read this piece: https://time.com /5900402/hathras-rape-case-india-violence/
3 SC and ST stand for Scheduled Caste and Scheduled Tribe, respectively.

Chapter 3: Can the Brahmin be Civil? The Ambiguous Repair of Caste Privilege

1 Often, Hinduism and the "Brahminical order" are treated as one and the same, while only the latter has had any conceptual coherence over time. So my choice here is deliberate.
2 "[Much] imprecision and difficulty arise from failing to distinguish in the 'individual': (1) The empirical agent, present in every society, in virtue of which he is the main raw material for any sociology. (2) The rational being and normative subject of institutions; this is peculiar to us [i.e., the modern Western society], as is shown by the values of equality and liberty: it is an idea that we have, the idea of an ideal" (Dumont 1970: 9).

213

NOTES TO PP. 73–94

3 I use the neologism "not-Brahmin," and not the more familiar "non-Brahmin," to (a) get away from the resonances of the Tamil context, but, more importantly, to (b) underscore the Brahmin power to render everyone else to a reductive category. The small-case "n" in the "not-Brahmin" is to further signal its reductiveness.

4 See the chapter titled "Modern World of Brahmins: A Schematic History" in Bairy (2010), where I describe the multiple ways in which, in the late nineteenth and early twentieth centuries, the mere invocation of one's Brahmin identity ensured access to crucial modern resources.

5 See Upadhya (2007) on the numerical preponderance of Brahmins in the globalizing software industry in Bengaluru, and Bairy (2010) on the renewed confidence these opportunities provided to the Brahmin.

6 In fact, at some other point in the interview, he began describing an incident by saying that in Udupi "there existed from the very beginning *class conscious* [he used the English phrase] between the Brahmin and non-Brahmin." I interjected correcting him, "*caste consciousness*, not *class*." He disagreed and offered a fine theoretical point for his use of "class" by saying, "'caste' means each caste has a different conscious, but 'class' means only one distinction exists: that the Brahmins are different from the non-Brahmin."

7 Billavas, the toddy-tapping caste, even as late as mid-twentieth century were treated as near untouchable in Udupi, something that the respondent too noted: in another context, he stated that they were "outcastes."

8 Indeed, my father was asked to stop his education after the fifth standard by his father so that he could take him to Bengaluru to work in the small restaurant where he was employed as a cook. It was at the insistence of his unlettered grandmother – who stated in no uncertain terms that he is good at school and must be educated further – that he went on to high school. I tried repeatedly to find out how and why she insisted on keeping him in school, but my father either did not see that as interesting or had no more information or willingness to reflect on it.

9 The Brahmin category is capacious, internally contested and negotiated, and includes a large number of endogamous groups, usually called jatis.

10 Matha-making/reviving has become an important project in contemporary Karnataka in the last many decades, particularly among non-Brahmin groups (see Bairy 2019).

11 Cf. Alexander's formulations of "dual membership" and of a certain paradox of "incorporation." For an early intimation of this, see Singer (1972).

Chapter 4: Civil Sphere versus Civil Religion: Hindutva and its Multiple Opponents in Karnataka

1 Hindutva thrives through its social (RSS) and political (BJP) organization in Karnataka, as is the case with the rest of India. RSS is denied the status of an association or social movement in civil society, and Rudolph (2000) suggests that the RSS does not constitute civil society due to its anti-Muslim discourse, as it fails to generate social capital for democracy.

2 Shankaracharya is the religious title given to heads of amnaya mathas in the Advaita Vedanta tradition of Brahmanism. The Shankaracharya of Puri is one of four main Shankaracharyas in India.

NOTES TO PP. 96–109

3 Pseudonym.

4 On the day of my visit to the center, I observed several Muslim patients. The head of Rashtrotthana informed me that close to 40 percent of beneficiaries at the thalassemia center were Muslims. This is a Trust-led initiative; therefore, they cannot exclude anyone on the basis of religion.

5 The list is not the standard range of north Indian eminent Hindus who represent the RSS's idea of national self-sacrifice and includes some local personalities like Bal Gandharva, Ramana Maharshi, and Obavva.

6 *Tapasya* refers to the meditation, austerity, and self-discipline that monks resort to for *moksha*. The students, too, are expected to achieve similar focus and self-discipline toward their goal of making it into IITs.

7 It is explained as five aspects of education – physical, emotional, psychological, intellectual, and spiritual.

8 Interview in July 2019, Bengaluru. All statements written as originally reported.

9 Singing *Vande Mataram* is also more of a passionate affair in Hindutva, as some Muslims refuse to sing *Vande Mataram* due to the call to worship the motherland in this song.

10 This was a crucial challenge to American civil religion as well. While by the late 1600s most colonies had extended full rights to non-Christians in the US, just who would be included as a "real American" was something civil religion was equivocal about, even making Catholics secondary citizens vis-à-vis Protestants.

11 Framed as a strategic plan of Muslims, the term refers to Muslim men tricking Hindu girls into marrying them so as to convert them to Islam.

12 Ahinda represents the non-party social solidarity of minorities, Dalits, tribals, and non-dominant backward castes in Karnataka that was formed and led by Siddaramaiah from kuruba (shepherd) caste. Siddaramaiah is influenced by the progressive Devaraj Urs, an ex-CM of Karnataka who advocated an alliance of non-dominant castes and played a crucial role in the radical land reforms of Karnataka. He began his political career with the Janata Party and later JDS (Janata Dal Secular) only to be ejected due to his growing popularity across Ahinda groups.

13 Valmikis are listed as a Scheduled Tribe in Karnataka. In the hierarchy of caste, they consider themselves higher than untouchables, though were identified as criminal tribes by the colonial government.

14 Personal interview in August 2015, Karnataka.

15 Despite being opposed to BJP, some Congress workers in Karnataka celebrated the defeat of the party in May 2023, by purifying the Karnataka Legislative Assembly with cow urine.

Chapter 5: The Authoritarian Civil Sphere, Populism, and Secular Sectarianism

1 The interface between cultural sociology and the civil sphere needs to be contextualized in order to make better sense of CST.

2 Geographer Michel de Certeau (2011) makes a distinction between "strategy" in urban planning (that standardizes/uniformity) and the "tactics" (random/contextual) of everyday practices.

NOTES TO PP. 110–116

3 Populist-authoritarianism in this chapter refers to the strategies and discourses of the ruling Bharatiya Janata Party (BJP), Rashtriya Swayamsevak Sangh (RSS), and other affiliated organizations that are referred to as the Sangh Parivar. Though there are differences and differentiated roles within each of the affiliated organizations, I do not venture there, but group them together under the rubric of populist-authoritarianism.

4 Karma philosophy is an important component of Hinduism that believes in re-birth and that the sins of past life are redeemed in the present life.

5 https://economictimes.indiatimes.com/news/politics-and-nation/terrorism-in -india-exported-not-home-grown-pm-narendra-modi/articleshow/43872192 .cms

6 Refer to Barrington Moore's *Social Origins of Democracy and Dictatorship* (1966) for an analysis of how Karma theory precluded peasant rebellions in India, unlike other South-East nations.

7 https://www.thehindu.com/news/cities/Kochi/article60062744.ece

8 For instance, in Maharashtra, the Shiv Sena engineered the "sons of soil" movement while the BJP got identified with the Hindi heartland. The logic seems to be the same for the BJP, supporting smaller states as they provide for a strong center by default.

9 A similar parallel could be drawn in the way they invoke Gandhi, to demonstrate how Hindus have been constrained and made "effeminate," and, because of which, Muslims take advantage and dominate them. In effect, invoking Gandhi becomes an invitation for violence.

10 I attempt to analyze this aspect of affective dimensions in my book *Politics, Ethics and Emotions in "New India"* (Routledge 2023).

11 In his celebrated book, *Event, Metaphor, Memory* (1995), Shahid Amin observes how nationalist politics in popular memory was filtered through local narratives.

12 A good instance of self-contradictory practices is how the BJP mobilizes in various regions with differentiated logics that run at cross-purposes. A BJP candidate in Kerala promised quality beef for his constituency, as did its unit in Meghalaya, even as mob lynchings by cow vigilantes continued in most of the Hindu heartland; but the electorate does not see this as contradictory or unacceptable.

13 Commonality of the civil sphere is decentered through contradictory and dispersed practices at one level and highly centralized effects at another. It could mark a split between the political and social domains, managed through "shifting contradictions" from one domain to the other or containing conflict in one through a narrative of commonality or unity in the other.

14 Refer to "A Rightward Shift in Dalit Politics" (Gudavarthy 2014).

15 I am referring here to an email communication with Jeffrey Alexander, drawing on his 2006 book.

16 Dr. Ambedkar, champion of anti-caste politics, suggested various means for "annihilation of caste," including inter-dining and inter-caste marriages. He later, realizing the stubborn rigidity of caste-based practices, moved on to suggest religious conversion from Hinduism to Buddhism. Later, in the 1970s, Dalit Panthers, fashioned after the Black Panthers, identified forging cross-caste and class solidarity of "all those dispossessed" as a radical means of questioning the hegemonic Brahminical order.

NOTES TO PP. 116–128

17 For my critique of such exclusionary claims, refer to "Gandhi, Dalits and Feminists: Recovering the Convergence" (Gudavarthy 2008).
18 Refer to Saba Mahmood's (2011) eloquently written book *Politics of Piety*, for a scholarly interpretation of Foucauldian notions of agency. Also refer to Partha Chatterjee's *Politics of the Governed* (2004) to understand the kind of shift I am suggesting here.
19 Jeffrey Alexander, in the introduction to *Performance and Power* (2011b), points to his critique of Foucault's emphasis on subjects, as against viewing them as actors.
20 For a more elaborate discussion on this refer to Ajay Gudavarthy, "Solidarity beyond Patronage" (2022).
21 To make sense of how populism creates a hegemonic unity, refer to https://www.telegraphindia.com/opinion/hindutva-hegemony-across-caste-and-class-lines-in-india/cid/1785729
22 https://scroll.in/article/863107/the-daily-fix-ban-on-meat-display-in-south-delhi-is-more-ideological-than-a-public-health-concern
23 Shankara Agraharam, "The Vedic Village," https://www.vedicagraharam.com/township/plots/?fbclid=IwAR0PW6yZVnlBu8KOL9srAR7zrT9aDfhThyHKHe2x2_3lZCQBFYQS-RAQCow; N. Bhanutej, "Housing Apartheid in Indian City," Al Jazeera, February 2014, https://www.aljazeera.com/features/2014/2/28/housing-apartheid-in-indian-city?fbclid=IwAR0fD6tFgDTj9ns3rd_cw7H-OD3pAFt-IEPVtUnhxLZoT8KbMuLWFyUvn2g
24 There is a need for a more elaborate discussion on the interface between the political and non-political – meaning the intimate and the spiritual. For more on this, refer to Prathama Banerjee *Elementary Aspects of the Political* (2021).
25 For a short review of my concept of secular sectarianism, refer to https://liveencounters.net/2020-le-mag/03-march-2020/professor-anindya-sekhar-purakayastha-subaltern-and-its-fragments-aporias-of-identity-politicsreview-of-dr-ajay-gudavarthys-book-secular-sectarianism
26 In an interesting response to Marx's writings on India, Ambedkar responded by arguing that what Marx understood as the division of labor was in the Indian context the "division of labourers."
27 For an assessment of the continued practice of untouchability in India, refer to https://www.epw.in/journal/2020/2/special-articles/continuing-practice-untouchability-india.html
28 For an overview of BJP's strategy of extending representation, refer to https://www.newindianexpress.com/nation/2022/mar/11/up-polls-bjps-caste-calculus-dominated-by-non-yadav-obc-communities-decimates-sp-2428991.html

Chapter 6: Building Solidarity, Attempting Civil Repair: Pious Altruism and Muslim Politics in Post-Babri Mumbai

1 Some exceptions to this pattern are other social groups excluded from the mainstream, who might share cultural food practices, for example, or have more porous faith boundaries.
2 Fieldwork was conducted in 2009–10, 2014–15, and 2016.
3 Alms given during the Islamic month of *Ramzan* as an obligation of Muslims to God.

NOTES TO PP. 129–146

4 A month in the Islamic calendar observed by Muslims worldwide as a month of fasting, prayer, reflection, and charity.

5 *Muharram* is the first month of the Islamic calendar and considered a holy month second to *Ramzan*. The tenth day of *Muharram*, known as *Ashura*, marks the martyrdom of Husain, the Prophet's grandson, and his family is commemorated through private and public acts of mourning.

6 *Urs* is a carnival to celebrate the birth of Sufi mystics that is often attended by Muslims of a variety of sects as well as non-Muslims.

7 Such events signaled the rise of an indigenous populace conscious of its force as a "people" with particular rights and claims to democratic participation. The Ganapati festival was a highly successful effort at utilizing these cleavages, transcending and combining the realms of rationality and ritual, making it a focal point for community and national identities in the making. See Kaur (2003).

8 A religious merit or reward followed by the performance of a good and pious deed. Although an Islamic obligation, the distribution of *zakat* is not always limited to Muslims living in poverty.

9 MIM is also a play on the Urdu alphabet *meem* (م) that refers to "Muslim." It is not uncommon to see several supporters of the party marking their vehicles (autorickshaws, motorcycles) with stickers bearing the alphabet *meem* in green.

10 *Bakri Eid* or *Eid al-Adha* (Feast of the Sacrifice) is a Muslim festival celebrated to commemorate Ibrahim's willingness to sacrifice his son in obedience to a command from God. It also marks the end of the annual Hajj pilgrimage to Mecca.

11 *Jai Bhim* refers to a popular slogan and a form of greeting or salutation among Ambedkarite movements, political parties, and individuals, which translates as the victory of Dr. B. R. Ambedkar and his ideology. Jai MIM refers to victory to Muslims. They are often used as phrases to represent the common political agendas of Dalits and Muslims by AIMIM in its political discourse.

Chapter 7: Financial Inclusion: Private Interventions in the Civil Sphere

1 Similarly, attention to culture allows for productive connections between CST and other analytic frameworks. For instance, while Alexander distinguishes his work from a class analytic (2006: 26–9), subsequent readers have pointed out that social class as an empirical reality, its multiple relations to the civil sphere (via the economy but also as a meaningful structure in the civil sphere), and the meaning-making processes of class communities, is amenable to empirical and theoretical examination via CST (Villegas 2023).

2 For a related discussion on "performativity" and the civil sphere see Egholm (2019). In my view, the two ontologies – the post-humanist *agencement* of actants and the human-centered logos of CST – are fundamentally irreconcilable, but that is a discussion for another time.

3 Nested within cultural sociology, this book contains multiple selections squarely addressing the civil sphere.

218

NOTES TO PP. 146–152

4 This was uncommon, as most discussions of microfinance at the time focused on credit and savings, and only occasionally, insurance.

5 See Saboo (2015) for another account, external to the CST framework.

6 With thanks to Carlo Tognato for formulating this insight about my work.

7 Clients of microfinance are difficult and expensive to reach, and typical loan sizes are small ($100–200). At the same time, the ultimate vision was to create clients for mainstream retail banking services in the long term. Another goal was to sell microfinance portfolios by creating a secondary market.

8 See *Dodge* v. *Ford* (1919) for the earliest and most succinct statement. For an overview see Allen (1992) and Berle (1931, 1932).

9 Also, development politics and planned economic growth are state approaches with aspects of "solidary criteria" (Alexander 2006: 208) expected to emerge in the civil sphere. We can also see them as "facilitating inputs" from one sphere into another.

10 Arteaga Botello and Arzuaga Magnoni's Mexican civil sphere exemplifies this "messiness" – the institution (the presidency) was non-civil but responded in a reformative way. Equally relevant, critique of the presidency was couched in a patrimonial rhetoric that would not resonate with CST (2018: 21–2, 32).

11 While the economic can always be interpreted via civil sphere logics, in our case, civil repair was based on translating civil motives into market discourse (i.e., discourse *internal* to the economic sphere became articulated in civil sphere cultural logic).

12 This is also true of the civil society and state boundaries, blurred through governmental technologies that create state-sponsored public spheres (Gupta 1995).

13 Financial exclusion is especially paradoxical, because banking infrastructure was created by regulatory mandate and inclusion was a central goal. The state created brick-and-mortar access to financial services through state-owned bank branches. It also directed banking activity by laying down "priority sector" targets (agriculture, housing, rural, microcredit) and creating specialized agencies (e.g., a National Bank for Agriculture and Rural Development).

14 It is instructive that we mentioned "caste" only twice in the position paper on the principles of microfinance, the challenges faced by the poor, and the growth agenda of our work (Ananth et al. 2002: 9).

15 Conceptually, this was similar to mortgage-backed securities that would bring financial markets to their knees in the crisis of 2007–8. Of course, our intention was not to sell loans without concern for client appraisal and recovery, and we did not have the lobbying power to create the regulatory environment that presaged the aggressive lending and excessive leveraging that culminated in the financial crisis (see Blackburn 2008 for an account of these mechanics).

16 We funded large-scale pilot projects on the strict condition of anonymity. That our research and funding was entirely separate from the corporate social responsibility of the bank further signified a serious long-term institutional commitment and not a piecemeal initiative to burnish the corporate brand.

17 This was the typical structure of Joint Liability Groups. Self-Help Groups were larger and met monthly.

NOTES TO PP. 152–165

18 For an overview, see Ananth 2005.

19 The models we deployed were documented by a US management scholar and fed back into the management discourse that inspired this work (Prahalad 2005).

20 While there are differences in political structure and economic scale, a similar consensus on developmentalism and planned, government-led industrialization existed in India as in South Korea (Lee 2019: 65–8).

21 I could not obtain a copy of this speech. Local staff relayed key themes, and the DC's talking points were repeated by others and featured in newspapers.

22 "We should answer concerns expressed by authorities and politicians through the media on 'usurious' interest rates, 'coercive' collection practices, 'poaching' SHG members [from state-run programs] and taking 'illegal' collaterals. The meetings should also be used to highlight the fact that MFIs are following RBI guidelines, reaching poor households whose credit needs are not being adequately fulfilled by SHG-Bank linkage [state-run programs], and MFIs are doing this without any subsidies from the government. Thus, their work needs to be encouraged. The action by certain officials to close MFI branches . . . will be detrimental to the cause of the poor, and to credit discipline" (notes from an email after the March 2006 meeting).

23 Destigmatizing the poor this way enables their passive presence.

24 This is why I propose a different "thickness" from Tognato, who locates institutional thickness in the overlap (2018: 150, 171–2); see its relevance for microfinance as a CST institution below.

Chapter 8: The British Raj and its Legacy for Democracy and Civil Society in India

1 Though we should note that to be ruled by "foreigners" was not so unusual in modern times (in pre-modern times we might say it was the norm). The Chinese were ruled by the "foreign" Manchus (the Qing dynasty) from 1644 to 1911; the English were ruled by Scots (Stuarts) for much of the seventeenth century and after a short hiatus of Dutch rule ("William and Mary"), by Germans (the Hanoverians).

2 This is an apt response to those who seek to "decolonize" the civil sphere, to see it as vitiated by its ignoring of the colonial context of the construction of its core values and practices (e.g., Hammer 2020). But to acknowledge the importance of empire in the development of some central Western ideas is not the same as seeing colonialism as *constitutive* of them, as so often claimed by the postcolonial school (e.g., Andrews 2021). There is often a colonial dimension to Western social thought; but the influence in most cases went from the imperial center to the peripheries, and then – sometimes – back again. This is clearly so in the case of the 1804 Haitian Revolution, a favorite example of the postcolonialists, which was fired by the example and ideas of the metropolitan French Revolution (where empire played its due part in the thinking of such Enlightenment philosophes as Diderot). This inspiration was freely and frequently admitted by its Black leader, Toussaint L'Ouverture. India provides another good example, as Christopher Bayly (2012) shows so well in his account of the impact of British liberal thought on Indian intellectuals and statesmen of the nineteenth and twentieth centuries, and their

220

NOTES TO PP. 171–184

creative variations on this inheritance. There was nothing in Western ideas of universality – as in the civil sphere concept – to prevent their expansion and extension to non-Western subjects, who of course often turned these ideas against their Western rulers.

3 For this dedication, Chaudhuri was dismissed from his post at All India Radio (Ferguson 2004: 217). He repeated the claim, to the chagrin of Indian nationalists, in his last book, *Thy Hand, Great Anarch!*: "No Indian with any education and some regard for historical truth, ever denied that, with all its shortcomings, British rule had, in the balance, promoted both the welfare and the happiness of the Indian people" (1987: 774).

4 Here is Nehru: "Nearly all our major problems today have grown up during British rule and as a direct result of British policy: the princes, the minority problem; various vested interests, foreign and Indian; the lack of industry and the neglect of agriculture; the extreme backwardness in the social services; and, above all, the tragic poverty of the people" (2010 [1946]: 333). One should also mention much earlier writings by Indian authors – duly acknowledged by Tharoor – that make many of the same charges as him, for instance Dadabhai Naoroji's *Poverty and Un-British Rule in India* (1901), and R. C. Dutt's *The Economic History of India in the Victorian Age* (1906), both of which draw upon the "drain theory" – that India's wealth was drained off to Britain – to explain India's poverty and backwardness. Another favorite of Tharoor's is the American writer Will Durant's hard-hitting, anti-British, *The Case for India* (1930).

5 This complexity is especially true of the measurement of the impact of British rule on the Indian economy, and of the importance of India to the British economy as a whole. For some helpful assessments, see the chapters by P. J. Cain, B. R. Tomlinson, and Avner Offner in Porter (1999). See also O'Brien (1988).

6 For an excellent example of this journalism, see the collection of articles from *The Indian Express* by the former diplomat and Congress Minister Mani Shankar Aiyar (2009).

Commentary: India and the Civil Horizons of Political Community

1 Several authors themselves recognize the limited traction. Chalwadi concludes, for example: "The societalization of the Hathras movement, however, has not been as successful in bringing about radical change due to the caste nature of Indian society; nevertheless, I argue, the movement has shown the presence of and possibilities for the Dalits in exerting civil power in the contemporary Indian civil sphere" (p. 55).

2 Mahajan observes that India's constitutional settlement of 1949 prefigured in some respects what some European and North American liberals would in the 1990s term multiculturalism. Notably, though, the direction of travel is one-way. There is little evidence that India's democratic discourse inflected and informed political and scholarly debates in the West and elsewhere.

3 Mahajan draws a fascinating contrast between Canada, where there are fierce controversies over the rights accorded to Francophone and Indigenous people but what is not disputed is that they are the salient minorities, and

NOTES TO PP. 186–187

India, where there is little consensus over *what* minorities are worthy of recognition, giving rise to endless claims and counter-claims that can only ever be resolved politically, producing in the process newer minorities.

4 The same might apply to Contractor's chapter. Contractor indicates that solidarity among poor urban Muslims is not only a function of class or minority status but is also made possible through long-standing civil elements in Islam. Islam, like Christianity and Hinduism, offers its own civil horizons.

5 This would appear to have caste implications, since while BJP representatives are often of lower castes or Dalits, RSS is generally led by Brahmins.

6 The chapters contain a wealth of material about the intricacies and tensions of civil *personae*. An example is Bairy's beautiful account of his Brahmin father's predicament: "Brahmins, because of both having anointed themselves the spokespeople for the nation-to-be and inhabiting the spaces of modern institutions, experience and enunciate great difficulty in being the bearers of two radically different ways of being human and associating with others and the world" (p. 76).

References

Aaj Tak. 2020. "Hathras Ground Report," Special coverage (in Hindi) by Shweta Singh for Aaj Tak, available at https://www.aajtak.in/programmes/desh-tak/video/what-hathras-people-think-about-gangrape-case-victim-family-and-accused-supporter-statements-ground-report-1141195-2020-10-06

Abhishek, K., and Sharma, S. 2020. "Would You've Cremated Your Own Daughter This Way, HC Ask UP ADG," *India Today*, October 13, available at https://www.indiatoday.in/india/story/hathras-case-lucknow-bench-allahabad-high-court-dm-victim-family-adg-1730906-2020-10-12

Abraham, J. 2014. "Contingent Caste Endogamy and Patriarchy," *Economic and Political Weekly* 49 (2): 56–65.

Ahmad, I. 2008. "Cracks in the 'Mightiest Fortress': Jamaat-e-Islami's Changing Discourse on Women," *Modern Asian Studies* 42 (2–3): 549–75.

Ahmad, I. 2009. *Islamism and Democracy in India: The Transformation of Jamaat-e-Islami*. Princeton, NJ and Oxford: Princeton University Press.

Ahmed, I. 1973. *Caste and Social Stratification among Muslims in India*. Delhi: Manohar.

Aiyar, M. S. 2009. *A Time of Transition: Rajiv Gandhi to the 21st Century*. New Delhi: Penguin Viking.

Aiyar, Y. 2023. "Citizen vs Labharthi? Interrogating the Contours of India's Emergent Welfare State," *The India Forum*, December 5, available at https://www.theindiaforum.in/public-policy/citizen-vs-labharthi

Aiyar, Y., and Venkat, R. 2024. "CASI Election Conversations 2024: Yamini Aiyar on the BJP's 'Techno-Patrimonial' Welfare Model," April 15, Center for the Advanced Study of India, University of Pennsylvania, available at https://casi.sas.upenn.edu/iit/election-conversations-2024-rohan-venkat-yamini-aiyar

Alexander, J. 2001. "Robust Utopias and Civil Repairs," *International Sociology* 16 (4): 579–91.

Alexander, J. C. 2002. "The Long and Winding Road: Civil Repair of Intimate Injustice," *Sociological Theory* 19 (3): 371–400.

Alexander, J. C. 2003a. *The Meanings of Social Life: A Cultural Sociology*. New York: Oxford University Press.

Alexander, J. C. 2003b. "On the Social Construction of Moral Universals: The 'Holocaust' from War Crime to Trauma Drama," pp. 27–84 in J. C. Alexander,

REFERENCES

The Meanings of Social Life: A Cultural Sociology. New York: Oxford University Press.

Alexander, J. C. 2004. "Toward a Theory of Cultural Trauma," pp. 1–30 in J. C. Alexander, R. Eyerman, B. Giesen, N. J. Smelser, and P. Sztompka (eds.), *Cultural Trauma and Collective Identity*. Berkeley, Los Angeles and London: University of California Press.

Alexander, J. C. 2005. "Contradictions in the Societal Community: The Promise and Disappointments of Parsons' Concept," pp. 93–110 in R. Fox, V. Lidz, and H. Bershady (eds.), *After Parsons: A Theory of Social Action for the Twenty-First Century*. New York: Russell Sage Foundation.

Alexander, J. C. 2006. *The Civil Sphere*. New York: Oxford University Press.

Alexander, J. C. 2009. "Postcolonialism, Trauma, and Civil Society: A New Understanding," pp. 221–40 in S. Koniordos et al. (eds.), *Conflict, Citizenship and Civil Society*. London: Routledge. Reprinted as "Partition and Trauma: Repairing India and Pakistan," pp. 136–54 in J. C. Alexander, *Trauma: A Social Theory*. Cambridge: Polity, 2012.

Alexander, J. C. 2010. *The Performance of Power: Obama's Victory and the Democratic Struggle for Power*. New York: Oxford University Press.

Alexander, J. C. 2011a. "Clifford Geertz and the Strong Program: The Human Sciences and Cultural Sociology," pp. 55–64 in J. C. Alexander, P. Smith, and M. Norton (eds.), *Interpreting Clifford Geertz: Cultural Investigation in the Social Sciences*. New York: Palgrave Macmillan.

Alexander, J. C. 2011b. *Performance and Power*. Cambridge: Polity Press.

Alexander, J. C. 2012. *Trauma: A Social Theory*. Cambridge: Polity Press.

Alexander, J. C. 2013. *The Dark Side of Modernity*. Cambridge: Polity Press.

Alexander, J. C. 2014a. "Glossary of Terms" (supplement) to "The Fate of the Dramatic in Modern Society: Social Theory and the Theatrical Avant-Garde," *Theory, Culture & Society* 31 (1): 3–24, available at https://www.theorycultu resociety.org/blog/glossary-of-terms-jeffrey-c-alexander

Alexander, J. C. 2014b. "Morality as a Cultural System: On Solidarity Civil and Uncivil," pp. 303–10 in V. Jeffries (ed.), *The Palgrave Handbook of Altruism, Morality, and Social Solidarity*. London: Palgrave.

Alexander, J. C. 2015. "Nine Theses on the Civil Sphere," pp. 172–90 in P. Kivisto and G. Sciortino (eds.), *Solidarity, Justice, and Incorporation: Thinking through the Civil Sphere*. New York: Oxford University Press.

Alexander, J. C. 2018. "The Societalization of Social Problems: Church Pedophilia, Phone Hacking, and the Financial Crisis," *American Sociological Review* 83 (6): 1049–78.

Alexander, J. C. 2019a. *What Makes a Social Crisis? The Societalization of Social Problems*. Cambridge: Polity Press.

Alexander, J. C. 2019b. "Frontlash/Backlash: The Crisis of Solidarity and the Threat to Civil Institutions," *Contemporary Sociology* 48 (1): 5–11.

Alexander, J. C. 2020. "Against the Idea of 'Western Modernity': Axial Foundations and Contemporary Civil Spheres in East Asia," *Culture: Newsletter of the Culture Section of the American Sociological Association* 32 (1): 10–13.

Alexander, J. C. 2024. "Introduction: Civil Repair and Social Theory," pp. 1–7 in J. C. Alexander, *Civil Repair*. Cambridge: Polity Press.

REFERENCES

Alexander, J. C. 2025a. *Frontlash/Backlash*. Cambridge: Polity Press.

Alexander, J. C. 2025b. "The Political Party between Democracy and Dictatorship," *Perfiles Latinoamericanos*.

Alexander, J. C., and Jaworsky, B. N. 2014. *Obama Power*. Cambridge: Polity Press.

Alexander, J. C., and Smith, P. 2003. "The Strong Program in Cultural Sociology: Elements of a Structural Hermeneutics," pp. 11–26 in J. C. Alexander (ed.), *The Meanings of Social Life: A Cultural Sociology*. New York: Oxford University Press.

Alexander, J. C., and Tognato, C. 2018a. "Introduction: For Democracy in Latin America," pp. 1–15 in J. C. Alexander and C. Tognato (eds.), *The Civil Sphere in Latin America*. New York: Cambridge University Press.

Alexander, J. C., and Tognato, C., eds. 2018b. *The Civil Sphere in Latin America*. New York: Cambridge University Press.

Alexander, J. C., Lund, A., and Voyer, A. 2019a. *The Nordic Civil Sphere*. Cambridge: Polity Press.

Alexander, J. C., Palmer, D. A., Park, S., and Shuk-mei Ku, A. 2019b. *The Civil Sphere in East Asia*. New York: Cambridge University Press.

Alexander, J. C., Kivisto, P., and Sciortino, G. 2020. *Populism in the Civil Sphere*. Cambridge: Polity Press.

Allen, W. 1992. "Our Schizophrenic Conception of the Business Corporation," *Cardozo Law Review* 14: 261–81.

Aloysius, G. 1998. *Nationalism without a Nation in India*. New York: Oxford University Press.

Ambedkar, B. R. 1944 [1936]. *The Annihilation of Caste*, available at https://ccnmtl.columbia.edu/projects/mmt/ambedkar/web/readings/aoc_print_2004_old.pdf

Ambedkar, B. R. 2016 [1936]. "Annihilation of Caste: An Undelivered Speech, 1936," pp. 205–317 in B. R. Ambedkar, *The Annihilation of Caste: The Annotated Critical Edition*. London: Verso.

Ambedkar, B. R. 1979 [1916]. "Castes in India: Their Mechanism, Genesis and Development," pp. 3–22 in *Dr. Babasaheb Ambedkar Writings and Speeches Vol. I*. Mumbai: Education Department, Government of Maharashtra.

Ambedkar, B. R. 1987. *Dr. Babasaheb Ambedkar: Writings and Speeches (Volume 3)*. New Delhi: Dr. Ambedkar Foundation, Ministry of Social Justice & Empowerment, Govt. of India.

Amin, S. 1995. *Event, Metaphor, Memory: Chauri Chaura 1922–1992*. Berkeley: University of California Press.

Anand, S. 2005. "Politics, Tamil Cinema Eshtyle," *Outlook*, May 30, available at http://www.outlookindia.com/article.aspx?227523

Ananth, B. 2005. "Financing Microfinance: The ICICI Bank Partnership Model," *Small Enterprise Development* 16: 57–65.

Ananth, B., Duggal, B., and Saboo, K. 2002. "Microfinance: Building the Capacity of the Poorest of the Poor to Participate in the Larger Economy," ICICI Working Paper Series.

Andersen, W. 1972. "The Rashtriya Swayamsevak Sangh: I: Early Concerns," *Economic and Political Weekly* 7 (11): 589–97.

Andersen, W. K., and Damle, S. 2019. *The RSS: View to the Inside*. New Delhi: Penguin.

REFERENCES

Anderson, P. 2018. "'An Abundance of Meaning': Ramadan as an Enchantment of Society and Economy in Syria," *HAU: Journal of Ethnographic Theory* 8 (3): 610–24.

Andrews, K. 2021. *The New Age of Empire: How Racism and Colonialism Still Rule the World*. London: Allen Lane/The Penguin Press.

Antipode Online. 2020. "Dalit Lives Matter! A Cry to Rage Against the Horrifying Violence of Saffron Terror in India," October 30, available at https://antipodeonline.org/2020/10/30/dalit-lives-matter/

Appleby, J. 1984. *Capitalism and the New Social Order: The Republican Vision of the 1790s*. New York: NYU Press.

Ara, I. 2020. "Aligarh Hospital MLC Report on Hathras Victim Shatters UP Police 'No Rape' Claim," *The Wire*, available at https://thewire.in/women/aligarh-jnmch-hathras-victim-mlc-report-up-police-rape

Arteaga Botello, N. 2020. "Solidary Cuisine: Las Patronas Facing the Central American Migratory Flow," pp. 183–202 in C. Tognato, N. B. Jaworsky, and J. C. Alexander (eds.), *The Courage for Civil Repair: Narrating the Righteous in International Migration*. New York: Palgrave Macmillan.

Arteaga Botello, N., and Arzuaga Magnoni, J. 2018. "The Civil Sphere in Mexico: Between Democracy and Authoritarianism," pp. 19–38 in J. C. Alexander and C. Tognato (eds.), *The Civil Sphere in Latin America*. New York: Cambridge University Press.

Aurobindo, S. 1998 [1906–8]. *Bande Mataram: Early Political Writings*. Pondicherry: Sri Aurobindo Ashram Publications.

Austin, G. 1999a [1966]. *The Indian Constitution: Cornerstone of a Nation*. New Delhi: Oxford University Press.

Austin, G. 1999b. *Working a Democratic Constitution*. New Delhi: Oxford University Press.

Bailyn, B. 1967. *The Ideological Origins of the American Revolution*. Cambridge, MA: Harvard University Press.

Bairy T. S., R. 2010. *Being Brahmin, Being Modern: Exploring the Lives of Caste Today*. New Delhi: Routledge.

Bairy T. S., R. 2019. "Thinking Religion Regionally: Hindu Institutions in Contemporary South India," paper presented at the Centre for Studies in Religion and Society, University of Victoria, Canada.

Bajpai, R. 2000. "Constituent Assembly Debates and Minority Rights," *Economic and Political Weekly* 35 (21/22): 1837–45.

Banerjee, D., and Copeman, J. 2018. "Ungiven: Philanthropy as Critique," *Modern Asian Studies* 52 (1): 325–50.

Banerjee, P. 2021. *Elementary Aspects of the Political: Histories from the Global South*. Durham, NC: Duke University Press.

Bardhan, P. 2022. "The 'New' India: A Political-Economic Diagnosis," *New Left Review* 136 (July–August): 5–27.

Barns, M. D. 1940. *The Indian Press: A History of the Growth of Public Opinion in India*. New York: G. Allen and Unwin.

Bate, B. 2009. *Tamil Oratory and the Dravidian Aesthetic*. New York: Columbia University Press.

Bauman, Z. 2001. *Community: Seeking Safety in an Insecure World*. Cambridge: Polity Press.

Bayat, A. 1997. *Street Politics: Poor People's Movements in Iran*. New York: Columbia University Press.

REFERENCES

Bayly, C. A. 1990. *Indian Society and the Making of the British Empire.* Cambridge: Cambridge University Press.

Bayly, C. A. 2012. *Recovering Liberties: Indian Thought in the Age of Liberalism and Empire.* Cambridge: Cambridge University Press.

Bayly, S. 1999. *Caste, Society and Politics in India from the Eighteenth Century to the Modern Age.* Cambridge: Cambridge University Press.

Becker, E. 2022. "Incivility and Danger: Theorizing a Muslim Undercaste in Europe," *American Journal of Cultural Sociology* 10: 398–431, https://doi.org/10.1057/s41290-021-00136-z

Bellah, R. N. 1967. "Civil Religion in America," *Daedalus* 96 (1): 1–21, https://www.jstor.org/stable/20027022

Bellah, R. N. 1970. "Civil Religion in America," pp. 168–89 in R. N. Bellah, *Beyond Belief: Essays on Religion in a Post-Traditional World.* New York: Harper and Row.

Bellah, R. N. 2011. *Religion in Human Evolution: From the Paleolithic to the Axial Age.* Cambridge, MA: Harvard University Press.

Bellah, R. N. 2015. "Religion and the Civil Sphere: A Global Perspective," pp. 32–56 in P. Kivisto and G. Sciortino (eds.), *Solidarity, Justice and Incorporation: Thinking through the Civil Sphere.* Oxford: Oxford University Press.

Berle, A. A. 1931. "Corporate Powers as Powers in Trust," *Harvard Law Review* 44 (7): 1049–74.

Berle, A. A. 1932. "For Whom Corporate Managers are Trustees: A Note," *Harvard Law Review* 45 (8): 1365–72.

Berlin, I. 2002. *Liberty.* New York: Oxford University Press.

Beteille, A. 1986. "Individualism and Equality," *Current Anthropology* 27 (2): 121–34.

Bhagat, R. B. 2001. "Census and the Construction of Communalism in India," *Economic and Political Weekly* 36 (46/47): 4352–6.

Bhalla, A., ed. 1994. *Stories about the Partition of India.* New Delhi: Indus/Harper Collins.

Bharathi, S. P. 2020. "Caste-Based Crimes Continue Unabated in Tamil Nadu During Lockdown," *The News Minute,* May 14, available at https://www.thenewsminute.com/article/caste-based-crimes-continue-unabated-tamil-nadu-during-lockdown-124558

Bhargava, R. 2000. "History, Nation and Community: Reflections on Nationalist Historiography of India and Pakistan," *Economic and Political Weekly* 35 (4): 193–200.

Bhatia, G. 2019. "Making the Path by Walking: The Supreme Court's Film Censorship Judgment," *Indian Constitutional Law and Philosophy,* April 14.

Bhattacharjee M. 2019. "Hindutva as a 'Sacred Form': A Case Study of Karnataka," pp. 108–23 in N. Kumar (ed.), *Politics and Religion in India.* Abingdon: Taylor & Francis.

Bianchi, L. 2017. "Come 'La Casta' ha Cambiato per Sempre l'Italia," *VICE,* April 17, available at https://www.vice.com/it/article/mgyeqx/la-casta-ha-cambiato-per-sempre-litalia [accessed November 11, 2023].

Biggar, N. 2023. *Colonialism: A Moral Reckoning.* London: Collins.

Biswas, S. 2024. "Free Water, Housing, Food: Modi's $400bn Welfare Bet to Win India's Elections," *BBC News,* May 9.

Blackburn, R. 2008. "The Subprime Crisis," *New Left Review* 50: 63–106.

REFERENCES

Bloch, R. 1985. *Visionary Republic: Millennial Themes in American Thought, 1756–1800*. New York: Cambridge University Press.

Bob, C. 2007. "'Dalit Rights are Human Rights': Caste Discrimination, International Activism, and the Construction of a New Human Rights Issue," *Human Rights Quarterly* 29 (1): 167–93.

Bose, M. 2018. "From Kaala's Reviews to Dhadak's Trailer, Dalit Assertion Ignored," *The Quint*, June 11, available at https://www.thequint.com/news/politics/kaala-sairat-strongest-theme-dalit-assertion-caste-blind-reviews-dhadak-trailer

Brown, J. M. 2003. *Nehru: A Political Life*. New Haven, CT: Yale University Press.

Buffett, W. 2002. *2002 Annual Report*, available at http://www.berkshirehathaway.com/2002ar/2002ar.pdf

Burke, E., and Lapidus, I., eds. 1988. *Islam, Politics and Social Movements*. Berkeley: University of California Press.

Carswell, G., and De Neve, G. 2014. "Why Indians Vote: Reflections on Rights, Citizenship, and Democracy from a Tamil Nadu Village," *Antipode* 46 (4): 1032– 53.

Carswell, G., and De Neve, G. 2015. "Litigation Against Political Organisation? The Politics of Dalit Mobilisation in Tamil Nadu, South India," *Development and Change* 46 (5): 1106–32.

Certeau, M. de. 2011. *The Practice of Everyday Life* (3rd edn.), translated by S. F. Rendall. Berkeley: University of California Press.

Chakrabarty, D. 2002. *Habitations of Modernity: Essays in the Wake of Subaltern Studies*. Chicago: University of Chicago Press.

Chakrabarty, D. 2007. *Provincializing Europe: Postcolonial Thought and Historical Difference* (new edn.). Princeton, NJ: Princeton University Press.

Chakravarty, S. 1991. *The Raj Syndrome: A Study in Imperial Perceptions*. Delhi: Penguin Books.

Chandrachud, D. 2020. "The Hues That Make India: From Plurality to Pluralism," P. D. Desai Memorial Lecture, Bujarat.

Chatterjee, P. 1993. *Nationalist Thought and the Colonial World*. Minneapolis: University of Minnesota Press.

Chatterjee, P. 2001. "On Civil and Political Society in Post-Colonial Democracies," pp. 165–78 in S. Kaviraj and S. Khilnani (eds.), *Civil Society: History and Possibilities*. Cambridge: Cambridge University Press.

Chatterjee, P. 2004. *The Politics of the Governed: Reflections on Popular Politics in Most of the World*. New York: Columbia University Press.

Chatterji, A. P., Hansen, T. B., and Jaffrelot, C. 2019. *Majoritarian State: How Hindu Nationalism is Changing India*. New York: Oxford University Press.

Chatterji, R., and Mehta, D. 2007. *Living with Violence: An Anthropology of Events and Everyday Life*. New Delhi: Routledge.

Chatterji, S. 2024. "How Rahul Gandhi Turned the Tide in Favor of Congress, INDIA Bloc Alliance," *Hindustan Times*, June 5, available at https://www.hindustantimes.com/india-news/how-rahul-gandhi-turned-the-tide-in-favour-of-congress-india-bloc-alliance-101717561727873.html

Chaudhuri, N. C. 1951. *Autobiography of an Unknown Indian*. London: Macmillan.

Chaudhuri, N. C. 1987. *Thy Hand, Great Anarch! India 1921–1952*. London: The Hogarth Press.

228

REFERENCES

Chishti, S. 2014. "Biggest Caste Survey: One in Four Indians Admit to Practising Untouchability," *New Indian Express*, November 29, available at http://indianexpress.com/article/india/india-others/one-in-four-indians-admit-to-practising-untouchability-biggest-caste-survey/

Choudhary, S. 2022. "Symbolism and Cultural Politics in Contemporary India," M.Phil. Dissertation, Jawaharlal Nehru University, pp. 37–69, available at http://etd.lib.jnu.ac.in/TH31250.pdf

Chowdhury, D. R. 2022. "Modi's India is Where Global Democracy Dies," *The New York Times*, August 25: A19.

Chowdhury, D. R. 2023. "Modi is Pushing India to the Brink," *The New York Times*, August 10: A19.

Chowdhury, D. R., and Keane, J. 2021. *To Kill a Democracy: India's Passage to Despotism*. Oxford: Oxford University Press.

Claveyrolas, M. 2023. "Hinduism and Caste System," pp. 235–46 in S. Jodhka and J. Naudet (eds.), *The Oxford Handbook of Caste*. New York: Oxford University Press.

Cohn, B. S. 1996. *Colonialism and its Forms of Knowledge: The British in India*. Princeton, NJ: Princeton University Press.

Collins, M. 2017. "Writing Dalit Assertion: Early Dalit Panther Politics and Legal Advocacy in 1980s Tamil Nadu," *Contemporary South Asia* 25 (3): 238–54.

Contractor, Q. 2012. "Quest for Water: Muslims at Mumbai's Periphery," *Economic and Political Weekly* 47 (29): 61–7.

Cooke, I. M. 2019. "Immoral Times: Vigilantism in a South Indian City," pp. 69–82 in A. P. Chatterji, T. B. Hansen, and C. Jaffrelot (eds.), *Majoritarian State: How Hindu Nationalism is Changing India*. Uttar Pradesh: HarperCollins.

Copeman, J., and Ikegame, A. 2012. "The Multifarious Guru: An Introduction," pp. 1–45 in J. Copeman and A. Ikegame (eds.), *The Guru in South Asia: New Interdisciplinary Perspectives*. Abingdon: Routledge.

Corbridge, S., and Harriss, J. 2000. *Reinventing India: Liberalization, Hindu Nationalism and Popular Democracy*. Cambridge: Polity Press.

CSCCL. n.d. "Study on Performance of Special Courts set up under the SC ST Prevention of Atrocity Act," Report prepared by Centre for Study of Casteism, Communalism and Law (CSCCL). Bangalore: National Law School, available at https://idsn.org/wp-content/uploads/user_folder/pdf/New_files/India/Perforrman_of_courts_SCST_act-_Study.pdf

Dahl, R. A. 1989. *Democracy and its Critics*. New Haven, CT: Yale University Press.

Dale, S. F. 2010. *The Muslim Empires of the Ottomans, Safavids, and Mughals*. Cambridge: Cambridge University Press.

Dalit Women Fight. 2020. "Mail UP Government, the Supreme Court of India, United Nations VAW, the Prime Minister of India and the National Commission for Scheduled Caste," September 2020 (campaign), *Jhatkaa.org*, available at https://act.jhatkaa.org/campaigns/235

Damodaran, K. 2018a. "Contentious Spaces: Caste, Commemorations and Production of Political Community in South India," Unpublished Ph.D. Thesis, University of Edinburgh.

Damodaran, K. 2018b. "Pariyerum Perumal: A Film That Talks Civility in an Uncivil, Casteist Society," *The Wire*, October 12, available at https://thewire.in/film/a-film-that-talks-civility-in-an-uncivil-casteist-society

REFERENCES

Damodaran, K., and Gorringe, H. 2017. "Madurai Formula Films: Caste Pride and Politics in Tamil Cinema," *South Asia Multidisciplinary Academic Journal*, available at http://samaj.revues.org/4359

Damodaran, K., and Gorringe, H. 2020. "Contested Narratives: Filmic Representations of North Chennai in Contemporary Tamil Cinema," pp. 19–35 in S. Velayutham and V. Devadas (eds.), *Tamil Cinema in the Twenty-First Century: Caste, Gender and Technology*. Abingdon: Routledge.

Darshan, N. 2019. "Sense of a Scene: Kaadhal Climax, Love in the Times of Caste," *The New Indian Express*, September 25, available at https://www.newindianexpress.com/entertainment/tamil/2019/sep/25/sense-of-a-scene-kaadhal-climax-love-in-the-times-of-caste-2038671.html

Darwin, J. 2013. "Empire and Ethnicity," pp. 147–71 in J. A. Hall and S. Malesevic (eds.), *Nationalism and War*. Cambridge: Cambridge University Press.

Das, V. 1982. *Structure and Cognition: Aspects of Hindu Caste and Ritual*. Delhi: Oxford University Press.

David, S. 2020. "How Dainik Jagran and TOI's Lucknow Editions Ignored the Hathras Rape," *Newslaundry*, October 1, available at https://www.newslaundry.com/2020/10/01/how-dainik-jagran-and-tois-lucknow-ditions-ignored-the-hathras-rape

Dayan, D., and Katz, E. 1992. *Media Events: The Live Broadcasting of History*. Cambridge, MA: Harvard University Press.

De, R. 2018. *A People's Constitution: The Everyday Life of Law in the Indian Republic*. Princeton, NJ: Princeton University Press.

Deeb, L. 2011. *An Enchanted Modern: Gender and Public Piety in Shi'i Lebanon*. Princeton, NJ: Princeton University Press.

Desai, S., and Dubey, A. 2011. "Caste in 21st Century India: Competing Narratives," *Economic and Political Weekly* 46 (11): 40–9.

Deshpande, P., and Chaturvedi, R., eds. 2024. *Bharat Jodo Yatra: Reclaiming India's Soul*. New Delhi: HarperCollins.

Deshpande, S. 1998. "Hegemonic Spatial Strategies: The Nation-Space and Hindu Communalism in Twentieth-Century India," *Public Culture* 10 (2): 249–83.

Devji, F. 2007. "Apologetic Modernity," *Modern Intellectual History* 4 (1): 61–76.

Dhanani, S. 2023. "India's Justice System is no Longer Independent: Part I", September 23, available at https://www.lawfaremedia.org/article/india-s-justice-system-is-no-longer-independent-part-i [accessed October 12, 2023].

Dickey, S. 1993. *Cinema and the Urban Poor in South India*. Cambridge: Cambridge University Press.

Dirks, N. B. 2001. *Castes of Mind: Colonialism and the Making of Modern India*. Princeton, NJ: Princeton University Press.

Dobbin, C. 1972. *Urban Leadership in Western India: Politics and Communities in Bombay City, 1840–1885*, vol. 55. Oxford: Oxford University Press.

Dodd, E. M. 1932. "For Whom are Corporate Managers Trustees," *Harvard Law Review* 45 (7): 1145–63.

Dodge et al. v. Ford Motor Co. [1919] *United States Reports*. Supreme Court.

Drèze, J. 2020. "The Revolt of the Upper Castes," *The Indian Forum*, February 18, available at https://www.theindiaforum.in/article/revolt-upper-castes

REFERENCES

Dumont, L. 1964. "The Functional Equivalents of the Individual in Caste Society," *Contributions to Indian Sociology (O.S.)* VIII: 85–99.

Dumont, L. 1970. *Homo Hierarchicus: The Caste System and its Implications.* Chicago: University of Chicago Press.

Dutta, A. 2022. "New India Leaders Less from English-Speaking World, so Judged Harshly: MEA Paper," *Indian Express.com*, December 28, available at https://indianexpress.com/article/express-exclusive/new-india-leaders-less-from-english-speaking-world-so-judged-harshly-mea-paper-7784564/

Economic and Political Weekly. 1973. "Gentlemen Killers of Kilvenmani," *Economic and Political Weekly* 8 (21): 926–8.

Egholm, L. 2019. "Complicated Translations," pp. 64–93 in J. C. Alexander, A. Lund, and A. Voyer (eds.), *The Nordic Civil Sphere.* Cambridge: Polity Press.

Eickelman, D. 1992. "Mass Higher Education and the Religious Imagination in Contemporary Arab Societies," *American Ethnologist* 19 (4): 643–55.

Eickelman, D., and Piscatori, J. 1996. *Muslim Politics.* Princeton, NJ: Princeton University Press.

Eisenstadt, S. N. 1982. "The Axial Age: The Emergence of Transcendental Visions and the Rise of the Clerics," *European Journal of Sociology* 23 (2): 299–314.

Ellis-Petersen, H. 2023. "India's Supreme Court Suspends Rahul Gandhi's Two-Year Defamation Jail Term," *The Guardian*, August 4.

Escobar, A. 1995. *Encountering Development: The Making and Unmaking of the Third World.* Princeton, NJ: Princeton University Press.

Eyerman, R. 2001. *Cultural Trauma: Slavery and the Formation of African American Identity.* New York: Cambridge University Press.

Falzon, M.-A. 2004. "Paragons of Lifestyle: Gated Communities and the Politics of Space in Bombay," *City & Society* 16 (2): 145–67.

Ferguson, J. 1990. *The Anti-Politics Machine: Development, Depoliticization, and Bureaucratic Power in Lesotho.* Cambridge: Cambridge University Press.

Ferguson, N. 2004. *Empire: How Britain Made the Modern World.* London: Penguin Books.

Ferry, M. 2018. "Cow Terrorism," *Books and Ideas*, March 26, available at https://booksandideas.net/Cow-Terrorism

Fitzgerald, T. 2007. *Discourses of Civility and Barbarism: A Critical History of Religion and Related Categories.* Oxford: Oxford University Press.

Frankel, F. R. 1978. *India's Political Economy: The Gradual Revolution.* Oxford: Oxford University Press.

Freeman, J. M. 1979. *Untouchable: An Indian Life History.* London: George Allen and Unwin.

Freitag, S. B. 1988. "The Roots of Muslim Separatism in South Asia: Personal Practice and Public Structures in Kanpur and Bombay," pp. 115–45 in E. Burke III and I. Lapidus (eds.), *Islam, Politics and Social Movements.* Berkeley: University of California Press.

Froerer, P. 2010. *Religious Division and Social Conflict.* New Delhi: Social Science Press.

Fuchs, M. 2001. "Religion for Civil Society? Ambedkar's Buddhism and the Imagination of Emergent Possibilities," pp. 250–73 in V. Dalmia, A. Malinar, and M. Christoff (eds.), *Charisma and Canon: Essays on the Religious History of the Indian Subcontinent.* Oxford: Oxford University Press.

REFERENCES

Fuller, C. J. and Narasimhan, H. 2014. *Tamil Brahmans: The Making of a Middle-Class Caste*. Chicago: Chicago University Press.

Gallo, E. 2017. *The Fall of Gods: Memory, Kinship and Middle Classes in South India*. New Delhi: Oxford University Press.

Gandhi, R. 2023. "Bharat Mata: The Voice of Every Indian," *Newsmeter Network*, August 15, available at https://newsmeter.in/nation/bharat-mata-the -voice-of-every-indian-rahul-gandhi-716453

Geertz, C. 1971. *Islam Observed: Religious Development in Morocco and Indonesia*, vol. 37. Chicago: University of Chicago Press.

Geertz, C. 1973. "Thick Description: Towards an Interpretive Theory of Culture," pp. 3–30 in G. Geertz, *The Interpretation of Cultures*. New York: Basic Books.

Geetha, V., and Rajadurai, S. V. 1998. *Towards a Non-Brahmin Millennium: From Iyothee Thass to Periyar*. Calcutta: Samya.

Geetha, V., and Rajadurai, S. 2011. *Towards a Non-Brahmin Millennium* (2nd rev. edn.). Calcutta: Samya.

George, A. 2006. "Reinventing Honorable Masculinity: Discourses from a Working-Class Indian Community," *Men and Masculinities* 9 (1): 35–52.

Go, J. 2016. *Postcolonial Thought and Social Theory*. New York: Oxford University Press.

Goody, J. 2001. "Civil Society in an Extra-European Perspective," pp. 149–64 in S. Kaviraj and S. Khilnani (eds.), *Civil Society: History and Possibilities*. Cambridge: Cambridge University Press.

Gooptu, N. 2001. *The Politics of the Urban Poor in Early Twentieth-Century India*, vol. 8. Cambridge: Cambridge University Press.

Gorringe, H. 2005. *Untouchable Citizens: Dalit Movements and Democratization in Tamil Nadu*. Los Angeles and London: Sage.

Gorringe, H. 2006. "Banal Violence? The Everyday Underpinnings of Collective Violence," *Identities: Global Studies in Culture and Power* 13 (2): 237–60.

Gorringe, H. 2017. *Panthers in Parliament*. Delhi: Oxford University Press.

Gorringe, H., and Waghmore S. 2019. "'Go Write on the Walls That You Are the Rulers of This Nation': Dalit Mobilization and the BJP," *Indian Politics and Society* 2 (1): 31–52.

Gorringe, H., Jeffery, R., and Waghmore, S., eds. 2016. *From the Margins to the Mainstream: Institutionalizing Minorities in South Asia*. London: Sage.

Gorski, P. S. 2010. *Civil Religion Today*. State College, PA: Association of Religion Data Archives, available at https://www.researchgate.net/profile/Philip-Gorski-2/publication/266329456_Civil_Religion_Today/links/56ab8aa60 8aed814bdea23b5/Civil-Religion-Today.pdf

Gorski, P. 2021. "The Past and Future of the American Civil Religion," pp 19–34 in R. Williams (ed.), *Civil Religion Today*. New York: New York University Press.

Gough, K. 1960. "Caste in a Tanjore Village," pp. 11–60 in E. Leach (ed.), *Aspects of Caste in South India, Ceylon, and North-West Pakistan*. Cambridge: Cambridge University Press.

Gouldner, A. W. 1979. *The Future of Intellectuals and the Rise of the New Class*. New York: Continuum.

Graham, B. 1990. *Hindu Nationalism and Indian Politics: The Origins and Development of the Bharatiya Jana Sangh*. Cambridge: Cambridge University Press.

232

REFERENCES

Green, N. 2011. *Bombay Islam: The Religious Economy of the West Indian Ocean, 1840–1915*. Cambridge: Cambridge University Press.

Green, N. 2019. "Proletarian Bodies and Muslim Festivals: Disciplining Pleasure in Colonial Bombay," in P. Kidambi, M. Kamat, and R. Dwyer (eds.), *Bombay Before Mumbai: Essays in Honour of Jim Masselos*. New Delhi: Oxford University Press.

Gudavarthy, A. 2008. "Gandhi, Dalits and Feminists: Recovering the Convergence," *Economic and Political Weekly* 43 (22): 83–90.

Gudavarthy, A. 2014. "A Rightward Shift in Dalit Politics," *The Hindu*, September 13, available at https://www.thehindu.com/opinion/op-ed/comment-a-rightward-shift-in-dalit-politics/article6405607.ece

Gudavarthy, A., ed. 2019. *Secular Sectarianism: Limits of Subaltern Politics*. New Delhi: Sage.

Gudavarthy, A. 2022. "Solidarity beyond Patronage," *Economic and Political Weekly* 57 (28).

Guha, R. 2007. *India after Gandhi: The History of the World's Largest Democracy*. New York: HarperCollins.

Gundimeda, S. 2023. "Debating Cow-Slaughter: The Making of Article 48 in the Constituent Assembly of India," *India Review* 22 (1): 1–27, https://doi.org/10.1080/14736489.2022.2142757

Gupta, A. 1995. "Blurred Boundaries: The Discourse of Corruption, the Culture of Politics, and the Imagined State," *American Ethnologist* 22 (2): 375–402.

Hall, J. 1998. "The Nature of Civil Society," *Society* 35 (4): 32–41.

Hammer, R. 2020. "Decolonizing the Civil Sphere: The Politics of Difference, Imperial Erasures, and Theorizing from History," *Sociological Theory* 38 (2): 101–21.

Hansen, T. B. 1999. *The Saffron Wave: Democracy and Hindu Nationalism in Modern India*. New Delhi: Oxford University Press.

Hansen, T. B. 2000. "Predicaments of Secularism: Muslim Identities and Politics in Mumbai," *Journal of the Royal Anthropological Institute* 6 (2): 255–72.

Hansen, T. B. 2001. *Wages of Violence: Naming and Identity in Postcolonial Bombay*. Princeton, NJ: Princeton University Press.

Hardgrave, R. 1979. *Essays in the Political Sociology of South India*. New Delhi: USHA.

Harriss, J. 2012. "Reflections on Caste and Class, Hierarchy and Dominance," *Seminar* 633, available at https://www.india-seminar.com/2012/633/633_john_harriss.htm

Hart, G. 2001. "Development Critiques in the 1990s: Cul de Sac and Promising Paths," *Progress in Human Geography* 24 (4): 649–58.

Hatch, N. O. 1977. *The Sacred Cause of Liberty: Republican Thought and the Millennium in Revolutionary New England*. New Haven, CT: Yale University Press.

Heesterman, J. C. 1988. "Householder and the Wanderer," in T. N. Madan (ed.), *Way of Life: King, Householder, Renouncer (Essays in Honour of Louis Dumont)*. Delhi: Motilal Banarsidass Publishers.

Hefner, R. W. 2000. *Civil Islam: Muslims and Democratization in Indonesia*. Princeton, NJ and Oxford: Princeton University Press.

REFERENCES

The Hindu. 2020a. "NHRC Notices Goes to U.P. Govt, Police on Hathras Case," *The Hindu*, September 30, available at https://www.thehindu.com/news /national/other-states/nhrc-notice-goes-to-up-govt-police-on-hathras-case/ article32734985.ece#:~:text.

The Hindu. 2020b. "Undying Embers: On Hathras Rape," *The Hindu* [online].

Hindustan Times. 2020. "'Unwarranted Comments': India Rejects UN Criticism of Violence against Women," *Hindustan Times*, October 5, available at https:// www.hindustantimes.com/india-news/unwarranted-comments-india-rejects -un-criticism-of-violence-against-women/story-alC071oosRAizeCehcA1YO .html

Holston, J. 2009. *Insurgent Citizenship: Disjunctions of Democracy and Modernity in Brazil.* Princeton, NJ: Princeton University Press.

Honneth, A. 2015. "Civil Society as a Democratic Battlefield," pp. 81–95 in P. Kivisto and G. Sciortino (eds.), *Solidarity, Justice, and Incorporation: Thinking through The Civil Sphere.* New York: Oxford University Press.

Human Rights Watch. 1999. *Broken People: Caste Violence Against India's "Untouchables."* Compiled by S. Narula. Washington: Human Rights Watch.

Inden, R. 1990. *Imagining India.* Oxford: Blackwell.

Inden, R. B. 2000. *Imagining India* (rev. edn.). Bloomington, IN: Indiana University Press.

Independent Initiative. 1999. *Report About Elections, Attacks on Dalits, Denial of Voting Right, Bogus Voting,* September. Published by Independent Initiative under instruction from V. I. Krishna Iyer.

India Today. 2020. "This is What AP Singh, Lawyer of Hathras Accused, Thinks of Women," *India Today*, October 6, available at https://www.indiatoday.in /india/story/lawyer-hathras-accused-ap-singh-controversial-commets-nirbhaya -case-trial-women-1728940-2020-10-06

Jaffrelot, C. 1996 [1993]. *The Hindu Nationalist Movement in India.* New York: Columbia University Press.

Jaffrelot, C. 2003a. *India's Silent Revolution: The Rise of the Low Castes in North India Politics.* Ranikhet: Permanent Black.

Jaffrelot, C. 2003b. *India's Silent Revolution: The Rise of the Lower Castes in North India.* New Delhi: Orient Blackswan.

Jaffrelot, C. 2007. *Hindu Nationalism.* Princeton, NJ: Princeton University Press.

Jaffrelot, C. 2011. *Religion, Caste, and Politics in India.* New York: Columbia University Press.

Jaffrelot, C. 2014. "Kejriwal Will Force Modi to Change His Electoral Campaign," *Rediff News*, January 16.

Jaffrelot, C. 2017. "India's Democracy at 70: Toward a Hindu State?" *Journal of Democracy* 28 (3): 52–63.

Jaffrelot, C. 2021. *Modi's India: Hindu Nationalism and the Rise of Ethnic Democracy.* Princeton, NJ: Princeton University Press.

Jaffrelot, C., and Anil, P. 2021. *India's First Dictatorship.* New York: Oxford University Press.

James, L. 1998. *Raj: The Making and Unmaking of British India.* New York: St. Martin's Press.

Jeffrey, C. 2001. "'A Fist is Stronger than Five Fingers': Caste and Dominance in Rural North India," *Transactions of the Institute of British Geographers* 26 (2): 217–36.

Jyoti, D. 2017. "'I'm not Afraid': Husband Murdered, Kausalya Fights

234

Honour Killings," *Hindustan Times*, August 13, available at https://www.hindustantimes.com/india-news/india-at-70-i-m-not-afraid-husband-murdered-kausalya-fights-honour-killings/story-tWtISLd4g1ONfQNap6uLzM.html

Kaur, R. 2003. *Performative Politics and the Cultures of Hinduism: Public Uses of Religion in Western India*. New Delhi: Permanent Black.

Kaushik, K., Chaturvedi, A., and Jayaram, K. 2024. "India's Supreme Court Scraps Opaque Election Funding System," *Reuters*, February 2.

Kaviraj, S. 2010. "The State of Contradictions: The Post-Colonial State in India," in S. Kaviraj (ed.), *The Imaginary Institutions of India: Politics and Ideas*. New York: Columbia University Press.

Keay, J. 1988. *India Discovered: The Achievement of the Raj*. London: HarperCollins.

Keay, J. 2004. *India: A History*. Uttar Pradesh: HarperCollins India.

Keer, D. 1954. *Dr. Ambedkar: Life and Mission*. Bombay: Popular Prakashan.

Kelly, C. 1995. "Civil and Uncivil Religions: Tocqueville on Hinduism and Islam," *History of European Ideas* 20 (4–6): 845–50, https://doi.org/10.1016/0191-6599(95)95820-7

Khan, D. 2019. "The Politics of Business: The Congress Ministry and the Muslim League in Bombay, 1937–39," in P. Kidambi, M. Kamat, and R. Dwyer (eds.), *Bombay before Mumbai – Essays in Honour of Jim Masselos*. New York: Oxford University Press.

Khan, F. 2022. "'All Lies': 2 Years since Hathras 'Rape', Thakurs in Victim's Village in Denial," *The Quint*, September 30, available at https://www.thequint.com/news/india/two-years-since-hathras-rape-village-supports-accused-thakur-men-deny-rape

Khosla, M. 2020. *India's Founding Moment: The Constitution of a Most Surprising Democracy*. Cambridge, MA: Harvard University Press.

Khosrokhavar, F. 2015. "The Civil Sphere and the Arab Spring: On the Universality of Civil Society," in P. Kivisto and G. Sciortino (eds.), *Solidarity, Justice, and Incorporation: Thinking through the Civil Sphere*. New York: Oxford University Press.

King, M. L. 2022 [1963]. *Dr. Martin Luther King Jr. I Have a Dream*. New York: HarperOne.

Kivisto, P., and Sciortino, G. 2015a. "Introduction: Thinking Through the Civil Sphere," pp. 1–31 in P. Kivisto and G. Sciortino (eds.), *Solidarity, Justice, and Incorporation: Thinking Through the Civil Sphere*. New York: Oxford University Press.

Kivisto, P., and Sciortino, G., eds. 2015b. *Solidarity, Justice, and Incorporation: Thinking Through the Civil Sphere*. New York: Oxford University Press.

Kivisto, P., and Sciortino, G. 2019. "Reflections on Radicalism and the Civil Sphere," pp. 268–83 in J. C. Alexander, T. Stack, and F. Khosrokhavar (eds.), *Breaching the Civil Order: Radicalism and the Civil Sphere*. Cambridge: Cambridge University Press.

Kivisto, P., and Sciortino, G. 2023. "From Author to Network: The Coming of Age of Civil Sphere Theory," *Cultural Sociology* 17 (1): 3–20.

Kothari, B. 1964. "The Congress 'System' in India," *Asian Survey* 4 (12): 1161–73.

Krishan, G. 2019. "Preventive Detention in India: A Legal Perspective," *International Journal of Reviews and Research in Social Sciences* 7 (2), https://doi.org/10.5958/2454-2687.2019.00036.4

REFERENCES

Kumar, A. 2016. "Why Dalit Youth Hacked to Death for Marrying Woman from a Higher Caste Won't Get Justice Anytime Soon," *Scroll.in*, March 19, available at http://scroll.in/article/805277/why-dalit-youth-hacked-to-death-for-marrying-woman-from-a-higher-caste-wont-get-justice-anytime-soon

Kumar, H., and Schmall, E. 2020. "Woman Dies in Delhi after Gang Rape, Fueling Outrage again in India," *New York Times,* September 30, available at https://www.nytimes.com/2020/09/30/world/asia/india-rape-caste.html

Kumar, K. 2021. *Empires: A Historical and Political Sociology.* Cambridge: Polity Press.

Kumar, V. 2014. "Inequality in India: Caste and Hindu Social Order," *Transcience 5* (1): 36–52.

Kumar, V. 2024. "BAMCEF: As a Civil Sphere of Indian Excluded Communities," *ATSK Journal of Sociology* 2 (1): 5–15, available at http://atsk.website/atsk-sociology-volume-2-issue-1/

Kurien, P. A. 2022. "The Racial Paradigm and Dalit Anti-Caste Activism in the United States," *Social Problems* 70 (3): 717–34.

Landau, D. 2013. "Abusive Constitutionalism," *UC Davis Law Review* 47 (1): 189–260.

Lapidus, I. 1988. "Islamic Political Movements: Patterns of Historical Change," pp. 3–16 in E. Burke III and I. Lapidus (eds.), *Islam, Politics and Social Movements.* Berkeley: University of California Press.

Lee, H.-J. 2019. "Boundary Tension and Reconstruction: Credit Information Crises and the Civil Sphere in Korea," pp. 60–83 in J. C. Alexander, D. A. Palmer, S. Park, and A. S.-M. Ku (eds.), *The Civil Sphere in East Asia.* Cambridge: Cambridge University Press.

Lee, J. 2021. *Deceptive Majority: Dalits, Hinduism and Underground Religion.* Cambridge: Cambridge University Press.

Leidig, E. 2020. "Hindutva as a Variant of Right-wing Extremism," *Patterns of Prejudice 54* (3): 215–37.

Leidig, E., and Mudde, C. 2023. "Bharatiya Janata Party (BHP): The Overlooked Populist Radical Right Party," *Journal of Language and Politics* 22 (3): 360–77.

Lijphart, S. 1977. *Democracy in Plural Societies.* New Haven, CT: Yale University Press.

Lok Sabha Debates. 2009. *Parliamentary Debates: Fifteenth Series, Vol. I, First Session, 2009.* New Delhi: Lok Sabha: No. 6, Monday June 8: pp. 189–91.

Macaulay, Lord T. B. 2003 [1835]. "Minute on Indian Education," pp. 227–45 in B. Harlow and M. Carter (eds.), *Archives of Empire, Volume I: From the East India Company to the Suez Canal.* Durham, NC: Duke University Press.

Mahajan, G. 2013. *India: Political Ideas and the Making of a Democratic Discourse.* London: Zed Books.

Mahapatra, J. 2024. "'Unconstitutional, Arbitrary': Supreme Court Junks Electoral Bonds 5-0," *Times of India,* February 6.

Mahmood, S. 2011. *Politics of Piety: The Islamic Revival and the Feminist Subject.* Princeton, NJ: Princeton University Press.

Mandela, N. 1995. *The Long March to Freedom.* Boston: Back Bay Books.

Manoharan, K. R. 2016. "The Missing Periyar and the Curious Tamil Nationalism of Kabali," *Economic and Political Weekly* 51 (33), August 13, available at https://www.epw.in/journal/2016/33/web-exclusives/missing-periyar-and-curious-tamil-nationalism-kabali.html

Manor, J. 2016. "Foreword," pp. xiii–xvi in H. Gorringe, R. Jeffery, and

REFERENCES

S. Waghmore (eds.), *From the Margins to the Mainstream: Institutionalizing Minorities in South Asia*. Los Angeles and London: Sage.

Manor, J. 2021. "Inter-Caste Accommodations and Minimal Civility," pp. 129–48 in S. Waghmore and H. Gorringe (eds.), *Civility in Crisis: Democracy, Equality and the Majoritarian Challenge in India*. Abingdon: Routledge.

Marriott, M. 1976. "Hindu Transactions: Diversity Without Dualism," in B. Kapferer (ed.), *Transaction and Meaning: Directions in the Anthropology of Exchange and Symbolic Behavior*, ASA Essays in Social Anthropology, I. Philadelphia: ISHI Publications Anthropology.

Marshall, T. H. 1965. *Class, Citizenship and Social Development*. New York: Free Press.

Mashal, M. 2024. "Vilification of Muslims is a Brazen Display of Modi's Power," *New York Times*, April 24: A5.

Mashal, M., Raj, S., and Singh, K. D. 2023. "With a Pliant Judiciary, Modi Tightens His Grip on India," *New York Times*, March 30: A4.

Masselos, J. 1976. "Power in the Bombay 'Moholla', 1904–15: An Initial Exploration into the World of the Indian Urban Muslim," *South Asia: Journal of South Asian Studies* 6 (1): 75–95.

Masselos, J. 1982. "Change and Custom in the Format of the Bombay Mohurrum during the Nineteenth and Twentieth Centuries," *South Asia: Journal of South Asian Studies* 5 (2): 47–67.

Mast, J. L., and Alexander, J. C. 2018. *Politics of Meaning / Meaning of Politics: Cultural Sociology of the 2016 U.S. Presidential Election*. Cham: Springer.

Masud, M. K. 2000. *Travellers in Faith: Studies of the Tablīghī Jamā'at as a Transnational Islamic Movement for Faith Renewal*. Leiden and Boston: Brill.

McClish, M. R. 2009. "Political Brahmanism and the State: A Compositional History of the Arthaśāstra," Ph.D. Dissertation, The University of Texas at Austin, available at https://repositories.lib.utexas.edu/handle/2152/10568

McCormack W. 1963. "Lingayats as a Sect," *The Journal of the Royal Anthropological Institute of Great Britain and Ireland* 93 (1): 59–71.

Mendelsohn, O., and Vicziany, M. 1998. *The Untouchables*. Cambridge: Cambridge University Press.

Metcalf, B. D. 1982. *Islamic Revival in British India: Deoband, 1860–1900*. Princeton, NJ: Princeton University Press.

Metcalf, T. R. 1997. *Ideologies of the Raj (The New Cambridge History of India*, III. 4). Cambridge: Cambridge University Press.

Michelutti, L. 2008. *The Vernacularisation of Democracy: Politics, Caste and Religion in India*. New Delhi: Routledge.

Mines, M. 1994. "Conceptualizing the Person: Hierarchical Society and Individual Autonomy in India," in R. T. Ames (ed.), *Self as Person in Asian Theory and Practice*. Albany, NY: State University of New York Press.

Mittermaier, A. 2014. "Beyond Compassion: Islamic Voluntarism in Egypt," *American Ethnologist* 41 (3): 518–31.

Modi, N. 2023. "PM's Remarks at the G20 Summit Session 1," Prime Minister of India, September 9, available at https://www.pmindia.gov.in/en/news_upda tes/pms-remarks-at-the-g20-summit-session-1/

Mody, A. 2023. *India is Broken: A People Betrayed, Independence to Today*. Redwood City, CA: Stanford University Press.

Mohan, J. A. 2023a. "Main Accused Convicted and Three Others Acquitted in

REFERENCES

Hathras Gang Rape and Murder Case," *Indian Express*, March 3, available at https://indianexpress.com/article/cities/delhi/hathras-gangrape-murder-case-up -court-convicts-main-accused-acquits-3-others-8475386/#:~:text

Mohan, J. A. 2023b. "In Hathras, 19-Year-Old's Family Unable to Move on," *Indian Express*, March 3, available at https://indianexpress.com/article/cities /delhi/in-hathras-19-year-olds-family-unable-to-move-on-8476573/#:~:text=

Moore, B., Jr. 1966. *Social Origins of Dictatorship and Democracy: Lord and Peasant in the Making of the Modern World*. Boston: Beacon Press.

Moore, R. J. 1999. "Imperial India, 1858–1914," pp. 423–46 in A. Porter (ed.), *The Oxford History of the British Empire, vol. III: The Nineteenth Century*. Oxford: Oxford University Press.

Mukhia, H. 2004. *The Mughals of India*. New Delhi: Wiley India.

Nagaraja, G. 2020. "Andhra: Police Tonsure Dalit Man for 'Unruly Behaviour' Towards YSR Congress Leader," *The Wire*, July 24, available at https://the wire.in/caste/andhra-pradesh-tonsure-dalit-ysr-congress

Naipaul, V. S. 1968. *An Area of Darkness*. Harmondsworth: Penguin Books.

Naipaul, V. S. 1991. *India: A Million Mutinies Now*. London: Mandarin.

Nandy, A. 1991. "Hinduism Versus Hindutva: The Inevitability of a Confrontation," *Times of India*, February 18.

Nandy, A. 2002. *Time Warps: Silent and Evasive Pasts in Indian Politics and Religion*. New Brunswick, NJ: Rutgers University Press.

Narayan, B. 2020. "Has the Pandemic Changed How Caste Hierarchies Play Out in India?" *The Wire*, June 20, available at https://thewire.in/caste/covid-19-pandemic-caste-discrimination

Natarajan, J. 2021 [1955]. *History of Indian Journalism*. Hassle Street Press.

NDTV. 2020. "Prime Time with Ravish Kumar: Hathras Rape Victim Cremated by Cops, Family Kept Out," available at https://www.youtube.com/watch?v= jCWBBWvbOCs

NDTV. 2022. "Braving the Rain, Rahul Gandhi Says Nothing Can Stop *Bharat Jodo Yatra*," October 3.

Nehru, J. 1947a. "Nehru to R. Prasad, 17 Sept.," J. Nehru Papers post-1947, 2nd Instalment, File No. 231, Correspondence with Prasad.

Nehru, J. 1947b. "Nehru to R. Prasad, 7 Aug.," Selected Works of Jawaharlal Nehru, 2nd Series, vol. 3: 189–92.

Nehru, J. 2010 [1946]. *The Discovery of India*. London: Penguin Books.

The New Indian Express. 2020a. "Hathras Gang Rape: Civil Society Members, Eminent Citizens Seek CM Yogi Adityanath's Removal," *The New India Express*, available at https://www.newindianexpress.com/nation/2020/Oct/06 /hathras-gang-rape-civil-society-memberseminent-citizens-seek-cm-yogi-aditya naths-removal-2206385.html

The New Indian Express. 2020b. "Need to Discipline Bureaucrats after Hathras Blot," *The New Indian Express*, available at https://www.newindianexpress .com/opinions/editorials/2020/Oct/15/need-to-disciplinebureaucrats-after-hathras-blot-2210438.html

News 18 Hindi. 2020a. हाथरस केस: पीएम मोदी और सीएम योगी को बदनाम करने में एमनेस्टी इंटरनेशनल और कुछ देशों का नाम आया सामने ["Hathras Case: Name of Amnesty International and Some Countries Surfaced in Defaming PM Modi and CM Yogi"], available at https://hindi.news18.com/news/nation/amnesty-international-and-islamic-country-involved-in-hathras-case-for-discredit-pm-modi-and -cm-yogi-dlnh-3280803.html

REFERENCES

News 18 Hindi. 2020b. हाथरस कांड में सामने आया नक्सल कनेक्शन, नकली भाभी बनकर साजिश रच रही थी महिला- सूत्र ["Naxal Connection Revealed in Hathras Incident, Woman Was Plotting by Posing as Fake Sister-in-Law – Sources"], available at https://hindi.news18.com/news/uttar-pradesh/hathras-naxal-connection-in-hathras-gang-rape-case-during-sit-investigation-upns-3288224.html

Newsclick Report. 2020. "TN: At Least 30 Major Incidents of Caste-based Violence During Lockdown, Says Study," *Newsclick*, May 13, available at https://www.newsclick.in/Tamil-Nadu-Caste-Based-Violence-COVID-19-Lockdown

NHRC (National Human Rights Commission). 2020. "NHRC Issued Notice to the Chief Secretary and DGP of Government of Uttar Pradesh over Reported Gang Rape and Brutality of 19 Year Old Women Belonging to Scheduled Caste in Hathras District, UP," September 30, available at https://nhrc.nic.in/media/press-release/nhrc-issued-notice-chief-secretary-and-dgp-government-uttar-pradesh-over

Nilsen, A. G. 2017. *Politics from Below: Essays on Subalternity and Resistance in India*. New Delhi: Aakar Books.

Noorani, A. G. 1969. *Badruddin Tyabji – Builders of Modern India*. New Delhi: Ministry of Information and Broadcasting, Government of India.

Nussbaum, M. C. 2007. *The Clash Within: Democracy, Religious Violence, and India's Future*. Cambridge, MA: Harvard University Press.

O'Brien, P. K. 1988. "The Costs and Benefits of British Imperialism 1846–1914," *Past and Present* 120: 164–200.

Olivelle, P. 1998. "Caste and Purity: A Study in the Language of the Dharma Literature," *Contributions to Indian Sociology (N.S.)*, 32 (2): 189–216.

Omvedt, G. 2012. *Understanding Caste: From Buddha to Ambedkar and Beyond*. Hyderabad: Orient Blackswan.

Orsi, R. 1999. *Gods of the City: Religion and the American Urban Landscape*. Bloomington and Indianapolis: Indiana University Press.

Osella, F. 2018. "Charity and Philanthropy in South Asia: An Introduction," *Modern Asian Studies* 52 (1): 4–34.

Osella, F., and Soares, B. 2010. *Islam, Politics, Anthropology*. Oxford: Wiley-Blackwell.

Osella, F., and Widger, T. 2018. "'You Can Give Even if You Only Have Ten Rupees!': Muslim Charity in a Colombo Housing Scheme," *Modern Asian Studies* 52 (1): 297–324.

Outlook India. 2020. "Forensic Report Confirms Victim Wasn't Raped, Says UP ADG Prashan Kumar," *Outlookindia.com*, October 1, available at https://www.outlookindia.com/national/india-news-hathras-rape-forensic-report-confirms-victim-wasnt-raped-says-up-adg-prashant-kumar-news-361281

Palepu, A., and Kay, C. 2024. "Billionaire Press Barons Are Squeezing Media Freedom in India," *Bloomberg*, February 26.

Palm, R. 2009. "Hegel's Concept of Sublation," Ph.D. Thesis, Institute of Philosophy, Leuven, Katholieke Universiteit Leuven.

Palmer, D. A. 2019. "Three Moral Codes and Microcivil Spheres in China," pp. 126– 47 in J. C. Alexander, D. A. Palmer, S. Park, and A. S.-M. Ku (eds.), *The Civil Sphere in East Asia*. New York: Cambridge University Press.

Pandey, G. 1983. "The Bigoted Julaha," *Economic and Political Weekly* 18 (5): PE19–PE28.

REFERENCES

Pandey, G. 1997. "In Defense of the Fragment," pp. 1–33 in R. Guha (ed.), *A Subaltern Studies Reader, 1986–1995*. Minneapolis: University of Minnesota Press.

Paz, O. 1997. *In Light of India*, translated from the Spanish by E. Weinberger. San Diego, CA: Harcourt Brace and Company.

Pernau, M. 2013. *Ashraf into Middle Classes: Muslims in Nineteenth-Century Delhi*. New Delhi: Oxford University Press.

Petras, J. 1999. "NGOs: In the Service of Imperialism," *Journal of Contemporary Asia* 29 (4): 429–40.

Pew Research Center. 2021. *Religion in India: Tolerance and Segregation*, June 29, available at https://www.pewresearch.org/religion/2021/06/29/religion-in -india-tolerance-and-segregation/

Polgreen, L. 2023. "India is Jettisoning Freedom and Tolerance," *The New York Times*, February 11: A18.

Porter, A., ed. 1999. *The Oxford History of the British Empire, volume III: The Nineteenth Century*. Oxford: Oxford University Press.

Porter, M. E., and Kramer, M. R. 1999. "Philanthropy's New Agenda: Creating Value," *Harvard Business Review* (November–December): 121–30.

Prahalad, C. K. 2005. *The Fortune at the Bottom of the Pyramid*. Upper Saddle River, NJ: Wharton School.

Price, P., and Ruud, A. E. 2010. "Introduction," in A. E. Ruud and P. Price (eds.), *Power and Influence in India: Bosses, Lords and Captains*. Abingdon: Routledge.

Puniyani, R. 2021. "The Politics behind Rising Atrocities against Dalits," *The Leaflet*, June 10.

Puri, J. 2019. "Sculpting the Saffron Body: Yoga, Hindutva, and the International Marketplace," pp. 317–31 in A. P. Chatterji, T. B. Hansen, and C. Jaffrelot (eds.), *Majoritarian State: How Hindu Nationalism is Changing India*. Uttar Pradesh: HarperCollins.

Rahman, F. 1983. "Some Key Ethical Concepts of the Qur'ān," *The Journal of Religious Ethics* 11 (2): 170–85.

Rai, P. [@Benarasiyaa]. 2020. "Demanding Capital Punishment for Hathras Gangrape...," [Tweet]. October 1, available at https://twitter.com/Benara siyaa/status/1311599823150215169

Rai, S. 2023. "Between the Divine and Digital: Parsing Modi's Charismatic Avatar," *Media, Culture, and Society* 46 (4): 834–50.

Rajagopal, A. 2001. *Politics after Television: Hindu Nationalism and the Reshaping of the Public in India*. Cambridge and New York: Cambridge University Press.

Rajagopal, K. 2023. "Supreme Court Stays Rahul Gandhi's Conviction in 'Modi Surname' Remark Criminal Defamation Case," *The Hindu*, August 4.

Rajagopal, K. 2024. "Supreme Court Declares Electoral Bonds Scheme Unconstitutional," *The Hindu*, February 15.

Rajasekaran, I. 2019. "Premature Release of all Melavalavu Murder Convicts Sparks Outrage in Tamil Nadu," *Frontline*, November 13, available at https:// frontline.thehindu.com/dispatches/article29963867.ece

Rajendran, S. 2017. "Sankar Verdict and Caste Pride: How Has Tamil Cinema Contributed to Glorifying Caste," *The News Minute*, December 14, available at https://www.thenewsminute.com/article/sankar-verdict-and-caste-pride -how-has-tamil-cinema-contributed-glorifying-caste-73165

REFERENCES

Ranganathan, M. 2019. "Mohammad Ali Rogay: Life and Times of a Bombay Country Trader," in P. Kidambi, M. Kamat, and R. Dwyer (eds.), *Bombay before Mumbai: Essays in Honour of Jim Masselos*. New York: Oxford University Press.

Rao, A. 2009. *The Caste Question: Dalits and the Politics of Modern India*. Ranikhet: Permanent Black.

Rao, S. 2019. "Introduction," in S. Rao (ed.), *Indian Journalism in a New Era: Changes, Challenges, and Perspectives*. New Delhi: Oxford University Press.

Ravikumar, D. 2009. *Venomous Touch: Notes on Caste, Culture and Politics*, translated by R. Azhagarasan. Kolkatta: Samya.

Rawls, J. 1971. *A Theory of Justice*. Cambridge, MA: Harvard University Press.

Rawls, J. 1993. *Political Liberalism*. New York: Columbia University Press.

Redacción BBC News Mundo. 2018. "Por qué en Colombia se Necesitan 11 Generaciones para Salir de la Pobreza y en Chile 6," *BBC News Mundo*, August 2, available at https://www.bbc.com/mundo/noticias-45022393 [accessed November 11, 2023].

Rediff.net. 1999. "Dalits, Vanniyars Clash as Post-Poll Violence Grips TN Town," *Rediff.net*, September 7, available at https://www.rediff.com/election /1999/sep/07clash.htm

Reetz, D. 2006. *Islam in the Public Sphere: Religious Groups in India, 1900– 1947*. New Delhi: Oxford University Press.

Republic Bharat. 2020. इंसाफ के नाम पर की बड़ी 'डील' बेनकाब, ने एक-एक कर किया खुलासा! ["Hathras Case: Congress – Arnab"], YouTube.

Reuters. 2013. "The Italians Have Caste Their Lot," *Reuters*, May 1, available at https://www.reuters.com/article/idUS163368496220130430 [accessed November 11, 2023].

Richards, J. F. 1995. *The Mughal Empire (The New Cambridge History of India, I.5)*. Cambridge: Cambridge University Press.

Roberts, N. 2016. *To Be Cared for: The Power of Conversion and Foreignness of Belonging in an Indian Slum*. Oakland: University of California Press.

Robinson, F. 2007. *The Mughal Emperors, and the Islamic Dynasties of India, Iran and Central Asia, 1206–1925*. London: Thames and Hudson.

Robinson, F. 2008. "Islamic Reform and Modernities in South Asia," *Modern Asian Studies* 42 (2–3): 259–81.

Rodrigues, U. M., and Ranganathan, M. 2015. *Indian News Media: From Observer to Participant*. Melbourne: Deakin University Press.

Rose, N. 1996. "Governing 'Advanced' Liberal Democracies," pp. 37–64 in A. Barry, T. Osborne, and N. Rose (eds.), *Foucault and Political Reason: Liberalism, Neo-Liberalism, and Rationalities of Government*. Chicago: University of Chicago Press.

Roy, A. 2023. "Modi's Model is at Last Revealed for What it is: Violent Hindu Nationalism Underwritten by Big Business," *The Guardian*, February 18, available at https://www.theguardian.com/commentisfree/2023/feb/18/naren dra-modi-hindu-nationalism-india-gautam-adani [accessed August 31, 2023].

Rudolph, L. I., and Rudolph, S. H. 2008. *Explaining Indian Democracy: A Fifty-Year Perspective, 1956–2006*. New Delhi: Oxford University Press.

Rudolph, S. H. 2000. "Civil Society and the Realm of Freedom," *Economic and Political Weekly* 35 (20): 1762–9.

Rushdie, S. 2006 [1981]. *Midnight's Children*. New York: Random House.

REFERENCES

Rutherford, S. 2000. *The Poor and their Money*. New Delhi: Oxford University Press.

Saboo, K. 2015. "Socially Responsible Investment and the Politics of Development in Microfinance: A Tale of Curious Intersections from India," *American Anthropologist* 117 (4): 789–94.

Sabrang. 2020. "Valmiki Sanitation Workers Go on Strike Demanding Justice in Hathras Case," *SabrangIndia*, October 5, available at https://sabrangindia.in/valmiki-sanitation-workers-go-strike-demanding-justice-hathras-case/

Sachs, W. 1992. *The Development Dictionary: A Guide to Knowledge as Power*. London: Zed Books.

Saraswati, S. D. 1972 [1875]. *Light of Truth. An English Translation of the Satyarth Prakash*. New Delhi: Jan Gyan Prakashan.

Sathaye, A. A. 2015. *Crossing the Lines of Caste: Visvamitra and the Construction of Brahmin Power in Hindu Mythology*. New York: Oxford University Press.

Satyanarayana, K. 2015. "Social Inequality and Human Dignity," *Seminar* 672, available at http://www.india-seminar.com/2015/672/672_k_satyanarayana.htm

Savarkar, V. D. 1967 [1942]. "Message on the Eve of 59th Birthday," pp. 2–3 in *For V. D. Savarkar*. Bombay: G. P. Parchure.

Savarkar, V. D. 1969 [1923]. *Hindutva: Who is a Hindu?* Bombay: S. S. Savarkar.

Sayer, R. A. 2005. *The Moral Significance of Class*. Cambridge: Cambridge University Press.

Schimmel, A. 2004. *The Empire of the Great Mughals: History, Art and Culture*. London: Reaktion Books.

Schoch, C., and Jaffrelot, C. 2021. *Modi's India: Hindu Nationalism and the Rise of Ethnic Democracy*. Princeton, NJ: Princeton University Press.

Scroll. 2020. "Hathras Case is 'Shocking, Extraordinary', Says Supreme Court Seeks Witness Protection Plan from UP," *Scroll.in*, October 6, available at https://scroll.in/latest/975042/hathras-case-is-shocking-extraordinary-says-supreme-court-seeks-witness-protection-plan-from-up

Scroll. 2022. "Hathras Gangrape: Allahabad HC asks UP Government to Provide Job to Family Member of the Woman," *Scroll.in*, July 28, available at https://scroll.in/latest/1029244/hathras-gangrape-allahabad-hc-asks-up-government-to-provide-job-to-family-member-of-the-woman

Seal, A. 1968. *The Emergence of Indian Nationalism: Competition and Collaboration in the Late Nineteenth Century*. Cambridge: Cambridge University Press.

Sen, A. 2005. "The Argumentative Indian," pp. 3–33 in A. Sen, *The Argumentative Indian: Writings on Indian History, Culture, and Identity*. New York: Picador.

Sen, A. 2021. "Illusions of Empire: Armartya Sen on What British Rule Really Did for India," *The Guardian*, June 29.

Sen, B., and Roy, A., eds. 2014. *Channeling Cultures: Television Studies from India*. New Delhi: Oxford University Press.

Sen, M. 2017. *Haunting Bollywood: Gender, Genre, and the Supernatural in Hindi Commercial Cinema*. Austin: University of Texas Press.

Sengupta, I. 2013. "Monument Preservation and the Vexing Question of Religious Structures in Colonial India," pp. 171–85 in A. Swenson and P. Mandler (eds.), *From Plunder to Preservation: Britain and the Heritage of Empire, c. 1800–1940*. Oxford: Oxford University Press.

REFERENCES

Shaikh, F. 1989. *Community and Consensus in Islam: Muslim Representation in Colonial India, 1860–1947*. Cambridge: Cambridge University Press.

Sharma, J. 2015. *Hindutva: Exploring the Idea of Hindu Nationalism*. Uttar Pradesh: HarperCollins.

Sharma, J. 2019. *M.S. Golwalkar, the RSS and India*. New Delhi: Westland Books.

Sharma, P. 2020. "AP Singh, Lawyer of Nirbhaya Convicts, to Defend Hathras Gangrape Case Accused," *India Today*, available at https://www.indiatoday.in/india/story/ap-singh-lawyer-nirbhaya-convicts-to-defend-hathras-gangrape-case-accused-1728616-2020-10-05

Shekhar, G. 2020. "Darkness Talks Back," *Outlook*, March 16, available at https://www.outlookindia.com/magazine/story/entertainment-news-darkness-talks-back/302920

Singer, A. 2008. *Charity in Islamic Societies*. Cambridge: Cambridge University Press.

Singer, M. 1972. *When A Great Tradition Modernizes: An Anthropological Approach to Indian Civilization*. New York: Praeger Publishers.

Singh, M. 2005. "Address by Dr Manmohan Singh, Prime Minister of India, in Acceptance of Honorary Doctorate from Oxford University," July 8, available at http://www.funnotes.net/tofpages/TopicOfFortnight.php?tofTpcFl=topicof fortnight8

Sirsiya, R. [@RamSirsiya]. 2023. योगी सरकार ने हाथरस पीड़िता का 11 दिन बाद . . . ["Yogi Government got the Hathras Victims"] [Tweet]. Twitter, March 3, available at https://twitter.com/RamSirsiya/status/1631555074970521600?s=20

Skinner, Q. 1978a. *The Foundations of Modern Political Thought, vol. 1: The Renaissance*. Cambridge: Cambridge University Press.

Skinner, Q. 1978b. *The Foundations of Modern Political Thought, vol. 2: The Age of Reformation*. Cambridge: Cambridge University Press.

Sonamandan. 1999. "Will There Be Re-Polls in Chidambaram?" *Nandan* (Tamil Journal), September 16–30: 13–14, 36.

Sonwalker, P. 2019. "From *Akhbarat* to Print: The Hybridity of News Culture in Early Modern India Journalism," pp. 17–36 in S. Rao (ed.), *Indian Journalism in a New Era: Changes, Challenges, and Perspectives*. New Delhi: Oxford University Press [Kindle edn].

Srinivas, K. R., and Kaali, S. 1998. "On Castes and Comedians: The Language of Power in Recent Tamil Cinema," pp. 208–27 in A. Nandy (ed.), *The Secret Politics of our Desires: Innocence, Culpability and Indian Popular Cinema*. New Delhi: Oxford University Press.

Stack, T. 2019. "Wedging Open Established Civil Spheres: A Comparative Approach to their Emancipatory Potential," pp. 11–41 in J. C. Alexander, T. Stack, and F. Khosrokhavar (eds.), *Breaching the Civil Order: Radicalism and the Civil Sphere*. Cambridge: Cambridge University Press.

Stack, T., and Luminiello, R. 2022. *Engaging Authority: Citizenship and Political Community*. Lanham, MD: Rowman & Littlefield.

Stack, T., Goldenberg, N. R., and Fitzgerald, T. 2015. "Religion as a Category of Governance and Sovereignty," in A. W. Hughes, R. McCutcheon, and K. von Stuckrad (eds.), *Supplements to Method & Theory in the Study of Religion* (vol. 3). Leiden: Brill.

Stella, G., and Rizzo, S. 2007. *La Casta: Perchè i Politici Italiani Continuano ad Essere Intoccabili*. Milano: Rizzoli.

REFERENCES

Stepan, A. 2015. "India, Sri Lanka, and the Majoritarian Danger," *Journal of Democracy* 26 (1): 128–40.

Still, C. 2011. "Spoiled Brides and the Fear of Education: Honour and Social Mobility among Dalits in South India," *Modern Asian Studies* 45 (5): 1119–46.

Stokes, E. 1959. *The English Utilitarians and India*. Oxford: Clarendon Press.

Subramanian, A. 2019. *The Caste of Merit: Engineering Education in India*. Cambridge, MA: Harvard University Press.

Sundar, N. 2023. "The Supreme Court in Modi's India," *Journal of Right-Wing Studies* 1 (1): 106–44.

Supreme Court of India. 2017. "Writ Petition (Civil) No 494 of 2012," July 17.

Supreme Court of India. 2020. "Sexual Harassment at Workplace Violates Women's Fundamental Rights," *Scroll.in*, April 23.

Tagore, R. 1917. *Nationalism*. New York: The Macmillan Company.

Taskin, B. 2023. "Politics of Showing Dalits Their Place – Hathras Victim's Family Slams Acquittals of 3 Thakur Men," *The Print*, available at https://theprint.in/india/politics-of-showing-dalits-their-place-hathras-victims-family-slams-acquittals-of-3-thakur-men/1412127/

Taylor, C. B. 2018. "Receipts and Other Forms of Islamic Charity: Accounting for Piety in Modern North India," *Modern Asian Studies* 52 (1): 266–96.

Telegraph India. 2020a. "Twisted Plot: Conspiracy and the Hathras Case," *Telegraph India*, available at https://www.telegraphindia.com/opinion/twisted-plot-conspiracy-and-the-hathras-case/cid/1794244

Telegraph India. 2020b. "Just so: Crimes against Dalits," *Telegraph India* [online].

Thapar, R. 2020. *Voices of Dissent: An Essay*. Calcutta: Seagull Books.

Tharoor, S. 2017. *Inglorious Empire: What the British Did to India*. Melbourne: Scribe.

Thirumavalavan, R. 2004. *Uproot Hindutva: The Fiery Voice of the Liberation Panthers*, compiled and translated by M. Kandasamy. Kolkata: Samya.

Thorat, A., and Joshi, O. 2020. "The Continuing Practice of Untouchability in India," *Economic & Political Weekly* 55 (2): 36–45.

Tognato, C. 2011. "Extending Trauma across Cultural Divides: On Kidnapping and Solidarity in Colombia," pp. 191–212 in J. C. Alexander, R. Eyerman, and E. Butler Breese (eds.), *Narrating Trauma: Studies in the Contingent Impact of Collective Suffering*. Boulder, CO: Paradigm Publishers.

Tognato, C. 2018. "The Civil Life of the University: Enacting Dissent and Resistance on a Colombian Campus," pp. 149–76 in J. C. Alexander and C. Tognato (eds.), *The Civil Sphere in Latin America*. New York: Cambridge University Press.

Tognato, C. 2020. "Understanding Civil Courage in International Migration," pp. 1–33 in C. Tognato, B. N. Jaworsky, and J. Alexander (eds.), *The Courage for Civil Repair: Narrating the Righteous in International Migration*. Cham: Palgrave Macmillan.

Travelli, A., and Kumar, H. 2023. "Ethnic Violence on Rise in Modi's Divided India," *New York Times*, August 2: A9.

Travelli, A., and Raj, S. 2023. "In Fast Stroke, Modi's Backers Banish Gandhi," *New York Times*, March 25: A1.

Travelli, A., Raj, S., and Kumar, H. 2023. "New Delhi Police Raid Journalists' Workplaces," *The New York Times*, October 4: A7.

REFERENCES

Upadhya, C. 2007. "Employment, Exclusion and 'Merit' in the Indian IT Industry," *Economic and Political Weekly* 42 (20): 1863–8.

Vaasanthi. 2006. *Cut-Outs, Caste and Cine Stars: The World of Tamil Politics.* New Delhi: Penguin.

Vaishnav, D. 2020. "'This isn't a Case of Rape': Arnab Goswami Rubbishes Hathras Horror as a 'Manohar Kahani'," *Newslaundry,* available at https://www.newslaundry.com/2020/10/08/this-is-not-a-case-of-rape-arnab-goswami-rubbishes-hathras-horror-as-a-manohar-kahani

Van der Veer, P. 1994. *Religious Nationalism: Hindus and Muslims in India.* Berkeley, Los Angeles, and London: University of California Press.

Van der Veer, P. 2002. "Religion in South Asia," *Annual Review of Anthropology* 31 (1): 173–87.

Varshney, A. 2014. *Battles Half Won: India's Improbable Democracy.* New York: Penguin Viking.

Varshney, A. 2019. "Modi Consolidates Power: Electoral Vibrancy, Mounting Liberal Deficits," *Journal of Democracy* 30 (4): 63–77.

Varshney, A. 2022. "India's Democratic Longevity and its Troubled Trajectory," pp. 34–72 in S. Mainwaring and T. Masoud (eds.), *Democracy in Hard Places.* New York: Oxford University Press.

V-Dem Institute. 2023. *Democracy Report 2023: Defiance in the Fact of Autocratization,* available at https://www.v-dem.net/documents/30/V-dem_democracyreport2023_highres.pdf

Villegas, C. M. 2023. "The Civil Sphere and Social Class," *Cultural Sociology* 17 (1): 62–78.

Vincentnathan, S. G. 1996. "Caste, Politics & the Panchayat," *Comparative Studies in Society and History* 38 (3): 484–502.

Viswanathan, G. 1990. *Masks of Conquest: Literary Study and British Rule in India.* London: Faber and Faber.

Viswanathan, N. 2018. "Voice for Special Law against 'Honour' Killing Grows Louder," *New Indian Express,* November 25, available at http://www.newindianexpress.com/states/tamil-nadu/2018/nov/25/voice-for-special-law-against-honour-killing-grows-louder-1903004.html

Vivekananda, S. 1999 [1951]. *The Complete Works of Swami Vivekananda.* Calcutta: Advaita Ashrama.

Waghmore, S. 2013. *Civility Against Caste: Dalit Politics and Citizenship in Western India.* New Delhi: Sage.

Waghmore, S. 2019. "Community, Not Humanity: Caste Associations and Hindu Cosmopolitanism in Contemporary Mumbai," *South Asia: Journal of South Asian Studies* 42 (2): 375–93, https://doi.org/10.1080/00856401.2019.1577944

Waghmore, S. 2022. "From Castes to Nationalist Hindus," pp. 199–218 in T. Hansen and S. Roy (eds.), *Saffron Republic: Hindu Nationalism and State Power in India.* Oxford: Oxford University Press.

Waghmore, S., and Contractor, Q. 2015. "On the Madness of Caste: Dalits; Muslims; and Normalized Incivilities in Neoliberal India," pp. 223–40 in B. Mohan (ed.), *Global Frontiers of Social Development in Theory and Practice: Climate, Economy, and Justice.* New York: Palgrave Macmillan.

Waghmore, S., and Gorringe, H., eds. 2020. *Civility in Crisis: Democracy, Equality and the Majoritarian Challenge in India.* New Delhi: Routledge.

REFERENCES

Wallen, J. 2020. "'They Said They Would Murder Me': Pandemic Sees Rise in Attacks against India's Lowest Caste," *The Telegraph*, June 29, available at https://www.telegraph.co.uk/global-health/science-and-disease/said-would-murder-pandemic-sees-rise-attacks-against-indias/

Walzer, M. 1965. *The Revolution of the Saints: A Study of the Origins of Radical Politics*. Cambridge, MA: Harvard University Press.

Washbrook, D. A. 1999. "India, 1818–1860: The Two Faces of Colonialism," pp. 395–421 in A. Porter (ed.), *The Oxford History of the British Empire, Vol. III: The Nineteenth Century*. Oxford: Oxford University Press.

Watt, C. A. 2005. *Serving the Nation: Cultures of Service, Association, and Citizenship in Colonial India*. New Delhi: Oxford University Press.

Weiner, M. 1989. *The Indian Paradox: Essays in Indian Politics*. New Delhi: Sage.

Welchman, L., and Hossain, S. 2005. "'Honour', Rights and Wrongs," pp. 1–21 in L. Welchman and S. Hossain (eds.), *'Honour': Crimes, Paradigms, and Violence Against Women*. London: Zed Books.

Wilson, J. 2016. *India Conquered: Britain's Raj and the Chaos of Empire*. London: Simon and Schuster.

Wilson, N. H. 2023. *Modernity's Corruption: Empire and Morality in the Making of British India*. New York: Columbia University Press.

The Wire. 2020a. "Hathras Case: At Massive Janta Mantar Protest, Opposition Leaders Demand Yogi's Resignation," October 3, available at https://thewire.in/women/uttar-pradesh-hathras-media-politicians-barred

The Wire. 2020b. "Yogi Govt Enlists PR Firm to Push 'Hathras Girl Was Not Raped' Story Line with Foreign Media," October 3, available at https://thewire.in/government/adityanath-government-hathras-case-rape-pr-firm

The Wire. 2020c. "Hathras Case: UP Govt Smells International Conspiracy Files 19 FIRs," October 5, available at https://thewire.in/rights/hathras-case-up-govt-smells-international-conspiracy-files-19-firs

Yamunan, S. 2018. "'Catastrophic Crisis for Rule of Law': Supreme Court Cracks down on Khap Panchayats, 'Honour Crimes'," *Scroll.in*, March 28, available at https://scroll.in/article/873523/catastrophic-crisis-for-rule-of-law-supreme-court-cracks-down-on-khap-panchayats-honour-crimes

Yasir, S. 2024. "Indian Opposition Parties Face Trouble as Vote Nears," *New York Times*, March 22: A9.

Yuval-Davis, N. 1997. *Gender and Nation*. London: Sage.

Zaman, M. Q. 2002. *The Ulama in Contemporary Islam: Custodians of Change*. Princeton, NJ: Princeton University Press.

Zavos, J, Wyatt, A., and Hewitt, V., eds. 2004. *Politics of Cultural Mobilization in India*. New Delhi: Oxford University Press.

Zee News. 2020. *DNA: मीडिया खबर बताएगा या खबर बनाएगा?* ["DNA: Will the Media Tell the News or Create the News?"], YouTube, available at https://www.youtube.com/watch?v=yekxj5LYo24

Index

Aaj Tak, 67
Abhinav Bharat Mandir, 14
Abraham, J., 48
Adityanath, Yogi, 20, 62
adivasi movements, 88, 94
affirmative action, 5, 41, 86, 132, 200
African National Congress (ANC), 10
Ahinda coalition, 31, 102, 103, 104, 106
Aiyar, Yamini, 21
Akhil Bharatiya Kshatriya Mahasabha (ABKM), 64
Alexander, Jeffrey
  on the Civil Rights movement, 45, 145–6, 180, 181
  civil sphere theory, 41, 55, 70, 76, 88, 90–1, 95, 108, 127, 130, 144–6, 164–5, 180–2, 186, 191, 192
  on constitutions, 199
  on cultural structures, 86, 108
  on democracy, 198, 199
  on fictional media, 42, 50–1
  on media, 47, 63
  regional applications of CST, 146, 191

  on social movements, 41, 63, 164–5
  on societalization, 55, 63, 192
  on solidarity, 50, 127, 130
  on universalism, 108
Aligarh movement, 131
All India Kshatriya Council *see* Akhil Bharatiya Kshatriya Mahasabha (ABKM)
All India Majlis-e-Ittehadul Muslimeen (AIMIM), 138–40
Ambedkar, B. R.
  Buddha–Basava–Ambedkar ideology, 104–5, 106
  on the caste system, 6, 39, 40–1, 43, 52, 55, 72–3, 92–3, 101, 103, 115–16, 184
  and the Constitution, 39, 40–1, 53, 102, 103, 106, 198, 199–200
  conversion to Buddhism, 95
  and Dalit movements, 52–3
  on democracy, 39, 40–1, 198, 206
  dress, 51
  on inequality, 43, 115–16
  Phule–Ambedkarite ideology, 93, 101, 103

INDEX

Ambedkar, B. R. (*cont.*)
  and political representation,
    122
  symbolic uses of words and
    image, 52–3, 102, 106
American Revolution, 11, 163
Amnesty International, 67
Amritsar massacre, 169
Anand, S., 50
Anglicization, 164, 170
Anjuman-e-Islam, 132
anti-caste movements, 7–10, 21,
    55–7, 88, 93–4, 96, 101–6,
    116, 192, 202
anti-elitism, 110, 111
architecture, 163, 168
art, 163, 168
Arteaga Botello, N., 192, 194
Arya Samaj, 14
Aryans, 12, 14
ashraf Muslims, 132, 133
Ashoka, 171
assassinations, 15, 18, 19
assembly, freedom of, 22
assimilation, 34, 45, 167
association, freedom of, 5
Association of National
    Volunteers *see* Rashtriya
    Swayamsevak Sangh (RSS)
Attakathi (2012), 51
Aurobindo, Sri, 13
Austin, Granville, 5, 122
authoritarianism, 31, 109–24,
    180–1, 185–8, 192–3, 196–7,
    205–6
Ayodhya, 128

Babri mosque, 128
backlash
  against civil repair, 5, 9–11,
    17–20, 26–7, 30–1
  cultural backlash, 17–20

against Dalit movements, 9–10,
    26–7, 42–5
frontlash/backlash dynamic,
    9–10, 26–7, 192, 206
against Hathras movement, 29,
    54, 63–8, 192
and Hindutva, 11–15, 17–20,
    30–1
layered nature of, 10–11
violent backlash *see* violence
Bahujan Samaj Party (BSP), 122
BAMCEF, 8
Bangalore, 119
Bangladesh, 150, 175
banks, 33–4, 146, 147–8, 151–61
Bardhan, Pranab, 206
Basava, 104–5, 106
Basaveshwara, 96
BASE coaching company, 99
Bate, B., 44
Bauman, Zygmunt, 107
Bayly, Christopher, 172
Becker, E., 190
Bellah, Robert, 11, 31, 88, 89–93,
    95, 102, 105, 106, 186, 192
Bengal Asiatic Society, 166
Bengaluru, 75, 77, 78, 79–81, 97,
    98, 99, 102
Besant, Annie, 169
Bhagavad Gita, 117
Bhagwat, Mohan, 94
Bhakti movements, 93, 96
Bhalla, Alok, 16–17
Bharat Jodo Yatra, 22–3, 31, 103
Bharathi, S. P., 40
Bharatiya Janata Party (BJP)
  anti-Muslim stance, 21, 31,
    96–7, 101, 163
  and authoritarianism, 196–7,
    205–6
  and Brahmins, 30, 84–5, 97
  Clean India Campaign, 4, 119

INDEX

and corruption, 96–7, 102, 206
and cow sacrality, 103
Dalit opposition to, 57–8
electoral defeats in 1990s and
2000s, 21
electoral losses (2024), 26, 206
electoral success (2014), 4, 21,
57, 196, 204
electoral success (2019), 21, 57,
196, 204, 205
founding of party, 20, 57, 204
and Hindutva, 12, 20, 21,
30–1, 89, 95, 96, 163, 186–8,
204–6
ideology building, 95
and Lingayatism, 106
Modi's leadership *see* Modi,
Narendra
and neoliberalism, 205, 206
opening to lower-caste groups,
30–1, 84–5, 205
organizational effectiveness, 20,
21
populism, 10, 21, 204–5
relationship with the RSS, 97,
186–7, 204
support for in Karnataka, 89,
96–7
suppression of civil sphere
institutions, 10, 21–4, 205
symbolic tropes used by, 31–2
and violence, 31, 57, 175
welfare policies, 21
Bhargava, Rajeev, 17
Bharatiya Jana Sangh (BJS), 204
Billavas, 77, 78
binary codes, 28–9, 55, 62, 91,
111, 144, 145, 199
Black Lives Matter, 67
Bombay *see* Mumbai
Bose, M., 51
boundary relations, 33, 145–7,

149–50, 159–60, 180, 192–4
boycotts, 57, 121
Brahmanism, 92–3, 101, 103,
105, 204
Brahmins, 13, 29–30, 70–87, 94,
97, 100, 103, 116, 119, 194,
202, 203
Brazil, 178–9, 202
British Broadcasting Corporation
(BBC), 174, 183, 190
British empire, 2, 165, 166, 168,
169, 171, 176–7, 188
British parliamentary system, 172,
174
British Raj, 15, 34–5, 130,
162–77, 182–3, 193
Broken People report (HRW), 45
Buddha, 56, 104–5, 106
Buddhism, 92–3, 95, 105
Bunts, 75, 78, 79–81

Calcutta, 16, 168
Cambridge University, 168–9
capitalism, 34, 121, 123, 146,
149, 163, 164, 180, 206
Carswell, G., 46–7
caste closure, 117, 187
caste discrimination, 40–2, 57,
101, 115–17, 121, 184–5,
193, 202
Catholicism, 180, 185
censorship, 201
Central Bureau of Investigation
(CBI), 67, 69
centralization, 114, 179, 200, 206
Chakrabarty, Dipesh, 17
Chandrachud, Dhananjaya, 25–6
charity, 3, 32, 128, 130, 133, 134;
see also zakat
Chatterjee, Partha, 34, 111, 122,
165, 179, 182, 183, 188
Chaudhary, Sudhir, 66–7

249

INDEX

Chaudhuri, Nirad C., 171
Chennai, 44
Chidambaram, 45–7
China, 181, 202, 205
Chowdhury, Debasish Roy, 197
Christianity
  and civil religion, 89, 90
  connections with democracy,
    11, 89
  connections with republicanism,
    11
  and education, 132, 165
  Hindutva resentment for, 12,
    15, 31, 89, 94, 95, 101, 192
  lack of conversions to, 170
  missionaries, 12, 132, 165,
    203
  othering of Christians, 31, 89,
    94, 95, 203
  and segregation, 185
cinema, 17, 42, 43–4, 50–2, 53,
    192
Citizen Welfare Associations,
    82–3
citizenship, 3, 40, 52–3, 101, 112,
    120, 141, 165, 178–80, 184,
    186
Citizenship Amendment Act
    (CAA), 101, 102, 123, 179,
    187–8
civil disobedience, 121, 123, 187
civil horizons, 179–80, 181, 183,
    184, 187, 188–9
civil religion, 11, 31, 88–95,
    98–106, 186, 192
civil rights, 4–5, 9–10, 52, 169,
    197, 200
Civil Rights movement (US), 9,
    45, 145, 180, 181
civil solidarity see solidarity
civil translation, 63, 145, 147,
    159, 160, 195

civilizing mission, 164, 182
Claveyrolas, M., 92
Clean India Campaign, 4, 119
Clive, Robert, 166
collective conscience, 88, 97
collective subconscious, 112
Colombia, 190, 202
Commission on International
    Religious Freedom (US), 57
communal violence, 16–17, 20,
    123, 128, 138, 141, 175
communism, 49, 121, 203
Confucianism, 181, 202
Congress party
  alignment of social movements
    with, 102
  alleged involvement with
    Hathras movement, 67
  British influences, 169
  and corruption, 4
Congress party (*cont.*)
  and cow sacrality, 103–4
  decline of, 19–20, 22
  dominant position in first
    decades of independence,
    18–19
  electoral defeat (1989), 4
  electoral gains (2024), 26
  establishment of, 3, 169, 173,
    198
  joins I.N.D.I.A. electoral
    coalition, 22
  leadership succession, 19–20
  and Lingayatism, 104–6
  organizational effectiveness,
    18–20, 21
  repression of RSS, 14–15, 204
  revival of, 20, 22–4, 26
  support for in Karnataka,
    102–3, 105
  welfare policies, 103
consensus, 121–2, 132–3

250

INDEX

conspiracy theories, 62, 66, 67
Constituent Assembly, 40–1, 174, 183–4, 198, 199–200
Constitution
  and affirmative action, 5, 41
  British influences, 174, 176, 182–3, 193, 198–9
  and the caste system, 7, 41, 52
  drafting and ratification, 4, 122, 183–4, 199–200
  "Emergency" clause, 19, 172, 174, 201
  idealistic nature of, 5–6
  protection of cows, 103
  rights set out in, 4–5, 22, 44–5, 52, 200
  source of legitimacy for Dalit movements, 44–5, 48, 52, 53, 102
constitutional morality, 43, 53, 111
constitutionalism, 102, 105, 111, 120, 123, 169, 183, 186–8
constructive work, 121
conversion, 57, 94, 95, 97, 101, 170
corruption, 4, 28, 96–7, 102, 201, 206
courts
  appeals, 23–4
  backlogs, 22
  colonial courts, 172, 173
  independence, 1, 5, 24–5
  influence of British justice system, 171
  judgment in Hathras case, 68–9
  judgments against political opponents, 22, 23–4
  slowness of decision-making, 22
  state interventions, 22, 23–4

statements on Hathras case, 28, 59, 60
statements on honor killings, 27, 49
Supreme Court, 24–5, 27, 28, 49, 59, 61, 179, 181
Uttar Pradesh High Court, 28, 59, 60
  see also judiciary
Covid-19 pandemic, 40, 42, 119, 191
cow sacrality, 103–5
cow slaughter bans, 97, 101
cow vigilantism, 103–4, 205
credit, 33–4, 146–8, 150–61, 194
cremation, 28, 54, 58–60, 104
cricket, 169, 176
crony capitalism, 206
cross-caste marriage, 41, 47–9, 79, 191
cross-caste solidarity, 31, 43, 47, 116
cultural backlash, 17–20
cultural codes, 55, 91, 94, 107, 109–12, 118, 124, 145, 158, 201
cultural legitimacy, 44, 49, 52, 184
cultural nationalism, 110
cultural sociology, 31, 119, 145
cultural sphere, 184, 187
cultural structures, 71, 86, 92, 107–11, 118, 120–1, 123–4, 145, 160, 187
Curzon, George, Lord, 167, 175

Dahl, Robert, 197
Dainik Jagran, 58, 66
Dalit Panthers, 7, 43, 44–7, 52, 116
Dalit Women Fight Twitter account, 61

251

INDEX

Dalits
  backlash against, 9–10, 26–7, 42–5
  cinematic representations, 42, 50–2, 53
  and the Covid-19 pandemic, 40, 191
  and cross-caste marriage, 41, 47–9
  Dalit movements, 7–10, 26–7, 41–7, 49, 51–3, 55–7, 116, 191
  discrimination against, 40–1, 42, 57, 110
  education access, 8
  exclusion of, 31, 56–8, 110, 114
  government employment, 8
  opposition to BJP, 57–8
  political participation, 8, 26–7, 138
  political parties, 8, 27, 45–7, 122
  political representation, 41, 45–7, 114, 122, 123, 179, 200
  sects and subcastes within, 114, 179
  social movements *see* Dalit movements
  solidarity among, 7, 8, 116
  support for democracy, 7–8
  village council presidencies, 9, 26–7, 42–5
  violence against, 9, 27, 31, 40–7, 54, 57–69, 110, 119, 191
Darwin, John, 176
David, S., 58
De, Rohit, 3
De Neve, G., 46–7
decentralization, 114, 179

decolonization, 110, 115, 117, 118, 111, 183, 193
Delhi, 54, 58, 62, 96, 119
Delhi Sultanate, 162
deregulation, 146
derivatives, 146, 150, 152
detention
  of journalists and newspaper editors, 172
  over-representation of Muslims in prison population, 138
  of political opponents, 22, 23–4, 201
  political prisoners, 201
developmentalism, 149
Dewey, John, 39, 198
Dhanani, Saraphin, 205
diaspora, 202
dictatorship, 19, 201; *see also* authoritarianism
diet, 81, 100, 103–4, 117, 119, 123
discrimination
  on basis of sexual orientation, 25–6
  caste discrimination, 40–2, 57, 101, 115–17, 121, 184–5, 193, 202
  against Dalits, 40–1, 42, 57, 110
  gender discrimination, 77, 121
  against Muslims, 32, 110
  racial discrimination, 49
  religious discrimination, 110
  socioeconomic discrimination, 32, 129
diversity, 32, 112–14, 117, 120, 131–2, 184–5, 186, 203
dominion status, 169
Draupathi (2020), 52
Dravidian movement, 43–4
Drèze, J., 57

INDEX

dualism, 115–19
duality, 115–19
Dumont, L., 72
Durkheim, Émile, 91

East India Company, 2, 15, 34
economic growth, 150, 205
economic liberalization, 146, 151, 154
Economist Intelligence Unit, 197
education
  access to, 8, 31, 75, 77, 97–100
  for Brahmins, 30, 75–6, 77–8
  British education, 5, 35, 164, 167, 168–9, 171, 174, 176, 182, 183
  demands for common school system, 123–4
  English-medium education, 98, 168–9, 171
  failure to counter caste hegemony, 51
  higher education, 8, 31, 35, 98–100, 168–9, 172, 176
  Institutes of Technology, 31, 98–100
  Muslim educational institutions, 132
  primary schools, 75
  public schools, 35, 168–9
  quotas for lower-caste participation, 8
  and secularism, 17, 77
  subsidization, 76
  Super 30 program, 99
  Tapas program, 31, 97–101, 186–7
education (*cont.*)
  universities, 17, 31, 35, 61, 168–9, 172, 176, 205
Egholm, L., 195

elections
  by-elections, 62
  campaign donations, 24–5
  Dalit participation, 8, 26–7, 138
  electorate size, 200
  independence of election machinery, 17–18
  influence of British system, 174, 183
  intimidation of voters, 27, 45–7
  local elections, 3, 9, 42–7, 156
  Muslim participation, 113, 138
  national elections, 3, 4, 8, 12, 17, 21–2, 26, 196–7, 200, 204–6
  proportional representation, 122, 200
  as regulative institutions, 2, 17–18, 30, 46
  reserved constituencies, 122
  separate electorates, 122, 168, 175
electoral bonds, 24–5
Elphinstone, Mountstuart, 166
Emergency Rule, 19, 172, 174, 197, 201
employment, 8, 75, 77, 78–9, 134, 138
English civil war, 11
English language
  English-language media, 21, 43, 66, 67, 174, 193
  English-medium education, 98, 168–9, 171
  as legacy of British Raj, 167, 170–1, 176
equality
  and citizenship, 39, 43, 52–3, 184
  class equality, 88
  and the Constitution, 5, 52, 183

253

INDEX

equality (*cont.*)
  and democracy, 25, 39
  and duality, 115–16, 117
  gender equality, 26, 88
  and Hindutva, 30–1, 93, 94–5
  and Islam, 141
  before the law, 5, 111, 173
  and Lingayatism, 106
  in schools, 78
  and secular sectarianism, 120
  social movements advocate for,
    7, 43, 52–3, 88
  see also inequalities
European Enlightenment, 163
Evidence NGO, 40
exceptionalism, 73–4, 86
exclusion
  and the authoritarian civil
    sphere, 107, 110–11, 113–22,
    192–3
  and binary codes, 2, 91, 111,
    144
  caste as metaphor for, 190
  of Dalits, 31, 56–8, 110, 114
  and duality, 115–19
  financial exclusion, 147, 150,
    151, 158, 161
  and Hindutva, 21, 31–2, 95
  of migrant workers, 190
  of Muslims, 21, 31, 32, 95,
    110, 130, 139
  and secular segregation,
    119–24
  vertical exclusion, 115, 116,
    192

fake news, 60, 65–7
farmers, 8, 19, 23, 123, 146, 204
fascism, 102, 203
federalism, 200, 206
feminism, 26, 56, 145; *see also*
  women's rights

fictional media, 2, 17, 42; *see also*
  cinema; literature
film *see* cinema
first information reports (FIRs),
  62, 155
First World War, 169
folk politics, 111
food *see* diet
foreign direct investment (FDI),
  146
Foucault, Michel, 116
founding fathers, 5, 6, 14, 35, 176
Freedom House, 197
French Revolution, 163, 200
friendship, 30, 78–9, 82
frontlash, 9–10, 26–7, 206

Gallo, Esther, 73
Gandhi, Indira, 19, 172, 174, 197,
  201
Gandhi, Mohandas
  assassination, 15, 18
  and diet, 103
  and the Dominion status model,
    169
  and dress, 51
  education, 169, 175, 198
  mobilization strategies, 121–2,
    187
  and nationalism, 15, 90, 169
  social standpoints, 121–2
  village republics proposal, 121,
    200
Gandhi, Rahul, 20, 22–4, 26, 31,
  102–3
Gandhi, Rajiv, 4, 19
Gandhi, Sanjay, 201
Gandhi, Sonia, 19–20
Geertz, Clifford, 145
gender
  feminist movements, 53, 56,
    145

254

INDEX

gender discrimination, 77, 121–2
gender equality, 26, 88
violence against women, 27–9, 54, 58–69
women's rights, 5, 26, 53, 136
George, A., 48
Germany, 190, 203
global civil sphere, 45, 49, 61, 109, 206
Global South, 190, 194
globalization, 127, 148
Godse, Nathuram, 14–15
Golden Age, 13, 14
Golwalkar, M. S., 14, 15, 97, 203
Goody, Jack, 34, 165
Gorringe, Hugo, 7–8, 9
Gorski, Philip, 90, 95
government employment, 8, 35, 75, 77, 138, 168, 170; *see also* Indian Civil Service
Government of India Act, 15, 167, 174, 175, 183, 199
Governor-Generals, 164; *see also* Viceroys
graded inequalities, 43, 115–16, 118, 120, 185
Grameen Bank, 150, 161
grassroots mobilization, 20, 23, 42
grhasta stage of life, 73
Guha, Ramchandra, 102
Gujarat, 20, 23, 93
Gupta, Naresh, 46

Habermas, Jürgen, 109
Hastings, Warren, 166
Hathras case, 27–9, 54–69, 192
Hazare, Anna, 4
healthcare, 76, 98, 138–40
Hedgewar, Keshav Baliram, 14

Hefner, R. W., 141
hegemony, 10, 31, 50, 63, 110, 116, 117
hierarchical solidarities, 113–14, 118
higher education, 8, 31, 35, 98–100, 168–9, 172, 176; *see also* universities
hijab bans, 97, 101
Hindu, The, 4, 24, 28, 60
Hindu cosmopolitanism, 117–18, 187
Hindu identity, 94, 110, 112, 114, 123, 175, 185, 203
Hindu nationalism, 26, 57, 84, 94–5, 102, 127–9, 196–7, 202–6; *see also* Hindutva
Hindu revival, 12–13, 16, 57
Hindu Right, 83–5, 129, 138
Hindu solidarity, 88–95, 101, 105–6
Hindutva, 11–15, 17–21, 25, 29–31, 88–106, 141, 163, 185–9, 192, 202–6; *see also* Hindu nationalism
Holston, J., 178–9
home ownership, 75
Honneth, Axel, 108
honor killings, 27, 40, 47–9, 52, 191
horizontal solidarity, 7, 8, 116
Hossain, S., 48
human rights, 27, 28, 45, 49, 59, 117, 118, 180
Human Rights Watch (HRW), 45
Human Solidarity Forum *see* Manava Bandhutva Vedika
Hume, Allan Octavian, 169
humiliation, 16, 28, 41, 48, 52, 58, 59
Hyderabad, 138–40, 170

INDEX

Ibrahim, Dawood, 141
ideological capture, 21
ideology building, 95
Ilbert Bill, 173
illiberal democracy, 196–7
imprisonment *see* detention
impurity, 31, 40, 55, 90, 93, 97, 103, 104; *see also* pollution; purity
inclusion
  and the authoritarian civil sphere, 107, 111, 113–23, 192–3
  and binary codes, 2, 91, 111, 144
  and cinema, 50–1
  and cross-caste marriage, 48–9
  of Dalits, 48–9, 50–1, 191
  and duality, 115–19
  financial inclusion, 151–2
  and Hindutva, 95
  moderate inclusion, 115, 192–3
  and secular sectarianism, 119–24
  and the Tapas program, 100–1
  universal inclusion, 107, 113–14, 120
independence
  of the courts and judiciary, 1, 5, 24–5
  of election machinery, 17–18
  of the media, 1, 21–2; *see also* press freedom
I.N.D.I.A. coalition, 22
Indian Civil Service, 35, 169, 170, 176; *see also* government employment
Indian Home Rule, 169
Indian independence, 2, 14, 166, 167, 176
Indian Mutiny, 34, 167, 175, 176
Indian National Congress (INC)

  see Congress party
Indian nationalism, 4, 90, 95, 169–70, 175, 176, 179
Indian Penal Code, 25, 64
individual rights, 28, 88, 105, 106
individuality, 29, 70–2, 77–8, 86, 88, 100, 106, 121, 164, 184, 200
Industrial Revolution, 163
industrialization, 132, 163, 177
inequalities, 41, 43, 91, 115–16, 118, 120, 122, 185, 202, 206; *see also* equality
Institute of Rural Management, 151
Institutes of Technology (IITs), 31, 98–100
insurance, 146, 150, 152
interest rates, 34, 155–6
International Finance Corporation, 146
International Women's Day, 154–5, 158
interstitial thickness, 147, 160
intimidation, 27, 44–7, 50, 123
Ireland, 169
Irwin Declaration, 167
Islam *see* Muslims
Islamic Congregation of India *see Jama'at-e-Islami Hind*
Islamic law, 141
Islamic nationalism, 15–16
Islamic reform movements, 131, 134
Islamic symbols, 133, 141
Islamism, 129, 131
Italy, 190, 203

Jaffrelot, Christophe, 8, 57, 197, 201, 203
Jama'at-e-Islami Hind, 129, 131
James, Lawrence, 175

256

INDEX

Janata Dal Secular (JDS), 96
Jarkiholi, Satish, 104–5
jati associations, 82–3, 85
jatis, 6, 8, 13, 82–3, 85, 111
Jinnah, M. A., 16, 175
Joint Entrance Examination (JEE), 31, 98–100
Jones, Sir William, 166–7
journalism *see* media; newspapers
judaism, 180, 203
judiciary, 1, 5, 22–6, 49, 69, 176, 180, 201, 205; *see also* courts
justice system *see* courts; judiciary; police

Kaadhal (2004), 50
Kaala (2018), 51
Kaali, S., 50
Kabali (2016), 51
Kanpur, 133
karma, 113, 116
Karnataka, 30–1, 71–2, 74–5, 83, 85, 89, 96–106, 186
Kashmir, 22
Keane, John, 197
Kerala, 56, 79, 97, 113
Khan, Firdaus, 140
Khan, Yasmin, 136–7
Khosla, Madhav, 200
King, Martin Luther, 10
Kshatriya, 13, 54, 64, 72, 100
Kumar, A., 48
Kumar, Anand, 99
Kumar, Prashant, 59–60
Kurubas, 104

labor migration, 40, 128, 190
land ownership, 6, 75, 80, 199
Landau, David, 205
Laxkar, Praveen, 60
Left, the
  far left, 10

left-leaning media, 63, 66
left/right social pendulum, 10, 11
left social movements, 93, 102
  see also socialism
legal profession, 3
liberal imperialism, 34–5, 167
liberalism, 11, 19, 93, 106, 165, 167
Liberation Panther Party *see* Viduthalai Chiruthaigal Katchi (VCK)
Lijphart, Arend, 200
Lingayats, 96, 98, 104, 105–6
literature, 163, 167
local media, 23, 43, 46–7, 154–6, 174, 193
localism, 114, 179
Lok Sabha, 46, 52, 174, 184, 193
"love jihad", 101, 205
lynchings, 31, 104, 110, 119, 181, 205

Macaulay, Thomas, 35, 164, 167, 170, 182
Madras, 168
Madras (2014), 51
Mahabharata, 13, 117, 118
Mahajan, Gurpreet, 183–5
Maharashtra, 93
majoritarianism, 196, 204
Malcolm, Sir John, 167
Manava Bandhutva Vedika, 104
Mandalization, 12
Mandela, Nelson, 10
Manoharan, K. R., 51
Manor, James, 8, 9
marginalization
  of Dalits, 44, 184
marginalized caste groups, 84–5, 184–5
and microfinance, 151

257

INDEX

marginalization (*cont.*)
  of Muslims, 32, 128–30, 134, 137–8, 142
  and political representation, 122
  and secular sectarianism, 120, 185
  socioeconomic marginalization, 142, 151
markets, 33–4, 146, 148, 149, 154, 160, 161, 194
marriage, 41, 47–9, 79, 112, 163, 191
Marshall, T. H., 5
Marxism, 33, 91, 109, 183, 203
masculinity, 13
master spheres, 180
mathas, 82–3, 85
media
  British influences, 174, 183, 193
  British repression of, 172
  broadcasting system, 174, 183, 193
  censorship, 201
  coverage of Hathras case, 28, 29, 58–61, 62–3, 65–8, 69
  coverage of microfinance institutions, 154–6, 158
  coverage of Rahul Gandhi's Yatra, 23
  coverage of VCK party, 27, 46–7
  development and expansion, 3–4, 165, 172
  English-language media, 21, 43, 66, 67, 174, 193
  independence, 1, 21–2
  and the independence movement, 3–4
  international media, 23, 65
  investigative journalism, 4, 28
  left-leaning media, 63, 66

local media, 23, 43, 46–7, 154–6, 174, 193
misconduct, 180
neutralized by Modi government, 21–2, 205
news channels, 4, 58–61, 63, 66–8
newspapers, 3–4, 21–3, 28, 43, 58–63, 65–6, 119, 154–6, 172, 174, 193
media (*cont.*)
  press conferences, 33–4, 59–60, 154–5
  press freedom, 5, 35, 118, 174–5, 176, 193, 205
  press releases, 29, 65
  relation to public opinion, 47, 181
  right-leaning media, 63
  state interventions, 21–2, 201, 205
  support for those with grievances, 181–2
  television, 4, 22, 58–61, 63, 66–7, 174, 183, 193
  see also fictional media; social media
Melavalavu massacre, 9, 42–5
memory, 22, 28, 32, 60, 109–10, 111–12
Mendelsohn, O., 9
merit, 74, 77, 98, 99, 116, 136
Metcalf, Thomas, 167
Mexico, 181, 192, 194, 202
MICO, 75, 79
microfinance, 33–4, 147–8, 150–61, 194
microfinancing institutions (MFIs), 33–4, 152–61, 194
migrant workers, 40, 128, 190
migration, 40, 128, 130, 132, 180, 190, 192

258

INDEX

military, 165, 170, 174, 183
Mill, James, 164
Ministry of External Affairs (MEA), 118
missionaries, 12, 132, 165, 203
mobility, 57, 75, 103, 111, 116–17, 120, 177, 190, 205
modernity, 31–2, 70, 74, 86, 89, 118, 121, 131, 163, 170
modernization, 3, 70, 74, 76, 86, 103, 114, 131, 167, 177, 197
Modi, Narendra
  attitude towards Muslims, 20, 187–8
  attributes and political skills, 20, 188, 204–5
  authoritarianism, 185–6, 187–8, 196–7, 205–6
  and Brahmins, 30, 84–5
  Chief Minister of Gujarat, 20
  electoral losses (2024), 26, 206
  electoral success (2014), 4, 21, 57, 196, 204
  electoral success (2019), 21, 57, 196, 204, 205
  and Hindutva, 20, 21, 185–8, 192, 204–6
  and neoliberalism, 205, 206
  neutralizing of the media, 21–2, 205
  poll ratings, 21
  populism, 10, 21, 204–5
  RSS membership, 204
  suppression of civil sphere institutions, 10, 21–4, 205
  and violence, 20, 175, 205
  see also Bharatiya Janata Party (BJP)
Mody, Ashoka, 197
Mohan, G., 52
moneylenders, 152, 156, 159

Montagu–Chelmsford Reforms, 167
morality
  and Brahmins, 30, 81, 86
  and civil religion, 90
  constitutional morality, 43, 53, 111
  and Muslim politics, 140–1, 142
  and pious altruism, 134–5, 136, 137–8
  and political community, 179
  universal morality, 30, 86, 89, 108, 200
Morley–Minto Reforms, 175
mosques, 15, 128, 134
Mughal empire, 15, 21, 34, 101, 130–1, 162–3, 166, 168, 170–1, 175, 193
multiculturalism, 144
Mumbai, 32, 62, 94, 127–9, 131–7, 168
Munusamy, Kiruba, 60
murders, 9, 15, 16, 20, 27–9, 40, 42–3, 57, 68–9, 104; *see also* assassinations; honor killings; lynchings; violence
Murugesan, 9, 42, 45
Muslim League, 16, 175
Muslims
  anti-Muslim nature of Hindutva, 21, 31–2, 89–90, 94–7, 101, 103, 105–6, 187, 203
  anti-Muslim stance of BJP, 21, 31, 96–7, 163
  and the colonization of India, 15, 130–1, 162–3, 170
  demands for independent state, 16, 175
  diet, 103, 104
  discrimination against, 32, 110

259

INDEX

Muslims (*cont.*)
distinct identity from Hindus, 112–13, 185
educational institutions, 132
erasure of Muslim history, 163
exclusion of, 21, 31, 32, 95, 110, 130, 139
government employment, 138
Islamic cultural influences, 93
Islamic reform movements, 131, 134
Islamic symbols, 133, 141
Islamism, 129, 131
Modi's attitude towards, 20, 187–8
mosques, 15, 128, 134, 136
Muslim identity, 112–13, 128–9, 133, 138–9, 141, 175, 185
othering of, 31, 83, 89, 94, 95, 103, 104, 110, 203
and Partition, 16–17, 18, 175, 198
political participation, 113, 138
political parties, 32, 129, 138–41
political representation, 122, 132
and poverty, 32–3, 128–30, 133–8, 141, 142
protests against Citizenship Amendment Act, 123, 187–8
solidarity among, 32–3, 128–30, 142, 193–4
treatment under the Raj, 15
violence against, 16–17, 20, 31, 104, 110, 119, 123, 128, 196, 205
violence committed by, 16–17, 141
zakat, 32, 128, 129–30, 133–7
Mussolini, Benito, 203

myth, 14, 32, 109, 111–12, 117, 118, 202

Naipaul, V. S., 176
Nairs, 79
Nandan magazine, 46
Nandy, Ashis, 94, 113, 169
Narayan, Badri, 40
Narayanan, K. R., 43
National Commission for Scheduled Caste, 61
National Dalit Movement for Justice (NDMJ), 40
National Human Rights Commission (NHRC), 28, 59
national identity, 90, 110, 112–13, 196, 202–4
national movement, 2–3, 5–6, 15, 19, 88
National Register of Citizenship (NRC), 123, 187–8
nationalism *see* cultural nationalism; Hindu nationalism; Indian nationalism; Islamic nationalism
Naxalism, 66
Nazism, 203
NDTV, 60
Nehru, Jawaharlal
on British rule, 162, 164, 166–7, 173
on communal violence, 16
and the Constitution, 200
education, 35, 169, 175, 198
on Mughal rule, 163–4
on Partition, 16
and socialism, 90, 106
succession, 19
suppression of RSS, 15
neoliberalism, 33, 127, 146, 149, 161, 196, 205, 206

INDEX

New Indian Express, 28, 60
New York Times, 23, 65, 197
news channels, 4, 58–61, 63, 66–8
News 18 Hindi, 66, 67
Newsom, Gavin, 202
newspapers, 3–4, 21–3, 28, 43, 58–63, 65–6, 119, 154–6, 172, 174, 193; *see also* media
Noble Society *see* Arya Samaj
non-bank finance companies (NBFCs), 152
non-civil spheres, 1, 33, 50, 108, 115, 145, 150, 160
non-governmental organizations (NGOs), 40, 45, 96–7, 136, 150–2, 204, 205

opinion polls, 17, 21; *see also* public opinion
Orientalism, 164
origin myths, 14
"Other Backward Classes" (OBCs), 8, 9, 40, 100, 114, 122, 179
othering, 31, 83, 89, 94, 95, 103, 104, 110, 203
Owaisi, Akbaruddin, 138–40
Owaisi, Asaduddin, 138–40
Oxford University, 35, 168–9, 175–6

Pakistan, 15, 174, 175
Palmer, David, 181, 202
Pandey, Gyanendra, 17
paramilitary groups, 203, 204
Paris Principles of Human Rights, 59
parliamentary system, 172, 174, 183, 193
Parsons, Talcott, 9
particularism, 92, 95, 106, 107, 192, 194

Partition, 16–17, 18, 110, 175, 198, 203–4
patriarchy, 28, 61, 63
Paz, Octavio, 162, 176
performance, 18, 20, 32, 62, 86, 91, 108–12, 118, 121, 145, 187
Periyar, 43
Pew Research Center, 112, 185
Phule, Jyotirao, 56, 93, 101, 103
pious altruism, 129–30, 133–8
pluralism, 90, 118, 165, 197, 201
polarization, 10, 18–19, 68, 113–14
Polgreen, Lydia, 197
police
  British influences, 176
  corruption, 28
  and Dalit movements, 27, 44, 46, 52
  and election interference, 46
  and the Hathras case, 28–9, 54, 58–61, 62, 64–6
  and microfinancing institutions, 154–5, 157
  policing of political rallies, 139
  political control of, 22
political authority, 178–81, 186, 188
political community, 178–89
political opponents, 22, 23–4, 111, 196, 201, 205
political participation, 8, 26–7, 113, 138
political parties
  corporate donations to, 24–5
  Dalit parties, 8, 27, 45–7, 122
  and discourses on the poor, 150
  Dravidian parties, 43–4

261

INDEX

political parties (*cont.*)
  Hindu Right parties, 83–5, 129, 138
  influence of British party political system, 170–1, 174, 183, 193
  leadership succession, 19–20
  and microfinance institutions, 156
  Muslim parties, 32, 129, 138–41
  organizational effectiveness, 18–21
  as regulative institutions, 2, 3
  secular parties, 26, 138, 140–1
  staffing, 18, 19, 20
  symbolic tropes used by, 31–2, 43–4, 129, 141
political prisoners, 201
political representation, 41, 45–7, 114, 121–3, 132, 168, 172, 179, 200
political rights, 5, 45, 52, 197, 200
political sphere, 131, 184, 187, 188
pollution, 2, 6, 25, 52, 56, 63, 73, 79, 95, 101, 144, 184; *see also* impurity
populism, 10, 21, 109–24, 190, 192–3, 202, 204–5
postcolonial theory, 32, 34, 91, 111, 115–18, 173, 183, 193
poverty, 32–4, 128–30, 133–8, 141–2, 146–61, 190, 197–8
poverty alleviation, 33, 146–7, 149–50, 154, 155
Prasad, Rajendra, 16
prejudice, 29, 49, 112, 114–15, 116–17, 120, 124, 193
press *see* media; newspapers

press conferences, 33–4, 59–60, 154–5
press freedom, 5, 35, 118, 174–5, 176, 193, 205
press releases, 29, 65
primordial attachments, 6, 70, 72, 76, 88, 106
privacy, right to, 25–6
private property, 164, 182
private sphere, 86
Proclamation (1858), 173
proportional representation, 122, 200
Protestantism, 185
public opinion, 3, 6, 18, 27, 33–4, 46–7, 55, 59, 112–13, 120, 172, 181
public relations (PR), 29, 33–4, 65, 155
public sphere, 3, 86, 109
purity, 25, 29, 40, 73, 79, 94, 95; *see also* impurity

quotas, 8, 12
Quran, 141

Railway Mail Service (RMS), 75, 77, 81
Rajendran, S., 49
Rajinikanth, 51
Rajputs, 64, 67, 135
Ramyana, 117, 118
Ranjith, Pa., 51
Ranganathan, M., 4
Rao, A., 48
rape, 29, 54, 58–69, 192
Rashtriya Swayamsevak Sangh (RSS), 14–15, 18, 23, 94–8, 100–1, 106, 186–8, 203–4
Rashtrotthana, 31, 97–101
Ravidas Jayanti, 94
regionalism, 114, 179

INDEX

religion, freedom of, 5, 28
Reporters Without Borders, 205
Republic Bharat, 67
Republic TV, 67
republicanism, 11, 74, 106
Reserve Bank of India (RBI), 154, 156, 157
reserved constituencies, 122
revolution, 5, 11, 163
Right, the
  backlash against civil repair, 9–10
  decolonial discourses, 117
  far right, 10
  Hindu Right, 83–5, 129, 138
  and populist-authoritarianism, 109, 202
  right-leaning media, 63
  right/left social pendulum, 10, 11
righteous lawlessness, 31, 110
riots, 16, 57, 62, 66, 67, 123
Ripon, George, Lord, 173
Rodrigues, U., 4
Roy, Lajapathi, 44
Roy, Rajan, 59, 60
rule of law, 27, 35, 164, 174, 176, 182, 193, 200–1

Saharanpur anti-Dalit riot, 57
Sakthivel, Balaji, 50
Samajwadi Party (SP), 139, 140
samrastha, 109, 114, 117
Sangh Parivar, 204
Sanskrit, 12, 20, 96, 97, 103, 116, 166, 202
sanskritization, 103, 116
Saraswati, Dayananda, 12–13
Satyanarayana, K., 52
Savarkar, Vinayak Damodar, 14, 202–3
savings, 146, 150, 152

Sayer, Andrew, 113
Scheduled Caste/Scheduled Tribes Act, 44, 57
secularism
  and Brahmins, 74–5, 77, 83
  and civil religion, 89–91, 92, 102
  civil sphere as secular, 11–12, 31, 91, 92, 108, 110–11, 186
  and the Constitution, 57, 120, 123, 187
  and education, 17, 77
  and Hindutva, 12, 31, 57, 95, 186, 187–8
  institutional secularism, 130
  and the national movement, 15, 201
  opposition of the BJP and RSS to, 12, 31–2, 57, 95, 206
  and populism, 110–11
  secular political parties, 26, 138, 140–1
secularism (*cont.*)
  secular sectarianism, 118, 119–24, 187
  secular solidarity, 71
  secularization, 31, 108, 114, 115
segregation, 32, 112–14, 117, 119–20, 128, 185, 189
self-help groups (SHGs), 3, 34, 155, 156
self-interest, 127, 149, 205
Sen, Amartya, 17
separate electorates, 122, 168, 175
seva, 3, 97, 101
sexual harassment, 26
sexual orientation, 25–6, 144
sexual violence, 29, 54, 58–69, 192
Shah, Mehboob, 134–6

263

INDEX

Sharma, Jyotirmaya, 12
Shudras, 13, 104, 116
Siddaramaiah, 103–5
Sikhism, 19, 168
Singh, A. P., 64
Singh, Charan, 8
Singh, Jaspreet, 59
Singh, Manmohan, 35, 175–6
Singh, V. P., 12
slum neighborhoods, 128–9,
  134–8, 142
social criticism, 129, 136, 142,
  194
social Darwinism, 116
social democracy, 95, 121, 202
social justice, 122, 141, 145, 159
social media, 23, 48, 61, 65
social movements
  adivasi movements, 88, 94
  anti-caste movements, 7–10, 21,
    55–7, 88, 93, 94, 96, 101–6,
    116, 192, 202
  Dalit movements, 7–10, 26–7,
    41–7, 49, 51–3, 55–7, 116,
    191
  feminist movements, 53, 56,
    145
  Hathras movement, 27–9,
    54–69, 192
  Islamic reform movements, 131,
    134
  left movements, 93, 102
  national movement, 2–3, 5–6,
    15, 19, 88
  and populist-authoritarianism,
    109, 120, 121
  Women's Liberation
  Movement, 53
social pendulum, 10, 11
social power, 85, 121–3
social rights, 5, 200
social solidarity, 33, 133, 142–3

social welfare, 21, 96, 103, 180
socialism, 3, 12, 19, 90, 106, 151,
  206; *see also* left, the
societalization, 28–9, 55–6, 58–9,
  62–3, 68, 158, 160, 192
solidarity
  and Brahmins, 29–30, 70–6, 80,
    81, 85–6
  civil solidarity, 6, 16–17, 41,
    64, 71, 80, 91, 93, 106–9,
    115, 120, 128–30, 135,
    141–2
  and the Covid-19 pandemic,
    40
  cross-caste solidarity, 31, 43,
    47, 116
  among Dalits, 8, 116
  as defining quality of civil
    sphere, 1–2, 108, 127, 144,
    145
  hierarchical solidarities,
    113–14, 118
  Hindu solidarity, 88–95, 101,
    105–6
  horizontal solidarity, 7, 8, 116
  impact of Partition, 16–17
  incompatibility of caste system
    with, 6, 39
  and individuality, 70–1, 72, 86
  material solidarity, 6
  among Muslims, 32–3, 128–30,
    142, 193–4
  national solidarity, 3, 7
  social solidarity, 33, 133,
    142–3
  universal solidarity, 88, 89,
    107, 109, 110, 113
South Africa, 10, 169
Special Rapporteur on Violence
  against Women (UN), 61
speech, freedom of, 5, 172
spirituality, 23, 121

264

INDEX

sport, 169, 176
Srinivas, K. R., 50
Stalin, M. K., 47
state languages, 198, 200
State Level Bankers Committee, 156
state violence, 28, 54, 58–60, 63
Stepan, Alfred, 196
strikes, 28, 62
structural adjustment programs (SAPs), 146, 149
sublated Hinduism, 31, 100–1, 106
subsidization, 76
Sudamani, 53
Sufism, 130, 132, 134
Super 30 program, 99
superstition, 12, 92, 104–5
Supreme Court, 24–5, 27, 28, 49, 59, 61, 179, 181
symbolism, 31–2, 43–4, 51, 89, 90, 101–3, 106, 119, 121, 129, 133, 141, 145

Tagore, Rabindranath, 162, 164, 169, 178
Tamil Maanila Congress, 45
Tamil Nadu, 7, 9, 22, 26–7, 42–52, 185
Tapas program, 31, 97–101, 186–7
taxation, 22, 96, 121
Telegraph India, 62–3
television, 4, 22, 58–61, 63, 66–7, 174, 183, 193
terrorism, 113
textile industry, 121, 171
Thakurs, 54, 64, 69
Thapar, Romila, 112
Tharoor, Shashi, 171–5
Thevars, 9, 43, 47–8, 50
thick description, 145, 197

Thirumavalavan, Thol., 7, 43, 44–6, 52, 184
Times of India, 25, 58
Tocqueville, Alexis de, 92
Tognato, Carlo, 147, 195
transcendental justice, 109, 127
Trump, Donald, 90
trusteeship, 121
Twitter, 61

Una flogging case, 57
United India March *see Bharat Jodo* Yatra
United Nations (UN), 49, 61, 65
United States
    American Revolution, 11
    application of civil sphere theory to, 45, 145, 180, 181, 182, 186, 191
    Black Lives Matter movement, 67
    caste discrimination lawsuits, 202
    civil religion, 89, 90, 92, 102
    Civil Rights movement, 9, 45, 145, 180, 181
    Commission on International Religious Freedom, 57
    funding raised in, 99
    microfinance provision, 148
    migration to, 192
    Trump presidency, 90
    universities, 61
Universal Declaration of Human Rights, 45
universal morality, 30, 86, 89, 108, 200
universal solidarity, 88, 89, 107, 109, 110, 113
universalism, 6, 17, 48–9, 51, 88–9, 92, 106, 107–10, 117–21, 144, 194

265

INDEX

universities, 17, 31, 35, 61, 168–9, 172, 176, 205; *see also* higher education
untouchability, 5, 41, 43, 52, 55–6, 93, 184
Upanishads, 13, 93
utilitarianism, 164
utopianism, 1–2, 5, 23, 53, 91, 109
Uttar Pradesh, 20, 27–9, 58–69, 122, 182
Uttarakhand, 67

Valmikis, 54, 61–2, 104
Vanniyars, 46
varnas, 6, 13, 92–3, 117
varnashrama dharma, 92, 94, 117
Varshney, Ashutosh, 198, 200
vasudaivika kutumbakam, 110, 114, 118
V-Dem Institute, 197
Vedas, 12–14, 20, 202
vegetarianism, 81, 100, 103, 119, 123
Vemula, Rohit, 57
Venkatesh, K., 104
vertical exclusion, 115, 116, 192
Viceroys, 167, 172, 173
Victoria, Queen, 173
Vicziany, M., 9
Viduthalai Chiruthaigal Katchi (VCK), 27, 45–7, 53
vigilantism, 103–4, 197, 205
village councils, 9, 26–7, 42–5, 156
village republics, 121, 200
Villegas, C. M., 161
violence
    assassinations, 15, 18, 19
    and the BJP, 31, 57, 175, 205

communal violence, 16–17, 20, 123, 128, 138, 141, 175
    during Covid-19 lockdowns, 40, 42
    against Dalits, 9, 27, 31, 40–7, 54, 57–69, 110, 119, 191
    against Hindus, 16–17
    honor killings, 27, 40, 47–9, 52, 191
    lynchings, 31, 104, 110, 119, 181, 205
    and Modi, 20, 175, 205
    murders, 9, 16, 20, 27–9, 40, 42–3, 57, 68–9, 104
    against Muslims, 16–17, 20, 31, 104, 110, 119, 123, 128, 196, 205
    and Partition, 16–17, 18, 175, 198, 203–4
    and the RSS, 14–15, 203–4
    sexual violence, 29, 54, 58–69, 192
    state violence, 28, 54, 58–60, 63
    against women, 27–9, 54, 58–69, 192
Vivekananda, Swami, 13, 15
Vokkaligas, 96, 98, 104, 105
volunteerism, 134–7
vote banks, 19, 20, 122, 140

Waghmore, Suryakant, 1, 9, 117, 165, 186–7
Wallen, J., 40
Walzer, Michael, 11
waqf, 134
Watt, C. A., 3
wealth distribution, 6, 86, 134–7
Weber, Max, 19
Wedderburn, William, 169
Weiner, Myron, 201
Welchman, L., 48
welfare payments, 21, 96, 103

INDEX

Western epistemologies, 32, 115, 164, 182
Westernization, 164
Wire, The, 65
witness protection, 28, 59
Women's Liberation Movement, 53
women's rights, 5, 26, 53, 136; *see also* feminism
World Bank, 154

Yamunan, S., 49
Young India Society *see* Abhinav Bharat Mandir
YouTube, 23
Yule, George, 169
Yunus, Mohammad, 150, 161

zakat, 32, 128, 129–30, 133–7
Zapatistas, 181
Zee News, 66–7